Problem-Based Learning
A Research Perspective on Learning Interactions

Problem-Based Learning
A Research Perspective on Learning Interactions

Edited by

Dorothy H. Evensen
The Pennsylvania State University

Cindy E. Hmelo
Rutgers University

LEA LAWRENCE ERLBAUM ASSOCIATES, PUBLISHERS
2000 Mahwah, New Jersey   London

Lawrence Erlbaum Associates, Inc., Publishers
10 Industrial Avenue
Mahwah, NJ 07430

Cover design by Kathryn Houghtaling Lacey

Library of Congress Cataloging-in-Publication Data

Problem-based learning : a research perspective on learning interactions / edited by Dorothy H. Evensen, Cindy E. Hmelo.
p. cm.
Includes bibliographical references and index.
ISBN 0-8058-2644-0 (cloth : alk. paper) — ISBN 0-8058-2645-9 (pbk. : alk. paper)
1. Problem-based learning. 2. Learning–Research. I. Evensen, Dorothy H. II. Hmelo, Cindy E.
LB1027.42.P78 2000
371.39—dc21   99-048613
                                                 CIP

Books published by Lawrence Erlbaum Associates are printed on acid-free paper, and their bindings are chosen for strength and durability.

Printed in the United States of America
10 9 8 7 6 5 4 3 2

Contents

Foreword

There are many antecedents to problem-based learning in the writings of Bruner, Gagne, and Dewey and it is logical to think that their work inspired its development as an educational method in medicine in the late 1960s. However, its origins were very pragmatic. In 1968, 4 years before the first class entered the new medical school at McMaster University, its education committee undertook the design of the school's curriculum. The physician who was the initial chair of the committee indicated that all members were "frustrated with some aspects of traditional medical education ... ."(Spaulding, 1991). Students were passive and exposed to too much information, little of which seemed relevant to the practice of medicine. They were bored and disenchanted when medical education should have been exciting. The committee noted that medical education didn't become exciting for students until residency training, when they were working with patients trying to solve their problems. They decided that from the beginning of school, learning would occur around a series of biomedical problems presented in small groups with the faculty functioning as "tutors or guides to learning." No background in educational psychology or cognitive science guided them, just the expressed hope that students would be stimulated by this experience, would see the relevance of what they were learning to their future responsibilities, would maintain a high degree of motivation for learning, and would begin to understand the importance of responsible professional attitudes. In this way, problem-based learning, as a defined curricular method, was born over 3 decades ago.

In the mid 1970s, while attempting to study this seemingly new method in which we were immersed at McMaster, I searched for prior studies about educational methods similar to problem-based learning. The most relevant that could be found at that time was a study by W. H. O. Schmidt from Natal University, South Africa, published in 1965. He used a variation of Katona's (1940) progressive card problems and described the problem-solving ability of a problem-based learning group, as compared to a group taught to memorize how to solve one problem in the initial set of card problems and to another group given only the principles on which the initial set of problems were based. Each group was given progressively more difficult problems based on the same principles in the initial set and then, unknown to the participants, problem sets were given requiring different principles for their solution. He provided a glimpse of what has subsequently been found about the performance of problem-based students compared with traditionally educated students; that is, that the problem-based students were able to solve problems based on progressively more complex principles whereas the other groups could not go beyond the initial context. A paper written by Shoemaker at George Washington University published in 1960 also seemed relevant. It had the forward-looking title, "The Functional Context Method of Instruction." He was frustrated by the results of traditional approaches to teaching radio repair personnel in the military, so on the first day of class he put malfunctioning radios on the benches of students and told them that they had to fix them. Learning resources were available as needed about the various components of radios. Shoemaker described the improved performance of those students who used what we would now call performance-based testing.

After McMaster's example, two more new medical schools, one in Maastricht and another in Newcastle, developed problem-based learning curricula. Later, a few established medical schools started alternative or parallel problem-based curricula. Problem-based learning was not a popular idea among medical school faculty. The usual reasons given for lack of interest were, to the effect, "Why fix something that isn't broken?" (the McMaster committee felt that something was broken) and "How will students learn what is important if we don't give it to them?" Slowly the method was adopted in different ways by many medical schools around the world and since the mid-1980s, has spread beyond the confines of medicine to all levels of learning in many different disciplines and professions.

Small studies evaluating the method as it was carried out in various schools began to appear. As more educational researchers have shown an interest in problem-based learning valuable new information began to appear. Now medical educational journals have papers devoted to problem-based learning in every issue. There were sufficient evaluative studies performed with modest numbers of students 25 years after its debut to permit meta-analyses of problem-based learning's effectiveness as an educational technique. And now, as testimony to the maturity of this method and to the general interest in it, this book appears with a wide range of authors studying many of the cognitive and social perspectives of two components of this method—the group process and self-directed learning.

The wide dissemination of problem-based learning has spawned so many mutations that the genus "problem-based learning" now has an almost unclassifiable array of species. The species are so variable that it may be necessary for some group to define the criteria for a method to be considered problem-based learning. Short of this happening, it is important for teachers to understand that it is not a monolithic method and that different studies are carried out on different species of the method with many variables. For example, the design of problem formats, the emphasis on teaching problem solving, the training and role of the facilitator, the composition and responsibilities of the small group members, the process and sequence of learning activities, the problem-solving and self-directed learning methods encouraged, the use of reflection and assessments, and the degree of student-centeredness can be variables. Keeping in mind these variations, the information in this book will be very helpful to anyone who is designing a problem-based learning curriculum or who is responsible for maintaining and improving a problem-based learning curriculum.

Some of the authors in this book, such as Henk Schmidt, who has provided us with valuable research information about problem-based learning since the early 1980s, have been working in this area for a long time. Some are relatively new to problem-based learning and bring exciting new perspectives. Other authors, well known in cognitive science, bring outside perspectives about the phenomena occurring in problem-based learning.

—Howard Barrows
Southern Illinois University

REFERENCES

Katona, G. (1940). *Organizing and memorizing: Studies in the psychology of learning and teaching.* New York: Columbia University Press.

Schmidt, W. H. O. (1965). Processes of learning in relation to different kinds of materials to be learnt. In J. V. O. Reid & A. J. Wilmont (Eds.), *Medical education in South Africa* (pp. 228–232). Pietermaritzburg, South Africa: Natal University Press.

Shoemaker, H. (1960). *The functional context method of instruction.* Human Resources Research Office, George Washington University. IRE Transactions and Education, V-E-3(2), 52–57. Alexandria, VA.

Spaulding, W. B. (1991). *Revitalizing medical education: McMaster Medical School, the early years 1965–1974.* Philadelphia: B. C. Decker.

Preface

Problem-based learning (PBL) has been mostly associated with medical education since the late 1960s. As we move into the 21st century, however, many of the advantages of a problem-based approach have become the generally articulated outcomes of education, especially education in the professions: an understanding of one's own knowledge needs, application of knowledge to novel problem situations, collaboration, and lifelong learning. Furthermore, these goals are not restricted to adult or to postsecondary learning populations. We see evidence of students collectively problem-solving, researching new areas of interest, and reflecting on their learning processes in high school, in middle school, and even down through the lower elementary years.

However, like many curricular reforms, PBL runs the risk of becoming something it is not through misunderstandings of its philosophical and epistemological underpinnings and of misapplication through the use of highly simplified methods. One particular danger, indeed one not unknown in medical education, is the assumption that the journey from problem to learning outcome is uncomplicated or that given a compelling problem, students will naturally want to work together to solve it.

This volume challenges such faulty assumptions by collecting research dealing with the two highly complex entities that are vital to the operation of a problem-based curriculum: group collaboration and self-directed learning. Together, these entities provide evidence of the social and psychological dimensions of the learning interactions afforded by this curricular reform. Although we separate them in forming the two sections of the volume, the contents of the chapters themselves illustrate the interrelatedness of the group- and the self-directed processes. Some of this research is preliminary and serves to point out specific instances when the group meeting and individual learning go well or go amiss. Other studies pit PBL against traditional curricula to reveal both its advantages and its disadvantages. The authors attempt to guide the readers' interpretations of findings and convince them that PBL is more than a package that can be picked up and applied to any classroom situation. Rather, it is a sophisticated design that requires attention to learner and to teacher, to content and to context. Ours is a decidedly constructivist perspective that conceptualizes learning as effort, and it might be appropriately abbreviated by the maxim, "A problem is an opportunity in work clothes." The "problem" in PBL requires ownership not only by the learner, but also by the teacher.

Our intended audience is both researchers and practitioners. For the former, we provide thorough explications of the development of our research questions and methodologies, in addition to discussions of how certain lines of research might be pursued. For the latter, we hope to offer information that can be used to inform curricular decisions and to guide practice. Graduate students dealing with issues of teaching and learning seem appropriate consumers of this work. As implied previously, we believe that PBL curriculum is applicable to all levels and facets of the educational spectrum. We contend that the inside looks into medical schools and close-ups of medical students serve to highlight the similarities between this group and other learners.

ACKNOWLEDGMENTS

There are many persons we thank for helping us realize this project. First, we thank the contributors and commentators who not only shared their work, but who also were willing to revise their manuscripts in ways that would bring coherence to the volume. We also recognize the hundreds of medical students, many of them now novice physicians, who were willing to somewhat interrupt their already overburdened schedules to help us understand the learning experiences in which they were engaged. It is worth commenting that many of these students demonstrated a pronounced concern for the state of medical education and understood that only research could provide the information necessary for medical curricula to change. We, the co-editors, met at an annual meeting of the American Educational Research Association and this project has benefitted from our associations with members of Division I, Research in the Professions, and the special interest group in PBL. Furthermore, some chapters in this volume represent work that was funded by the Spencer Foundation through their postdoctoral fellowship program; we are particularly grateful for such support.

We acknowledge our editor at Lawrence Erlbaum Associates, Naomi Silverman, and her assistant, Lori Hawver, for their patience, encouragement, and assistance. We thank our families: The Evensens—Carl, Andy, and Lori—for understanding that Dorie needed to retreat to her third-floor office to work on " the book"; The Hmelos—Laura and Samantha— for their patience while Cindy worked on this longstanding project. We also thank Trudi Haupt, staff assistant in Penn State's program in higher education for helping to format the final manuscript.

Last, we acknowledge Howard Barrows, who graciously agreed to preview this volume and provide us with our foreword. His scholarship and efforts to clarify PBL for a larger audience have contributed enormously to an understanding of what PBL is about and what it takes to make this model work well (or not). His encouragement and enthusiasm have contributed, directly and indirectly, to many of the chapters in this book.

Chapter 1

INTRODUCTION
Problem-Based Learning: Gaining Insights on Learning Interactions Through Multiple Methods of Inquiry

Cindy E. Hmelo
Rutgers University

Dorothy H. Evensen
The Pennsylvania State University

The workplace of the 21st century requires professionals who not only have an extensive store of knowledge, but who also know how to keep that knowledge up-to-date, apply it to solve problems, and function as part of a team. This revised view of the workplace compels educators to rethink and reinvent the ways in which professionals are prepared. Schooling, in particular, must extend beyond the traditional preparatory goal of establishing a knowledge base. Concomitantly, it must actively engage preservice doctors, lawyers, teachers, and businesspersons in opportunities for knowledge seeking, for problem solving, and for the collaborating necessary for effective practice. To realize such experiences, educators have looked to constructivist pedagogical designs that are based on the assumption that learning is a product of both cognitive and social interactions in problem-centered environments (Greeno, Collins, & Resnick, 1996; Savery & Duffy, 1994). Problem-based learning (PBL) is an example of such a design.

PBL can be used to refer to many contextualized approaches to instruction (Bruer, 1993; Williams, 1993). What all of these methods have in common is that they anchor much of the learning and instruction in concrete problems. There are five objectives that PBL is most likely to address for medical students (Barrows, 1986): construction of clinically useful knowledge, development of clinical reasoning strategies, development of effective self-directed learning strategies, increased motivation for learning, and becoming effective collaborators. Barrows (1986) has identified two factors that affect the probability that any of these objectives might be achieved: the nature of the case: whether it is a complete case, a vignette, or a full problem simulation; and the locus of control of learning: whether it is teacher-centered, student-centered, or mixed.

What has become known as a classic version of PBL is described by Barrows (1985, 1988). This model has two key features: a rich problem is used that affords free inquiry by students, and learning is student-centered.

In this approach, a group of five to seven medical students and a facilitator meet to discuss a problem (Barrows, 1986). The facilitator provides the students with a small amount of information about a patient's case, and then the group's task is to evaluate and define different aspects of the problem and to gain insight into the underlying causes of the disease process. This is accomplished by extracting key information from the case, generating and evaluating hypotheses, and formulating learning issues. Learning issues are topics that the group deems relevant and in need of further explication. The group members divide up the learning issues among themselves and research them. They then share their information and use it to explain the patient's disease process. At the completion of the cycle, the students reflect on what they learned from the problem. The facilitator's role is to help the students' learning processes by modeling hypothesis-driven reasoning for the students and by encouraging them to be reflective.

At the heart of PBL is the tutorial group. The PBL tutorial consists of several phases: introductions and climate setting, starting a problem, problem follow-up, and post-problem reflection (Barrows, 1988). Before beginning to grapple with a problem as a group, students must get to know each other, establish ground rules, and establish a comfortable climate for collaborative learning. Meeting in a small group for the first time, students introduce themselves, stressing their academic backgrounds to allow facilitators and each other to understand what expertise might potentially be distributed in the group. The other important function of this preproblem-solving phase is to establish a nonjudgmental climate in which students recognize and articulate what they know and what they do not know (Barrows, 1988).

The actual problem-based episode begins by presenting a group of students with minimal information about a patient's case. The students then query the case materials to determine what information is available and what they still need to know and to learn to solve the problem. During this phase students typically take on particular roles.

One student takes on the role of scribe. The scribe records the groups' problem solving on whiteboards or on easel paper where they list the facts known about the problem, students' ideas or hypotheses, additional questions about the case, and the learning issues generated throughout ensuing discussion. This written record (which usually remains visible during the entire discussion around the case) helps the students keep track of their problem solving and provides a focus for negotiation and reflection. At several points in the case, students reiterate this process: pausing to reflect on the data collected so far, generating additional questions about that data, and hypothesizing about the problem and about possible solutions. In addition, the facilitator models metacognitive questions to encourage reflective thinking by asking students to explain why they consider a particular solution to be good, or why they need a particular piece of information about the problem.

As the students work on the problem, they identify concepts they do not sufficiently understand and so need to learn more about to solve the problem (the "learning issues"). Early in the PBL process, the facilitator may question students to help them realize what they don't understand. For example, he or she may ask puzzled students whether or not a particular issue should be added to the growing list of learning issues posted on the board. As students become more experienced with the PBL method and take on more of the responsibility for identifying learning issues, the facilitator is able to fade this type of support, or scaffolding. After the group has developed its initial understanding of the problem, the students divide up and independently research the learning issues they have identified. The learning issues define the group's learning goals and help group members work toward a set of shared objectives. These objectives can also help the facilitator to monitor the group's progress and to remind members when they are getting off course, or alternately, to ask if they need to revise their goals (Barrows, 1988).

In the problem follow-up phase, the students reconvene to share what they have learned, to reconsider their hypotheses, or to generate new hypotheses in light of their new learning. These further analyses, and accompanying ideas about solutions, allow students to apply their newly acquired knowledge to the problem. Students share what they have learned with the group as they coconstruct the problem through the lens of their newly accessed information. At this point, it is important for the students to evaluate their own information and that of the others in their group. In the traditional classroom, information is often accepted at face value. In the PBL tutorial, the students discuss how they acquired their information and critique their resources. This process is an important means of helping the students become self-directed learners.

The emphasis in PBL is not necessarily on having students solve the problem; rather, it is on having them understand the cause of the problem. During postproblem reflection, students deliberately reflect on the problem to abstract the lessons learned. They consider the connections between the current problem and previous problems, considering how this problem is similar to and different from other problems. This reflection allows them to make generalizations and to understand when this knowledge can be applied (Salomon & Perkins, 1989). Finally, as the students evaluate their own performance and that of their peers, they reflect on the effectiveness of their self-directed learning and their collaborative problem solving.

Both cognitive constructivist and sociocultural theories provide insights into the learning mechanisms of PBL (Greeno et al., 1996). In terms of individual learning, PBL situates learning within the context of medical practice. Problems give rise to epistemic curiosity (Schmidt, 1993) that will, in turn, trigger the cognitive processes of accessing prior knowledge, establishing a problem space, searching for new information, and reconstructing information into knowledge that both fits into and shapes new mental models. At the same time, proceeding through the PBL process requires the learner's metacognitive awareness of the efficacy of the process. In this regard, PBL is inherently self-regulated. Yet, PBL does not exist in a vacuum. Rather, it is a social system within a larger cultural context. The knowledge that the learner seeks is embedded in and derives from social sources—in this case, the world of medical practice. From this perspective, the learner is seen as both transforming and as transformed as the processes of practice and their underlying symbol systems are internalized through dialectical activity (John-Steiner & Mahn, 1996). In this sense, learning is not an accumulation of information, but a transformation of the individual who is moving toward full membership in the professional community. This identity-making is marked by observing the facility with which cultural tools, or the ways of thinking and using language, are invoked. The sociocultural context of PBL is the group meeting that simulates the social process of medical problem solving in a scaffolded way.

Although theoretical grounding provides an important starting point for educational initiatives, what is also required is an ongoing research agenda. Indeed, PBL has received a large amount of research attention since the late 1980s; however, although much research has focused on knowledge acquisition and problem-solving advantages of PBL, few studies have targeted self-directed learning or group interactions, which are equally important components of the curriculum. By narrowing the scope of inquiries to cognitive variables, studies have often bypassed or bracketed the social and pragmatic aspects of these key components. Assumptions are made that enhanced understanding develops in conjunction with self-regulation and with group participation, but theories remain vague about how these interactions are practiced or which aspects of the interactions differentially affect learning.

What we hope to do in this volume is to present empirical work that scrutinizes these two crucial components of PBL, revealing the complexity of each. The learning advantage of PBL is theorized as being embedded in the interactional dynamics between group processes and individual study; however, the mere presence of these entities cannot guarantee departure from traditional practices. It has been argued that surface differences do not necessarily mean substantive differences, and that what may appear to be transformational learning practices might actually reflect conventional transmission teaching models (Pea, 1993). This possibility adds impetus to the argument that PBL might just be old wine in new casks, an idea anathema to PBL proponents. Decades of research on cooperative learning continues to result in ambiguous findings pointing to both advantages and disadvantages of working in groups (see McCaslin & Good, 1996). But what's more important is that the educational research community is just beginning to ask how self-regulatory functions interact with group dynamics to enhance goal setting, planning, execution, and evaluation of learning issues in social relations (Schunk & Zimmerman, 1997). Hence, what we attempt to do in this volume is to get closer to PBL-in-practice.

The research reported here derives from constructivist traditions that employ a variety of methods to focus on learning processes and seek to discover ways of documenting change and transformation within learning contexts. Constructivism is represented by a range of perspectives that situate the individual learner, epistemological beliefs, and the sociocultural context of learning in different relations to each other (see Prawat, 1996). The contributing authors of this volume assume different constructivist perspectives ranging from information processing to social reconstructivist. As a result, each sheds light on different aspects of learning interactions. Likewise, different perspectives employ different methods of inquiry. The studies that follow use self-reports, interviews, observations, and microanalyses to find ways into the psychological processes and sociological contexts that constitute the world of PBL in medical education.

To a large extent, these studies are derived from empirical work conducted within a variety of disciplines. For example, many of the authors from Part I credit the work of researchers who studied cooperative learning in K–12 settings (D. W. Johnson & Johnson, 1987; Slavin, 1983), whereas many in Part II refer to work in self-directed learning emanating from adult education (e.g., Candy, 1991). But at the same time, these studies are situated within the literature of PBL, especially the body of work representing the field of medical education. That work tends to focus on the effects of PBL, particularly how engagement with PBL curricula affects both the methods of knowledge construction and performance that requires the application of knowledge.

PBL AND KNOWLEDGE CONSTRUCTION

Research in psychology predicts several advantages for students in PBL curricula compared with those in traditional medical education contexts (Norman & Schmidt, 1992). PBL students may be more highly motivated, better at problem solving and self-directed learning, better able to learn and recall information, and better able to integrate basic science into the solutions of clinical problems. PBL students may also be better at collaboration.

PBL provides an appropriate situation for learning basic science because all of the content is learned in the context of a clinical problem, which should enhance recall of this information when it is needed (Adams et al., 1988; Needham & Begg, 1991; Perfetto, Bransford, & Franks, 1983). Norman and Schmidt (1992) reported several direct tests of the effect of PBL on recall. These studies indicate that PBL students' initial learning is not as good as students in a conventional curriculum but their long-term retention is superior.

In addition to facts, medical students need to learn the principles and concepts of the basic biomedical sciences. These concepts are typically taught in the first 2 years of medical school with the assumption that students will be able to transfer them into their clinical practice. However, students need to learn more than science; they need to learn how science can be used as a tool that can be applied in subsequent clinical practice. Barrows and Feltovich (1987) argued that because clinical reasoning processes and scientific knowledge are inextricably linked, educational strategies should be used that teach embedded knowledge construction in the clinical reasoning context.

Thus it is hypothesized that if students in a PBL curriculum learn basic science concepts in the context of a clinical problem, they should be better able to integrate concepts into the solution of other clinical problems. Patel, Groen, and Norman (1991, 1993) asked students from conventional and from PBL curricula to solve a clinical problem and to then integrate passages of relevant basic science information into their pathophysiological explanations of the problem. The PBL students incorporated many more causal explanations than did the students from the conventional curriculum. In a similar pathophysiological explanation task, Hmelo (1998) demonstrated that, when compared with students in a traditional curriculum, PBL students were more likely to use basic science as a tool for problem solving.

Much evaluation of PBL has examined traditional academic outcome measures such as examination scores. Schmidt, Dauphinee, and Patel (1987) reviewed 15 studies of PBL on several outcome measures. They found that the PBL students tended to score slightly lower on traditional measures of academic achievement such as the National Board of Medical Examiners (NBME) Part I (see also Albanese & Mitchell, 1993; Goodman et al., 1991; Mennin, Friedman, Skipper, Kalishman, & Snyder, 1993; Vernon & Blake, 1993). They found that PBL students performed slightly better at tasks related to clinical problem solving such as the NBME III, the portion of the licensing examination that deals with clinical practice. This research suggests that problem-based curricula encourage a more intentional style of learning, with the students attempting to integrate their prior knowledge with what they are learning, to understand the meaning, and to look for explanations underlying concepts rather than facts to be mastered (Schmidt et al., 1987).

Some recent research has focused on PBL outcomes from a cognitive perspective; these have focused largely on measures of problem solving. Patel and colleagues' research suggests that students in a PBL curriculum do not outperform students in a conventional curriculum, and, in fact, they may do worse on a task requiring diagnostic explanation. Patel, Groen, and Norman (1991, 1993) compared beginning, intermediate, and senior level medical students at two Canadian medical schools, one using a conventional medical curriculum and the second using a PBL curriculum. The students were asked to provide diagnostic explanations of a clinical case, both before and after being exposed to relevant basic science information.

The results showed that students in the PBL curriculum were more likely to use hypothesis-driven reasoning (as they were taught) than were students in the conventional curriculum. The students in the conventional medical school used predominately data-driven reasoning, a pattern that is more characteristic of experts. The PBL students' explanations, although more error-prone, were also more elaborated. The authors concluded that the PBL students are at a disadvantage because, although basic science and clinical knowledge acquisition are both goals of a medical education, basic sciences should not be taught in the context of a clinical case because the knowledge structures are different. Patel, Groen, and Norman (1993) argued that this is because learning how to make a diagnosis is different from learning how to explain what causes a disease.

In two different studies, Hmelo (Hmelo, 1998; Hmelo, Gotterer, & Bransford, 1997) examined the effects of PBL on problem solving. In the first study (Hmelo et al., 1997), students taking a PBL elective were compared with students taking other electives as a supplement to a traditional curriculum. This study demonstrated that the PBL students transferred their problem-solving strategies to new problems and that they constructed more coherent explanations. Hmelo (1998) demonstrated similar effects in a longitudinal study that also compared students in a full-time problem-based curriculum with a traditional curriculum. The PBL students were more accurate, more likely to use the hypothesis-driven reasoning strategies that they were taught, and constructed better quality explanations than the comparison students. It was concluded that hypothesis-driven reasoning strategies are appropriate for novice and for intermediate students to be using because they must invoke their causal knowledge in lieu of clinical knowledge. It is noteworthy that this type of reasoning is also used by experts when faced with an unfamiliar or a difficult problem (Norman, Trott, Brooks, & Smith, 1994).

The research that focuses on reasoning strategies clearly addresses PBL's goals, but ultimately the gold standard for performance is what do doctors know: can they accurately make diagnoses? Schmidt and colleagues (1996) compared PBL and traditional students on diagnostic accuracy for 30 case vignettes. They found that the PBL students were more accurate than students in a traditional curriculum. Finally, measures of clinical performance have also tended to favor PBL, although these studies have some methodological limitations (Albanese & Mitchell, 1993; Vernon & Blake, 1993).

It is also increasingly clear that PBL students are more satisfied with their curriculum than are students in a traditional curriculum (Vernon & Blake, 1993). They are more likely to attend class, to see what they are learning as more clinically relevant, and are more confident in their problem solving (Blumberg & Eckenfels, 1988; Hmelo, 1994; Nolte, Eller, & Ringel, 1988; Vernon & Blake, 1993).

So what do we know about PBL? We know a lot about the effects of PBL on problem solving and on test performance. We know that PBL is motivating. We know less about how PBL students learn to become good collaborators and self-directed learners. That, then, is the goal of this book. Some of the studies that follow use qualitative methods that allow us to look into the group meeting or to accompany medical students as they make decisions about what, when, where, and how to study. Others survey students to elicit their perceptions of group effectiveness and retrospections on study habits. Still others use online probes of problem solving to detect what differences might coincide with curricular effects. This work, we argue, is just the beginning of the research that needs to be done to develop more comprehensive theories of PBL and other constructivist learning environments. In light of that, we additionally offer chapters that suggest an array of methodological approaches to the study of PBL. Taken as a whole, we hope that this volume can serve to update educators of the advances in understanding of PBL processes, while at the same time afford researchers multiple methodologies to facilitate the study of learning in relation to this curricular design.

CHAPTER OVERVIEWS

Part I: The Group Meeting

In chapter 2, Schmidt and Moust review the body of literature that has come out of Maastricht University in The Netherlands dealing with the factors that affect learning in PBL groups. Maastrict has not only situated problem-based curricula as the centerpiece of its numerous professional programs, but it has also sponsored a rigorous research agenda that provides empirical support for worldwide PBL efforts. In this review, the authors question the influences of the problem, the learners' cognitive processes and motivations, and the tutor on students' learning. They then summarize empirical work that first takes up and then addresses these questions. The picture that emerges is complex yet clearly supports the premise that problem-based curricula provide a learning advantage when certain characteristics of the learning environment are maintained. For example, it is most likely the quality of the problem that initially stimulates learners toward "theory construction." This, in turn, lays the foundation on which certain cognitive activities, not typically observed in traditional education contexts, commence. Concurrently and collectively, the text of the problem and the affordance of collaborative cognitive activity enhance learners' motivations. All the while, learning is buttressed when the presiding tutor holds a certain degree of subject expertise and is both socially and cognitively congruent with learners. The chapter ends by pointing out the boundaries of our current understandings of group learning and where new research efforts might be focused. Many of the chapters that follow attempt to address these expressed needs.

In chapter 3, Koschmann, Glenn, and Conlee take issue with the term "tutorial," and through microgenetic analysis, first describe and then evaluate the tutor's role in the generation of learning issues during the PBL group meeting. Using "Knowledge Display Segments" (KDSs) as the unit of analysis, these authors demonstrate how a highly skilled tutor provides a framework within which students' collective knowledge becomes synthesized and wherein limitations of students' knowledge become salient. This process is then compared with more traditional forms of classroom tutorial discourse where tutors' interactions are more directive and are often oppositional to student-centered learning. In conclusion, the authors argue for the adoption of new terminologies to better capture the essence of the interactive roles played in the PBL group.

The title of chapter 4 asks, "Whose group is it anyway?" and Duek proceeds to find an answer to the question by investigating participatory patterns, roles, and tutors' responses to students in terms of gender and ethnicity. What emerges from her analyses are examples of practices that serve to maintain the dominance of majority groups. Although tutors appear to be doing little to "level the playing field" for, especially, persons of color, the study also points out that students themselves, through their adoptions of stereotypical social and academic roles, contribute to the maintenance of group inequities.

Chapter 5 also looks at aspects of group dynamics, or what is known as group processing. Faidley and colleagues, however, focus on methodologies that can be used to assess this aspect of the group meeting. Two instruments are introduced: one is an easy-to-administer survey through which group members evaluate participation and perceived effectiveness; the other is an observational checklist that facilitates the discovery of participatory patterns and targeted behaviors. The authors synthesize the information from these two data sources with postsession discussions of group processing to construct descriptions of four different PBL groups. They conclude that such instruments are useful to both curricular designers and to researchers of PBL.

Chapter 6 presents an exercise that took place at the 1996 meeting of the American Educational Research Association. Again, we focus on a segment of a PBL session, but this time encounter not one perspective, but five. In short, five researchers known for their diverse analytical orientations of the discourse of group interactions provide different "takes" on the same segment of a PBL meeting. Taken separately, these perspectives open avenues on which those who research group interactions can travel. Taken together, along with questions and comments from audience members, they provide a rare look at the richness of the data and what necessarily has to be the narrowness of any single interpretation.

The final chapter in this section on groups, chapter 7, begins and ends with the same hypothesis: The structure and function of PBL groups are directly related to the outcomes achieved. The study presented in this chapter, however, does not set out to test this hypothesis but to survey North American medical schools to discover the extent of schools that report "doing PBL," the outcomes valued in those schools, and the degree to which they adhere to elements of the group process that are theoretically related to learning outcomes. Kelson and Distlehorst identify three parameters of collaboration: learning, problem solving, and working collectively toward individual outcomes. Survey data indicate that many programs hold to a common set of outcomes while creating conditions that most likely jeopardize those outcomes. These data lead to the conclusion that defining PBL remains problematic, calling into question the meaningfulness of findings that purport to assess its effectiveness.

Part II: Self-Directed Learning

In chapter 9, Blumberg begins the section on self-directed learning (SDL) by surveying the landscape of the SDL research and the nature of SDL itself. She has developed a useful framework from which to view the existing research, one that takes into account the dimensions of learning processes, strategies, and outcomes. Several perspectives are important to consider in understanding the SDL process: the students themselves, the curriculum planners, the facilitators, and, we would add, educational researchers with an interest in teaching and in learning. This chapter recognizes the importance of being a reflective practitioner who sees the need to acquire new knowledge and who reflects on that knowledge before applying it (Schön, 1987). The literature shows that students and faculty perceive that PBL fosters the development of self-directed learning. In addition, converging evidence from students' reports and from library usage indicate that PBL students are more active library users who use a diverse set of information resources, and that students adapt their resource use to the subject matter being studied. The learning strategies that PBL students use tend to favor deep-level processing.

Despite knowing quite a bit about the SDL of medical students, Blumberg concludes that there is still a good deal to learn and lays out a research agenda. We still do not know enough about the learning process in PBL—how students construct learning issues, plan their SDL, and implement their learning plans. We do not have a good understanding of which features of PBL are essential to foster the development of self-directed learners. Finally, we need to learn more about the long-term effects of PBL in creating lifelong learners. The chapters in the SDL section of this book attempt to tackle the first two issues of this agenda.

In chapter 10, Hmelo and Lin use information processing and constructivist theories to examine a component process model of the SDL process. The authors argue that learners, when faced with a novel problem, must use metacognitive strategies to identify what they don't know and what they need to learn more about to solve the problem. In addition, learners need to figure out what resources they will need to remedy their knowledge deficits. Finally, the new knowledge must be evaluated to determine whether it is the appropriate knowledge and to integrate it with prior knowledge to solve the problem. Hmelo and Lin use methods of protocol analysis from cognitive psychology to compare problem-based and traditional students' SDL processes on a novel problem-solving task. They examine several of the individual component processes in SDL, such as how students generate learning issues and plan their learning, as well as how well they use new knowledge in problem solving. They find that the PBL students acquire effective SDL strategies, transfer these strategies to new problems, and effectively integrate their new learning into their problem solving.

In chapter 11, Dolmans and Schmidt examine the validity of a commonly held assumption in the PBL approach; namely, that it is the problem content and ensuing discussions that direct SDL. In questioning this assumption, they concomitantly ask what other curricular elements might direct SDL. The PBL students at their institution receive course objectives, a limited number of lectures, tests, and suggested references. Over-reliance on these external elements, they reason, might impede the development of SDL skills. To examine this, they gave first- through fourth-year students a questionnaire with items relating to the different curricular elements. They found that problem discussion and course objectives had the greatest influence on SDL. Tests and lectures had the least influence. Moreover, over the 4 years of the curriculum, students increased their emphasis on the functional knowledge they needed as physicians and decreased their reliance on external elements such as tests. These results indicate that over time, students in a PBL curriculum become more self-reliant.

In chapter 12, Evensen examines SDL in context. The ethnographic approach used in this chapter zooms in on two students who are beginning PBL and investigates how their learning strategies evolve. Evensen uses this approach to paint a rich portrait of how SDL is practiced in PBL. This study examines the reciprocal interactions of academic self-concept, learning strategies, program affordances, and evaluation mechanisms. In the two case studies, Evensen describes students' strategies for coping with challenges to their self-efficacy, the reflection on (and pride in) their learning, and information-seeking strategies. This work provides a glimpse into the lives of two students learning to adapt to the SDL demands of a PBL program. Several generalizations arise from this study. Students bring strategies and beliefs about learning to a new situation. This is not surprising, as medical students generally have been successful learners throughout their school careers. However, prior ways of learning are not transported intact to this new learning environment; rather, good self-directed learners are proactive in achieving their goals. That is, these successful learners adapt their personal strategies to the situational demands. This is not a trivial matter in that SDL does not impose structure, and learners must impose their own structure to make it manageable. A major portion of the case studies attempts to document how these students use reflection to negotiate and renegotiate their self-directed positions. This work suggests that the more self-reflective one is about SDL, the more likely one is able to modify or to invent strategies for SDL. Evensen concludes that SDL may well be an individual characteristic but one that needs to be carefully nurtured.

Each of the previously mentioned sections closes with a commentary. Bereiter and Scardamalia consider PBL related to the work they have pursued in collaborative knowledge building. They speculate how components of PBL could be carried out within computer-supported environments, and they discuss empirical projects that might be undertaken to inform continuously better models of PBL. Zimmerman and Lebeau synthesize the findings from the chapters in Part II to construct a model that considers how specific PBL curricular influences affect SDL processes. They relate this model to theories of self-regulated learning and conclude that these two research strands might well be combined to provide a conceptual basis within which to conduct future studies of PBL.

Our final chapter, an epilogue, is included in this volume to remind readers that the best curricular intentions are oftimes foiled by incongruent methods of assessment. Indeed, why should students grapple with the demands of group collaboration and pursue learning issues along multidisciplinary lines and through multiple sources when performance is determined by traditional, teacher-made tests. Kelson outlines the impact of assessment on both the curriculum and student epistemologies. She posits that if lifelong learning is to become an actual goal of educational efforts, then it is essential that curricular designers find ways of embedding factors related to lifelong learning into assessment activities. Kelson proposes that PBL has the potential of achieving such a goal because it is neither teacher- nor student centered. Rather, the assumption of PBL is that problems drive learning both within the classroom and into professional practice. Hence, the outcomes of the curriculum and the goals of assessment need to be one and the same: to insure that students become sensitive to the learning affordances of problems and that they have the tools necessary to pursue such learning. Kelson concludes her chapter by describing the system of assessment in place at Southern Illinois University and stresses that such a system is very much a "work in progress."

CONCLUSION

Although the studies contained in this volume are all situated within the context of medical education, we invite readers from other communities, be they professional or general education communities, to locate their own issues within the ones presented. The fact that these groups of students are meeting around problems related to medical diagnosis can, in one sense, be seen as coincidental—they could as well be undergraduates meeting to address problems related to the interpretation of poetry, elementary school students considering how to apply mathematical operations to a real-world problem, or high school students debating the causes of certain economic conditions. Likewise, self-direction in learning can be investigated by following any student—the medical student pursuing information needed to understand the mechanisms of infection, the law student grappling to comprehend the hierarchical system of jurisdictions, or the fifth grader in search of finding out which groups of European explorers made it to the New World first and what social conditions enabled them to do so.

We believe that problems themselves are crucial to the process of PBL and that educators need to strive to construct problems that can serve as the necessary impetus to begin the process of learning. Equally important are facilitator and institutional roles in creating a climate for effective PBL. It is incumbent on educators to recognize that the dynamics at work within groups and the motivations and practices of individual group members will be equally important to the learning process. The processes of the group meeting and SDL serve as the connective events between the problem and the learning outcomes. The operations of these events, as is demonstrated by much of the research contained in this volume, can be highly variable and, thus, differentially effective. But we hope that this research reveals both the components and interrelations of PBL systems that will lead to refine theoretical understandings and methodologies through which theory testing can proceed.

REFERENCES

Adams, L., Kasserman, J., Yearwood, A., Perfetto, G., Bransford, J., & Franks, J. (1988). The effect of fact versus problem oriented acquisition. *Memory & Cognition, 16,* 167–175.

Albanese, M. A., & Mitchell, S. (1993). Problem-based learning: A review of literature on its outcomes and implementation issues. *Academic Medicine, 68,* 52–81.

Barrows, H. S. (1985). *How to design a problem-based curriculum for the preclinical years.* New York: Springer.

Barrows, H. S. (1986). A taxonomy of problem-based learning methods. *Medical Education, 20,* 481–486.

Barrows, H. (1988). *The tutorial process.* Springfield IL: Southern Illinois University Press.

Barrows, H. S., & Feltovich, P. J. (1987). The clinical reasoning process. *Medical Education, 21,* 86–91.

Blumberg, P., & Eckensfels, E. G. (1988, November). *A comparison of student satisfaction with their preclinical environment in a traditional and a problem-based curriculum.* Paper presented at the meeting of the American Association of Medical Colleges, Research in Medical Education, Chicago, IL.

Bruer, J. T. (1993). *Schools for thought.* Cambridge MA: MIT Press.

Candy, P. C. (1991). *Self-direction for lifelong learning.* San Francisco: Jossey-Bass.

Goodman, L. J., Erich, E., Brueschke, E. E., Bone, R. C., Rose, W. H., Williams, E. J., & Paul, H. A. (1991). An experiment in medical education: A critical analysis using traditional criteria. *Journal of the American Medical Association, 265,* 2373–2376.

Greeno, J. G., Collins, A. M., & Resnick, L. (1996). Cognition and learning. In R. C. Calfee & D. C. Berliner (Eds.), *Handbook of educational psychology* (pp. 15–46). New York: Simon & Schuster Macmillan.

Hmelo, C. E. (1994). *Development of independent thinking and learning skills: A study of medical problem-solving and problem-based learning.* Unpublished doctoral dissertation, Vanderbilt University.

Hmelo, C. E. (1998). Problem-based learning: Effects on the early acquisition of cognitive skill in medicine. *Journal of the Learning Sciences, 7,* 173–208.

Hmelo, C. E., Gotterer, G. S., & Bransford, J. D. (1997). A theory-driven approach to assessing the cognitive effects of PBL. *Instructional Science, 25,* 387–408.

John-Steiner, V., & Mahn, H. (1996). Sociocultural approaches to learning and development: A Vygotskian framework. *Educational Psychologist, 31,* 191–206.

Johnson, D. W., & Johnson, R. T. (1987). *Joining together: Group theory and group skills* (2nd ed.). Englewood Cliffs, NJ: Prentice Hall.

McCaslin M., & Good, T. L. (1996). The informal curriculum. In R. C. Calfee & D. C. Berliner (Eds.), *Handbook of educational psychology* (pp. 622–670). New York: Simon & Schuster Macmillan.

Mennin, S. P., Friedman, M., Skipper, B., Kalishman, S., & Snyder, J. (1993). Performances on the NBME I, II, and III by medical students in the problem-based and conventional tracks at the University of New Mexico. *Academic Medicine, 68,* 616–624.

Needham, D. R., & Begg, I. M. (1991). Problem-oriented training promotes spontaneous analogical transfer. Memory-oriented training promotes memory for training. *Memory and Cognition, 19,* 543–557.

Nolte, J., Eller, P., & Ringel, S. P. (1988). Shifting toward problem-based learning in a medical school neurobiology course. *Proceedings of the Annual Conference on Research Medical Education, 27,* 66–71.

Norman, G. R., Trott, A. D., Brooks, L. R., & Smith, E. K. (1994). Cognitive differences in clinical reasoning related to postgraduate training. *Teaching and Learning in Medicine, 6,* 114–120.

Norman, G. T., & Schmidt, H. G. (1992). The psychological basis of problem-based learning: A review of the evidence. *Academic Medicine, 67,* 557–565.

Patel, V. L., Groen, G. J., & Norman, G. R. (1991). Effects of conventional and problem-based medical curricula on problem solving. *Academic Medicine, 66,* 380–389.

Patel, V. L., Groen, G. J., & Norman, G. R. (1993). Reasoning and instruction in medical curricula. *Cognition & Instruction, 10,* 335–378.

Pea, R. D. (1993). Practices of distributed intelligence and designs for education. In G. Salomon & D. Perkins (Eds.), *Distributed cognitions* (pp. 47–87). New York: Cambridge.

Perfetto, G. A., Bransford, J. D., & Franks, J. J. (1983). Constraints on access in a problem solving context. *Memory & Cognition, 11,* 24–31.

Prawat, R. S. (1996). Constructivisms, modern and postmodern. *Educational Psychologist, 31,* 215–225.

Salomon, G., & Perkins, D. N. (1989). Rocky roads to transfer: Rethinking mechanisms of a neglected phenomenon. *Educational Psychologist, 24,* 113–142.

Savery, J. R., & Duffy, T. M. (1994). Problem-based learning: An instructional model and its constructivist framework. *Educational Technology, 35*(5), 31–38.

Schmidt, H. G. (1993). Foundations of problem-based learning: Some explanatory notes. *Medical Education, 27,* 422–432.

Schmidt, H. G., Dauphinee, W. D., & Patel, V. L. (1987). Comparing the effects of problem-based and conventional curricula in an international sample. *Journal of Medical Education, 62,* 305–315.

Schmidt, H. G., Machiels-Bongaerts, M., Hermans, H., ten Cate, T. J., Venekamp, R., & Boshuizen, H. P. A. (1996). The development of diagnostic competence: Comparison of a problem-based, an integrated, and a conventional medical curriculum. *Academic Medicine, 71,* 658–664.

Schön, D. A. (1987). *Educating the reflective practitioner: Toward a new design for teaching and learning in the professions.* San Francisco: Jossey-Bass.

Schunk, D. H., & Zimmerman, B. J. (Eds.; 1997). *Self-regulation of learning and performance.* Hillsdale, NJ: Lawrence Erlbaum Associates.

Slavin, R. E. (1983). *Cooperative learning.* New York: Longman.

Vernon, D. T., & Blake, R. L. (1993). Does problem-based learning work? A meta-analysis of evaluative research. *Academic Medicine, 68,* 550–563.

Williams, S. M. (1993). Putting case based learning into context: Examples from legal, business, and medical education. *Journal of the Learning Sciences, 2,* 367–427.

Part I

THE GROUP MEETING

Chapter 2

Factors Affecting Small-Group Tutorial Learning: A Review of Research

Henk G. Schmidt
Jos H. C. Moust
University of Maastricht

INTRODUCTION

In this chapter we review a number of studies, conducted by a group of Dutch educational researchers, that were aimed at uncovering the factors that affect small-group tutorial learning in problem-based curricula. These studies deal with four different aspects of problem-based instruction. These aspects are as follows:

1. The role of problems used to stimulate the learning of students: We argue that the nature of the problems presented to students has a far more pervasive influence on learning than is generally assumed in the literature.

2. The cognitive processes elicited by small-group discussion and their effects on achievement: Emphasis here is on problem discussion as a means of activating prior knowledge. It is shown that activation of, and elaboration on, previously acquired knowledge has strong facilitative effects on subsequent self-directed learning (SDL). In addition, we will present results of studies that attempted to capture the individual's thinking processes while discussing a problem in a small group.

3. Motivational influences: It is generally assumed that problem-based learning (PBL) is intrinsically motivating for students. We investigate to what extent this expectation is warranted.

4. The influence of the tutor on students' learning: This part of our review summarizes a large number of studies carried out at Maastricht

University. We present studies on tutors' expertise and on differences between staff and peer tutoring, in addition to evidence supporting a particular model of tutor functioning in problem-based contexts.

Throughout the chapter, we assume that PBL is a form of constructivist learning. Students are engaged in constructing theories about the world, represented by the problems presented. They do so collaboratively and in a meaningful context provided by those same problems. While doing so, they construct new knowledge about the world using a variety of informational resources. Our perspective, therefore, can be described as "information-processing constructivism," as opposed to more philosophical brands that particularly emphasize the social nature of learning and knowledge. Unlike other authors (Barrows & Tamblyn, 1980; Boud & Feletti, 1992), we do not emphasize PBL as a method of acquiring professional reasoning skills. In our view, PBL is, first and for all, a special way of acquiring subject matter knowledge of a domain. Whether it also fosters thinking and reasoning skills remains to be seen (Schmidt & Moust, 1999).

The next section is devoted to describing the context in which most of the research was carried out: the various curricula of Maastricht University. In addition, we provide a brief overview of activities of students and teachers involved in PBL. This description sets the stage for most of the theoretical ideas that were tested in the studies subsequently reviewed.

THE CONTEXT: PBL AT MAASTRICHT UNIVERSITY

In 1974, PBL was introduced in the Netherlands by faculty of the then new medical school of Maastricht University. The approach was adopted from the health sciences program of McMaster University, located in Hamilton, Canada. Between 1974 and 1994, six additional programs were established: health sciences, law, economics, liberal arts, knowledge engineering, and psychology. These six programs all adopted PBL as their educational approach, emphasizing collaborative learning stimulated by meaningful problems, by self-directed study, and by team teaching.

The ways in which students are prepared for university training in the Netherlands differs from those in Northern America. In principle, university training is open to all students passing secondary school final examinations. There is no entrance examination, nor are other ways of selection employed. There is no preparatory college education. (However, Dutch secondary education generally concentrates more on academic subjects than American high schools.) Therefore, university students in the Netherlands are younger than their colleagues in the USA and are relatively less well-equipped with SDL skills. This state of affairs has forced teachers at Maastricht University to provide students with some more structure, in particular in the first year of training. The problems that are used tend to be more focused and less complex; students receive extensive training in discussing problems, in chairing meetings, in reporting findings from the literature, and in using the library. Frequent assessment monitors students' progress.

The Process of PBL at Maastricht

All learning in a problem-based curriculum starts with a problem. A problem, written by a team of teachers, aims to guide students toward certain subject matter. A problem usually describes some phenomena or events that can be observed in daily life, but it can also consist of the description of an important theoretical or practical issue (Schmidt, 1983b). Table 2.1 shows several examples of problems that students are offered in the various curricula of several Maastricht faculties.

Problems are the starting point of students' learning processes. A problem is presented to students for discussion in a small tutorial group generally made up of 8 to 10 students. Usually the students have to explain the phenomena or events presented to them in terms of their underlying mechanisms, principles, or processes. The students do not prepare themselves for the initial discussion of the problem. They come into the situation equipped only with their prior knowledge. This knowledge may have been acquired through formal education, through the mass media, or may have been derived from their own personal experiences of a similar situation.

While discussing a problem, the group employs a specific procedure that all students are taught shortly after entering a problem-based curriculum. This procedure is called the "Seven Jump" (Schmidt, 1983b). The Seven Jump consists of seven steps to be completed by a tutorial group to take maximal learning advantage of a problem. Table 2.2 gives an overview of the procedure.

The procedure guides the small-group members from the initial clarification of terms through a phase of problem definition to a phase of brainstorming in which they bring forward their initial ideas. Students then have to elaborate on their initial ideas and critically evaluate what they know and do not know. Finally, they have to formulate their learning issues for self-directed study. After about 2 days of SDL, the members of the tutorial group meet again to report and synthesize their findings in relation to the original problem. The goal here is to make sure that they now have gained a better, deeper, and more detailed understanding of the (causal) mechanisms or processes underlying the problem. The discussion

TABLE 2.1
Examples of Problems Offered to Students in the Various
Problem-Based Curricula of Maastricht University

Little monsters[1]

Coming home from work, tired and in need of a hot bath, Anita, an account manager, discovers two spiders in her tub. She shrinks back, screams, and runs away. Her heart pounds, a cold sweat is coming over her. A neighbor saves her from her difficult situation by killing the little animals with a newspaper.
Explain.

The miserable life of a stomach[2]

The protagonist of our story is the stomach of a truck driver who used to work shifts and who smokes a lot. The stomach developed a gastric ulcer and so the smoking stopped. Stomach tablets are now a regular part of the intake.

While on the highway in southern Germany, our stomach had to digest a heavy German lunch. Half an hour later, a severe abdominal pain developed. The stomach had to expel the meal. Two tablets of acetyl salicylic acid were inserted to relieve the pain (the truck driver had forgotten his stomach tablets!).

A second extrusion some hours later contained a bit of blood. In a hospital in Munich an endoscope was inserted. The stomach needed to be operated upon in the near future.
Explain.

The death penalty[3]

A U.S. serviceman, stationed at the NATO base in Soesterberg, the Netherlands, has been arrested and detained by the Public Prosecutor's office on charges of homicide. Pursuant to the NATO Status Forces Agreement, the United States requests that the man be handed over to the U.S. authorities who claim exclusive criminal jurisdiction in the case. The serviceman is liable to be subjected to the death penalty in the United States. The question arises as to whether the Netherlands authorities, in view of the existing law and the practice developed under the European Convention, should comply with the request by the United States. Take into account the judgement by the European Court of Human Rights of 7 July 1989 in the Soering case.

---

[1]From the introductory course of the psychology curriculum, Maastricht University, 1995–1996.
[2]Adapted from a course on abdominal complaints, medical curriculum, Maastricht University, 1993–1994.
[3]Adapted from a course on human rights, law curriculum, Maastricht University, 1994–1995.

in the tutorial group is chaired by a student. The chairperson ensures that the meeting proceeds in an orderly fashion through introducing new topics for discussion, summarizing the students' contributions, and making certain that the group achieves its goals. Thus the discussion of a problem is not a spontaneous ad hoc process, but proceeds along prescribed lines.

A tutorial group is supported by a staff member, known as a tutor. The role of the tutor is to facilitate students' learning processes and to stimulate students to collaborate in effective ways. The contributions of a tutor are geared toward challenging the students to clarify their own ideas,

TABLE 2.2
The Seven Jump

---

1. Clarify unknown terms and concepts in the problem description.
2. Define the problem; that is, list the phenomena to be explained.
3. Analyze the problem; "brainstorm"; try to produce as many different explanations for the phenomena as you can. Use prior knowledge and common sense.
4. Criticize the explanations proposed and try to produce a coherent description of the processes that, according to what you think, underlie the phenomena.
5. Formulate learning issues for SDL.
6. Fill the gaps in your knowledge through self-study.
7. Share your findings with your group and try to integrate the knowledge acquired into a comprehensive explanation for the phenomena. Check whether you know enough now.

---

inciting students to elaborate on the subject matter, questioning ideas, looking for inconsistencies, and considering alternatives. By doing so, he or she helps the students to organize their knowledge, to resolve their misconceptions, and to discover what is not well understood. Apart from sufficient knowledge of the subject under discussion, the tutor should be capable of understanding the frame of mind of the students while discussing the problem and the subject matter to which it refers. A tutor should be able to imagine how people think if they only have a limited knowledge of a subject or a field. To stimulate students' collaboration in a tutorial group, a tutor should also be able to manage interpersonal dynamics in the group, to be sensitive to group development processes, and to handle interpersonal conflicts.

The Process of Problem-Based Learning in Theory

What, now, are the main factors affecting the learning and collaboration processes in the small-group tutorial? First of all, there is the prominent *role of the problem*. The problem is supposed to trigger the students' learning processes. To do so, high demands are placed on its quality. Problems should be adapted to the knowledge level of the students. They must be transparent as to what is expected from students without "giving away the solution." Finally, the problem should not be overly complex.

Second, the attempts made by the students to make sense of the phenomena or events described in the problem can be considered a process of *theory construction*. While discussing the problem, students engage in formulating a theory that may explain the phenomena or events presented to them. (For instance, students may explain Anita's fear of spiders as an evolutionary remnant of a justified fear for hairy, fast-moving insects that may have threatened the lives of our forebears millions of year ago, and they may become engaged in explaining the genetic mechanisms that may have helped this trait to survive.) As students are not supposed to prepare themselves prior to encountering the problem in the group tutorial, they construct this theory based on prior knowledge, on common sense, and on logical thinking. Prior knowledge mobilized by one participant tends to activate what might have been inaccessible knowledge in another participant. Once collective knowledge is accessed, learners also begin to elaborate on what they know and try to build bridges between their knowledge and the phenomena described in the particular problem. Typically, in a small-group session much elaboration based on what the participants already know can be observed. Their attempts to account for the problem may lead to a first reconstruction of what they know, and the emergence of a new problem-oriented knowledge structure. Because different students tend to know somewhat different things or to think somewhat differently, theory construction becomes a collaborative effect that may lead to new insights that were not present in the individual participants before the analysis of the problem began.

The collaborative effort, by which students help each other in clarifying the issues, is a central element of problem-based groups. In the course of the discussion, however, questions come up that cannot be answered by any of the participants in the group, or several alternatives are proposed between which the students are unable to choose, or students conclude that they only have a vague idea of the explanation of a phenomenon or an event. In these cases, a gap between what is known and understood and what is not understood will be experienced. This perceived cleft induces *an intrinsic motivation to learn* (Hunt, 1971). As D. W. Johnson and Johnson (1979) have shown, group discussion is an excellent vehicle to help students perceive gaps in their knowledge and, hence, to be motivated to search for additional information. The issues in need of further clarification are taken as cues for SDL activities and students spend considerable time with various resources sorting out these issues. On returning in the tutorial group, the new knowledge acquired is applied to the problem at hand to check whether the explanatory theory constructed can better deal with the phenomena presented than the original ideas produced during the previous session. Usually, further elaboration takes place to tune the theoretical notions that have evolved as a result of the ongoing learning even more closely to the problem-at-hand. If this is the case to a sufficient extent, the tutorial group will move to the next problem. In summary, PBL, conceptualized in this way, is an collaborative form of learning in which active construction of coherent mental models of knowledge, rather than simple processing of subject matter, is the focus of the activities. It is also a form of contextual learning, because principles, ideas, and mechanisms are not studied in the abstract but in the context of a concrete situation that can be recognized as relevant and interesting; at best, a situation that resembles future, professional situations in which the knowledge acquired must be applied.

RESEARCH QUESTIONS INVESTIGATING FACTORS OF PBL

This conceptualization of problem-based learning immediately induces a series of questions about its purported effects on students' learning. Among the questions raised may be the following:

1. How important is the nature of the problems presented to students? How do problems affect learning and achievement?
2. To what extent does elaboration on prior knowledge, both before and after new knowledge has been acquired, stimulate active construction of new knowledge?
3. What about motivational processes in PBL, in particular its influence on students' intrinsic motivation?
4. What does the tutor contribute to the learning?

This latter question is particularly pertinent because teachers, acting as tutors, are rarely content experts in the all disciplines studied during problem-based courses. This is due to the fact that students are offered subjects in an interdisciplinary way. Often, tutors may be specialists in one field of study (e.g., physiology in a medical curriculum or private law in a law curriculum), but less, if at all, in another academic discipline (e.g., pathology in the medical curriculum or administrative law in the law curriculum). Not surprisingly, one of the questions that continues to surface again and again is, "To what extent should tutors be subject matter experts?" and, even more important, "Which behaviors characterize an effective tutor?"

These and other questions are addressed in the following sections. We almost exclusively draw on studies carried out by the Maastricht Educational Research Group (MERG). In some cases, we add findings by other research teams. In addition, the reader is referred to the other chapters in this book.

To What Extent Do Problems Influence Students' Achievement?

Surprisingly, PBL literature devotes scant space to the role of problems. Barrows (1985) spent four pages on problem selection and preparation. Kaufman (1985) confined himself to giving a number of examples. Boud and Feletti (1992) presented a short introductory chapter. This lack of attention for the role of problems contrasts sharply with the focus on the tutor role by researchers as well as by teachers. Researchers have given much attention to the level of expertise and the way in which tutors perform effectively, as we see later in this chapter. When teachers new to PBL are confronted with this approach for the first time they also tend to focus on the small-group tutorial and to identify the tutor as the key element of problem-based learning. In the literature of PBL the tutor role is also heavily emphasized. Phrases like "The skill of the tutor is the backbone to problem-based learning" (Barrows, 1985, p. 93) and ". . . no single element is as critical to program success as the quality and preparation of its tutors" (Lucero, Jackson, & Galy, 1985, p. 53) seem to support this view. Is this opinion correct? Is the quality of the problems we offer to students in a problem-based context perhaps not equally important as a stimulus of learning?

Research relevant in this respect was conducted by Gijselaers and Schmidt (1990) and by Schmidt and Gijselaers (1990). These authors studied the contributions of various elements of PBL on learning outcomes such as knowledge and increased interest in subject matter. As a result of these activities, the researchers formulated a theory of PBL. This theory fits in with the models-of-school-learning tradition represented by such authors as Carroll (1963), Bloom (1976), and Cooley and Leinhardt (1980). The latter investigators maintained that learning in the school setting can be described by three categories of variables. The first category is that of the input variables, such as students' characteristics, teachers' behavior, and the adequacy of the learning materials. The second category is comprised by the intervening or process variables, such as learning activities carried out by the students, the amount of time they spend on the learning task, and characteristics of the instructional process, such as grouping of students or time on task. The third category, finally, consists of cognitive output variables (e.g., achievement) and affective outcomes, such as interest in subject matter studied. Schmidt and Gijselaers implemented these ideas in a model of PBL represented in Fig. 2.1.

In this theory, it is assumed that the way in which a tutorial group functions is mainly affected by the amount of prior knowledge that students bring to the learning situation, the quality of the problems presented to them (expressed as the amount of calibration to the current levels and needs of the students, their representativeness regarding the objectives of the course, and other facets), and the way the tutor deals with students and with the learning situation in general. The functioning of the tutorial group, in turn, would influence the interest that students would display regarding the topics studied and it would influence the amount of time they would spend on those topics. Time on task then would influence achievement of these students. If one thinks of the elements of our theo-

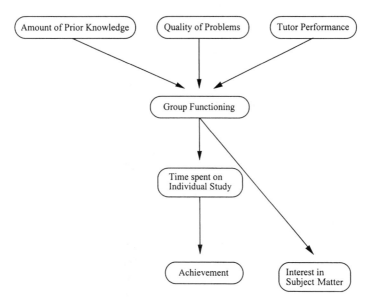

FIG. 2.1.   Theoretical model of PBL (adapted from Schmidt & Gijselaers, 1990).

ry as variables, that is, as entities that can have higher or lower values, the model outlined can be considered a causal and quantitative representation of the learning going on within a problem-based context. According to the model, an increase in the magnitude of one of the variables characteristically causes an increase of the magnitudes of other variables. The arrows indicate the direction of the causal influence. For instance, this theory predicts that an improvement in the quality of the problems presented to students, all other things being equal, will result in improved group performance. Better executed small-group tutorials, in turn, influence study time, which leads to higher achievement of the students involved. The role of the other variables involved can be interpreted in much the same way. For instance, the better the tutor guides the group, the better it will function.

The investigators subjected this model to a series of tests in which they measured each of the variables involved and studied their relations. The quality of problems used in a problem-based course, for instance, was measured by asking students to rate them. All items on which the problems in a course were rated consisted of a statement and a so-called Likert scale ranging from 1 (*totally disagree*) to 5 (*totally agree*) to which the students could respond by circling a number. In Table 2.3, sample statements used for the problem rating task are displayed. The scores were averaged over items, producing a "quality of problems" score. The other variables

TABLE 2.3
Sample Items Used for the Rating of the Quality of Problems

The problems were clearly stated.
The problems were suitable for applying a systematic work procedure.
The problems sufficiently stimulated group discussion.
The problems gave sufficient opportunities for formulating learning goals.
The problems sufficiently stimulated SDL.

---

in the model were measured in similar ways. Achievement was measured by using the end-of-course test. Data from 20 courses of the Maastricht University medical curriculum and additional data from the health sciences curriculum of the same university were analyzed. The statistical technique used to test our theory was structural equations modeling (Bentler, 1989; 1990), which enables the investigator to check to what extent the actual data fit his theoretical model and to estimate the strengths of the causal relations hypothesized. Figure 2.2 displays the results of our analyses. The original model, as displayed in Fig. 2.1, proved to be too restrictive, but a less stringent, more "relaxed" model fit the data quite well. The values accompanying the arrows are "path coefficients" and can be interpreted as beta weights in multiple regression analysis. They have a maximum value of 1.00 and a minimum of –1.00. The actual values represent the strength of the causal paths. Here, quality of problems exerts an influence of .43 on group functioning, whereas the magnitude of the influence of tutor performance on the same variable is .31. Most of the path coefficients found can be considered reasonably high. This is, in particular, the case for the paths emerging from the quality of problems factor. Quality of problems does not only affect the functioning of the tutorial group; it influences two other elements of the model as well—time spent and interest in subject matter. This suggests that the higher the quality of the problems used, the better the group works, the more time is spent on SDL activities, and the more interest is raised in the materials studied. Indeed, problems seem central to the learning in problem-based curricula. Compare their influence with the influence of the tutor. Tutor performance only directly affects group functioning; all other influence is indirect, namely via group functioning. Problems, by contrast, influence almost all elements of the learning in a direct fashion.

These findings imply two things for the implementation of PBL. The first is that poor problems present at least an equally serious hazard to students' learning as the presence of a poor tutor. The second is that improving the quality of problems is bound to have beneficial effects on learning at least to the same extent as extending tutor training activities to improve

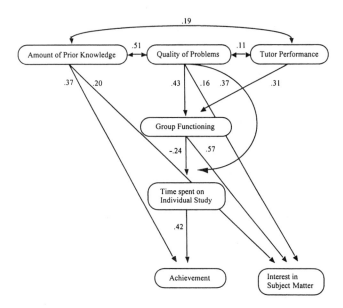

FIG. 2.2.   Causal paths for a model of PBL.

tutors' performance. In addition, experience shows that it is easier to improve on problem quality than it is to ensure consistently good performance of tutors.

To What Extent Does Problem-Based Learning Affect Cognitive Processing?

In this section, research will be discussed demonstrating various cognitive effects of problem-based learning on students.

Activation of Prior Knowledge.   Schmidt (1984) presented small groups of students attending higher professional training with the following problem: "A red blood cell is put in pure water under a microscope. The cell swells and eventually bursts. Another blood cell is added to an aqueous salt solution. It shrinks. Explain these phenomena." A few years prior to this study, during their high school years, the students involved had all been acquainted with the subject of osmosis, which is the underlying explanatory mechanism for the phenomena described in the problem. Half of the students discussed the blood cell problem, while the other half discussed a problem about factors affecting an airplane taking off. Both groups then read a text on osmosis and diffusion. At a subsequent "free-recall" test,[1] the group that had discussed the blood cell problem remembered almost twice as much information about osmosis as the other group. This demonstrates that problem analysis in a small group indeed has a strong activating effect on prior knowledge.

Effects of Prior Knowledge Activation on the Processing of New Information. In another study Schmidt, De Volder, De Grave, Moust, and Patel (1989) presented the blood cell problem to novices, 14-year-old high school students, who had never studied the subject concerned. Therefore, the theory that these students developed about the mechanisms and processes that could be responsible for the phenomena described in the problem was expected to have a commonsense character. In an attempt to account for the swelling of the blood cell, one group assumed, for instance, that the membrane probably had valves that would let the water in but would prevent it from escaping again. Another group explained the shrinking of the cell by assuming that salt has hygroscopic characteristics. According to them, the salt "soaked up" fluids from the cell in the way that it would with a wine-stained tablecloth. Table 2.4 represents several ideas and the elaborations on these ideas of these students.

Subsequent to the discussion, a six-page text about osmosis was distributed, both to groups that had tackled the blood cell problem and to a control group that had discussed a neutral topic. The group that had discussed the blood cell problem prior to reading the text remembered significantly more about the text than the group that had studied an unrelated topic. These findings indicate that activation of prior knowledge through problem analysis in a small group definitely facilitates understanding and remembering new information, even if that prior knowledge is only to a small extent relevant to understanding the problem—and sometimes even incorrect. What's interesting, students who studied the topic of osmosis a few weeks before the experiment was conducted (called the "experts" by the authors) did not profit as much by the experimental treatment as compared to the novices, indicating that problem analysis is most helpful if students have only limited knowledge of the subject.

Contribution of Group Discussion to the Effect of PBL. Individual prior knowledge activation can be performed in several ways; for example, by giving students questions or by asking them to write down every-

---

[1]Free recall is a procedure in which a participant is instructed to write down everything that he or she remembers about a certain topic without the aid of further information. It is considered by educational researchers as a measure of both amount and coherence of the knowledge a participant has.

TABLE 2.4
Naive Ideas and Elaborations of High School Students
Discussing the Blood Cell Problem

Action	Explanations
Swelling	The cell is filled with tiny sponges absorbing the water.
	The cell absorbs water by means of an unidentified mechanism because the wall is porous. However, the wall contains valves that prevent the water from escaping.
	Red blood cells carry oxygen. The cell extracts oxygen from the water and swells.
	The cell contains salts dissolved in liquid. The solution exerts pressure on the wall larger than the outside pressure exerted by pure water.
	The absorption of water triggers an unknown chemical reaction within the cell.
Bursting	Blood cells usually take in small quantities of liquids, because the human body contains many cells. In this particular case, there is only one cell that has to absorb too much water.
	Animate objects only have a limited life span.
Shrinking	Water or other fluids are extracted from the cell because of the hygroscopic properties of salt.
	Salt water exerts a higher pressure on the wall than the content of the cell.
	The salt corrodes the wall by affecting the wall's molecules. The cell then begins to leak.
	The salt enters into the cell and digests the cell from within.
Swelling and shrinking in combination	The cell contains salt that extracts water from its environment because of its hygroscopic properties. If the water in the environment contains a higher concentration of salt, however, fluids will be extracted from the cell.

Note. Taken from Schmidt, Spaay, and De Grave (1988).

thing they remember about a topic. Does group discussion contribute more? De Grave, Schmidt, Beliën, Moust, De Volder, and Kerkhofs (1984) have compared effects of problem analysis in a small group with individual problem analysis and direct prompting of knowledge about osmosis. They discovered that small-group analysis had a larger positive effect on remembering a text than individual problem analysis. Simply prompting already available knowledge had the smallest relative effect. The investigators concluded that the confrontation with a relevant problem and small-group discussion of that problem each have an independent facilitating effect on prior knowledge relative to direct prompting of prior knowledge. Group discussion had, in particular, a considerable effect, suggesting that elaboration on prior knowledge and learning from each other, even before new information is acquired, are potent means to facilitate understanding of problem-relevant information.

Cognitive Processing While Involved in Problem Discussion. Students are, of course, not always involved to the same amount of overt verbalization of information in a small-group discussion. What happens to those who participate less actively in the tutorial group? Do students who elaborate less verbally—the silent students—learn less? Research by Moust, Schmidt, De Volder, Beliën, and De Grave (1986) demonstrated that the quantity of one's contribution to the discussion and its quality were unrelated to achievement. This led the researchers to the conclusion that subjects not or less participating in the discussion elaborate as much as those who do participate without verbalizing their elaborations to the same extent as the latter. The more silent students were involved in what they called "covert elaboration." In other words, these students are elaborating without sharing their conclusions with their fellow students. According to these authors it would otherwise be hard to understand how these students would profit from the experience.

In an exploratory study, Geerligs (1995) investigated to what extent students participating in tutorial groups where really task-focused; for example, were actually involved in the thinking about the problem at hand. He followed five tutorial groups during 10 subsequent sessions in the first and second year of the health sciences curriculum. Geerligs used the technique of thought sampling for his study. At irregular intervals a beeper was activated and the tutor asked the students to write down their thoughts just before the beeper was heard. The results showed that 74% of students' thoughts were task-related, whether content-related (55%), procedure-related (11%) or reflective thoughts (8%). Task-irrelevant thoughts accounted for 16%, whereas 10% of students' thoughts were classified as miscellaneous or as reflecting an absence of thought. This research seems to suggest that students in a problem-oriented environment are, most of the time, actively involved in the processing of problem-relevant information. The research of Geerligs did, however, not provide records of the nature and sequence of subjects' mental processes or whether active students were more task-oriented than more silent students. Nevertheless, in particular the Moust and colleagues (1986) study suggests that, contrary to popular belief, more silent students do not appear to be less task-oriented.

Evidence for Constructive Processes in Small-Group Tutorials. To date, only a few studies document the emergence of problem-oriented knowledge structures as a result of PBL, that is, as a result of problem discussion. There is, however, some evidence for problem-oriented tuning as a result of problem analysis per se. Table 2.4 summarizes explanations of secondary education students regarding the blood cell problem. These explanations were compiled from taped discussions of six tutorial groups (some groups produced several explanations). The explanations given suggest that students indeed adapt their general prior knowledge to fit the problem at hand, or that they attempt to construct a theory that deals with the phenomena provided in terms of an underlying process that explain these phenomena (if only partially in most cases). The participants involved had never before been confronted with a similar problem; therefore, the assumption that general world knowledge is indeed restructured to make it suitable for the problem presented does not seem far-fetched.

In a recent study, De Grave, Boshuizen, and Schmidt (1996) investigated the ongoing cognitive and metacognitive processes during the phase of problem analysis by analyzing the verbal communication among group members and their thinking processes. Thinking processes were tapped by means of a stimulated recall procedure. Directly after a tutorial session, each participant individually reviewed a videotape of the session and was requested to stop the tape whenever he or she would recall particular thoughts that came up during discussion. The investigators analyzed the verbatim transcripts or "verbal protocols" of the interaction in the tutorial group, and the "recall protocols" of individuals to study to what extent the ongoing processes could be described as theory construction, and whether there was evidence of conceptual change in small-group tutorials. The authors discovered that the verbal protocols were dominated by attempts at theory building, causal reasoning, and hypothesis testing. Considerable time was also spent on what the authors described as data exploration (finding out what the significance is of the various cues in the problem) and problem definition. Less attention was given to procedures and to metareasoning. By contrast, the recall protocols reflected metareasoning. Students evaluated the appropriateness of their prior knowledge, reflected on the learning process, and reflected on strategies of thinking. It seems that, while thinking, students prepare their utterances and assess to what extent they are relevant to the task at hand. They also pay thought to the process of collaboration, although this category hardly shows up in the actual verbal interaction. This indicates that students are sensitive to the way the group collaborates and take their own contributions in this respect into account. Theory construction and evaluation are also prevalent in the stimulated recall protocols. Interestingly, the investigators found "bursts" of theory construction, alternated by data exploration. It seems that ideas are proposed in a cyclical fashion that continues during the whole session. Even in the last three minutes of the 20-minute meeting, new ideas were proposed. In addition, the patterns of verbal interaction and individual thought were rather similar, thoughts being both a response to what is said and a precursor. Finally, the authors presented evidence for conceptual change as a result of initial problem discussion. Students evaluate what is proposed by other students and are influenced by the arguments exchanged, leading to conceptual change. This is a somewhat surprising finding, because it was expected that conceptual changes would result largely from reading the literature.

Long-Term Retention of Knowledge. Does PBL enhance students' long-term retention of information? An assumption of constructivist learning is that education becomes more personally meaningful. If this is so, then knowledge acquired should be retained over longer periods. To test this assumption, Tans, Schmidt, Schadé-Hoogeveen, and Gijselaers (1986) compared achievement of physiotherapy students randomly allocated to either a problem-based or to a lecture-based version of a course in muscle physiology. Students in the problem-based course performed significantly poorer on an immediate multiple-choice test. However, a free-recall test of core knowledge taken after 6 months showed the reverse effect: Students under the problem-based condition recalled up to five times more concepts than the control group. This finding, along with the findings of Martensen, Eriksson, and Ingelman-Sundberg (1985), and Eisenstaedt, Barry, and Glanz (1990), suggests that PBL induces students to retain knowledge much longer than under conventional teaching conditions. Results from these studies also seem to indicate that initial learning may be poorer, possibly because students under this condition learn less initially, but process the information more extensively.

To What Extent Does PBL Affect Intrinsic Motivation?

In a series of studies by De Volder and his colleagues (De Volder, Schmidt, De Grave, & Moust, 1989; De Volder, Schmidt, Moust, & De Grave, 1986), attempts have been made to see to what extent group discussion about a problem would increase intrinsic interest in problem-related subject matter. Groups were presented with either the blood cell problem or with a problem describing a plane taking off from Amsterdam airport. Immediately after the discussion, the students were asked to indicate to what extent they were interested in receiving information about osmosis. After having studied a text on the subject, they were asked whether they would like to read more about the subject and whether they were interested in additional information sent to them by the investigators. Before, as well as after having studied the text, the groups that had tackled the blood cell problem displayed significantly greater intrinsic motivation than the group that had studied the airplane problem. Schmidt (1983a) found that this higher intrinsic motivation also demonstrated itself in the fact that significantly more students participating in the blood cell discussion had signed up to attend a lecture about osmosis than those who had not participated in that discussion.

Other studies of the influence of PBL on motivation have been scarce. Program evaluations carried out routinely in the Maastricht curricula, however, suggest that students consider PBL highly motivating, a fact that is also demonstrated in consumer studies of higher education carried out nationally in the Netherlands. In these studies, Maastricht University curricula are mostly nominated number one in their category, primarily because of PBL.

Which Contributions Does the Tutor Make?

The question about the necessary level of a tutor's expertise has dominated, from the onset, the literature on the role of the tutor in PBL. In the first book about this educational approach, Barrows and Tamblyn (1980) described a study conducted at McMaster University Medical School with tutors who were more-or-less content experts in the field covered by the problem being discussed by the students. Barrows and Tamblyn concluded:

> This experiment thus showed that it is far better to have an expert working with the students, one who knows if the students are in a quandary or are going down the wrong track; but who also knows how to get them to discover this for themselves, to learn by making mistakes, and to reason their way to the right conclusions. Such an expert can provide the students with better evaluative feedback about their learning, relevant to their own objectives. (p. 106)

In a later publication, Barrows (1988) stated that, ideally, tutorial groups are best guided by experts. "There is no question that the ideal situation is for the tutor to be an expert both as a tutor and in the discipline being studied by the students" but "if this is not possible, the next best tutor is the teacher who is good at being a tutor, as described here, though not an expert in the discipline being studied" (p. 43). According to Barrows (1988), the worst thing to happen is confronting students with a tutor "who is an expert in the area of study, but a weak tutor" (p. 44). So, Barrows opts for a tutor who is competent in both areas—subject matter and tutoring skills. Of course, we all wish that all faculty involved in PBL would have the characteristics described by Barrows and by others, but reality shows otherwise. In fact, some feel that teachers who are both knowledgeable and proficient tutors are the exception rather than the rule. The question then becomes, "To what extent can students perform with nonsubject matter tutors, and even with nonexpert poor tutors?"

Although most advocates of PBL emphasize the importance of the tutor's role for students' learning in tutorial groups, until recently, there was almost no empirical data available concerning the question of tutors' expertise. In this contribution we present data on this topic collected in various academic programs at Maastricht University. First, we concentrate on findings regarding effects of expert or nonexpert staff tutors on their students' learning. Next, we review research comparing tutorial groups guided by either staff or by student tutors. In a subsequent section we attempt to explain differences in outcomes between the various studies. Finally, we make an effort to summarize the various findings in a comprehensive theory of tutor functioning and present data in support of that theory.

Research Comparing Expert and Nonexpert Staff Tutors. In an early study assessing the impact of content expertise on students' learning, Schmidt (1977) compared the levels of achievement of second-year medical students in three courses of Maastricht University's medical curriculum. In the comparison, about 150 students and 20 tutors were involved. Both students and tutors were randomly assigned to the tutorial groups. About half of the tutors were nonmedical, such as social science and basic science staff. They were considered the nonexperts regarding the topics at hand. Staff with medical degrees were considered the subject matter experts. End-of-course tests were used as the dependent variable. The study revealed no difference in levels of achievement related to content expertise of the tutor. In fact, one of the best performing groups was guided by a laboratory assistant (at the time, Maastricht University involved academic as well as nonacademic tutors in its curriculum).

De Volder and Schmidt (1982) studied a total of 125 groups from the first 4 years of the same school. They found that tutors' actual behaviors correlated significantly with their level of expertise. Tutors considered experts asked more stimulating questions and provided more explanations. In addition, students guided by experts performed somewhat better than students guided by nonexperts.

In another study carried out at the same institution, but conducted almost 10 years later, Swanson, Stalenhoef-Halling, and Van der Vleuten (1990) investigated the effects of expertise of 230 tutors on the performances of students, using end-of-course tests as the dependent measure. Because the particular curriculum integrated biomedical, clinical, and psychosocial aspects of medicine in each course, the investigators subdivided each end-of-course test according to these three categories and studied the impacts of tutors' professional backgrounds on students' performances on the resulting subtests. No effect of expertise was found.

In an extensive research effort, Schmidt, Van der Arend, Moust, Kokx, and Boon (1993) investigated the effects of tutors' subject matter expertise on students' levels of academic achievement in the problem-based health sciences curriculum of Maastricht University. Data were analyzed from 336 staff-led tutorial groups involving students participants in seven

4-year undergraduate programs. The results showed that students guided by subject matter experts achieved somewhat more than students guided by nonexperts tutors. The effect of subject matter expertise on achievement was strongest in the first curriculum year.

Another study by Schmidt (1994) also showed that students guided by expert tutors performed significantly better than students guided by nonexpert tutors. Data were analyzed from 1,800 Maastricht University health sciences students who participated in tutorial groups led by content-expert staff tutors, by nonexpert staff tutors, or by student tutors. The main effect of expertise level on achievement was statistically significant, showing that the higher the level of subject matter expertise of the tutor, the better the students' achievement.

Research Comparing Staff and Student Tutors. Research comparing tutorial groups guided by staff with those guided by student tutors has almost exclusively been conducted at Maastricht University as part of ongoing self-evaluation initiatives. In response to the influx of approximately 1500 students in each of the health sciences, law, and economics programs each year, the various faculty boards decided to investigate whether it would be possible to employ students to perform the tutor role. In all schools, the student tutors hired were advanced undergraduate students. For most programs there were no strict criteria for selecting student tutors. Students had to show a reasonable level of achievement and a positive attitude toward PBL. Before students were entitled to tutor they had to participate in workshops on tutoring skills. In the studies reviewed that follow, the student tutors can be considered relatively nonexpert as compared with the academic staff.

De Volder, De Grave, and Gijselaers (1985) compared achievement levels of health sciences students in three consecutive courses of the first curriculum year of the health sciences. In total, 17 student-guided groups were compared with 28 groups guided by staff tutors. Assignment to groups was random. The investigators found significant differences favoring staff tutors in one course but failed to discern differences in the other two. A follow-up study carried out in the subsequent year of study in this specific course period by De Grave, De Volder, Gijselaers, and Damoiseaux (1990) revealed no differences.

Gijselaers, Bouhuijs, Mulder, and Mullink (1987) compared 20 student-tutored groups with 26 staff-tutored groups in two courses within the economics program. The investigators found a difference in achievement levels favoring staff tutors in one of the courses. In the second course, however, no difference was found.

A study of law students by Moust, De Volder, and Nuy (1989), involving 10 student tutors and 10 staff tutors in a first-year course, revealed a significant difference supporting the hypothesis that tutors' subject matter expertise indeed facilitates student performance. A follow-up study in two other courses by Moust (1993), however, failed to replicate the findings of the previous study. No differences were found between student- and staff-guided groups.

Schmidt, Van der Arend, Kokx, and Boon (1994) studied the effects of students versus staff tutoring on students' learning in the health sciences program. Exam performance of 334 tutorial groups guided by staff tutors was compared with achievement of 400 groups guided by student tutors. Overall, students guided by a staff tutor achieved somewhat more. The difference was, however, fairly small.

Research on effects other than examination performance is rather scarce. Moust (1993) found differences in time spent on self-directed study in one course. Students guided by student tutors spent significantly less time on self-directed study than students guided by staff tutors.

In summary, the results of the studies comparing expert staff tutors and nonexpert staff tutors, as well as the research comparing staff and student tutors reviewed here, are generally inconclusive. This outcome is in line with research on this topic conducted in problem-based curricula elsewhere (Des Marchais & Black, 1991; Davis, Nairn, Paine, Anderson, & Oh, 1992; Davis, Oh, Anderson, Gruppen, & Nairn, 1994; Eagle, Harasym, & Mandir, 1992; Gruppen, Traber, Paine, Woolliscroft & Davis, 1992; Silver & Wilkerson, 1991; Wilkerson, Hafler, & Liu, 1991). Of the five studies comparing academic achievement levels of students guided by staff tutors of different levels of subject matter expertise, three (De Volder & Schmidt, 1982; Schmidt, 1994; Schmidt et al., 1993) demonstrated an effect in favor of the expert staff tutors. Two other studies (Schmidt, 1977; Swanson et al., 1990) showed no differences in achievement. Of the six studies comparing staff tutoring with student tutoring, one (Schmidt et al., 1994) demonstrated significant differences favoring students guided by staff students, three studies (De Volder et al., 1985; Gijselaers et al., 1987; Moust et al., 1989) showed mixed outcomes, and two studies (De Grave et al., 1990; Moust, 1993) did not reveal any differences at all.

Reasons for Inconclusive Results of the Tutor Expertise Studies. The question, of course, is how these contradictory results may be explained. Several reasons have been proposed in the literature (Moust, 1993; Schmidt, 1994; Schmidt et al., 1993).

The first reason may be related to the definition of what actually constitutes subject matter expertise in small-group tutoring. In some studies, an extremely stringent definition of what constitutes a content expert was applied: Expert tutors were those staff members who had an active research interest in the specific topic studied by the students. Nonexperts included all nonspecialists in the field concerned (Davis et al., 1992, 1994). Other studies (in the domain of medicine) divided the tutors in three broad subject matter categories: biomedicine, clinical medicine, and social sciences staff. Another group of studies defined expertise uniquely in relation to the course's content. Experts were those who had received training in the area covered by the course (e.g., biochemistry in a course about nutrition); nonexperts included all academic staff who had expertise only partially related to the topic at hand (e.g., family medicine, epidemiology, sociology). In the studies comparing staff with student tutoring, on the other hand, content expertise was considered equivalent to the level of training of the tutor and not so much to his or her specific knowledge (all academic staff were considered experts). This may imply that some staff tutors employed in these studies were not really content experts in the stricter sense of the word. In his study carried out in two consecutive courses, Moust (1993) did not find any differences in achievement between student-led groups and staff-led groups. However, after removing a number of nonexpert staff from his analyses, Moust demonstrated, a posteriori, that subject matter expertise indeed made a difference in terms of students' achievement.

A second reason for the inconclusiveness of the findings may be the magnitudes of the samples studied. Most studies examined effects of subject matter expertise in one single course (De Grave et al., 1990; Moust et al., 1989). Only two studies included an entire year or an entire curriculum (Schmidt et al., 1993; Swanson et al., 1990). Even if the subject matter expertise of the tutor makes a difference, its influence is bound to be small. Students spend relatively little time with their tutor and during these encounters and the verbal contributions of the tutor are mostly limited. Reliable effects, if any, will show up only when sufficient numbers of tutorial groups are included in the analysis; that is, if the power of the statistical test applied is sufficiently great. Studies employing large samples, however, also show contrasting results.

The extent to which students are exposed to PBL may also be a factor. Casual observations suggest that students who have little or no experience with PBL rely more heavily on their tutors as sources of guidance and information. If these tutors are familiar with the subject matter to be mastered, this may make a difference. These observations may explain why the positive findings reported were largely confined to first-year courses, or to courses in which students encountered PBL for the first time. Novice students may lean more on their tutors' expertise than do students in later years.

A fourth explanation, in agreement with the third, has been proposed by Schmidt (1994). Based on his earlier studies (in which he found effects of tutor expertise mainly in those cases in which students were largely novices to the domain), he conjectured that students in a problem-based curriculum need a minimum level of structure if any useful learning is to take place. This structure can be provided either internally, through the prior knowledge that students already have regarding the topic at hand, or externally, through the structure provided by the learning materials. If these kinds of structures are lacking, for some reason, students will seek structure from their tutor. Only under these conditions, a subject matter expert tutor may have a positive impact on student learning. Or to put it negatively, only under these circumstances students with a nonexpert tutor are handicapped as compared with their peers. In a study testing these hypotheses, Schmidt found the following:

1. Tutors' expertise particularly influenced students' achievement when the students had limited prior knowledge. When the level of prior knowledge was high, it was less important whether or not the tutor was a subject matter expert. Students were then able to organize the new information themselves.

2. The impact of tutors' expertise was also greater when the structure of the course materials was low, suggesting that tutors' expertise indeed compensates for lack of structure in the curriculum. Offering sufficient structure (e.g., through proper introductions, high-quality cases, and clear references to the literature) may help students to study on their own.

3. The impact of tutors' level of expertise was greatest in courses that were both poorly structured and that introduced topics unfamiliar to students.

These findings suggest that the tutor can be considered a last-resort device. Students seek guidance from their tutor mainly when everything else fails. In conditions where materials are sufficiently structured and prior knowledge is sufficient, the subject matter expertise of the tutor seems to play a limited role.

Differences in Actual Behavior Between Tutors. A final reason for the inconclusiveness of the findings in the tutor subject matter expertise studies may be that in some studies the experts did not behave differently from the nonexperts, whereas in other studies the experts behaved differently. Schmidt et al. (1993), for instance, found clear differences in behavior (as observed by students) between expert and nonexpert tutors in relation to students' achievement and study efforts. After each course, students were asked to rate their tutor's behavior on an 11-item Likert-type rating scale, ranging from 1 to 5. Each item consisted of a statement with which students could (strongly) agree or (strongly) disagree. The items dealt with various aspects of tutorial behavior: a four-item subscale dealt with tutors' "subject matter input" and a four-item subscale was directed to tutors' "process facilitation." The subject matter input scale contained items referring to the ways in which the tutor made use of his or her subject matter knowledge to help students; for example, "The subject-matter contributions of the tutor were relevant" and "The tutor displayed a fair understanding of this course's objectives." The process-facilitation scale was intended to measure the skills considered crucial to stimulating the collaborative processes; for example, "The tutor's questions stimulated the discussion" or "At regular intervals, the tutor evaluated with us the group's functioning." Schmidt and his colleagues found differences in ratings between expert and nonexpert tutors on a number of these criterial behaviors. Subject matter experts displayed a deeper understanding of the objectives of the particular course, appeared to be more knowledgeable about the subjects to be mastered by the students, and used their subject matter knowledge more frequently to help the students. In addition, their contributions in this respect were rated as being more relevant. The nonexpert tutors, on the other hand, evaluated the group's functioning more often. Schmidt and colleagues concluded that the data indicate that subject matter expertise is really what counts in small-group tutoring: subject matter experts display more content-related behaviors while tutoring, resulting in better achievement and greater effort by their students.

However, the process-facilitation behaviors are not irrelevant.

> One of the more intriguing results of the present study is that process-facilitation behaviors such as asking questions and evaluating the group's progress are causally related to achievement in much the same way as subject-matter-related behaviors. An effective tutor appears to be someone who uses his or her subject-matter knowledge and, at the same time, is able to ask stimulating questions. (Schmidt et al., 1993, p. 790)

Schmidt and his colleagues (1994) also studied differences in behavior between student and staff tutors. Schmidt and colleagues compared tutor's performance on four behaviors considered critical to facilitating students' learning of 334 tutorial groups guided by staff tutors and of 400 groups guided by student tutors. The investigators found that staff tutors made extensive use of their subject matter knowledge. Detailed inspection of the data, however, showed that student tutors are rated higher in this respect in the first year of study, whereas staff tutors get higher ratings in the 3 subsequent years. The same phenomenon was also observed in the data concerning "the relevance of the tutor's contributions" and "asking stimulating questions."

Moust (1993) and Moust and Schmidt (1994) studied differences in behavior of staff and student tutors in two subsequent courses of the first-year curriculum of the law school. Based on interviews with both students and their tutors, the investigators distinguished between two main components of tutor functioning: the way a tutor handles the knowledge that students must acquire (the subject matter input component) and the way a tutor establishes a personal relationship with the members of a tutorial group. Each component was assumed to have several subcomponents. The subject matter input component contained the following subcomponents: *use of expertise* (To what extent does a tutor use his or her subject matter expertise to help students?); *cognitive congruence* (To what extent is a tutor able to understand and to express him or herself at the students' level of knowledge, e.g., the ability to express oneself in the language of the students, using the concepts they use and explaining things in ways easily grasped by the students?); and *assessment orientation* (To what extent does a tutor stress the importance of the end-of-course-test to direct the students' learning?). The process facilitation component was subdivided into the following subcomponents: *use of authority* (To what extent does a tutor exercise his or her power to direct students' activities in the group?); *role congruence* (To what extent is a tutor able to show empathy with and to relate to students' life experiences, e.g., the willingness of the tutor to be a "student among the students," i.e., to seek an informal relationship with the students and to display an attitude of personal interest and caring?); and *focus on cooperation* (To what extent is a tutor interested in students' cooperation in the tutorial group?). For all components of tutor functioning, appropriate Likert-type rating scales were developed.

The results showed that as far as the subject matter input component was concerned, staff tutors proved to use their expertise more frequently; student tutors, however, displayed significantly more "cognitively congruent behavior" in a tutorial group (both courses showed significant differences in these respects). In other words, student tutors were better at understanding the nature of the cognitive problems that students faced in attempting to master the subject matter. In addition, the investigators found that student tutors referred more often to the end-of-course test than staff tutors to direct students' activities in the small-group tutorials. As for the process facilitation component, the researchers also found contrasts between staff and student tutors. Staff tutors showed more authority in both courses, whereas student tutors displayed more role congruence behavior; they were more interested in students' daily study experiences and their personality factors. As for attention to group cooperation, no differences appeared in groups led by a staff or a student tutor. The findings leave one with the impression that student tutors better understand the nature of the intellectual problems that first-year students face in the comprehension of the subject matter as well as the demands that an university education pose on them.

A THEORY OF THE EFFECTIVE TUTOR

Based on the findings reviewed here, in particular the differences in behaviors between expert, nonexpert, and student tutors, Moust (1993) and Schmidt and Moust (1995) have proposed a theory of tutor performance. The investigators framed their ideas in the context of the theory of PBL proposed by Schmidt and Gijselaers (1990), discussed earlier in this chapter.

A key concept in their theory of tutor performance is the concept of "cognitive congruence." As defined previously, cognitive congruence is a tutor's ability to understand and to express him or herself at the students' level of knowledge. To do this tutors have to express themselves in the language of the students, using the concepts they use and explaining things in ways easily grasped by them. If a tutor is not able to frame his of her contributions in a language that is adapted to the level of students' understanding of the subject matter studied, these contributions will go unnoticed. In addition, cognitive congruence assumes sensitivity of the tutor concerning the difficulties that students may come across while dealing with a problem or with the subject matter relevant to that problem. A tutor should know when to intervene and what to offer: asking for clarification, suggesting a counterexample, or providing some brief explanation. Cognitive congruence is a necessary condition for tutors to be effective. According to Moust (1993), a tutor can only be effective in this respect if he or she has relevant subject matter knowledge and, in addition, has an authentic interest in his or her students' lives and in their learning. Without appropriate subject matter knowledge it will be difficult to follow the students' line of reasoning or to actively contribute to it. Additionally, without a genuine and personal interest in the students and in their learning there would not be a compelling reason to help them carrying out their task, nor would their be a particular motive to understand the nature of the difficulties students meet with in a PBL context. Therefore, both subject matter expertise and interpersonal qualities are necessary conditions for cognitive congruence to occur. Figure 2.3 summarizes the Schmidt and Moust position on tutors' behavior and its effects on students.

The figure can be read as follows: The more socially congruent the tutor is, and the more he or she uses his or her subject matter knowledge, the more cognitively congruent he or she will be. Higher levels of cognitive congruence cause the tutorial group to function better, which expresses itself in more intrinsic interest in subject matter displayed by the students, extended self-study time, and higher achievement.

Research to test this theory of the effective tutor was done by Schmidt and Moust (1995) in Maastricht University's health sciences curriculum. To that end, data from 524 tutorial groups and their 261 tutors were studied.

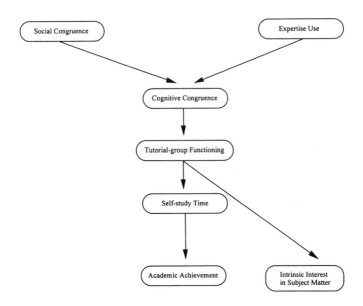

FIG. 2.3.   Theoretical model of tutor behaviors and their relation with other elements of PBL.

Students were asked to respond to items in a program evaluation questionnaire at the end of each course, in which the functioning of the tutor was an element. Social congruence was measured by five items, including the following: "The tutor demonstrated that he liked informal contact with us" and "The tutor showed interest in our personal lives." Use of subject matter expertise was measured by five items, such as "The tutor was sufficiently knowledgeable regarding the course's subject matter" and "The tutor used his subject-matter knowledge to guide the group." Cognitive congruence was measured by three items, among them the following: "The tutor displayed an understanding of our problems with the subject matter" and "The tutor succeeded in explaining things in a comprehensible way." Tutorial-group functioning was measured by two items inquiring whether students considered the group productive and whether they thought the meetings were agreeable. Self-study time was measured by asking students to give an estimate of the number of hours per week spent on SDL activities. Student achievement was measured after each 6-week course by 100 to 150 true–false items (in the first year) and short essay questions (in subsequent years). Finally, intrinsic interest in subject matter was measured by inquiring how interesting the students thought the course's subject matter was. The data were analyzed using a structural equations modeling approach. The authors' findings indicate that, while the model tested represents a reasonable first approximation of the structure underlying the data, the Moust (1993) model of effective tutor behavior does not adequately represent the data. (χ^2 = 46.89, df = 14, p < .001); Comparative Fit Index (CFI) = .97, Root Mean Square Residual (RMSR) < .07). Figure 2.4 shows the relevant path coefficients. These path coefficients indicate the strength of the causal relationship between any two variables. Only statistically significant path coefficients are displayed.

In comparison to prototypical findings using this technique, the causal influences of social congruence and expertise use on cognitive congruence, of cognitive congruence on group functioning, and of group functioning on intrinsic interest are fairly large. The influence of tutorial group functioning on self-study time is somewhat more limited and so is the influence of time-on-task on achievement. Note that the model as proposed only allows one-to-one relations. This may be an unnecessary restriction, because there is no compelling theoretical reason why, for instance, social congruence of the tutor could not influence the quality of tutorial functioning directly, in addition to an indirect influence via cognitive congruence. Assuming that social congruence not only contributes to higher levels of cognitive congruence in the tutor, but also may have a direct positive impact on the way the group members interact with each other, a direct path would be appropriate. In addition, one could assume that the use of expertise by the tutor would not only indirectly (through cognitive congruence and group functioning), but also directly affect the amount of time spent by students, or achievement.

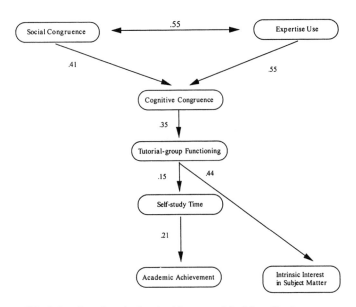

FIG. 2.4.   Causal paths for the Moust model of the effective tutor.

The investigators tested some of these alternatives and found that with a number of adaptations of the original model an excellent fit of the data could be established. The less restrictive model is displayed as Fig. 2.5. For this embellished model of the effective tutor, $\chi^2 = 15.36$ ($df = 11, p = .17$). In addition, CFI = .99 and RMSR < .07.

These findings complicate, but do not contradict Moust's (1993) original assumptions. Both social congruence and expertise use appear to be important constructs because they do not only affect cognitive congruence, as was hypothesized by Moust, but they also influence other variables in the model. Social congruence does not only help the tutor become more cognitively congruent with his or her students, but it also seems to facilitate group performance in a more direct way. Observations of small-group sessions have indeed documented immediate effects of tutoring style on the nature of student interactions (see e.g., Silver & Wilkerson, 1991), the more informal tutoring leading to higher levels of participation. In addition, students almost invariably report that they feel more free to contribute if a tutor displays an interest in what they do (Moust, 1993). Intriguing is the slightly negative influence of expertise on self-study time, suggesting that the more the tutor contributes to the discussion using his own subject matter knowledge, the less time students spend on SDL. Finally, the effect of the tutor's subject matter expertise on achievement has been demonstrated.

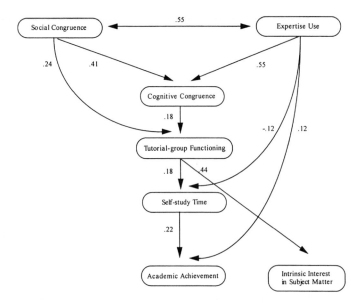

FIG. 2.5.   Less restrictive variant of the effective tutor model.

So, effective tutoring in the context of PBL seems to imply three distinct, though interrelated, qualities: the possession of a suitable knowledge base regarding the topic under study, a willingness to become involved with students in an authentic way, and the skill to express oneself in a language understood by students. This theory of the effective tutor merges two different perspectives prevalent in the literature. One perspective emphasizes the personal qualities of the tutor: his or her ability to communicate with students in an informal way, coupled with an empathic attitude that enables them to encourage students' learning by creating an atmosphere in which open exchange of ideas is facilitated. The other stresses the tutor's subject matter knowledge as a determinant for learning.

CONCLUSION

Understanding how PBL works is only in its preliminary stages. The reader may have noticed that most research cited has been conducted in the 1980s and the 1990s. This implies that only recently, researchers have begun to gain an understanding of what happens to the learner in problem-based curricula. It seems to us that four issues have been resolved fairly satisfactorily. First, in a number of studies it has been demonstrated that the initial analysis of a problem mobilizes prior knowledge among students that is used to construct a initial representation of the processes responsible for the phenomena or events described in it. We have chosen to assign to these collaborative cognitive processes the label of *theory construction*; students build a theory based on whatever they already know, suspect, and think about the problem. Second, it has been demonstrated that the construction of this initial theory facilitates the construction of problem-relevant new information, suggesting that PBL fosters a kind of cognitive process and subsequent learning that cannot be observed in more conventional curricula. These findings are mainly based on the so-called "red blood cell studies" conducted by Schmidt and his associates in the 1980s. These studies were conducted in carefully controlled experiments somewhat remote from actual educational contexts. Recently, however, De Grave (1998) has replicated these findings in a medical curriculum, using actual curricular materials. Third, the limited number of studies conducted regarding the role of (intrinsic) motivation all point in the same direction: PBL is highly motivating for students. These studies were mainly done under laboratory conditions. There is definitely a need for curriculum-based studies on motivational factors affecting learning in these contexts.

Fourth, we now know quite a lot about the behaviors of tutors that tend to be effective in guiding their students. Social congruence, subject matter expertise, and the ability to be cognitively congruent with one's students all seem to be crucial to effective tutoring. Furthermore, we seem to have gained an understanding of the conditions under which tutors are most effective. If insufficient structure is provided by the learning environment and if students' prior knowledge of the subject to be mastered is limited, a knowledgeable, socially congruent, and cognitively congruent tutor would tend to be most beneficial.

An area that deserves further study is the question, "What makes a problem useful?" We know that good-quality problems are important (Gijselaers & Schmidt, 1990), but we do not really know what constitutes a good problem. Preliminary studies into this area have produced disappointing results (e.g., Kokx & Schmidt, 1990), in the sense that it proves difficult to distinguish between good and poor problems based on textual characteristics alone. It seems that the quality of a problem can only be decided on in the context of a particular course, taking into account the prior knowledge of the students. Further research is recommended here.

A second area deserving attention is the question, "What exactly do students do while engaged in SDL activities?" We have only limited knowledge on the factors that influence what students do given a set of learning goals, and what we know about this leads to the conclusion that there is no straightforward relation between what is agreed on during initial problem analysis in the tutorial group and what students do subsequently (e.g., see chapters in Part II of this volume).

A third area of concern involves long-term effects of PBL. Some studies suggest that students in a problem-based curriculum learn less at the outset but remember more in the long run. This is an intriguing finding that should be elaborated on.

ACKNOWLEDGMENT

This chapter includes excerpts from articles published in Academic Medicine and Medical Education, reprinted with permission here.

REFERENCES

Barrows, H. S. (1985). *How to design a problem-based curriculum for the preclinical years*. New York: Springer.

Barrows, H. S. (1988). *The tutorial process*. Springfield: Southern Illinois University School of Medicine.

Barrows, H. S., & Tamblyn, R. M. (1980). *Problem-based learning, an approach to medical education*. New York: Springer.

Bentler, P. M. (1989). *EQS. Structural equation program manual*. Los Angeles, CA: BMDP Statistical Software, third print.

Bentler, P. M. (1990). Comparative fit indexes in structural models. *Psychological Bulletin, 107,* 238–246.

Bloom, B. S. (1976). *Human characteristics and school learning.* New York: McGraw-Hill.

Boud, D., & Feletti, G. (1992). *The challenge of problem-based learning.* London: Kogan Page.

Carroll, J. B. (1963). A model of school learning. *Teachers College Record, 64,* 723–733.

Cooley, W. W., & Leinhart, G. (1980). The instructional dimensions study. *Educational Evaluation and Policy Analysis, 2,* 7–25.

Davis, W. K., Nairn, R., Paine, M. E., Anderson, R. M., & Oh, M. S. (1992). Effects of expert and non-expert facilitators on the small-group process and on student performance. *Academic Medicine, 67,* 470–474.

Davis, W. K., Oh, M. S., Anderson, R. M., Gruppen, L., & Nairn, R. (1994). Influence of a highly focused case on the effect of small-group facilitators' content expertise on students' learning and satisfaction. *Academic Medicine, 69,* 663–669.

De Grave, W. S. (1998). *Probleemgestuurd leren als kennisconstructie. (Problem-based learning as knowledge construction).* Unpublished doctoral dissertation, Maastricht University, Maastricht, The Netherlands.

De Grave, W. S., Boshuizen, H. P. A., & Schmidt, H. G. (1996). Problem-based learning: Cognitive and metacognitive processes during problem analysis. *Instructional Science, 24,* 321–341.

De Grave, W. S., De Volder, M. L., Gijselaers, W. H., & Damoiseaux, V. (1990). Peer teaching and problem-based learning: Tutor characteristics, tutor functioning, group functioning and student-achievement. In Z. N. Nooman, H. G. Schmidt, & E. S. Ezzat (Eds.), *Innovation in medical education. An evaluation of its present status* (pp. 123–135). New York: Springer.

De Grave, W. S., Schmidt, H. G., Beliën, J. J., Moust, J. H. C., De Volder, M. L., & Kerkhofs, L. M. M. (1984). *Effecten van verschillende typen van activatie van voorkennis op recall, gemeten met een aanvultoets. (Effects of different types of activation of prior knowledge on recall, measured with a close procedure.)* Paper presented at the Onderwijs Research Dagen, Tilburg, the Netherlands.

De Volder, M. L., De Grave, W. S., & Gijselaers, W. H. (1985). Peer teaching: Academic achievement of teacher-led versus student-led discussion groups. *Higher Education, 14,* 643–650.

De Volder, M. L., & Schmidt, H. G. (1982). Tutor: Inhoudsdeskundige of procesbegeleider (Tutor: Resource person or facilitator)? In H. G. Schmidt (Ed.), *Probleemgestuurd onderwijs* (pp. 30–44). Harlingen, The Netherlands: Stichting voor Onderzoek van het Onderwijs.

De Volder, M. L., Schmidt, H. G., De Grave, W. S., & Moust, J. H. C., (1989). Motivation and achievement in cooperative learning. In J. H. C. van der Berchen, Th. C. M. Bergen, & E. E. I. de Bruyn (Eds.), *Achievement and task motivation* (pp. 123–127). Berwyn: Swets North America.

De Volder, M. L., Schmidt, H. G., Moust, J. H. C., & De Grave, W. S. (1986). Problem-based learning and intrinsic motivation. In J. H. C. van der Berchen, Th. C. M. Bergen, & E. E. I. de Bruyn (Eds.), *Achievement and task motivation* (pp. 128–134). Berwyn: Swets North America.

Des Marchais, J. E., & Black, R. (1991). *Effect of tutor content expertise on students academic achievement in the Sherbrooke problem-based curriculum.* Unpublished manuscript, Québec, Canada: Université de Sherbrooke.

Eagle, C. J., Harasym, P. M., & Mandin, H. (1992). Effects of tutors with case expertise on problem-based learning issues. *Academic Medicine, 67,* 465–469.

Eisenstaedt, R. S., Barry, W. E., & Glanz, K. (1990). Problem-based learning: Cognitive retention and cohort traits of randomly selected participants and decliners. *Academic Medicine (Supp), 65,* S11.

Geerlings, T. (1995). Students' thoughts during problem-based small-group discussions. *Instructional Science, 22,* 269–278.

Gijselaers, W. H., Bouhuijs, P. A. J., Mulder, M., & Mullink, J. (1987). Rapport: Experiment student- tutoren blok 1.5 en blok 1.6. (Findings on students as a tutor in courses 1.5 and 1.6). Maastricht, Universiteit Maastricht, Rapport FdEW—OC 87—237.

Gijselaers, W. H., & Schmidt, H. G. (1990). Towards a causal model of student learning within the context of a problem-based curriculum. In Z. N. Nooman, H. G. Schmidt, & E. S. Ezzat (Eds.), *Innovation in medical education. An evaluation of its present status* (pp. 95–114). New York: Springer.

Gruppen, L. D., Traber, P., Paine, M. E., Woolliscroft, J. O., & Davis, W. K. (1992, April). *Tutor-led and student-led small groups: No differences in learning?* Paper presented at the Annual Meeting of the American Educational Research Association, San Francisco, CA.

Hunt, J. McV. (1971). Intrinsic motivation: Information and circumstances. In H. M. Schroder & P. Suedfeld (Eds.), *Personality theory and information processing*. New York: Ronald.

Johnson, D. W., & Johnson, R. T. (1979). Conflict in the classroom: Controversy and learning. *Review of Educational Research, 49*, 51–69.

Kaufman, A. (Ed.; 1985). *Implementing problem-based medical education. Lessons from successful innovations*. New York: Springer.

Kokx, I. P. A., & Schmidt, H. G. (1990). The quality of problems in problem-based learning: Expert judgements. Paper presented at the Second International Symposium on Problem-Based Learning, Yogyakarta, Indonesia.

Lucero, S. M., Jackson, R., & Galey, W. R. (1985). Tutorial groups in problem-based learning. In A. Kaufman (Ed.), *Implementing problem-based medical education*. New York: Springer.

Martensen, D., Eriksson, H., & Ingelman-Sundberg, M. (1985). Medical chemistry: Evaluation of active and problem-oriented teaching methods. *Medical Education, 19*, 34–42.

Moust, J. H. C. (1993). *De rol van tutoren in probleemgestuurd onderwijs. Contrasten tussen student-en docenttutoren. (The role of tutors in problem-based learning: Contrasting student-guided with staff-guided tutorials.)* Unpublished doctoral dissertation, Universitaire Pers Maastricht, Maastricht, the Netherlands.

Moust, J. H. C., De Volder, M. L., & Nuy, H. J. P. (1989). Peer teaching and higher level cognitive learning outcomes in problem-based learning. *Higher Education, 18*, 737–742.

Moust, J. H. C., & Schmidt, H. G. (1994). Facilitating small-group learning: A comparison of student and staff tutor's behavior. *Instructional Science, 22*, 287–301.

Moust, J. H. C., Schmidt, H. G., De Volder, M. L., Beliën, J. J. J., & De Grave, W. S. (1986). Effects of verbal participation in small-group discussion on learning. In J. T. E. Richardson, M. E. Eysenck, & D. W. Piper (Eds.), *Student learning: Research in education and cognitive psychology* (pp. 147–155). Guilford, UK: Society for Research into Higher Education.

Schmidt, H. G. (1977). *Niet medici als tutor; maakt het een verschil? (Nonphysicians as a tutor: Does it make a difference?)*. Internal Report, Faculty of Medicine, Maastricht University, Maastricht, the Netherlands.

Schmidt, H. G. (1983a). Intrinsieke motivatie en studieprestatie: Enkele verkennende onderzoeken. (Intrinsic motivation and achievement: Some exploratory investigations). *Pedagogische Studiën, 60*, 185–195.

Schmidt, H. G. (1983b). Problem-based learning: Rationale and description. *Medical Education, 17*, 11–16.

Schmidt, H. G. (1984). Activatie van voorkennis en tekstverwerking. (Activation of prior knowledge and text processing). *Nederlands Tijdschrift voor de Psychologie, 39*, 335–347.

Schmidt, H. G. (1994). Resolving inconsistencies in tutor expertise research: Lack of structure causes students to seek tutor guidance. *Academic Medicine, 69*, 656–662.

Schmidt, H. G., De Volder, M. L., De Grave, W. S., Moust, J. H. C., & Patel, V. L. (1989). Explanatory models in processing of science text: The role of prior knowledge activation through small-group discussion. *Journal of Educational Psychology, 81,* 610–619.

Schmidt, H. G., & Gijselaers, W. H. (1990, April). *Causal modeling of problem-based learning.* Paper presented at the Annual Meeting of the American Educational Research Association, Boston, MA.

Schmidt, H. G., & Moust, J. H. C. (1995). What makes a tutor effective? A structural-equations modeling approach to learning in problem-based curricula. *Academic Medicine, 70,* 708–714.

Schmidt, H. G., & Moust, J. H. C. (1999). *Essentials of problem-based learning. Theory, research, practice.* Manuscript in preparation.

Schmidt, H. G., Spaay, G., & De Grave, W. S. (1988). Opsporen van misconcepties by middelbare scholieren. (Looking for misconceptions in high school students). *Tijdschrift voor Onderwijsresearch, 13,* 129–140.

Schmidt, H. G., Van der Ahrend, A., Kokx, I., & Boon, L. (1994). Peer versus staff tutoring in problem-based learning. *Instructional Science, 22,* 279–285.

Schmidt, H. G., Van der Ahrend, A., Moust, J. H. C., Kokx I., & Boon, L. (1993). Influence of tutors' subject-matter expertise on student effort and achievement in problem-based learning. *Academic Medicine, 68,* 784–791.

Silver, M., & Wilkerson, L. (1991). Effects of tutors with subject-matter expertise on the problem-based tutorial process. *Academic Medicine, 66,* 298–300.

Swanson, D. B., Stalenhoef-Halling, B. F., & Van der Vleuten, C. P. M. (1990). Effects of tutor characteristics on test performance of students in a problem-based curriculum. In W. Bender, R. J. Hiemstra, A. J. J. A. Scherpbier, & R. P. Zwierstra (Eds.), *Teaching and assessing clinical competence* (pp. 129–133). Groningen, the Netherlands: BoekWerk Publications.

Tans, R. W., Schmidt, H. G., Schadé-Hoogeveen, B. E. J., & Gijselaers, W. H. (1986). Sturing van het onderwijsleerproces door middel van problemen: Een veldexperiment (Directing the learning process by means of problems: A field experiment). *Tijdschrift voor Onderwijsresearch, 11,* 35–46.

Wilkerson, L., Hafler, J. P., & Liu, P. (1991). A case study of student-directed discussion in four problem-based tutorial groups. *Academic Medicine, 66S,* 9.

Chapter 3

When Is a Problem-Based Tutorial Not Tutorial? Analyzing the Tutor's Role in the Emergence of a Learning Issue

Timothy Koschmann
Phillip Glenn
Melinda Conlee
Southern Illinois University

INTRODUCTION

In the shared vocabulary of Problem-Based Learning (PBL), curricular meetings convened to explore a teaching case are referred to as *tutorials* and the faculty member responsible for facilitating these meetings is designated the *tutor*. Some (cf. Barrows, 1988; Koschmann, Kelson, Feltovich, & Barrows, 1996) have expressed dissatisfaction with this usage, expressing concerns that such terminology might provide a misleading picture of the faculty member's role and of the PBL process generally.

Tutorial, of course, had an established meaning well before PBL was introduced. The *Oxford English Dictionary*, for example, provides as one definition, "a period of individual instruction given by a college or university tutor to pupils, either singly or in small groups" (Vol. 16, p. 732). This denotes that a tutorial is a particular form of instructional activity, one in which a low ratio of learners to faculty affords special opportunities for individualized attention to learners' needs. By this definition, applying the label of tutorial to PBL group meeting might seem appropriate. Barrows (1988) has argued, however, that the PBL tutor should be more facilitory and less didactic, more guidelike and less directly instructive than a conventional tutor. To better understand these distinctions, we need to examine what tutors actually do, both in PBL meetings and in other settings.

In this chapter, therefore, we apply methods borrowed from studies of talk-in-interaction (Atkinson & Heritage, 1984) to document what actually occurs within PBL meetings in a medical school context. We focus on a particular segment of interaction in a tutorial meeting—interaction leading to the production of a *learning issue* (LI). Fox (1993) conducted similar analyses of one-on-one tutorial interactions involving graduate students and undergraduate tutees. Taking Fox's findings as representative of more conventional pedagogical approaches to tutoring, we make comparisons of the tutor's role across the two settings. In so doing, we hope to deepen our understanding of what it means to be a tutor and to participate in the joint activity known as a tutorial.

The Genesis of a Learning Issue

In the course of exploring a problem, the members of the PBL group inevitably discover areas in which their collective knowledge is deficient (Barrows, 1996). Recognizing such a deficiency, they may elect to treat it as an LI, that is, as a topic requiring further study outside of the tutorial meeting (Barrows, 1994). LIs have been shown to be critical determinants of student study outside of the meeting (Dolmans, Schmidt, & Gijselaers, 1994a, 1994c) and, on this basis, are an important contributor to self-regulated learning (Winne, 1995).

It is the policy of the particular implementation of PBL under study that LIs are always to be generated by the students in the PBL group, rather than determined in advance by the faculty.[1] Producing an LI is a collaborative enterprise, therefore, requiring the students to assess their current understanding and evaluate their current need to know. To become an LI a topic must satisfy three conditions: there must be a recognizable knowledge deficiency, the students must see the missing knowledge as relevant to or necessary for the eventual practice of medicine, and, there must be consensus about the timeliness of undertaking the study.

Students reveal many misconceptions and examples of incomplete understanding within their discussions of a problem. These only become LIs, however, when they are recognized by and become explicit for the group. The students must also grant the relevancy of the knowledge to clinical practice. Barrows (1994) suggested, "Those learning issues that are directly related to analyzing the problem are the most important" (p.

---

[1]This is not necessarily true of all PBL implementations (cf., Barrows, 1986). Implementations also vary in the ways in which the lists of LIs are utilized within the curriculum (Blumberg, Michael, & Zeitz, 1990; Coulson & Osbourne, 1984; Dolmans, Schmidt, & Gijselaers, 1994b).

63). This ensures the relevancy of the LIs not only to the problem, but also to eventual practice.

To better understand how this process of recognition and negotiation is accomplished, we undertook a study of a group's interaction leading up to the identification of an LI. We term this portion of the group interaction a *knowledge display segment* (KDS).

Knowledge Display Segments

We define a KDS to be a topic-delimited segment of discourse in which participants raise a topic for discussion and one or more members elect to display their understanding of that topic.[2] Note that in defining a KDS in this way, we do not stipulate that the discussion necessarily results in the generation of an LI. There are, in fact, many discussions within PBL meetings that satisfy the requirements of this definition, but within which one or more of the three conditions for the establishment of an LI are not met. We use the term *segment* to suggest that these activities happen over stretches of talk longer than a single sequence, but briefer than an entire interactional episode (Crow, 1994).

Our focus is on the ways in which the group (students and tutor) display understandings within the context of their ongoing deliberations of a case. Documenting how this is accomplished is an important contribution to our understanding of how participants engage in PBL, because it elucidates the mechanisms by which students evaluate their individual knowledge bases and their progress within the curriculum.

Unlike traditional classroom recitation (cf. Cazden, 1988; Mehan, 1978), talk within a PBL meeting is, for the most part, informally organized.[3] A broad set of conversational options are, therefore, open to a participant in a KDS. A respondent to an initial query, for instance, might supply an answer or restate the inquiry to clarify or modify it. Alternately, the respondent might present arguments for why the matter should or should not be treated as an LI. Often such arguments may be tacit. A KDS might be brought to a close, for example, simply by raising a new topic for discussion.

---

[2]In an earlier publication (Koschmann, Glenn, & Conlee, 1977), we had referred to segments of this type as *Knowledge Assessment Segments*. Because "knowledge display" appears to be more descriptive of what participants actually seem to do in these segments and because, in particular, what we see is different from assessment, especially in the way in which the term is used in conversation analytic research (cf., Pomerantz, 1984a), we decided to use a new term.

[3]Though not entirely so. See Barrows (1994, 1996) for a description of the ground rules governing participation in a PBL meeting.

THE STUDY

This study is part of a larger project that has involved videotaping numerous meetings within the PBL medical school curriculum over a period of approximately 5 years. Recorded sessions reflect a variety of circumstances, including early in the first year when students receive their first exposure to PBL and late in the second year when students are well acclimated to the method, both with novice and highly experienced tutors, and in meetings augmented with special technologies (cf. Koschmann et al., 1996). These studies vary in duration, ranging from a single case (2–3 meetings each of approximately 2 hours duration) to a complete unit lasting 12 weeks. From this growing corpus of observational data, we isolated specific segments for careful study.

Field notes and certain high-level representations of the group's deliberations (e.g., Conlee & Koschmann, 1997) are helpful in suggesting likely places where interactions of the type we have been describing might occur. Such segments tend to occur more frequently in the first and second meetings devoted to a case.[4] These isolated segments representing KDSs are generally quite brief (of 2–5 minutes in duration). The one selected for analysis here was transcribed using conversation analytic notational conventions developed by Jefferson and summarized in Appendix A (cf. Atkinson & Heritage, 1984; Goodwin, 1981). Referring back to the original videotape and field notes, we conducted a fine-grained analysis using the transcript as a guide and a resource. This was done first by the three authors to establish a shared interpretation of what was accomplished by the participants within the segment. Subsequently, we presented the segment in one of the weekly data analysis sessions of the Department of Speech Communication at Southern Illinois University to solicit alternate treatments and interpretations of the data.

We present here a detailed case analysis of a KDS. Following in the traditions of conversation analytic studies (cf. Schegloff, 1987), we provide a carefully constructed account of a single case rather than a summary of many cases taken in the aggregate. The segment analyzed here occurs late in the group's second meeting on a case involving an adolescent female patient presenting with a complaint of abdominal pain. The tutor (identified in the transcript as "Coach"; see closing discussion) is highly experienced and widely recognized for his skill in teaching in collaborative settings. The students (all identified by pseudonyms) are second-year medical students enrolled in a PBL curriculum. All participants provided written consent before being videotaped.

---

[4]See Barrows (1994) for a detailed description of the sequence by which PBL groups undertake a case.

We are cognizant, in presenting this sample, of the admonishment made by McDermott, Gospondinoff, and Aron (1978) that

> There is a requirement, often neglected, that such a description of behavior and its contexts be presented in a way that readers can decide for themselves whether or not to believe the analyst's account of what it is that a particular group of people is doing at any given time. (p. 245)

We propose to address this requirement, not only by providing the reader with a complete copy of the working transcript, as is usually done (see Appendix B), but also by providing access to a digitized copy of the video segment from which the transcript was prepared.[5]

"What Would Be the Risk?"   At the beginning of this segment, Joel asserts that performing a computerized axial tomography (CT) scan constitutes standard practice in cases of this kind. Patrick's response (in lines 5 and 7) raises a question of safety:[6]

Patrick: You think you can get
                can get a lot of risks doing a CT to the pelvis.

This potential objection (presented in a question) to performing a CT scan problematizes Joel's preceding proposal on the basis of safety. In so doing, it directs the focus of talk, momentarily at least, away from the patient and onto the procedure itself. It shifts the topic from the relevance of a CT scan for cases of this kind to risks in doing CT scans. We treat his utterance, therefore, as constituting a possible opening for a KDS and choose it as a starting point for our analysis.

Joel replies to the question, disagreeing with the premise that a pelvic CT scan carries "a lot of risks." His "why?" constrains Patrick to account for his preceding question. A pause follows, then Joel produces a more elaborate version of his question:

Joel: No why.
         (2.5)

---

[5]Instructions for obtaining a digitized copy of the video segment can be found at the following website: http://edaff.siumed.edu/dept/studies/xscript/risks.html. A transcript of the segment can be found in Appendix B.

[6]Note that ending punctuation in this transcription system indicates intonation, not grammatical category. Patrick's turn is a question (Joel treats it as such by providing an answer in line #6); the period at the end indicates a downward terminal intonation. In the transcript excerpts, word spellings reflect speaker variations in pronunciation and speech rhythm. These "nonstandard" forms are extremely common in spoken (as opposed to written) language. They should be viewed as examples of how language is actually used, particularly in informal settings, rather than flaws in performance.

Joel: What would be the risk.

One might expect this to be Patrick's question to answer, and Patrick's alone. However, Jackie speaks next. She seems to take the middle ground between Joel and Patrick: Yes, there are risks, but only under special circumstances:

Jackie: Wuh- only if it was ectopic.
           Or if she was <u>preg</u>nant

In this moment group members orient to foregrounding shared—group knowledge over individual knowledge. The point of the talk is not to see what Patrick or Joel knows; the point is to provide discursive space for any relevant information from any group member. Thus Jackie self-selects to answer the question.

Patrick (lines 18–20) then inquires about other possible risks, even if the patient were not pregnant:

Patrick: Well even even (.) well
           would you have (.) <u>dan</u>ger of X-raying (.) the
           ovaries °and that°

Patrick's follow-up query refines the focus of his earlier solicitation from risks "to the pelvis" more specifically to risks to "the ovaries and stuff." This would seem to suggest a broader domain for risks (to certain body areas without a particular conditions such as pregnancy being present) than did Jackie's answer.

Group members have provided different, even competing answers to whether the CT scan poses health risks, perhaps displaying collective uncertainty. At this point, the tutor enters into the discussion:

Coach: Is there a risk to CT?

While asking this question he makes a hand gesture similar to that of a crossing guard delaying oncoming traffic. He recycles Patrick's question with slight modification from the advisability of performing a CT scan on a particular patient to the more abstract consideration of the medical risks of CT.

As worded, his inquiry only calls for a "yes" or a "no" response that, after a brief pause, Jackie, Patrick, and Joel provide. He then asks another question that invites elaboration. Before the students can respond, however, he produces a different version of the question, once again slightly respecifying the issue under discussion:

Coach: I mean <u>what</u> is the risk in a CT, is there a
              difference between X-r-CT and an ordinary X-ray?

By setting up a contrast, he provides the students with a new framework for considering the risks of CT scans. He simultaneously expands (by bringing in conventional X-rays) and restricts (by focusing specifically on the contrast between the two imaging techniques) the scope of the original discussion.

Patrick (lines 33 and 36–38) attempts to respond to Coach's inquiry. Joel (lines 41 and 43) further refines the question raised by Coach (i.e., How does a CT scan compare to an X-ray?) by focusing specifically on differences in the amount of radiation used in the two techniques:

Joel: What is the dosage (1.2) relative to a normal
           X-ray to a CT

Joel then answers his own question, marking the answer as tentative by putting it in question form:

Joel: CT- serial CT um is serial X-rays is it not?

Jackie provides confirmation (line 47) and then constructs her own answer to Coach's question about the differences in the two forms of imaging:

Jackie: Right, you're taking slices
          ((*making chopping gesture with right hand*))
          so <u>natu</u>rally if you do: (0.8) <u>two</u> views of an
          <u>ab</u>domen with a <u>plane</u> film and you do (0.8) <u>fifteen</u>
          with the CT °I mean° but <u>I</u> don- <u>I</u> don't know <u>I</u>
          can't remember (.) the relative dosage for
          one slice of CT versus

She contrasts an abdominal X-ray, usually providing only two "views," with a CT scan involving 15 or more "slices." If each slice or view produces exposure equivalent to an X-ray, it would follow that a CT scan would place a patient at a higher risk than a single X-ray. She then expresses doubt about the relative dosage required for each, thereby claiming insufficient knowledge (Beach & Metzger, 1997) about the issue.

At this point the discussion has revealed a deficiency in the students' collective knowledge. Patrick, Joel, and Jackie have attempted collaboratively to construct a model of how CT scans are produced, but, by Jackie's admission, they are missing a crucial piece of information—the amount of radiation exposure produced by a CT scan. By the ground rules of the method, if other members of the group possessed further information, it would be their responsibility to share it (Barrows, 1988, 1996). Because no one in the group does, a collective knowledge deficiency appears to have been revealed, satisfying the first condition for the establishment of an LI.

Though Coach could now ask whether or not this item should be considered an LI, he instead encourages Jackie to continue to reason through her answer:

Coach: Wel-wt think-think it through what does the X-ray
beam have to <u>do</u> in ordinary X-ray, how much
en- what does the energy have to do,

Jackie's response focuses on the need for the X-ray beam to penetrate the body:

Jackie: Well it's gonna
penetrate the whole
<u>bo</u>dy. er I mean which ever way it's going through.

She illustrates this by bringing the backs of her hands together, pointing toward her midsection. As she speaks she draws her hands across her abdomen, fingers pointing inward, bringing them around to both sides of her body. She repeats the gesture as she attempts to repair her sentence.

Coach's single word utterance in line 60 solicits Jackie to extend her answer. Similarly, his "Right" (line #64) is less of an assessment than an invitation to continue. By initiating his next sentence with an "and" he marks his utterance as a collaborative continuation of Jackie's, "Well it's gonna penetrate the whole body."

Coach: Right
And change (.) the chemical (.)
constituents (.) in a film right?

The full stops following "change," "chemical," and "constituents" might be heard as an invitation for her (or for one of the other students) to finish the sentence. He tags his answer with the particle "right?" to solicit confirmation from the students, which Jackie and Joel provide in lines 67 and 68.

Having now led the group to consider the mechanism by which a conventional X-ray image is formed, he then asks them (line 69) to construct a similar model for the production of a CT scan. Joel (line 70) begins by expanding the acronym, and Jackie overlaps to provide agreement. Coach breaks in (lines 72–73) to redirect attention to the mechanism:

> Coach: =What's what's the re<u>ce</u>ptor then if it isn't a
>   f<u>i</u>lm, what <u>is</u> it

This query focuses specifically on the mechanics of how a CT scan is actually produced. Patrick, Joel, and Jackie offer an assortment of rather vague responses ("It's electronic," "Isn't it not an X-ray receptor," "It's computerized"). Coach (line 82) provides a confirmation.

In lines 83 and 84, Joel indicates his understanding that the radiation dosage associated with a CT scan is approximately equivalent to that of a single X-ray. This assertion constitutes a reply to the question he himself posed earlier in lines 41 and 43. He marks this knowledge as uncertain (and thus open to correction or criticism by others) by prefacing his claim with "I understand that. . . ."[7] When Coach (line 85) challenges his assertion, Joel expresses additional uncertainty with his response:

> Joel: That's what my understanding ↓is I- I'm not
>   I'm just saying (   )

He reinforces this impression with hand gestures that resemble the motions of someone juggling a set of balls.

Melissa proposes that this topic be recorded on the whiteboard as an LI. Joel and Jackie both concur:

> Melissa: <u>Why</u> don't we just put it up as a <u>lea</u>rning issue.
>
> Joel: >Let's throw that up<
>
> Jackie: Yeah.

Coach (lines 92–93) returns to Joel's claim about the radiation dosage of a CT scan. He asks Joel to quantify his degree of certainty:

> Coach: >I was going to say< how sure are you on a scale of
>   zero to ten.

Joel first answers facetiously (line 94) that he is not certain at all. The subsequent pause (line 95) suggests that Coach is seeking a more specific answer.[8] Joel then estimates his certainty as "Three," though his into-

---

[7]See Pomerantz (1984b) for a description of how evidence is presented in situations of doubt.

[8]See Schegloff, Jefferson, and Sacks (1977) for a discussion of the preference for self-correction in conversational repair.

nation marks this response as tentative. With a chuckle, Coach replies (lines 98–99) that perhaps it should be treated as an LI. Joel concurs (line 100).

By bringing ultrasound imaging into the discussion, Jackie's question in lines 101 and 104 might be seen as yet another respecification of the topic. Alternately, her inquiry could be construed as calling into question the need for the previous discussion. By asserting that there is an alternate imaging technique available that does not entail the risks of radiation, Jackie's question might be paraphrased more bluntly as, "Why do we need to know about CT scans when we already know that there is a safer alternative?" The fact that Jackie had initially suggested that ultrasound be used for this patient (lines 6, 8) supports this interpretation.

By his response (lines 105, 107, 109–112), Coach makes clear that he reads her inquiry in just this way, that is, as a metalevel critique of the group's need to know about the risks associated with CT scans. He argues that the group's hesitation about ordering a CT scan for a pregnant woman suggests a misunderstanding that has important implications for later practice. In line 113, Jackie concedes the point pertaining to the need to know, but reasserts in line 115 that an ultrasound would be the appropriate test to use. Brenda endorses this position (lines 114, 116) and Jackie (lines 120, 122–123) elaborates that any form of X-ray is contraindicated in pregnant women.

Although group members continue to provide information relevant to this topic, no one challenges the move to make this an LI. The students have shared what they know about the risks of CT scans and of X-rays, assessed their collective knowledge as deficient, and made the decision, under the guidance of Coach, to "throw that up" (that is, mark it on the board in the conference room) as an LI. This is a crucial moment in the PBL method. Its success in this instance relies, in part, on the ability of group members to assess not only the accuracy, but also the relative degree of uncertainty, of what they know.

Some Observations on Tutorial Practice

To summarize, Patrick initially raises a topic for discussion. His question focuses on the possible risks to the pelvis (which he later narrows to a risk to the ovaries) of the patient. Coach's question expands the topic to the risk of CT generally. To facilitate the students' reasoning about this question, he asks them to contrast CT scans with conventional X-rays. Joel refines this inquiry further by focusing on the differences in radiation exposure between the two imaging techniques. Coach, in his questioning, brings the students back to a discussion of the process by which images are produced in CT scans and in conventional X-rays. Melissa suggests that they make this an LI, and others agree. Coach asks them to assess the certainty of their knowledge; after hearing that they are not very certain, he concurs that this should be an LI.

Although we defined a KDS as a "topic-delimited" segment of talk, participants continuously renegotiate the boundaries of the topic through the course of the interaction. In general, any group member may clarify, expand, restrict, or otherwise alter a topic; hence, the topic is not static but is dynamic and emergent. Much of the conversational work that takes place within this segment is devoted to specifying just what the topic of the discussion actually is. This process is important, for it directly affects how a learning issue gets identified, which in turn will crucially influence the success of subsequent research on the issue. Coach's persistent efforts to refine the object of discussion can be seen as exemplary in this regard.

There is an extensive literature exploring the effect of tutor expertise on tutorial interaction and subsequent student performance (cf. Regehr et al., 1995). In an early study, Silver and Wilkerson (1991) found that in discussions in which tutors considered themselves to be experts, the tutors spoke more often, took longer turns at talk, and provided more direct answers to student queries; in short, they were considered to be more directive.

In the segment analyzed here, it is Coach's expertise that enables him to recognize the misconception underlying Patrick's initial query. Though his role in the ensuing discussion might be construed by some as directive, it is also clearly true that his facilitation was crucial to the students' learning in this situation. His leading questions provide a form of "scaffolding" (Wood, Bruner, & Ross, 1976) in that they offer a framework for reasoning about the topic and applying prior knowledge. The overarching goal is for the students to internalize this process of inquiry so they may eventually be able to incorporate it into their own independent problem solving (Barrows, 1994; P. Feltovich, Spiro, Coulson, & Feltovich, 1996). Further, when Coach asks Joel to estimate his degree of certainty (lines 92–93), he encourages a form of "thinking about thinking" (Olson & Astington, 1993) by pushing Joel and the group to reflect on what they do and do not know. The important question, therefore, is not whether expertise itself is necessarily obtrusive, or even if tutor-led inquiry is detrimental to the group process, but rather, in what settings and for what purposes does tutor inquiry serve the objective of advancing student-centered learning?

Schegloff (1995) has argued that "the absence of actions can be as decisive as their occurrence for the deployment of language and the interactional construction of discourse" (p. 186). Completely absent in this segment are any examples of Coach providing direct instruction. To see how the discussion might have played out differently had such action been taken, we turn now to Fox's analysis of more conventional tutorial interaction.

Conventional Tutorial Interaction

Fox (1993) conducted a study of a series of one-on-one sessions involving graduate student tutors and undergraduate tutees in a variety of domains (i.e., chemistry, physics, math, and computer science). Like the current study, she applied an analytic framework derived from ethnomethodological conversation analysis (Atkinson & Heritage, 1984; Psathas, 1995). For the purposes of the discussion that follows, we treat her description as representative of conventional tutorial interaction. As Fox described it, "Face-to-face tutoring consists mainly of two activities: description and explanation of some domain by the tutor, and working and solution of problems by the student" (p. 69). We examine each of these activities in turn and discuss how they are manifested in conventional and in PBL tutorials.

Because one of Fox's (1993) central interests was how tutees come to "situate otherwise abstract and a-contextual forms" (pp. 1–2), she provides few examples of tutors presenting extended descriptions and explanations. One of her transcribed segments, however, does provide a clear example of directed instruction. The segment is from a Calculus tutoring session and is presented as follows:

T: Okay, so (1.1) chain rule?
    (1.5)
T: Ring a bell?
S: Yeah, ⌈yeah chain rule rings a bell.
T: ⌊Okay.
T: Okay. So what that says is if you have (2.1) a function sitting inside of another function.
    (0.8)
S: Right
T: (And) to differentiate it, you take the outside derivative (1.0) the ef prime (1.7) and then you multiply it by the inside derivative, (0.6) the gee prime.
(pp. 23–24, transcription conventions modified)

This brief exchange can be seen to satisfy the requirements for a KDS, as defined earlier. Though it is much shorter than the KDS analyzed in the PBL tutorial, it has the same structural features—the tutor raises a topic for discussion, the tutee acknowledges the topic, and the tutor provides an expository description of the topic under discussion. In both cases, the participants can be seen to orient toward a joint activity of displaying their understanding of a specified topic. Unlike the "What would be the risk?" segment, however, the tutor brings the segment to an abrupt close by supplying her own description of the object (i.e., the chain rule), thereby preempting an opportunity for students' articulation.

The differences between the two segments highlight the fundamentally different pedagogical goals underlying conventional and PBL tutoring. Whereas the goal, from the tutor's perspective in a conventional tutorial, is to bring the tutee to a negotiated level of understanding,[9] the primary objective of the PBL tutorial is just to make deficiencies in the learner's understanding evident. These deficiencies need not, and usually are not, immediately redressed but instead are deferred as LIs for later independent study. Further, it can be seen that the PBL tutor is attempting to effect a more global change in the tutees' orientation toward learning and knowing. This is evident in the way in which Coach provides a framework for thinking about the question and in the way in which he probes the students concerning their confidence in their answers. Therefore, although KDSs may occur naturally within the discourse of both conventional and PBL tutorials, they tend to serve different purposes in these two settings.

This difference in goals can also be seen in the ways in which problem solving is approached in conventional and in PBL tutorials. Fox describes problem solving in tutorial interaction as proceeding

> with the student narrating steps, the tutor asking questions or making suggestions, the student asking for confirmation, the tutor checking understanding, and so on, in some cases with multiple levels of embedding, until the tutor and student agree they have come to an acceptable stopping point. (p. 23)

She provides an example of this process, as excerpted here:

T: And what are these, these are?
    (0.9) those aren't lengths, so what are they
S: That's the work?

---

[9]See Fox's (1993) discussion of the way in which it is meaningful to speak of the tutee's understanding "matching" that of the tutor (pp. 54–55).

T: Wor⌈k or e-nergy.
S: ⌊Energy?
T: okay? So this is an energy.
(p. 22, transcription conventions modified)

This exchange can be seen to follow the pattern of the well-documented IRE recitational sequence in which the instructor *I*nquires, the student *R*esponds, and the instructor *E*valuates (Cazden, 1988; Mehan, 1978).

Compare this to the more elaborate exchange in the "What would be the risk?" segment beginning at line 54 and continuing to line 85 in Appendix B. Here Coach begins by asking about how an ordinary X-ray image is produced. He inquires, "What does the energy have to do?" Jackie replies that the energy must penetrate through the body. Coach's "and" (line 60) encourages her to continue her narrative and explain what happens after the X-ray beam has passed through the body.

Jackie evidences some confusion when she says, "er I mean which ever its going through" and repeats the gesture she made previously. Coach's "Right" (line 64), therefore, is less of an evaluation of her answer than an instance of what is referred to in studies of tutorial dialogue as a "pump" (Graesser, personal communication, Sept. 19, 1998). He builds on her answer in lines 65 and 66, pausing repeatedly to provide her with opportunities to participate.

Coach then shifts the discussion to an exploration of what the X-ray beam must do in a CT scan. Joel provides an expansion of the acronym CT that Jackie endorses. Coach pushes the students to explain the mechanism for image production, just as he had done previously for ordinary X-ray images. Joel suggests that CT scans use an "electronic receptor" and Jackie allows that it's "computerized." As before, Coach's "Right" acknowledges their answers but does not necessarily imply endorsement.

Rather than attempt to elaborate on his answer, Joel states simply, "I understand that the CT is just about equivalent to an X-ray." By shifting the topic from the mechanism of production (back) to radiation exposure, Joel is conceding that he is unable to answer Coach's question. Coach's neutral "Is it?" neither confirms nor disconfirms Joel's assertion.

In comparing the problem solving exchange from Fox's study of one-on-one tutoring with this extended segment of interaction, several differences are apparent. Most important is the way in which the tutor in the PBL tutorial withholds assessment of the various answers provided by the students. In the conventional tutorial, the student's answer to the tutor's inquiry is produced and confirmed in the moment; in the PBL tutorial, the answer is deferred pending further study. Just as was the case with "description and explanation," the different strategies utilized by the tutors suggest that they are pursuing a different set of goals in the two settings.

CONCLUSIONS

Despite the differences between tutorial interaction as described by Fox (1993) and what we have observed in PBL tutorials, there are also important similarities—both entail teaching in the context of joint problem solving and both involve an asymmetric exchange in which the tutor assumes a distinguished role and is called on to model expert problem solving strategies. Further, as Fox observed, "Tutoring involves constant, and local, management. This requires a pervasive mutual orientation between tutor and student, such that every session (indeed, every utterance) is a thoroughly interactional achievement, produced by both tutor and student" (p. 3). Finally, her observation concerning the goal of tutoring being "to situate otherwise abstract and a-contextual forms" (p. 2) and her description of the general indeterminancy of language within tutorial dialogue both appear to apply with equal validity to PBL tutorials (cf. Glenn, Koschmann, & Conlee, in press).

Nonetheless, there remain marked differences between the roles of PBL and conventional tutors. Fox (1993) stipulated that there are a set of norms to which tutors and tutees "orient in interpreting and creating the contexts in and through which they act" (p. 114). It would appear to be the case, however, that there are norms that apply to the conduct of PBL tutorials that do not apply to more conventional tutorial interaction.

Newman, Griffin, and Cole (1989) suggested that introducing a new term "is a way to signal that old phenomena are being reconceptualized with a different kind of theory" (p. 59). Given the different set of norms by which tutors and tutees structure their interactions in conventional and in PBL tutorials, we reiterate the recommendation made previously (Koschmann et al., 1996) that a new title be given the faculty member in the PBL tutorial as a means of signaling that the tutor's role has been reconceptualized in this setting. We believe adopting the label *tutor/coach* or, more simply, *coach* would have this effect.

The norms that organize participation within PBL meetings are themselves abstractions that must be continually reinterpreted and made relevant within the bustle and confusion of the ongoing interaction. On cursory inspection, the discussions that take place may seem disorganized, even chaotic. Participants overlap each other, pause, stumble over words, express ideas in vague or uncertain ways, and laugh in response to some statements. Through the type of analysis conducted here, however, a more precise order can be seen to emerge. As McDermott et al. (1978) argued, "By pointing to the order in . . . apparently chaotic behavior, we . . . raise the possibility that most behavior is ordered in ways about which we as observers or participants are systematically inarticulate" (p. 246). By becoming more articulate about how PBL is enacted in practical settings, we come to develop a better understanding of PBL on a theoretical level, as well. Studies, such as the one reported here, therefore, begin to provide us with a foundation for understanding what it means to *do* PBL.

ACKNOWLEDGMENTS

The authors express their gratitude to Howard Barrows, both for reading and for commenting on an earlier version of this chapter and for allowing us to observe his tutorial group. This research was funded through a Spencer Postdoctoral Fellowship awarded to the first author and a series of small grants from the Abbott Foundation.

REFERENCES

Atkinson, J. M., & Heritage, J. (Eds.; 1984). *Structures of social action: Studies in conversation analysis*. Cambridge, U.K.: Cambridge University Press.

Barrows, H. S. (1986). A taxonomy of problem-based learning methods. *Medical Education, 20*, 481–486.

Barrows, H. S. (1988). *The tutorial process*. Springfield, IL: Southern Illinois University School of Medicine.

Barrows, H. S. (1994). *Practice-based learning: Problem-based learning applied to medical education*. Springfield, IL: Southern Illinois University School of Medicine.

Barrows, H. S. (1996). *What your tutor may never tell you*. Springfield, IL: Southern Illinois University School of Medicine.

Beach, W. A., & Metzger, T. R. (1997). Claiming insufficient knowledge. *Human Communication Research, 23*, 562–588.

Blumberg, P., Michael, J., & Zeitz, H. (1990). Roles of student-generated learning issues in a problem-based curriculum. *Teaching and Learning in Medicine, 2*, 149–154.

Cazden, C. (1988). *Classroom discourse: The language of teaching and learning*. Portsmouth, NH: Heinemann.

Conlee, M., & Koschmann, T. (1997). Representations of clinical reasoning in a PBL meeting: The inquiry trace. *Teaching and Learning in Medicine, 9*, 51–55.

Coulson, R., & Osborne, C. (1984). Insuring curricular content in a student-directed problem-based learning program. In H. Schmidt & M. De Volder (Eds.), *Tutorials in problem-based learning* (pp. 225–229). Assen, the Netherlands: Van Gorcum.

Crow, B. K. (1994). Conversational episode structure. In R. L. Conville (Ed.), *Uses of "structure" in communication studies* (pp. 155–184). Westport, CT: Praeger.

Dolmans, D., Schmidt, H., & Gijselaers, W. (1994a). The relationship between student-generated learning issues and self-study in problem-based learning. *Instructional Science, 22*, 251–267.

Dolmans, D., Schmidt, H. G., & Gijselaers, W. H. (1994b). Use of student-generated learning issues to evaluate problems in a problem-based curriculum. *Teaching and Learning in Medicine, 6*, 199–202.

Dolmans, D., Schmidt, H. G., & Gijselaers, W. H. (1994c). What drives the student in problem-based learning? *Medical Education, 28*, 372–380.

Feltovich, P., Spiro, R., Coulson, R., & Feltovich, J. (1996). Collaboration within and among minds: Mastering complexity, individually and in groups. In T. D. Koschmann (Ed.), *CSCL: Theory and practice of an emerging paradigm* (pp. 25–44). Mahwah, NJ: Lawrence Erlbaum Associates.

Fox, B. (1993). *The human tutorial dialogue project.* Hillsdale, NJ: Lawrence Erlbaum Associates.

Glenn, P., Koschmann, T., & Conlee, M. (in press). Theory sequences in a problem-based learning group: A case study. *Discourse Processes.*

Goodwin, C. (1981). *Conversational organization: Interaction between speakers and hearers.* New York: Academic Press.

Jefferson, G. (1984). Transcription notation. In J. Atkinson & J. Heritage (Eds.), *Structures of social action* (pp. ix–xvi). New York: Cambridge University Press.

Koschmann, T., Glenn, P., & Conlee, M. (1997). Analyzing the emergence of a learning issue in a problem-based learning meeting. *Medical Education Online, 2*(1) [available at: http://www.utmb.edu/meo/res00003.pdf].

Koschmann, T., Kelson, A. C., Feltovich, P. J., & Barrows, H. S. (1996). Computer-supported problem-based learning: A principled approach to the use of computers in collaborative learning. In T. D. Koschmann (Ed.), *CSCL: Theory and practice of an emerging paradigm* (pp. 83–124). Mahwah, NJ: Lawrence Erlbaum Associates.

McDermott, R., Gospodinoff, K., & Aron, J. (1978). Criteria for an ethnographically adequate description of concerted activities and their contexts. *Semiotica, 24,* 245–275.

Mehan, H. (1978). *Learning lessons.* Cambridge, MA: Harvard University Press.

Newman, D., Griffin, P., & Cole, M. (1989). *The construction zone: Working for cognitive change in school.* New York: Cambridge University Press.

Olson, D., & Astington, J. (1993). Thinking about thinking; Learning how to take statements and hold beliefs. *Educational Psychologist, 28,* 7–23.

Oxford English Dictionary (2nd ed.). (1989). Oxford, U.K.: Clarendon Press.

Pomerantz, A. (1984a). Agreeing and disagreeing with assessments: Some features of preferred/dispreferred turn shapes. In J. M. Atkinson & J. Heritage (Eds.), *Structures of social action: Studies in conversation analysis* (pp. 57–101). Cambridge, UK: Cambridge University Press.

Pomerantz, A. (1984b). Giving a source or basis: The practice in conversation of telling "how I know." *Journal of Pragmatics, 8,* 607–625.

Psathas, G. (1995). *Conversation analysis: The study of talk-in-interaction.* Thousand Oaks, CA: Sage.

Regehr, G., Martin, J., Hutchison, C., Murnaghan, J., Cusimano, M., & Reznick, R. (1995). The effect of tutor's content expertise on student learning, group processes and participant satisfaction in a problem-based learning curriculum. *Teaching and Learning in Medicine, 7,* 225–232.

Schegloff, E. (1987). Analyzing single episodes of interaction: An exercise in conversation analysis. *Social Psychology Quarterly, 50,* 101–114.

Schegloff, E. (1995). Discourse as an interactional achievement III: The omnirelevance of action. *Research on Language and Social Interaction, 28,* 185–212.

Schegloff, E., Jefferson, G., & Sacks, H. (1977). The preference for self-correction in the organization of repair in conversation. *Language, 53,* 361–382.

Silver, M., & Wilkerson, L. (1991). Effects of tutors with subject expertise on the problem-based tutorial process. *Academic Medicine, 66,* 298–300.

Winne, P. (1995). Inherent details in self-regulated learning. *Educational Psychologist, 30,* 173–187.

Wood, D., Bruner, J. S., & Ross, G. (1976). The role of tutoring in problem solving. *Journal of Child Psychology and Psychiatry, 17,* 89–100.

APPENDIX A

Transcription Conventions

The notational scheme employed in this data was originally developed by Jefferson (1984). All symbols used in the representation of the data are defined below.

Symbol	Name	Function
[ ]	Brackets	Marks the beginning (and end) of overlapping utterances
=	Equal sign	Indicates the end and beginning of two "latched" utterances that continue without a pause
(1.8)	Timed Pause	Measured in seconds, this symbol indicates intervals of silence occurring within and between same or different speaker's utterances
(.)	Micropause	A brief pause of less than (0.2)
.	Period	Indicates a falling pitch or intonation
?	Question Mark	Rising vocal pitch or intonation
,	Comma	Indicates a continuing intonation; with slight upward or downward contour
-	Hyphen	An abrupt halt of sound, syllable, or word
< > < >	Greater than/less than signs	Portions of an utterance delivered at a noticeably quicker (> <) or slower (< >) pace than surrounding talk
° °	Degree signs	Marks texts spoken at a lower volume than surrounding talk
	Capitalized text	Represents speech delivered more loudly than surrounding talk
_	Underscore	Underlined word or syllable indicates stress
↑↓	Arrows	Marks a rise or fall in intonation
:::	Colon(s)	Prolongation of previously indicated sound, syllable, or word
(hhh)		Audible exhalation (linguistic aspiration)
(.hhh)		Audible inhalation
( )	Parentheses	Spoken text in which the transcription is in doubt
(( ))	Double parentheses	Annotations describing nonverbal aspects of the interaction (text italicized)

APPENDIX B

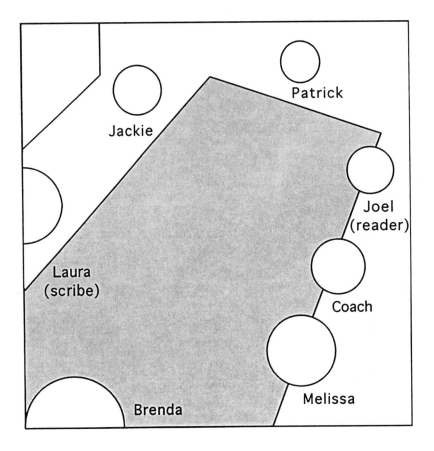

1	Joel:	They did talk about doing a CT along with
2		along with it if you feel there are abcesses
3		but it's low yield unless you feel there are
4		abcesses=
5	Patrick:	=You think you can ⌈get- (can you get)- lot ⌉=
6	Jackie:	⌊And an ultrasound can be⌋
7	Patrick:	of ⌈risks doing a CT to ⌉the pelvis.
8	Jackie:	=⌊used for that reason.⌋
9	Patrick:	⌊Can get a lot a r̲isks doing a CT to the pelvis.
10		(0.5)
11	Joel:	No why.
12		(2.5)
13	Joel:	What would be the r̲isk.

```
14   Jackie:    Wuh- only if it was ⌈ectopic.
15   Patrick:                      ⌊Yeah
16   Jackie:    ⌈Or if she was pregnant⌉ (.) (but probly)
17   (?)        ⌊(                    )⌋=
18   Patrick:   =Well even even (.) well
19              would you have (.) danger of X-raying (.) the
20              ovaries °and that°
21   Coach:     ⌈Is there a ↑risk to CT?        ⌉
22              ⌊((with arresting hand gesture))⌋
23   Jackie:    °Hm°
24              (0.9)
25   Patrick:   Sure.
26   Joel:      It's an ↑X-r⌈ay.
27   Jackie:               ⌊Yea⌈h
28   Patrick:               ⌊It's an X-ray, there's always a risk
29              to an X-ray.
30              (0.5)
31   Coach:     I mean what is the risk in a CT, is there a
32              difference between X-r-CT and an ordinary X-ray?
33   Patrick:   ⌈Yeah (0.5) a CT is (.) um (.) in a plane.
34              ⌊((opening hand gesture))
35   Coach:     Yeah?
36   Patrick:   So I would think that the CT (0.9) would be (1.0)
37              instead of just a plane film (0.4) would be more
38              ⌈X-rays (being used)
39              ⌊((circular hand gesture))
40              (1.9)
41   Joel:      ⌈↑What is the dosage (1.2) relative to a normal
42              ⌊((spreading hands palms up))
43              X-ray to a CT CT- ⌈↑serial CT um is serial X-rays
44   Patrick:                     ⌊(       )
45   Joel:      ⌈is it not?
46              ⌊((making slicing motion with hand))
47   Jackie:    ⌈Right, you're taking slices
48              ⌊((making chopping gesture with right hand))
49              so naturally if you do: (0.8) two views of an
50              abdomen with a plane film and you do (0.8) fifteen
51              with the CT °I mean° but I don- I don't know I
52              can't remember (.) the relative dosage for
```

```
53                    ┌one slice of CT versus
54    Coach:         └Wel-wt think-think it through what does the X-ray
55                    beam have to do in ordinary X-ray, how much
56                    en- what does
57                    ┌the energy have to do,
58    Jackie:        └Well ┌it's gonna penetrate the whole
59                          └((draws both hands across abdomen))
60    Coach:    And.
61    Jackie:   body. er I mean ┌which ever way
62                              └((repeats previous gesture))
63              it's going ┌through.
64    Coach:               └Right
65              And change (.) the chemical (.)
66              constituents ┌(.) in a film rig┌ht?
67    Jackie:               └Hm mm          └Hm m┌m
68     Joel:                                      └Hm mm
69    Coach:    °What does CT have to do.°
70     Joel:   Computer axial t-tomography it puts ┌it in a (  )
71    Jackie:                                       └Right it's=
72    Coach:    =What's what's the receptor then if it isn't a
73              film, what is it
74    Patrick:  It's a-it's a much more sensitive receptor,
75              °idn-it?°
76              (1.3)
77     Joel:   It's an electronic recep┌tor
78    Jackie:                          └It's com-
79     Joel:   Isn't it not an x-ray receptor so it's going to be
80              very very low ┌(           voltage)
81    Jackie:                └It's computerized.
82    Coach:    Right.
83     Joel:   I understand that the CT is ↑just about equivalent
84              to an X-↓ray.
85    Coach:    Is it?
86     Joel:   That's what my understanding ↓is I- I'm not
87              ┌I'm just saying (      )
88              ├((making juggling motion with hands))
89    Melissa:  └Why don't we just put it up as a learning issue.
90     Joel:   >Let's throw that u┌p<
91    Jackie:                     └Yeah.
```

```
92    Coach:    >I was going to say< how sure are you on a scale
93              of zero to ⌐ten.
94    Joel:              └(not)
95              (0.6)
96    Joel:     Three?
97              (0.8)
98    Coach:    Think we oughta make a ↑learning issue out
99              of it. ⌐Hheh heh heh
100   Joel:            └Ha (maybe we ought to)
101   Jackie:   But we all know ⌐that ultrasound isn't radiation
102   Melissa:              └(Joel) ⌐this is from the (        )
103                                └((passing papers to Joel))
104   Jackie:   Right?=
105   Coach:    =No, ↓ultrasound isn't rad⌐i↑ation.
106   Jackie:                        └Everybody knows that.
107   Coach:    But if you're gonna get- ⌐hesitate
108   Jackie:                        └So what I'm gonna ↑say,
109   Coach:    doing a CT scan, because the woman might be
110             pregnant then I think you oughta know if the CT
111             scan is to be of concern or ↑not when doing it on a
112             preg⌐nant woman.
113   Jackie:      └Ri::ght.
114   Brenda:   Well I kn⌐ow from last year=
115   Jackie:           └°Well we'll do an ultrasound then°=
116   Brenda:   =CT is contraindicated when a woman's pregnant
117             (0.9)
118   Brenda:   Remember when we had that c⌐ase last year when-
119   Jackie:                          └Right.
120   Jackie:   Yeah, anything is, any X-ray is if ⌐she's pregnant,
121   Brenda:                              └°Yeah°
122   Jackie:   un the, until the very end sometimes they do
123             some.
```

Chapter 4

Whose Group Is It, Anyway?
Equity of Student Discourse in
Problem-Based Learning (PBL)

JodyLee Estrada Duek
FRESCO

From the premed college years and perhaps even earlier, the prospective physician learns competition in the classroom and in the laboratory and carries it over into medical school, into residency, and into practice. This competitive history is driven, in part, by the fact that there are far too many applicants for the limited seats in North American medical schools (Nolan, 1970). Precisely 45,365 students applied for 17,317 seats in the U.S. medical class of 1998 (beginning their studies in 1994); 5,600 students applied for the 145 slots at UCLA (Association of American Medical Colleges, 1996; UCLA, 1994). At the same time that these students are doing academic battle with each other, they are also looking to professors to tell them what they need to know to gain the coveted spots. Here, the characteristics of conformance and compliance form the basis of the stereotype of the medical student who can retain vast amounts of prescribed information long enough to spew it back on a test. Indeed, it is not unusual to find that the newly certified M.D. is an expert at taking multiple-choice examinations, but is still a novice when it comes to problem solving, to using symptoms and medical tests as evidence to build a diagnostic theory, or to sharing information in a collaborative style with colleagues and patients. Unfortunately, the traditional medical curriculum does not foster these skills (Coombs, May, & Small, 1986).

As Bruffee (1993) stated in his book, *Collaborative Learning: Higher Education, Interdependence, and the Authority of Knowledge*:

For a decade or more, reports . . . have complained that many undergraduates tend to be authority-dependent, passive, irresponsible, overly competitive, and suspicious of their peers. Similar complaints have been made about students in professional training, especially those preparing for professions, such as medicine . . . that require them to interact constructively with other human beings. These complaints will persist as long as we fail to understand interdependence and constructive human interaction as part and parcel of knowledge and learning. (p. 8)

How can medical schools counter the cultural forces that foster competition and compliance, and instead, prepare learners to be competent, caring, creative, and cooperative? What type of supportive context will afford medical students the opportunity to work together equitably to achieve constructive interdependence?

Predicated on the principles of cooperation and inclusion, Problem-Based Learning (PBL) has the hallmarks of a method that can help students achieve these goals. To what degree, however, is PBL successful in adhering to its principles? The research reported in this chapter attempts to address this question. The study, which took place at the UCLA School of Medicine, focused on the quality of group interactions in three PBL groups during a Clinical Applications of Basic Sciences (CABS) course. Specifically, my aim was to detect patterns of participation among group members and the role of a faculty tutor within the group learning process. It was hypothesized that if groups are performing in optimal ways, then evidence of "interdependence and constructive human interaction" would be observable. How such constructs are operationalized and the theoretical justifications of the study are discussed next.

LEARNING IN GROUPS

Johnson and Johnson differentiate between atheoretical versions of group learning (i.e., simply clustering students into groups without changing other aspects of a curriculum) and what they call "cooperative learning" (D. W. Johnson, 1990; D. W. Johnson & Johnson, 1989, 1991, 1992, 1993; D. W. Johnson, Johnson, Holubec, & Roy, 1984).

As a result of their research findings they have identified criteria that are necessary to the functioning of cooperative groups. These include the following:

1. Positive interdependence: Each individual is concerned about performance of all other members of the group.
2. Individual accountability: Each student's mastery is assessed, including skills in self-assessment and in giving feedback to each group member.

3. Heterogeneity: Members need to be diverse in terms of ability and personal characteristics.
4. Dispersed leadership: All members need to perform leadership actions.
5. Developing social skills: All members need to possess high degrees of communication skills, trust, conflict management, and leadership. These skills are to be both explicitly and implicitly taught.
6. Reflection: Times and procedures are needed for dealing with group processing, with evaluating and modifying personal and collaborative effectiveness.

In short, their model of cooperative learning promotes what they and others have come to call "constructive socialization" (D. W. Johnson et al., 1984; Joyce, Weil, & Showers, 1992; Wood, 1988), which relies on a theory of social interdependence. They have stated that social interdependence exists when the outcomes of individuals are affected by others' actions. This is in contrast to social independence, when one person's outcome is unaffected by the actions of another (D. W. Johnson & Johnson, 1992). In most classroom contexts there is usually interdependence, but it is often what the Johnsons term "negative interdependence"; if one student performs "better" and receives a higher grade, it is at the expense of one or more other students. Alternately, if everyone can contribute to the whole, and all are enhanced by the interaction of the parts, then this is "positive interdependence." In a meta-analysis of studies that focused on small group learning, Johnson and Johnson (1974) concluded that learning in small groups was nearly always more effective than learning in isolation, if, and only if, there was positive interdependence evidenced within the group. The goal of positive interdependence cannot be realized unless *all* members of a group participate and are recognized to be constructively participating in the learning process. If even one member is marginalized or is permitted to absent himself or herself from the group activity, then positive interdependence is jeopardized and learning suffers.

Interdependence in PBL Groups

Within PBL curricula the group meeting is the obvious site in which to observe interdependence, and it can likewise be the context in which to gauge group effectiveness. Group effectiveness can be deconstructed into three separate components. The first component is the group's knowledge, which is conceptualized as not only the aggregate of individual knowledge, but as collective knowledge that is the result of group cognitive activity. It is organized as a shared mental model that allows the group to understand the problems and to resolve the tasks at hand. This is the *content construct.* Several scholars have studied the content construct in PBL, looking at the effectiveness of the group in identifying faculty-designated learning issues (Duek & Wilkerson, 1995; Duek, Wilkerson, & Adinolfi, 1996), the amount of structure necessary in the composition of a problem (Davis, Oh, Anderson, Gruppen, & Nairn, 1994), and the level and type of expertise of the faculty tutor (Schmidt, 1994; Schmidt & Moust, 1995; Silver & Wilkerson, 1991; Wilkerson, 1994, 1995).

The second component of group effectiveness is the *affect construct*. This concerns the feelings and attitudes of group members toward the group as a whole and toward their respective places and functions within the group. Only a few researchers have done work on the affect construct. Bouhuijs, Gijselaers, and Kerkhofs (1984) looked at the effect of individual students on group function and found that no one student appeared to have a consistent negative effect on all groups in which that student participated, even though he or she might have had a consistent negative effect in one group. Another study was done on the attitudes of students in traditional and in problem-based medical programs (Kaufman & Mann, 1996). These researchers found that PBL students had significantly more positive attitudes toward the learning environment and the curriculum. Traditional students, however, were found to be significantly more positive on the student-interaction scale, and further analysis indicated that "cliques tended to form in the PBL class" (p. 1097). There was no significant difference found on any subscale measuring attitudes toward social issues in medicine.

The third construct for group effectiveness is the *process construct*; it concerns how group members work together. Small groups can vary in many ways. In PBL, for example, one person, the tutor or a student, could take control of the group and direct all activities, essentially resolving problems by fiat. At the opposite end of the spectrum, each person could take on numerous flexible roles, doing whatever needed to be done at any given moment to best accomplish the group's tasks, with the tutor standing by to serve as resource or guide if needed. Members of groups might work at cross-purposes, unable (or unwilling) to refrain from competition. At another extreme, group members might defer to or even patronize each other out of fear of offense. Benne and Sheats (1978) divided group process into distinct roles, ways in which individuals participate, which either help or hinder the group task (see Table 4.6 later in this chapter).

Within the process construct, which is the area of concern in this chapter, Bossert (1989) has identified four mediating explanations that account for the enhanced learning associated with cooperative groups. These are higher order reasoning strategies; constructive controversy; cognitive processes of rehearsal, elaboration, and integration; and peer encouragement and involvement in learning.

To achieve these goals, however, groups need to function in equitable ways. Indicators of PBL group effectiveness that directly relate to the issue of equity among group members and between tutors and students include the equality of discourse, in length, type, and frequency, among the students; the equality of asking questions among the students; and the equality and distribution of feedback from the tutor to the students (Cariaga-Lo, Conner, & Springer, 1996; Duek, 1996a, 1996b; Tipping, Freeman, & Rachlis, 1995; Wilkerson, Hafler, & Liu, 1991).

In its 1995–1996 annual report, the Association of American Medical Colleges (AAMC; 1996) states its concern with "protecting diversity in the health professions" (p. 8) and goes on to delineate projects undertaken during the year to enhance diversity both within the AAMC and within its member colleges. Given the fact that diversity in institutions of higher education and medical education is a major concern (AAMC, 1996; Bowles & Gintis, 1976; Rosser, 1997; Sleeter & McLaren, 1995) the term "equality" assumes a meaning beyond measures of equal attendance. Gender, race, ethnicity, and socioeconomic status are considerations that must be recognized when we attempt to assess whether groups are indeed affording equal opportunities to all members. Hence, within PBL groups, attention must be directed at levels of participation of women, people of color, persons who speak English as a second language, and students who are first-generation college graduates. The present study takes up all but the last of these issues.

Gender, Ethnicity and Equity in Groups

Although today's classroom might not be considered an overtly hostile environment for young women, it is certainly not a place where they are encouraged to engage in rigorous intellectual activity. M. Sadker and Sadker (1994) conducted two major studies of gender equity. First, they studied over 100 elementary school classrooms, in three states and in the District of Columbia, for a 3-year period. Next, they studied college classrooms for a further 2 years. In a recent report based on these and other studies, the Sadkers concluded that a clear "gender message" is palpable. They claim:

> The classroom consists of two worlds: one of boys in action, the other of girls' inaction. Male students control classroom conversation. They ask and answer more questions. They receive more praise for the intellectual quality of their ideas. They get criticized. They get help when they are confused. They are the heart and center of interaction. (p. 42)

Orenstein (1994) noted the lowered expectations for young women during adolescence and the gender bias in the classroom with teachers encouraging assertive behavior in boys and giving boys more attention.

Specifically, in studies conducted among both suburban and inner-city communities, Orenstein found that boys received five times the amount of classroom conversational space and teacher attention as did girls. Meanwhile girls show a precipitous drop in interest and in feelings of capability regarding math and science. Orenstein concluded what has been shown in other research—that the loss of confidence in math and science *precedes* the drop in achievement.

These early patterns do not disappear as we move through the educational hierarchy to the higher grades, to college, and to graduate school. Patricia Ireland, president of the National Organization for Women, reported she "learned the hard way" that although she paid the same tuition, the college world that she lived in was different from the one attended by her male classmates. She recollects the remark of one professor, when she asked a question on the first day, ". . . announcing to everyone, 'Why do they expect me to teach calculus to girls?'" She never asked him another question, and subsequently dropped out of calculus, to her much later regret (M. Sadker & Sadker, 1994, pp. 161–162). Krupnick's (1992) study of the effects of gender on classroom participation at Harvard revealed that the most academically talented women in the nation were interrupted, cut off, and silenced; males performed and females watched. This issue of the "silent" female student has become the refrain of those who study the psychosocial development of women in academic settings.

In *Women's Ways of Knowing*, Belenky, Clinchy, Goldberger, and Tarule (1986) found that women in learning environments repeatedly speak of feeling "deaf and dumb." Their informants speak of having become accustomed to someone (usually men) in authority guiding every academic move. They admit to having become passive recipients of knowledge, not actively engaging in dialogue and attempting to understand and utilize it.

This problem becomes exacerbated for women of color. bell hooks (1989) explained the difficulty women of color experience in obtaining a clear "voice" in academic conversations. She recounts that it

> . . . was born in me the craving to speak, to have a voice . . . that could be identified as belonging to me . . . punishments . . . seemed endless. They were intended to silence me—the child—and more particularly the girl child. Had I been a boy, they might have encouraged me to speak . . . for talking girls, no legitimized, rewarded speech. The punishments I received . . . were intended to suppress all possibility that I would create my own speech. (pp. 5–6)

hooks sees the goal of her teaching as assisting all students to feel empowered in a rigorous, critical discussion. She contrasts this with the occurrences from her own life, and those of young women she studied, who received subtle messages from professors who "avoided looking at you, pretending they do not hear you when you speak, and at times ignoring you altogether" (p. 57).

M. Sadker and Sadker (1994) charged that "at the highest educational level, where the instructors are the most credentialed and the students the most capable, teaching is the most biased" (p. 168). Regarding medical schools, they noted, ". . . the profession has been extremely effective at deflecting the aspiration of medically-minded women . . . female medical students report greater loneliness, role conflict, and depression" (p. 190). Although this work pertains to large classroom situations, instances of bias, marginalization, and silencing have also been witnessed in studies of smaller group situations.

Rosser (1997) looked at the participation of women and of minorities in small groups studying science. She cautioned that often, an "equitable" division of a few women and minority students into groups composed primarily of White males results in a phenomenon she calls "spotlighting." These isolated students often felt excluded and were either silenced or dropped out altogether. Based on her findings, Rosser suggested that groups should include two or more women or minorities to safeguard against such isolation. This may leave some groups more homogeneous than others; however, Rosser stated that this is generally less detrimental to the learning of the minority members.

Theorists from the critical perspectives warn that the continued silencing of what now is more than half of the total academic population is incompatible with democratic ideals. Sleeter and McLaren (1995) pointed to ways to change this situation:

> As educated whites, we can speak to an educated white audience and attempt to contribute to dialog and praxis oriented around the deconstruction of white supremacy. . . . We want . . . readers to examine our own collective positions of privilege, identify actions we can take to share power. . . . In part, this involves learning to share, listen, step aside. . . . (It also) means supporting the ideas, perspectives . . . of colleagues of color . . . men and women. (pp. 22–23)

These same ideals are affirmed in the writings of Friere (1998), who succinctly stated:

> No one lives democracy fully, nor do they help it to grow, if, first of all, they are interrupted in their right to speak, to have a voice, to say their critical discourse, or, second, if they are not engaged, in one form or another, in the fight to defend this right, which, after all, is also the right to act. (p. 65)

This literature on gender, ethnicity, and equity in groups suggests that creating a climate of positive interdependence in PBL groups may not occur automatically or be easy to achieve.

Investigations into the Process of PBL Groups

The general methods of PBL call for cooperating with a group, teaching each other key information, and trusting one another to be thorough in finding the relevant portion of the needed information. The cases for any given course are chosen to direct the students' self-learning of issues that the faculty deem important, and students are tested on information and procedures that it is assumed they have found, taught, and learned together. PBL is an excellent mechanism for group work, based on sound premises. Unfortunately, PBL is offered to a group that has spent the past 8 or 10 years of their schooling self-selecting for independence and competitiveness (negative interdependence). In addition, certain members retain privileged positions within groups, creating a dominance that can predictably curtail equal participation among members.

Furthermore, the group process can become imperiled by an overly directive tutor, who, like students, has been enculturated in traditional ways of pedagogy. Barrows (1986) warned, "If the students (do not) . . . reason and learn on their own because of an overly directive tutor . . . then objectives (of PBL) are compromised" (p. 485).

Cox (1996) studied 107 medical students enrolled in a hybrid PBL curriculum at the end of their first year at St. George's University, Trinidad, West Indies. She found that males enjoyed the PBL group sessions more than females (50% to 36%). Additionally, 68% of students said they were sometimes bored, whereas 24% were reluctant to make contributions to discussions. Nearly one third, 31% of the respondents, reported that they would hesitate to say that they did not understand a point during a discussion, and 32% said that they would not ask questions at all. The percentages on these last two categories were distinctly higher for female students than for male students. Racial or sexual discrimination against students by faculty was reported by 29% of women and by 15% of the men.

Cox (1996) summed up by stating that these factors, including ". . . racial and sexual discrimination were apparent and may have led to the poor attendance in (PBL) groups and lectures noted by administrators" (p. 20). In other words, many students, and a disproportionate number of women and minorities, elected to opt out or to become silent rather than to assert their right to be active members of the group.

Wilkerson and colleagues (1991) studied case-based learning groups at Harvard Medical College and discovered patterns of practices that compromised student ownership of the group. In one group, "the tutor frequently interrupted with questions, speaking loudly to be heard above the students" (p. S79). In another group the session began with students working together,

... however, his (the tutor's) comments increased in length and frequency as the tutorial progressed. He asked factual questions, occasionally interrupting students to do so. He called on students by pointing. Their answers were brief and followed by "yes" or "no" from the tutor. Time ran out and no agenda was set. After the tutor left, the students complained that they had not taken a systematic approach to the session. (p. S80)

Wilkerson and colleagues (1991) also noted differences in tutors' questions, with two tutors using questions to guide group process, probe, and clarify (open-ended questions), and the other two asking questions regarding specific facts (closed-ended questions). Concerning the latter, the authors noted, "Their questions required only brief answers and often served to stop, rather than to advance, discussion" (p. S80).

Two of the groups were characterized by silences (a period of 3 seconds or more with no discourse) that might imply more thought. Silence was "virtually nonexistent" in the other two groups, where exchanges were typified by interruptions. The tutors of these two groups admitted that they felt uncomfortable with extended silence and would begin to speak rather than wait. The authors conclude that

Smooth-turn-taking (is) the social lubricant that promotes a well-oiled discussion. Students form judgments of one another and of their relationship to the tutor based on the pattern of the conversational exchanges that occur. When a group member consistently interrupts, he or she may be labeled domineering, uncaring, or even rude. When a tutor interrupts, this behavior not only signals a struggle for control of the discussion but also sets a standard for acceptable interactive behavior in the group. (Wilkerson et al., 1991, p. S81)

Students' acceptance of ownership of the group and of their own learning should change this paradigm to exemplify a more "well-oiled" discussion, with students asking and answering a higher proportion of the questions, and with questions being characterized by a more substantive and open-ended nature. Likewise, fewer interruptions, and less off-task, digressive behavior should be hallmarks of groups more strongly committed to student directedness of the small group process and to awareness of a commitment to equitable access to the discourse.

RESEARCH QUESTIONS

This study proceeded from several questions about equity among group members. Would observations of PBL groups show that all members took equal responsibility for discussion, and for asking questions? If a PBL group truly functions on a level playing field, for example, encouraging participation by every student, I expected to see relatively equivalent numbers of questions and amounts of discourse for each member. If this equal participation is not seen, then is the difference related to any gender and or ethnic differences within the group?

The PBL course observed used alternating formats. The case began in Session A where students met without a tutor and it continued through Session B with a tutor present. Hence, a second set of research questions focused on possible differences in discourse among students at the two sessions: Were there differences in discourse among students affected by the presence or absence of the tutor? If so, were these differences related to any gender and or ethnic differences within the group?

A goal of PBL is to foster group cooperation and positive interdependence. I asked, therefore, whether students are sharing roles and taking on primarily positive ones. If not, are the roles taken related in any way to gender and or ethnic differences within the group? This was my third area of interest.

Fourth, an important issue in PBL is how well the tutor fosters group cooperation. To address this, I examined whether all group members would receive an equal amount of feedback from the tutor during the sessions the tutor attended. In particular, is there a difference in the amount of positive feedback? If there are differences, then are they related to any gender differences, to ethnic differences, or to both?

METHODS

The Course

The PBL course investigated here was begun as a small-group discussion portion of the Gross Anatomy course. At UCLA this course is called Clinical Applications of the Basic Sciences (CABS). Students in the CABS course were assigned to groups (consisting of 9–12 students in 1994) by computer to achieve, as nearly as possible, a representative distribution of students into groups with respect to gender and ethnicity (C. Hodgson, personal communication, 1995). The groups met once a week for 2 hours' work on the current case. Each case required two sessions, one each week for 2 weeks. A faculty tutor was assigned to each group; if the tutor was unable to be present a substitute tutor attended. As noted earlier, only Session B was attended by the faculty tutors; the students met without the tutor at Session A. Students were given no specific instructions on how to conduct Session A, although they had gone through a preliminary case with a tutor present to demonstrate a general format for exploring a case.

At the first session for a particular case the students opened the week's materials distributed to each classroom from a central office. The materials they received included individual copies of the case handout (usually 2–5 pages) and one copy of any test results, X rays, magnetic resonance images (MRIs), or photos. The case handout was narrative in form, giving the history and usually at least a portion of the patient's physical examination. Students then posted several large, newsprint "tear-sheets" (about 24″ by 36″) and wrote items under four column headings: (1) Findings, (2) Hypotheses, (3) Additional Information, (4) Learning Issues (LI). After some discussion of the items under the four headings, each student chose one or more LIs to study for the following session.

At the second session, which the tutor attends, students taught each other the things they learned during independent study (the items designated as "Learning Issues") and then re-examined the case in light of their new knowledge to resolve their understanding of the patient's problem(s). In most cases students also discussed proposed treatment(s), possible patient compliance problems, and psychosocial issues.

The tutor's task was conceptualized as that of a coach who corrects and redirects ideas. In addition, the tutor might introduce additional concepts that the students may have missed. Theoretically, according to the principles of PBL, the tutor spends very little time speaking; his or her job is not to teach the students but to assist them with their organization and resolution of the problem, to "coordinate the flow" as needed.

At the end of Session B the tutor handed out the last portion of the case and students assessed their accuracy in evaluating the problem and the treatment. Students were encouraged to discuss how they performed, both as learners and as group members, although at UCLA this is not a requirement as it is in some schools. Also, at this point, some tutors reassigned topics that they thought were still not clearly understood, but this was not the rule. Generally the case was considered finished at the end of the second session.

Students were graded on attendance and on contribution to the discussion (during Session B only) by the tutor, and that represented a small portion of the total Gross Anatomy (CABS) grade (Adinolfi, personal communication, December, 1994).

The Participants

For this study I randomly selected 3 out of 15 CABS groups with the prerequisites that each group had a tutor who was not a novice tutor, and each met on a different day. These groups are referred to as Group P, Group Q, and Group R, facilitated by Tutors P, Q, and R, respectively. The distribution of gender and ethnicity for each group is shown in Table 4.1. Tutors P, Q, and R were White males.

TABLE 4.1
Distribution of Participants by Group, Gender, and Ethnicity

Group	Ethnicity	Male	Female	Males + Females
P	Asian	2	0	2
n = 10	Black	0	0	0
	Hispanic	1	2	3
	White	4	1	5
Q	Asian	2	0	2
n = 12	Black	2	2	4
	Hispanic	3	0	3
	White	2	1	3
R	Asian	3	0	3
n = 10	Black	0	0	0
	Hispanic	3	1	4
	White	1	2	3
Totals for				
all groups	Asian	7	0	7
	Black	2	2	4
	Hispanic	7	3	10
	White	7	4	11
Total by Gender		23	9	32

Permission was obtained for access to students' ethnicity data and the case transcripts could be sorted by gender and by ethnicity to observe possible differences in students' behaviors. In the case of Hispanic students, they were further sorted into the categories of "ethnic appearance and speech patterns" and "nonethnic." Seven of the students designated as Hispanic in the official records were born in Spanish- or in Portuguese-speaking countries, had strongly melanistic skin tones, had dark hair, and spoke a distinctly accented English. The remaining three Hispanic-designated students were born in the United States, had much lighter skin and hair color, and spoke a more conventional English with no detectable accent beyond one associated with a U.S. region. For the purposes of observing both group interactions and tutors' feedback, it seemed appropriate to consider these two groups separately. Therefore, for comparative purposes, three students were designated "nonethnic Hispanic" and were associated with the majority group.

The Procedure

I attended and audiotaped the three CABS groups during a single case (two sessions) each. Because each case involved two sessions (A and B) lasting 2 hours per session, my taping of the 3 groups covered 4 hours per group for a total of 12 hours. Observations were conducted over a 6-week period in the Fall 1994 semester.

I also individually interviewed each tutor and at least three members of each CABS group. The interviews were informal with notes taken during each interview and elaborated immediately afterward. Tutor interviews lasted about 5 to 10 minutes, and student interviews lasted from 10 minutes to over an hour, depending on each individual's willingness to share his or her perspective. General questions were asked about how students saw the group, how well they felt the group interacted to resolve each case, and how each individual felt about his or her participation.

As the audiotapist and observer I used one large, central tape recorder placed on the table around which discussion was held and a second hand-held recorder. The recorder on the table produced a high-quality recording of the conversation, and the second allowed me to keep a running account of who was speaking and of any other commentary I wished to include such as movements, facial expressions, and off-task behaviors. To preserve anonymity a clockwise identification system with a one-letter identifier for each participant (A through L as needed, plus T for tutor) was devised. All audiotapes were completely transcribed. After several reviews of the data, including listening to each audiotape on at least three occasions, transcribing the tapes, and reading the pages of the transcriptions several times, patterns were detected. Tutors' feedback to students in response to a statement or to an answer given by a student was also noted, including the kind of feedback such as a nod, a noncommittal nonverbal noise, or spoken feedback of a positive, neutral, or negative tone. The pattern of tutors' feedback was noted—to which students and how often it was given. This, along with the tutors' interviews, helped form an idea of how the tutors viewed individual students. There was essentially no negative feedback, and the neutral or noncommittal feedback was at a level too low to analyze. The feedback that was of most interest, therefore, was the positive, verbal feedback. In addition, several students demonstrated particular behavioral patterns that were noted for later consideration and analysis.

I began to generate categories of students' behaviors that were, in most cases, closely related to the theoretical group processing categories proposed by Benne and Sheats (1978). These categories are listed in the next section. Categories of questions were clarified, and all questions were sorted, whether asked by the tutor or the students, into these categories. Questions of little substance ("what did you say?" "which page?" "really?") and repetitive asking of an unanswered question are not included in the question analysis sections of this chapter.

RESULTS AND DISCUSSION

Students' Participation

Student talk was calculated in "turns" that could range from a single comment to an extensive discourse when, for example, students took turns
presenting the findings from their independent inquiries during Session
B. Tables 4.2 and 4.3 show the mean calculations of students' turns at talking as a function of gender and of ethnicity. This talk occurred under two
conditions: tutor absent (Session A) and tutor present (Session B).

The means of the total talk for Session A show no gender differences;
some differences in terms of ethnicity were observed. Black females and
Asian and Hispanic males performed, as a group, below the mean. Black
males and one Hispanic female, however, participated well above the mean.

TABLE 4.2
Mean Number of Turns Taken as a Function of Gender, Ethnicity, and Tutor's Presence

Gender	Ethnic Group	Tutor Absent Session Mean #	Tutor Present Session Mean #	N
Female	Asian	n/a	n/a	0
	Black	13.50	12.00	2
	Ethnic Hispanic	41.00	17.00	1
	Nonethnic Hispanic	33.50	22.50	2
	White	34.67	12.50	3/4
	All female	29.88	15.11	8/9
Male	Asian	12.29	7.86	7
	Black	82.00	27.50	2
	Ethnic Hispanic	7.80	12.83	5/6
	Nonethnic Hispanic	80.00	19.00	1
	White	35.43	25.43	7
	All male	28.05	25.42	22/23
Totals		28.53	16.25	31/32

TABLE 4.3
Mean Number and Rank of Turns by Ethnic Group, and Tutor's Presence

Ethnic Group	Tutor Absent Session Mean #	Tutor Present Session Mean #
Asian	12.29	7.86
Black	47.75	19.75
Ethnic Hispanic	13.33	13.43
Nonethnic Hispanic	49.00	21.33
White	35.72	20.73

Participation in Session A within particular groups is noteworthy. In Group P, 63% of the 369 total turns were taken by two White males and by one nonethnic Hispanic male. Two Black males came close to dominating the time in Group Q. Their back-and-forth comments and banter accounted for 45% of the 363 total turns taken. Finally, in Group R, the least active group where the total turns numbered only 124, two White females used 42% of the turns. In light of these observations, it seems that neither gender nor ethnicity accounted for participation differences except to say that Asian and Hispanic minorities appeared less inclined to participate.

A notable difference occurred, however, when the tutor was present. First of all, the tutors themselves claimed a significant portion of the discourse. In Group P, the tutor took 28% of the turns; in Group Q he took 49%; in Group R he took 40%. Tables 4.2 and 4.3 also show the drop in the mean number of turns for all groups of students. Here, an effect on gender is seen, with females almost reducing by half the number of turns taken during the session. Also striking is the drop taken by Black males (although one of them still participated above the mean).

Looking at each group during Session B, it was noted that in all three groups, the dominant speaker (other than the tutor) was a White male. Specifically, for Groups P, Q, and R, one White male accounted for 21%, 29%, and 26% of the total group comments, respectively. In Group R, one White male jumped from 10 to 50 turns between Sessions A and B. In Group Q, one White female fell silent after a White male Hypercontributer presented her assigned topic, thus reducing her turns from 52 in Session A to 5 in Session B.

In summary, relative to total talk, participation seemed equal in terms of gender without the tutor present. With the tutor present, students' participation decreased for all, but significantly more so for females. Regarding participation by ethnicity, Asians and Hispanics lagged behind other groups including Blacks and nonethnic Hispanics. However, if we collapse ethnic groups into majority and minority categories and consider nonethnic Hispanics as majority individuals, a more striking disparity is detectable. In Fig. 4.1, participation is divided into three parts: the area around the median, a high area, and a low area, and percentages of participation by majority and by minority membership are designated. This division clearly shows the overrepresentation of the majority students on the high end and the overrepresentation of minorities on the low end.

Question asking was also affected by the presence of the tutor as shown in Tables 4.4 and 4.5, but there does not appear to be an overall gender or ethnicity effect here. The drop in question asking was greatest for the Black students. In particular, the two Black male students in Group Q went from asking 59 to 14 questions between Sessions A and B. Questions

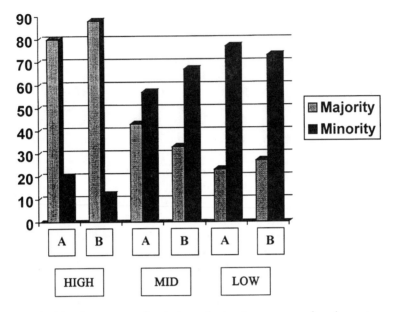

FIG. 4.1. Percentages of majority and minority group members in areas of high, median, and low participation by session.

TABLE 4.4
Mean Number of Questions Asked as a Function
of Gender, Ethnicity, and Tutor's Presence

Gender	Ethnic Group	Tutor Absent Session Mean #	Tutor Present Session Mean #	N
Female	Asian	n/a	n/a	0
	Black	4.00	3.00	2
	Ethnic Hispanic	9.00	0.00	1
	Nonethnic Hispanic	7.50	8.50	2
	White	8.33	3.00	3/4
	All female	7.13	3.89	8/9
Male	Asian	2.71	2.14	7
	Black	29.50	7.00	2
	Ethnic Hispanic	1.60	2.50	5/6
	Nonethnic Hispanic	11.00	0.00	1
	White	9.15	4.57	7
	All male	7.32	3.30	22/23
Totals		7.27	3.47	31/32

TABLE 4.5
Mean Number of Questions Asked by Ethnic Group

Group	Tutor Absent Mean #	Tutor Present Mean #
Asian	2.71	2.14
Black	16.75	5.00
Ethnic Hispanic	2.83	2.14
Nonethnic Hispanic	8.67	5.67
White	8.90	4.00

also shifted more toward asking the tutor to define, explain, or expand on some item, rather than asking fellow students to elaborate or clarify ideas presented. In Group P, a nonethnic Hispanic female asked one third of the total questions (8 out of 24) in Session B (tutor present). Eleven of the remaining 16 questions were asked by the two White males. In Group Q, a White male asked 14 of 43 questions, and in Group R, a nonethnic Hispanic female asked 9 of the 44 questions, followed by a White female who asked 8 questions and an Hispanic male who also asked 8 questions.

Roles and the Interdependence of Students

The third research question had to do with whether students were truly cooperating and sharing the various roles and tasks in a positively interdependent way. If not, could the roles that various students assumed in the group be related to gender differences, to ethnic differences or to both?

Terms Relating to Group Tasks

To talk about roles it becomes necessary to introduce some terminology for the roles that were observed within groups. Some are positive group roles, nearly mandatory for group function. Other roles are positive group roles that are useful but are not required for efficient group function. Finally, there are several roles that were seen to hinder groups in a variety of ways—by taking up time, by distracting one or more group members from the primary task, or by setting some members in opposition to others. These terms were both induced from the data and gleaned from several sources read during the coding phase of the study to achieve theoretical sensitivity, after the manner of Strauss and Corbin (1990).

As I watched the groups I noticed several participatory roles that seemed to occur regularly, and as I listened to and transcribed the tapes and reread the transcripts, other roles began to emerge from the data. None of the groups had explicitly assigned roles for members, either permanent or changing for each session, yet all of the groups had some members who self-selected certain roles. These roles and behaviors are presented in Table 4.6. The first term in each category denotes my original terminology. Subsequent terms following the slash mark "/" indicate terms derived from other sources who have also named these roles (see Benne & Sheats, 1978).

Observing Roles

Tabulations of who spoke and how often they spoke provided one perspective on overall group participation. Another perspective could be dis-

TABLE 4.6
Terms Relating to Group Roles and Behaviors

Group Functioning Roles

Group Leader, Discussion Dominator/Coordinator: The person who directs the discussion.
Reference Person: One individual who takes responsibility for looking up items and reading them aloud.
Scribe/Recorder: A person who stands at the tear sheets and does the writing for the group.
Task Organizer: A person who obtains or organizes handouts, materials.

Group Processing Behaviors

Aggressing: An attempt to run group without the consent of others. This may include Hypercontributing, Lecturing, and Overtalking.
Derailing/Blocking: Making comments or asking questions that may completely remove the group from task-related behaviors for a period of time. This might include jokes and off-topic comments.
Encouraging/Energizing: A form of feedback during the conversation that has the result of encouraging the current speaker. An indirect form of Forwarding. (See also Placeholding for contrast)
Facilitating/Orienting–clarifying: Asking probing or clarifying questions.
Forwarding/Initiating–contributing: Taking a leadership role in moving toward task completion.
Gatekeeping: Encouraging quieter members to participate.
Hypercontributing/Dominating: Speaking frequently or at length on his or her own or on others' topics.
Hypocontributing, Withdrawing/Following: This could be active listening, passive listening, or total uninvolvement. (See also Observing)
Observing, Participating Peripherally: Paying attention to proceedings without contributing.
Overtalking: Interrupting, or talking more loudly than a current speaker.
Placeholding: Making noncommittal or repetitive noises or comments. (See also Encouraging for contrast)
Recognition Seeking: Trying to gain recognition or approval from the tutor or the group.
Undertalking: Carrying on *sotto voce* conversations with neighbors; usually off-task.

cerned by attending to the types of roles assumed by group members. To discover roles the inquiry needed to move beyond simply counting turns and look for distinct patterns in the content of the discourse, the manner in which it was undertaken, and how role adoption affected other group members. Some of the more notable and consistent roles included the following:

The Discussion Dominators. The membership of the three groups was fairly well balanced by race (Asian, Black, Hispanic, White) and by gender, but individual contributions to the discourse varied along lines of both gender and ethnicity. In Group P, a White male "expert" on certain topics frequently steered the conversation into areas where he was knowledgeable and would then go on at some length "lecturing" the other students on something that was peripherally related. Two Black males in Group Q spoke more often than other members of the group during the tutorless Session A, frequently playing off each other's comments and working as a team. A White male in this group also spoke at length about many topics. Between the frequent contributions of the first two males, and the less frequent but quite lengthy contributions of the third male, the rest of the members of the group spoke very little in Session A. The two Black males were quieter in Session B in front of the tutor, speaking about the same number of times as other members of the group. The White male, however, continued to speak frequently and at length in Session B. In Group R, one White male dominated the Session B activity, continuing to talk about many of the topics without letting the person who had studied that topic have a turn. Except for the two Black males in Group Q, who spoke frequently during the tutorless session, the rest of these discussion dominators were White males. Common behaviors included Aggressing, Hypercontributing, Overtalking, Placeholding, and Recognition Seeking.

The Hypercontributors. In two of the three groups there was a "holistic big-picture" or "hypercontributing" student who would study the entire case rather than their assigned portion. Although this practice might be seen as valuable and admirable, these individuals tended to take over the group, "teaching" the group not only their assigned piece of the case, but going on at length teaching the remaining portions, leaving other students with nothing to add to the discourse. Each time this occurred the tutor did nothing to discourage this behavior or to suggest that the hypercontributor should use this big-picture viewpoint more constructively; for example, speaking last to "fill in the holes" left by others. In individual interviews (some reported later in this chapter), several students expressed frustration with hypercontributors, reporting that such behavior left them feeling powerless and unheard despite having prepared a presentation. However, most critics felt that it was up to the faculty tutor to intervene. One female went so far as to exclaim, during Session B, "Well, *you* already *took* my topic!" and then she gave a short laugh and shrugged. The tutor said nothing, so when her turn came she distributed a prepared handout and spoke for a minute on one minor aspect of her topic that the hypercontributor had not covered. She did not speak again for the remainder of the session. In another group one Black male said "Hey, that's my topic!" when the hypercontributor began to talk, but both the hypercontributor and the tutor ignored the outburst. The Black student was then silent, but was apparently angry, judging from the manner in which he shuffled his papers together, brusquely and noisily putting them back in his folder. Both of these hypercontributors were White males. The most frequent behaviors observed within this role type were Aggressing and Overtalking.

The Referencer and the Silent Scribe. Each group also had a self-appointed student whose major contribution was to look terms up in the medical dictionary that was provided with the case materials and to read the definitions aloud. In each group, this "referencing" role was held by a female student (one ethnic Hispanic, one nonethnic Hispanic, and one White) who spoke infrequently, except to present her piece of the case in session B and to read definitions. A similar behavior that I called "silent scribe" was evident in one group where an Asian male wrote on the tear sheets during Session A, spending the entire time standing before the group and writing the group's notes on the case. He made no verbal contributions to the discussion. Hypocontributing and Observing were the hallmarks of these behaviors.

Observing Behaviors

Beyond the roles discussed previously there were also patterns of behaviors discerned, and although these were not exclusively practiced by particular group members, they were frequently observed across members. These included the following:

Overtalking. In nearly every group one or two students frequently interrupted others, talking over them to make a comment. Students who were thus interrupted usually relinquished their space in the conversation. In all but one instance these overtalkers were White males. Aggressing also characterized this behavior.

Withdrawing. Some students divorced themselves both mentally and physically from the proceedings. They placed themselves either in a chair far removed from the rest of the group, or, in one case, a student spent both sessions lying on a sofa a few feet from the table and chairs where the other group members were working. These students participated only minimally. One of these students, a White male, only evinced this behavior during the tutorless Session A. During the tutor session (Session B) he sat with the group and participated well above the norm. These students engaged in Hypocontributing.

Participating Peripherally. Other students were physically within the group but participated almost as infrequently as the withdrawing students. They, however, appeared to be attending to the discussion, simply not offering anything. They seemed to be engaged in "peripheral participation" because gestural responses such as head nodding and maintaining eye contact with other group members was observed. Persons demonstrating these behaviors included two Asian males, two Black females, one Hispanic female, and two Hispanic males. There were no White males or females in this category. Other behaviors of these students included Hypocontributing, Observing, and Placeholding.

Undertalking. Each of the groups had some students who would frequently "tune out" the dominant conversation and begin holding their own discussion. Sometimes this would be a few whispered words; on other occasions they would talk in normal tones, at some length. This was occasionally related to the topic at hand but more frequently appeared to be social discourse, sarcasm, questions about other matters, and generally nontask-oriented remarks. These behaviors were noted for one Black female, two White females, and two White males on a regular basis; sometimes they would get others to join them in conversation, other times they spoke and someone else merely nodded or smiled to indicate that they had heard. Derailing/Blocking and Recognition Seeking (from individuals) were other behaviors seen in this set of students.

In summary, it appeared that there were distinct roles, and that most students chose one role, either contributory to the group or not, and maintained that role throughout a session. In each group there was usually one person who dominated the discourse in a number of ways. In five of the six observed sessions this person was a White male, although the pattern was somewhat reduced during the sessions in which the tutor was present. The exception to this pattern was evidenced in the tutorless session in Group Q where two Black males codominated, but this behavior was significantly curtailed when the tutor was present.

It is notable that four students, two Hispanic females, one White female, and one Asian male, chose to participate in very "low risk" ways—by writing on the tear-sheets and by looking up terms in the provided dictionary. In later interviews they stated that this was comfortable for them. Three of them cited it as a way to contribute but to insure that they would not be interrupted; two said that it was nice to participate without running the risk of saying something incorrect. To investigate the reasons behind the choice of roles I interviewed all tutors and about 40% of the students. Some of the most informative interviews are summarized in the following section.

Interviews

Tutor Interviews

The tutors reported that they enjoyed their groups and felt that the groups were doing well. In all instances the tutors mentioned that they had some students who participated more than others. None of them mentioned the various roles or behaviors listed previously: the Hypertopic or "big-picture" student presenting the topics of others, the Overtalkers, the Referencers, the Hypocontributors (withdrawing and peripherally participating), or the Undertalkers (carrying on side conversations). When these roles were suggested, none of the tutors said that he had noticed anything other than that some students participated more than others. The tutors did not appear to believe that it was part of their job to equalize the conversation, leveling down the Hypercontributors and Overtalkers, discouraging the Undertalkers from fragmenting the group, and encouraging the Referencers or Hypocontributors to become more involved. The tutors did not seem to have considered the matter, but by their conversation I inferred an implicit belief on their part that the hands-off nature of being a PBL tutor meant that they should let the group dynamic evolve without trying to change it, just as the tutors believed that they let the conversations evolve.

Student Interviews

As noted earlier I approached between three and six students from each group for informal interviews, which ranged from 10 minutes to over 1 hour.

Conversation with a Referencer. I spoke at length with one Referencing student, an ethnic Hispanic female. She reported that she was unused to speaking out in a conversation because this was not the model in her home where her father and brothers dominated the discourse. She chose to participate in the group in what she felt was a useful role and was comfortable with this level of contribution. She said that she would like to speak more but noticed that certain others dominated the conversation. She added that she found it difficult to begin a sentence because it would mean talking over others' voices, and she found it even more challenging to finish a sentence before someone interrupted her. She reported feeling frustrated but did not believe that she had the power to change these patterns. Rather, she felt that it was up to the tutor to change it and "allow" her to talk; in other words, the tutor was in charge. She felt far more comfortable when the tutor spoke, telling the students the facts of the case and indicating which concepts were important. This passivity on her part was "a more familiar method of learning."

Some Average Participants. Several interviews were held with group members who appeared to contribute to their respective groups without dominating them. Those in a group with one Hypercontributor expressed great frustration that this person's behavior interfered with completion of the case under study. Again, however, they did not feel that they had the power to rectify the situation. They, too, felt that the faculty tutor should say something. Three members in another group with a discussion dominator and several Undertalkers expressed deep dissatisfaction with the group dynamics without seeing any way in which they might alter it. The possibility of taking ownership, and responsibility for changing the group dynamic, did not occur to them.

A Hypercontributor Speaks. One of the Hypercontributors, although he stated that he was very busy and would probably not have time for an interview, did spend a few minutes in the hallway chatting with me about his group and his role. He saw students' presentations of learning issues as the equivalent of "book reports." According to him, each student read a prepared paper, no one listened to anyone else, and no one tried to make sense of the whole. He felt that he was the only one in the group who tried to go beyond his own little piece of information and tie it all together. He viewed his role as essential to the group's understanding of the case. Several members of his group confided that they found it frustrating to have him continually usurp their selected topics. These mismatched perceptions of the group process led to increased dissatisfaction of several students in this group as the semester went on.

A "Natural Leader" Grasps the Reins of Group Control. One White male, who appeared to lead his group rather ably, was happy to speak with me at great length. He reported that he attended a small, East Coast liberal arts college as an undergraduate and was quite used to participating in small-group discourse. At the beginning of the semester he admitted to having "seized" leadership of the group, and admitted seeing himself as a "natural leader." In the student-led sessions he could be found standing in front of the rest of the students, directing the discussion, calling on others, writing on the tear-sheets, organizing and assigning the Learning Issues, and summarizing the session at the end. During the tutor-led session he would not stand, but he still maintained group leadership and discourse dominance. He felt that, as the student most comfortable with small-group tutorials, it was his "duty" to organize and to lead. Unfortunately, this also meant dominating the conversation. However, as the more peripheral members of the group became familiar with the format in subsequent weeks and wished to increase their participation, he appeared reluctant to relinquish his central position. Other group members confided in interviews that, by the third case (5th week of the semester), the group began to resent his dominance and a power struggle ensued, which was finally resolved by the end of the semester with access to leadership roles more distributed. This struggle seriously detracted from the on-task time and energy put forth on three of the cases.

The View of an Occasional Withdrawer. One of the extremely withdrawn students spoke to me briefly, indicating that the entire group process was a waste of his time. He said that he had always studied material on his own, and he saw this as his only reliable method of learning new information. He attended the group sessions because it was required.

It should be noted that this particular student, although both physically and socially withdrawn from the rest of the group during Session A, was an Overtalker and a Hypercontributor in Session B when the tutor was there and was presumably assessing their performance for grading purposes. The other students in his group did not seem to have a clear picture of his strategy; they only knew that they did not like having him in the group and felt angry when he interrupted or presented their information in front of the tutor.

Some Tentative Conclusions Regarding Students' Beliefs about PBL and the Tutor's Responsibility

It was clear both from interviews and from demonstrated behaviors that many students believed the following:

1. Groups are the responsibility of the faculty tutor, who should ask students to speak or refrain from speaking; ask and answer clarifying questions; and keep the group on task.
2. The faculty tutor's job is to provide the important knowledge, *the* right answer, for the group.
3. Learning from each other is not a reliable method.

Tutors, on the other hand, stated that they were not responsible for group dynamics or for equalizing participation, but only for ensuring the accuracy of information and thorough coverage of the case material.

It was clear that despite the best intentions of the course designers, the ideals of PBL—student-centeredness, self-directed learning, situated learning, and problem solving—were not being fully realized. The students saw the groups as being only as effective as the faculty tutor. Thus, the data were next examined for tutors' behaviors that might encourage or discourage participation. Again, to investigate the question of equity, tutors' feedback behaviors were observed regarding individual students.

Investigating PBL Tutor Activities

In the final research question the intent was to inspect portions of the session that involved tutors' feedback to individual students. Was tutors' feedback limited to a few students or disseminated among all present? Specifically, was there a pattern of distribution for the types of feedback, with some students receiving a disproportionate share of the most positive types of feedback and encouragement?

The literature shows that, in K–12 classrooms, teachers (of both genders) tend to call on boys more frequently and tend to give boys more positive feedback about the content of their answers. This differential attention appears even more extreme when student–teacher interactions are assessed along ethnic lines. Some have speculated that a teacher's reluctance to call on foreign-born students might be due to the problems associated with pronouncing names or to a desire on the teacher's part to shelter the student who has limited English proficiency from embarrassment. The literature is clear, however, that positive feedback encourages student talk (Orenstein, 1994; Rosser, 1997; M. Sadker & Sadker, 1994; Sleeter & Grant, 1994). Hence, it is appropriate to look at this variable across gender and ethnic lines when attempting to understand group dynamics.

The aggregate amount of positive feedback is shown in Table 4.7. There were some differences detected between the amount of positive feedback that male and female students received. This mean difference was less than it might have been, due in large part to the nonethnic Hispanic female in Group P who received 8 of the 13 positive feedback remarks in her group (the other two females in the group received no positive feedback). Ethnic Hispanic, Black, and Asian students received less positive feedback than their White and nonethnic Hispanic counterparts. Two White male students received 18 total positive feedback comments between them, while of the other 21 male students, 7 received no positive feedback at all (including 3 of the 7 Asian males), 5 received one positive comment, and 5 received two positive comments each.

It might be argued that students received positive feedback in proportion to their participation within the group, and that, in a self-fulfilling prophecy, those who participated more received more feedback, so they continued to participate. However, all students spoke in Session B, and the frequency of their participation, particularly for ethnic students, was

TABLE 4.7
Positive Tutor Feedback by Gender and Ethnicity

Gender	Ethnicity	Mean Number of Positive Feedback Responses
Female	Asian	n/a
	Black	1.00
	Ethnic Hispanic	0.00
	Nonethnic Hispanic	6.50
	White	3.75
	All females	3.33
Male	Asian	1.43
	Black	1.00
	Ethnic Hispanic	2.00
	Nonethnic Hispanic	1.00
	White	3.29
	All males	2.09
Combined	Asian	1.43
	Black	1.00
	Ethnic Hispanic	1.71
	Nonethnic Hispanic	4.67
	White	3.45
	All students	2.44

not reflected in the frequency of tutors' feedback. In Group P, for example, a Hispanic female spoke 17 times of the 126 verbalizations made in her group during Session B. This is slightly above the mean (12.6 per student, for 10 students) number of talk events for her group. She received no positive feedback from the tutor. Meanwhile, a nonethnic Hispanic female student, who spoke 20 times, received eight positive feedback responses from the tutor.

As we see in Tables 4.2 through 4.5, the students participated unequally when the tutor was present, and from Table 4.7 we see that they received unequal amounts of positive feedback that were not necessarily in proportion to their participation. This finding corresponds to patterns noted in other studies (Belenky et al., 1986; hooks, 1989; Orenstein, 1994; M. Sadker & Sadker, 1994). Status characteristic theory (Cohen, 1994; Cohen & Lotan, 1995) provides a way to understand the phenomenon. Cohen (1994) explains:

> Status characteristics . . . are defined as socially evaluated attributes of individuals for which it is generally believed that it is better to be in the high state than the low state. Status generalization is the process by which status characteristics come to affect interaction and influence so that the prestige and power order of the group reflects the initial differences in status. . . . The net effect is a self-fulfilling prophecy . . . (high status students) become

more active and influential . . . low status students are cut off from access to the resources of the group, (and) . . . the group lacks the contributions and ideas of all its members. (p. 24)

Cohen (1994) argues, however, that teachers possess the means through which status can be redistributed among diverse group members. Specifically, she advocates methods of assigning competence to low-status students through specific, favorable, and public evaluations of good performance, thus enhancing their status in others' eyes. In other words, it is positive feedback that serves to help equalize an initially uneven playing field.

In the present study, however, it was mostly the already high participators, particularly White students and nonethnic Hispanics, who were encouraged when they spoke. Other high or medium participators, and most low participators, particularly those of non-White groups, received little or no encouragement and continued to be peripheral participants with only minimal conversational input. It is particularly disturbing that the Black students who were active in the group received little positive feedback (the four Black students received only four positive feedback comments in total). Second, Asian males received little or no positive feedback (a total of 10 positive comments for seven Asian males; three of them received no positive comments). Although their average input to the group was determined to be minimal, still, this lack of positive feedback could serve to negatively reinforce their minimal input. Of the nine females, two received no positive feedback and two received only one positive comment each. Conversely, of the White males, only the extremely withdrawn White male, who spoke very little in either session, received no positive tutor feedback. The other six White males received an average of 3.83 positive tutor feedbacks, compared to the whole group average of 2.44 positive tutor feedbacks. The highest number of positive tutor feedbacks (11) went to one of the White male Hypercontributors.

Thus it would seem that positive tutor feedback might play a role in encouraging and discouraging participation. In this instance, and consonant with the findings of Cohen (1994; Cohen & Lotan, 1995), status appears to be reinforced by the observed actions of the tutor rather than being redistributed. Although positive feedback might have been a way to equalize the uneven playing field, its underutilization with women and minorities precluded its possibility of doing so.

Limitations

This study was conducted over a 6-week period in 1994, with three groups of first-year medical students observed for two sessions each. One concern was that these "snapshots" might not be reflective of the true group inter-action even though the entire 2-hour session was audiotaped and tran-scribed for each session.

In 1995, three more "natural" or untrained groups were chosen in a similar fashion to the 1994 cohort; they were observed and audiotaped for three 2-hour sessions per group, producing an additional 18 hours of tapes. During that year, all groups had tutors present at all sessions. All observations were done in Session B of each case, and all nine sessions had a tutor present, although in several cases there was a substitute tutor. These data showed the same behavioral patterns as the 1994 groups. There were, in addition, three groups trained in cooperative group skills in 1995. They were also observed and audiotaped for three 2-hour ses-sions each, for a total of 18 hours. The majority of the data and results from this portion of the study are reported elsewhere (Duek, 1998). However, it may be useful to note here that the trained groups, from 1995, appeared to take more ownership and responsibility and to answer far higher percentages of student-asked questions (Duek, 1996a, 1996b; Duek, 1998). The trained groups also had significantly fewer incidents of Overtalking and engaged in more equitable patterns of discourse, with all students' participation being significantly closer to the mean, rather than having a few frequent participants and a few nonparticipants as was observed in all untrained groups (Duek, 1998).

CONCLUSIONS

In this study, students did not participate equally in the group discourse, nor did they ask equivalent numbers of questions. The distributional pat-terns were skewed; some ethnic groups, Asians and Hispanics, never par-ticipated as fully as others, whether the tutor was present or not. The Black students participated more fully in the absence of the tutor than when the tutor was present. White males were the largest contributors and question-askers, followed by White females and the two nonethnic Hispanic females. Nearly all White females decreased their participation in the presence of the tutor. With the exception of the two White males who dominated the discourse in Session A for Group P, all White males maintained the same amount of talk or increased, in some cases dramati-cally, during the tutor-led Session B. Of the two exceptions, one decreased from contributing 22.7% of the total student talk events (in a group of 10 students) to 21.4%, whereas the other dropped from 18.9% to only 5.5%.

In considering the findings of the study, the question arises as to what components of the interaction might serve to maintain unequal relations. The analysis leads to the conclusion that the inequality of participation may relate to four factors: traditional roles, students' expectations, tutors' presence, and tutors' feedback.

Some students revealed in the interviews that they tended to view themselves both in home and in school settings as either full or peripheral participants. Particularly Hispanic females told of households where male voices dominated. In school settings, they reported feeling uncomfortable with vying to gain the group's attention. Furthermore, they pointed out that if they attempt to speak and someone else Overtalks, they stop. Asian males also voiced their dissatisfaction and tendency to defer to more powerful voices. In addition, many from these minority groups sought the safety of "safe" roles—the Scribe or the Referencer. Exacerbating this problem is the assumption of leadership roles by some of the White males. This is particularly apparent in the case of the "natural leader," the White male who saw himself as the only one able to organize and direct his group. Hence, there seems to be a proclivity for students to adopt "traditional" active or passive roles, and when these are conjoined through group dynamics, it results in more extreme positions.

A second factor relates to students' expectations of "how to do school." Many of these students came from undergraduate institutions where teachers were perceived as givers of knowledge, and students were its passive recipients. Some students, particularly women, seemed willing to speak out in the tutorless group, but retreated into more passive, silent roles when the tutor was present, awaiting the "correct" version of the facts to write down and memorize for the exam. For them, this appeared to be a more familiar, comfortable, and preferred way of learning.

Third, the tutor's presence implies that the tutor will be assessing the students, and some individuals saw this as a time to perform for the authority figure—to "stand out" by speaking out. Some students, particularly White males, reported speaking in the presence of the tutor, not necessarily to resolve the case, but to convey a positive impression. In terms of motivation theory, these students chose to adopt a performance goal rather than a mastery goal (Nicholls, 1984). This was certainly the case with the White male in Group R, the "occasional withdrawer," who saw the tutorless session as a waste of his time but who dominated the conversation, contributing over 25% of the total student discourse, in the tutor-led session.

It is interesting to note that many students, females in particular, perceived themselves as being dependent on the tutor for effective group management. This includes the tutor's dissemination of content knowledge, the tutor's process strategies for encouraging everyone to participate, and the tutor's evaluative feedback. The tutors, meanwhile, tended to see content coverage as their primary task. These perceptions resulted in a mismatch between what students see as the tutor's role and what tutors perceive as their role, and an even greater mismatch between the students' and tutors' expectations and the stated goals of PBL.

Finally, tutors' feedback, which can serve to reinforce or to redistribute status in the group (status characteristic theory, discussed earlier), appeared to be distributed in a manner that served to maintain the status quo. If members of some ethnic groups are selectively not empowered in this manner, this may be one force acting to marginalize their participation and to disallow their acquisition of agency. This may have been particularly the case for the Black females and the Asian males observed.

There are, of course, many other factors affecting these students' behaviors in a group: perceived personal ability and self-concept, current health, past interactions with other group members, past experiences with groups in general, and so forth.

The four factors identified through this research might point to ways educators can work to address issues of group dynamics through individual participation. For example, it would be beneficial to share findings about roles with tutors and to make them aware of students' behaviors such as overtalking or peripherally participating. It might also be valuable to show them ways to recognize and redirect students who are reading "lists and descriptions" that cannot be of any use to others, either in learning content or in solving the problem. One student did this repeatedly, speaking 58 times in one session, reading from texts, describing a diagram, and giving lists of nerves and sinuses of the head. By the time he was nearing the end of his exposition the other students were fidgeting, grooming, doodling, and otherwise indicating inattention.

A course for tutors to help them to understand students' needs and to improve their tutoring methods might be a valuable addition to any program. It seems reasonable to infer that these marked patterns of unequal participation and unequal feedback serve to perpetuate the privileged status quo. Awareness of the distribution of participation and of the use of feedback as a way to bring about participation should to be brought to the attention of tutors, encouraging them to be more skillful group managers. It would be beneficial to the group process if the tutors were more aware of their role in providing access to the group collaboration. Tutors play an important part in encouraging (and indirectly, therefore, privileging) students to articulate their thoughts and findings, allowing them to recast their knowledge and coconstruct the dialogue (polylogue), solidifying their understanding and ability to hypothesize about and solve patients' cases.

Likewise, students should be made aware of group dynamics and should be empowered to take responsibility for their own participation and contribution to the group. If we wish to create skilled problem solvers, then training the students in effective group participation would be an important component of the first weeks of the course. Assisting students to be metacognitive about the course, the group, and their role(s) in the group may allow them to take more responsibility for the group and how it functions. They would then be able to take "ownership" of the group and of their own learning, becoming less dependent on a tutor. In this way, students could learn the value of positive interdependence and become increasingly metacognitive, self-directed learners.

Both students and tutors need not only an initial orientation to the purposes and techniques of PBL but also reinforcement of the goals, perhaps in the form of an evaluative questionnaire to be used frequently. This would both remind them of the program goals and subtly prompt them to change their behaviors and become more self-directed.

These findings emphasize the importance of continuing, and refining, the techniques involved in PBL. Unfortunately some of the original goals and purposes of this format have been mislaid, and some reorientation of the tutors, along with the teaching of metacognitive group strategies to both students and tutors, may be useful in promoting a forum for collaborative group work that is truly equally accessible to all. When we ask the question, "Whose group is it?" the clear answer should be "the students'— ALL of the students."

REFERENCES

Association of American Medical Colleges. (1996). *Facts: Applicants, matriculants, graduates: 1990–1996*. Washington, DC.

Barrows, H. (1986). A taxonomy of problem-based learning methods. *Medical Education, 20,* 481–486.

Belenky, M. F., Clinchy, B. M., Goldberger, N. R., & Tarule, J. M. (1986). *Women's ways of knowing: The development of self, voice, and mind.* New York: Perseus Books.

Benne, K. D., & Sheats, P. (1978). Functional roles of group members. In L. P. Bradford (Ed.), *Group development* (pp. 52–61). La Jolla, CA: University Associates.

Bossert, S. T. (1989). Cooperative activities in the classroom. In E. Z. Rothkopf (Ed.), *Review of research in education* (pp. 225–250). Washington, DC: American Educational Research Association.

Bouhuijs, P. A. J., Gijselaers, W., & Kerkhofs, B. (1984). The use of group data to trace the influence of individual students on group functioning. In H. G. Schmidt & M. L. d. Volder (Eds.), *Tutorials in problem-based learning: New directions in training for the health professions* (pp. 221–224). Maastricht/Assen, The Netherlands: Van Gorcum.

Bowles, S., & Gintis, H. (1976). *Schooling in capitalist America: Educational reform and the contradictions of economic life.* USA: HarperCollins.

Bruffee, K. A. (1993). *Collaborative learning: Higher education, interdependence, and the authority of knowledge.* Baltimore: The Johns Hopkins University Press.

Cariaga-Lo, L., Conner, D., & Springer, C. (1996, July). *Learning behaviors of students in a problem-based learning curriculum: Videotape studies.* Paper presented at the meeting of The 7th Ottawa conference, Maastricht, The Netherlands.

Cohen, E. G. (1994). Restructuring the classroom: Conditions for productive small groups. *Review of Educational Research, 64,* 1–35.

Cohen, E. G., & Lotan, R. (1995). Producing equal-status interaction in heterogeneous classrooms. *American Education Research Journal, 32*, 99–120.

Coombs, R. H., May, D. S., & Small, G. W. (Eds.; 1986). *Inside doctoring: Stages and outcomes in the professional development of physicians.* New York: Praeger.

Cox, C. A. (1996, April). *Student responses to problem-based learning in the Caribbean.* Paper presented at the meeting of Research in Medical Education, Association of American Medical Colleges, San Francisco, CA.

Davis, W. K., Oh, M. S., Anderson, R. M., Gruppen, L., & Nairn, R. (1994). Influence of a highly focused case on the effect of small-group facilitators' content expertise on student learning and satisfaction. *Academic Medicine, 69*, 663–669.

Duek, J. L. E. (1996a). *Reflective questioning: Interactions among students in problem-based learning sessions.* Paper presented at the meeting of Research in Medical Education, Association of American Medical Colleges, San Francisco, CA.

Duek, J. L. E. (1996b). *When is equal access not? A qualitative look at problem-based learning (PBL) group interactions.* Paper presented at the meeting of The 7th Ottawa conference, Maastricht, The Netherlands.

Duek, J. L. E. (1998). *Conversational effectiveness in problem-based learning groups.* Unpublished doctoral dissertation, UCLA, Los Angeles.

Duek, J. L. E., & Wilkerson, L. (1995, April). *Learning issues identified by students in tutorless problem-based tutorials.* Paper presented at the meeting of the National Association for Research in Science Teaching, San Francisco, CA.

Duek, J. L. E., Wilkerson, L., & Adinolfi, A. (1996). Learning issues identified by students in tutorless problem-based tutorials. *Advances in Health Sciences Education, 1*, 29–40.

Freire, P. (1998). *Teachers as cultural workers: Letters to those who dare teach.* Boulder, CO: Westview Press.

hooks, b. (1989). *Talking back: Thinking feminist, thinking Black.* Boston: South End Press.

Johnson, D. W. (1990). *Reaching out: Interpersonal effectiveness and self-actualization* (4th ed.). Edina, MN: Interaction Book Company.

Johnson, D. W., & Johnson, R. T. (1974). Instructional goal structure: Cooperative, competitive, or individualistic. *Review of Educational Research, 44*, 213–240.

Johnson, D. W., & Johnson, R. T. (1989). *Cooperation and competition: Theory and research.* Edina, MN: Interaction Book Company.

Johnson, D. W., & Johnson, R. T. (1991). *Active learning: Cooperation in the college classroom.* Edina, MN: Interaction Book Company.

Johnson, D. W., & Johnson, R. T. (1992). Positive interdependence: Key to effective cooperation. In R. Hertz-Lazarowitz & N. Miller (Eds.), *Interaction in cooperative groups: The theoretical anatomy of group learning* (pp. 174–199). Cambridge: Cambridge University Press.

Johnson, D. W., & Johnson, R. T. (1993). *Circles of learning* (4th ed.). Edina, MN: Interaction Book Company.

Johnson, D. W., Johnson, R. T., Holubec, E. J., & Roy, P. (1984). *Circles of learning: Cooperation in the classroom.* New York: Association for Supervision and Curriculum Development.

Joyce, B., Weil, M., & Showers, B. (1992). *Models of teaching* (4th ed.). Boston: Allyn and Bacon.

Kaufman, D. M., & Mann, K. V. (1996). Comparing students' attitudes in problem-based and conventional curricula. *Academic Medicine, 71*, 1096–1099.

Krupnick, C. (1992). Unlearning gender roles. In K. Winston & M. J. Bane (Eds.), *Gender and public policy: Cases and comments.* Boulder, CO: Westview Press.

Nicholls, J. G. (1984). Achievement motivation: Conception of ability, subjective experience, task choice, and performance. *Psychological Review, 91*, 328–346.

Nolan, W. A. (1970). *A surgeon's world.* Greenwich, CT: Fawcett.

Orenstein, P., in association with the American Association of University Women (1994). *School girls: Young women, self-esteem, and the confidence gap.* New York: Doubleday.

Rosser, S. V. (1997). *Re-enginnering female friendly science*. New York: Teachers College Press.

Sadker, M., & Sadker, D. (1994). *Failing at fairness: How our schools cheat girls*. New York: Simon & Schuster.

Schmidt, H. G. (1994). Resolving inconsistencies in tutor expertise research: Does lack of structure cause students to seek tutor guidance? *Academic Medicine, 69*, 656–662.

Schmidt, H. G., & Moust, J. H. C. (1995). What makes a tutor effective? A structural-equations modeling approach to learning in problem-based curricula. *Academic Medicine, 70*, 708–714.

Silver, M., & Wilkerson, L. (1991). Effects of tutors with subject expertise on the problem-based tutorial process. *Academic Medicine, 66*, 298–300.

Sleeter, C. E., & Grant, C. A. (1994). *Making choices for multicultural education: Five approaches to race, class, and gender* (2nd ed.). New York: Macmillan.

Sleeter, C. E., & McLaren, P. L. (Eds.; 1995). *Multicultural education, critical pedagogy, and the politics of difference*. Albany, NY: State University of New York Press.

Strauss, A., & Corbin, J. (1990). *Basics of qualitative research: Grounded theory, procedures, and techniques*. Newbury Park, CA: Sage.

The University of California at Los Angeles. (1994). *UCLA School of Medicine Announcement, 1994–95*. Los Angeles, CA: Author.

Tipping, J., Freeman, R. F., & Rachlis, A. R. (1995). Using faculty and student perceptions of group dynamics to develop recommendations for PBL training. *Academic Medicine, 70*, 1050–1052.

Wilkerson, L. (1994). The next best thing to an answer about tutors' content expertise in PBL. *Academic Medicine, 69*, 646–648.

Wilkerson, L. (1995). Identification of skills for the problem-based tutor: Student and faculty perspectives. *Instructional Science, 22*, 303–315.

Wilkerson, L., Hafler, J. P., & Liu, P. (1991). A case study of student-directed discussion in four problem-based tutorial groups. *Academic Medicine, 66*, 579–581.

Wood, G. (1988). Democracy and the curriculum. In L. E. Beyer & M. W. Apple (Eds.), *The curriculum: Problems, politics, and possibilities* (pp. 166–187). Albany, NY: State University of New York Press.

Chapter 5

How Are We Doing?
Methods of Assessing Group
Processing in a Problem-Based
Learning Context

Jeff Faidley
Dorothy H. Evensen
The Pennsylvania State University

Jill Salisbury-Glennon
Auburn University

Jerry Glenn
The Pennsylvania State University

Cindy E. Hmelo
Rutgers University

> *If I wanted to learn basic science in a weird way, I may as well have taken traditional.*

So remarked Carol,[1] a first-year medical student who had elected to participate in a problem-based learning (PBL) track that provided an alternative to a "traditional" curriculum at an Eastern medical college (Evensen, 1999). What Carol interpreted as "weird" was the group meeting, which was not going well for her. The experience failed to meet the expectations of collegiality and collaboration that had prompted her to select the PBL track, and it had become the source of almost daily frustration that led her to doubt her ability to effectively operate on an interpersonal level, a characteristic she believed to be crucial to medical practice. Carol acknowledged that she was learning basic science, but she reported also learning to selectively "keep your mouth shut" or "tune out" in group meetings. Over the course of her first semester, Carol struggled to assess the group situation and to devise strategies to deal with the prob-

---

[1]Throughout this report, pseudonyms are used.

lems she faced in the PBL group. To an extent she was successful. But her struggle, like her learning, remained an individual effort, and it did not result in bringing out into the open the issue of how the collaborative process, with its ensuing benefits, was not being realized for this learner.

A critical feature of PBL is the collaborative structure, which can entail numerous learning advantages. First, collaboration distributes the cognitive load among the members of a group and allows the group as a whole to tackle problems that necessitate the access of knowledge beyond that possessed by any individual group member (Pea, 1993; Salomon, 1993). Second, collaboration takes advantage of the groups' distributed expertise; as the students divide up the learning issues, they become "experts" in particular topics. Third, small-group discussions encourage individuals to coordinate different points of view, enhancing reasoning and higher order thinking skills that promote shared knowledge construction (Blumenfeld, Marx, Soloway, & Krajcik, 1996; Brown, 1995; Vye, Goldman, Voss, Hmelo, & Williams, 1997). Concurrently, collaborative discussions result in members talking each other out of their unshared biases and presuppositions (Abercrombie, 1960) as they discover that some of their beliefs and opinions are not socially defensible. In short, collaboration engages learners in cognitive activities that could not be realized individually; the social interaction sets the stage on which a shared cognition occurs.

But beyond being shared, the cognitive activity is also situated both historically and culturally (Brown, Collins, & Duguid, 1989). Collaboration grounds knowledge within a community of practice (Lave & Wenger, 1991) and serves to model an aspect of professional expertise associated with teamwork and consultation (Eraut, 1994). Finally, the phenomenon of collaboration requires a new level of self-consciousness—a way to reflect on both the individual and the collective activities during and after knowledge construction. Such a process reflects what Schön (1983) referred to as *reflection-in-action*, and necessarily involves learners' perceptions that, as Schunk (1992) concluded from a review of research on students' motivations, can be as important in predicting performance in academic achievement settings as abilities.

Research investigating the relations between learning in groups and student achievement has demonstrated that the discussion of group interactions and how they might be improved, or *group processing*, is a necessary component of group learning activity, and it contributes to improved achievement (Yager, R. T. Johnson, Johnson, & Snider, 1986). It is still not fully understood, however, how groups might best engage in, and thus benefit from reflective activities (Webb & Palincsar, 1996).

In the ideal PBL model, students deliberately reflect on the problem to abstract both substantive and procedural lessons (Hmelo & Ferrari, 1997). They consider the connections between the current problem and previous problems, determining how this problem is similar to and different from other problems (Barrows, 1988). This reflection allows them to make generalizations and to understand when and under what circumstances this knowledge can be applied (Salomon & Perkins, 1989). Within this recursively reflective process, students evaluate their own performance and that of their peers; they reflect on the effectiveness of their self-directed learning and their collaborative problem solving. This latter aspect of reflection helps students to think about and improve their learning and collaborative strategies.

In practice, this ideal model of PBL is coconstructed by the group facilitator. Hence, the literature that describes the facilitator's role stresses the importance of helping the student group manage its own interpersonal dynamics (Barrows, 1988). Barrows maintained the necessity of having students bring their problems out into the open and working them through. This may be accomplished both implicitly and explicitly, and it may occur during the time when problems are being discussed and at the culmination of a problem-based session. For example, if a facilitator notices a problem in a newly formed group, he or she might model the behavior that the students should acquire within the context of the group discussion. In the initial stages of a group, then, the facilitator might be the one to explicitly point out, "We seem to have a problem as a group." As time proceeds, the facilitator would fade this modeling back using only metacognitive prompts when the students themselves notice a problem. In this case, the facilitator might ask, "What shall we do about the problem (that the students noticed)?" Students are thus scaffolded (Bruner, 1977), or implicitly taught to become more attuned to the group dynamics as they reflect on their learning and their problem solving.

Facilitators are encouraged to ensure that time is reserved at the end of each session to reflect on group processing dynamics. Here, students comment on their own contribution to the group, after which their peers are invited to comment on the self-evaluation before assessing their own performance. Initially, students are expected to be reluctant to disagree with others in their group (unless they are being overly self-critical). Again, the facilitator is encouraged to model the kinds of comments that students should learn to give to group members whose performance is problematic. Barrows (1988) gave such examples as "Those resources you went to seemed to be rather superficial and you didn't bring the information we needed to really understand" and "You seemed to want to take over the group's thinking and tell everyone what should be asked and how it should be put together" (p. 42). Once the students become comfortable expressing their opinions about each other and realize their dependence on the quality of each other's work, they should become more critical in their comments, helping to enhance the group's function.

Some research has been done on the aspects of reflection outlined previously. The implicit modeling of reflective techniques by facilitators during the discussion of a case has been found through microgenetic analyses like those presented in chapters 3 and 4 of this volume (see Koschmann et al.; Koschmann & Evensen). This work has demonstrated how faciltators embed both cognitive and metacognitive cues into the discourse of the group meeting to affect substantive thoroughness and procedural efficiency in dealing with complex problems, especially to the end of identifying learning issues.

Other studies have looked at how reflection is practiced either at the end of PBL sessions or after a case had been completed. Some of this research reports disturbing findings. In a qualitative study that included semester-long observations of six students in PBL groups, Evensen (1999) found that this component of the meeting was often performed in a perfunctory way if not totally overlooked. Indeed, one participant felt so ill-equipped to evaluate his own performance that he reported that he had essentially mimicked the faculty facilitator's evaluation of himself.

Tipping, Freeman, and Rachlis (1995) compared interviews with 27 first-year PBL students and three faculty facilitators on their perceptions of group procedural effectiveness with videotapes of actual sessions. Although all informants reported that groups worked "well as a team," data collected from videos indicated gross imbalances of participation and communication generally directed at the faculty facilitator. In some instances students were found sleeping during the PBL session, and some members of groups were egregiously neglected. These researchers noted no evidence of any periods of reflection during or after the group session. Although these findings may very well be specific to this particular PBL program, they still point out that contradictions can exist between subjective reports of group processing and more objective observations.

Because any possibility of rectifying group interactions, thus improving collaborative learning, is dependent on students' first having a clear understanding of how their groups work, it is important to find ways of making students' perceptions of group processing salient. Although the mechanism of the round-robin, postsession reflection has the potential of bringing to the fore issues related to group processing, the scant research on this component of PBL suggests that this method might not be accomplishing its goal. It appears that the postsession reflection perhaps has become so routine that it has deteriorated into a refrain of "I'm ok, you're ok." However, even if it were achieving the desired end of exposing group processing issues, it remains a singular method that, in terms of research criteria, should be compared, or triangulated, with measures obtained from other sources (Lincoln & Guba, 1985).

This research project sets out to explore both alternate and supplementary methods that might be used in PBL groups, thus leading to ways of opening up meaningful discussions of group processing. In short, two instruments were used to provide information on how four PBL groups performed in terms of group processing components. One instrument was adapted from an existing survey used primarily in business contexts. The aim of this survey was to identify students' perceptions of group performance and effectiveness. The second instrument was developed in consultation with stakeholders at the institution under study. This tool was designed to be used by nonparticipant observers to yield data about group performance.

Although both of these instruments provided numerical data, interpretive rather than statistical analyses were performed for two reasons. First, this study was intended to be a pilot designed not to validate an assessment instrument but to determine whether the assessments are methodologically feasible and conceptually interrelated in ways that would make them useful in PBL settings. Second, the number of groups under study (four) is too few to meet the criteria for statistical inference. The reason for including a report of this work in the present volume is to offer the readers, both those who conduct inquiries in PBL environments and those who are responsible for the design and implementation of PBL curricula, access to tools that might forward their research efforts.

METHOD

Participants

A total of 20 first-year medical students agreed to participate in this study. All students had met regular admission standards at the medical school and had self-selected the PBL option.[2] Students met in one of four PBL groups facilitated by one or two faculty members who were either physicians on staff at the teaching hospital or persons who held doctorates in particular scientific fields. Groups were reconfigured at the beginning of

---

[2]At this medical college, PBL is made available to about 20% of the first- and second-year classes. The remaining students followed a traditional curriculum characterized by discipline-based, lecture and lab subjects. Once enrolled in PBL, students are committed to remaining in that curricular option during the second year of study. Students are apprised that if more than this percentage of students requests the PBL option, then a lottery is held. At the point in which the study was conducted, the number of requests had not exceeded availability.

every 8-week "block." Data collection took place about midway through the third block, so these particular groups of students had been meeting together for 3 to 4 weeks but had been meeting in groups for about 20 weeks. One component of the PBL group meeting in this medical college required groups to reserve the final 10 or 15 minutes of a session to reflect on how the group functioned both in terms of individual and collective performance. In addition, facilitators were responsible for collecting students' responses to questions with which to evaluate the case. This latter task was to be completed at the end of the final session on each case.

Materials

Survey Instrument. A customized version of a larger survey, called the *CWG Survey, University Edition, Form A* (Connolly & Wilson, 1992)[3] was constructed to assess aspects of this particular learning situation. The reported purpose of the CWG survey was to provide a psychometric instrument that can "enable people to adjust their own behavior to enhance their contributions to the goals and objectives of their organization" (Wilson, 1995, p. 58). Reliability and validity of particular subscales of the survey are reported to range between .75 and .95 with lower estimates occurring with negative scales (Wilson). This survey instrument is used mainly in business settings, but its usefulness within contexts that rely on collaborative group efforts has been documented (Wilson).

In the case of PBL, individual group members are responsible for contributing to the conditions that will support group learning. Thus, the items drawn from the CWG survey focused on those behaviors and attitudes that would be seen as important to group learning. The resulting survey was called the *Learning Team Survey* (LTS) and was constructed by Performance Programs, Inc. in consultation with the first author. The LTS was administered during the first 15 minutes of a group session at the end of the third week of the third block. This instrument provides scores that reflect individual and group perceptions of process and performance. Seven subscales that included 38 items from the survey were administered. These subscales were titled as follows: Commitment to Purpose; Commitment to a Common Approach; Complementary Skills; Accountability; Team Conflict; Team Performance; Overall Team Satisfaction (see the Appendix for a complete listing of items). To complete the survey, group members were asked to provide Likert ratings of 1 (*never*) through 7 (*always*) for items within each target category. Response sheets from the survey were returned to Performance Programs, Inc. for scoring and reports were prepared for each group.

---

[3]Further information about this and similar instruments is available from Performance Programs, Inc, Old Saybrook, CT 06475.

Observational Checklist.   An observational checklist of group interaction variables was designed to be used to score targeted behaviors observed in videotapes of PBL sessions dealing with one case. The construction of the checklist involved a series of steps. First, the two PBL co-coordinators at the medical college were asked to list behaviors that they believed were important to the functioning of a PBL group. They were asked to think about behaviors in two ways: first, *substantive behaviors*—those that aligned with the objectives of PBL curricula; second, *group processing behaviors*—those that related to group procedures and to social interactions. Using responses to this open-ended prompt, a checklist of group processing and substantive behavioral variables was constructed. The survey included 12 items under each of the two behavioral categories. The survey was distributed to 15 experienced PBL facilitators and was returned by 13.

Next, these experienced facilitators were asked to determine the importance of the various substantive and group processing behaviors. In this particular PBL setting, facilitators rated student group members on a daily basis, and the final facilitator rating for each of the four blocks per year is worth 10 percent of the total block grade, the same percentage as the final exam. Hence, the facilitator's evaluation of students' behavior is highly valued in this educational context. Facilitators were asked whether certain behaviors, or practices, were "essential," "relevant" (but not essential), or "irrelevant" to the PBL process. Once completed, a second step was required wherein facilitators were asked to rank order each set of 12 items in each category. This process yielded a Content Validity Ratio (Lawshe, 1975) that assigned weights to each item allowing us to determine the three most valued practices in each behavioral category. These are listed in Table 5.1.

The practice of connecting principles of basic science to the case under study was deemed the most important substantive variable by facilitator respondents. This behavior could be indicated, for example, by a group's

TABLE 5.1
Most Valued Substantive and Group Processing
Behaviors to be Used for Observational Checklist

Substantive Behaviors	*Group Processing Behaviors*
Practice of connecting principles of basic science to case under study.	Practice of relatively equal participation of all group members.
Practice of assessing what knowledge is needed to understand the case under study.	Practice of questioning or challenging information or reasoning processes of group members.
Practice of hypothesizing from a particular set of facts concerning a case.	Practice of recognizing contributions of individual group members (complimenting, encouraging, etc.).

review of the biochemistry of the male hormone testosterone and their subsequent discussion of its physiologic role in the development and function of the prostate gland. The next most important behavior was the practice of assessing what knowledge is needed to understand the case under study. This, in fact, is the process of determining the learning objectives, or learning issues, for the case. Finally, respondents noted the importance of hypothesizing from a particular set of facts concerning the case. All three of these behaviors are central components to the practice of PBL; hence, it was not surprising that they were so prominently represented among the responses.

The valued group processing behaviors primarily featured the practice of relatively equal participation of all group members. In this PBL setting, each group member was expected to be prepared in terms of content and to be willing to equally participate in each group meeting. The practice of questioning or challenging information and reasoning processes of group members was also evaluated as important. Students were expected to model their interactions on those demonstrated by facilitators, who are known as practitioners or researchers in the field of medicine. In particular, students were expected to internalize the discursive patterns that operate within this field, and the PBL session is, to a large extent, a training ground for this. Finally, experienced facilitators also valued the practice of recognizing contributions of individual group members. The PBL context requires constructive controversy (Bossert, 1988–1989), but is not designed to be adversarial or competitive. Therefore, it is important to contest a colleague's opinion, while at the same time recognizing its validity and merit.

Once the behaviors listed previously were identified, we were ready to use them to assess the group interactions as captured on the videos.

Design and Procedure

As mentioned earlier, the LTS was administered at the end of the third week and was then sent out for scoring. Meanwhile, at the beginning of the fourth week of the third block, all groups were beginning a new case dealing with suspected prostate cancer. The case was scheduled to be discussed during three group sessions. It was to be introduced during the last half hour of the first session, it was the scheduled topic of the entire 3 hours of the second session, and it was to be completed during the first hour or so of the third session after which another case was introduced. Arrangements were made to audiotape the first session and to videotape each of the remaining sessions with each of the four PBL groups.

The entire case, both audio and video portions, was reviewed by the first author. It was decided that only the second and third sessions would be used for coding. Almost no variations were observed in the first session; all groups used essentially the same process to read the case, extract relevant facts, and determine the initial learning objectives. From the two remaining target sessions, six 7-minute segments were identified for coding—two at the beginning, two near the middle, and two at the end. Thus, 42 minutes of group interactions were available for coding and for comparison. Once segments were identified, two independent coders viewed each series of segments and used the behavioral checklist to make note of targeted practices. Both coders were highly familiar with the case under discussion because each had conducted the videotaping for one group. Before tallying the behaviors of interest, however, coders viewed the segments without interruption to get a holistic sense of the group discussion. Once that was completed, coders viewed each segment and first calculated participation among group members, including the facilitator(s). Aggregate time was recorded for each participant, and a tally was made of the number of "turns" taken by each group member. The second set of codes required an additional viewing of all segments and dealt with the two other dynamic targets. The number of questions or challenges and instances of recognition were tallied for each group member. The overall level of agreement between raters for the combined categories was .91.

Substantive behaviors—connecting clinical to basic science, assessing knowledge needed, hypothesizing—were also calculated. The unit of analysis for this measure was the number of discrete topics discussed, and the total number of units was assessed for the group, not for individuals. Topics initiated by facilitators, however, were not included in the tally. For example, if students hypothesized that a 1 cm nodule on the right lobe of the prostate during a rectal exam was prostate cancer, the group would have been assigned one point for "hypothesizing." If the hypothesis was later linked with the same symptom, no additional points were assigned. However, if the cancer hypothesis was additionally generated after noting the patient's complaint of back pain, an additional point would be assigned. Again, for the substantive behaviors, two independent raters coded the video segments and their average level of agreement was greater than .90.

RESULTS

In this section we first present the group mean scores and standard deviations obtained on the seven subscales of the LTS. Individual scores for "overall team satisfaction" are presented in graph form to allow for visual between-group comparisons. Next, we look at each group separately and discuss our findings related to the three group processing variables identified as important to the performance of a PBL group. In doing this, we interpret how these behaviors might relate to particular subscale or item scores on the LTS. We then assess how perceptions of group performance on the LTS and interpretations of group performance gleaned from observed group dynamic variables relate to the occurrence of substantive learning behaviors identified as highly valued within this learning context. In the final section, we present findings obtained through analysis of the postcase discussion, a curricular component prescribed by this medical college's version of PBL.

Learning Team Survey Results

As indicated in Table 5.2, a marked difference in group perceptions was noted in subscale results from the LTS. At the time the survey was completed by the student members of the PBL group, they had been working together for 3 weeks and had completed six cases. The overriding question answered in the survey could be seen as "How are we doing?" as a learning team. A review of the subscale means indicate that the student respondents perceived some groups as doing well and others as not doing so well. Moreover, standard deviation data suggest that individual members in some groups had similar perceptions, whereas others were more disparate.

To more directly see the level of agreement among group members, Fig. 5.1 is provided. It allows for visual analysis of the overall team satisfaction for group and individual scores. Differences are notable both in terms of levels of satisfaction among groups and in levels of agreement within groups.

Figure 5.1 shows that, in general, Group 2 appeared to be the most satisfied and its members seemed to be in relative agreement. Group 4 indicated the greatest level of discontent, but the degree varied among group

TABLE 5.2
Means and (Standard Deviations) by Group for Subscales of the LTS

Subscale	Group			
	1	*2*	*3*	*4*
Commitment to Purpose	5.3 (.5)	6.0 (.7)	5.9 (.6)	3.8 (.9)
Commitment to Common Approach	4.8 (.7)	6.7 (.4)	6.0 (.6)	3.6 (.7)
Complementary Skills	5.1 (.4)	6.6 (.4)	5.7 (1.3)	3.9 (.5)
Accountability	5.4 (.7)	6.5 (.5)	5.9 (.8)	4.8 (1.1)
Team Conflict	2.4 (1.0)	1.2 (.2)	1.4 (.3)	4.5 (1.3)
Team Performance	5.4 (.8)	6.7 (.4)	4.8 (1.7)	3.2 (.6)
Overall Team Satisfaction	4.5 (.7)	6.8 (.2)	5.3 (1.9)	2.8 (1.3)

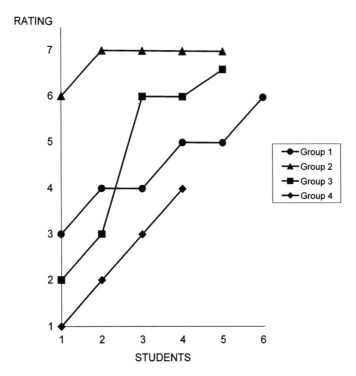

FIG. 5.1.   Individual student within-group responses to overall satisfaction
component of LTS.

members from extreme to moderate. Group 1 and Group 3 appeared
moderately satisfied, but again, individual levels of satisfaction varied particularly in Group 3, which showed one person as extremely satisfied,
whereas another person indicated significant dissatisfaction.

In the following section, we present the results of the analyses of videotaped segments of the group meetings. This assessment was designed to
answer the question of "What are we doing?" as a learning team. As part
of the analysis, we compare sections or items from the LTS and speculate
about how certain behaviors might relate to assessed perceptions. Because
this inquiry is pilot work, we make inferences that would require additional support to be considered valid claims.

Observation of Targeted Behaviors

Group Processing Behaviors Observed in Video Segments.   The inquiry
now turns to the data provided in the videotapes to determine whether
the group differences outlined previously can be explained by attending
to the behavioral variables deemed important by persons serving as facil-

itators in the PBL program. We look at each group separately to determine whether group processing, or behavioral differences might contribute to levels of satisfaction and perceptions of effective performance. In addition, we inductively labeled each group in terms of its most salient features.

Before presenting each group profile, we provide the information in Tables 5.3 and 5.4 that summarizes observed behaviors in raw scores. These tables should be referred to while reading the narratives on each group.

Table 5.3 represents the participation patterns in terms of number of turns found in each group over the 42 minutes of videotape analyzed. Reading across groups differences can be seen. For example, the facilitator in Group 1 stands out as having been the most active. Group 2 demon-

TABLE 5.3
Participation Patterns in Number of Turns Taken by Individual Group Members

	Group			
Individuals	1	2	3	4
Facilitator 1	60	16	21	21
Facilitator 2	8		0	
Male 1	14	27	39	52
Male 2	28	31	40	47
Male 3				29
Female 1	22	4	40	40
Female 2	19	39	52	
Female 3	30	26	28	
Female 4	6			
Total turns	187	143	220	189

TABLE 5.4
Dyanmic Behaviors: Challenging or Questioning and Recognizing in Raw Scores for Faculty (fac) versus Students (st), and Male (m) versus Female (f) Students

	Group			
Behavior	1	2	3	4
Challenging or				
Questioning	55	27	42	60
Fac vs. St	45/10	7/20	6/36	12/48
M vs. F	5/5	7/13	12/24	35/13
Recognizing	40	26	29	24
Fac vs. St	10/30	2/24	1/28	3/21
M vs. F	9/21	12/12	15/13	13/8

strates fewer aggregate turns that could either mean that members were taking longer turns or were tolerant of periods of silence. Finally, it appears that the bottom range of female participation exceeded that of males.

Table 5.4 presents the data on the two remaining group processing variables—challenging or questioning and recognizing. Taken together, these factors have the potential to enhance the level of discussion without resorting to undue competitiveness. On the one hand, facilitators should model, and students are encouraged to adopt, interactive strategies that will contest each other's positions so that new learning objectives are identified or possible misconceptions are resolved; on the other hand, students should learn a collaborative civility that guards again denigrating another person's contribution. In Table 5.4, the total number of challenging or questioning and recognizing behaviors are presented. Again, differences can be noted across groups; in particular, Group 1 appears to have engaged in both behaviors more than others, whereas Group 4 students challenged or questioned without a proportionate balance of recognizing. The data are further broken down in a way to compare faculty's versus students' behavior and male versus female behavior. Here again we see the facilitator for Group 1 as having been the most active challenger or questioner among the other facilitators. Patterns between male and female group members, however, do not point to any compelling inferences to be made among the groups. Rather, gender-related behaviors are discussed in the following sections that present individual group profiles.

Group 1: Teacher-Dominated or Socratic. Group 1 was made up of a highly experienced male facilitator, a male faculty observer, two male students, and four female students. What differentiated Group 1 from all the others was the dominance of the facilitator, who talked about one third of the time and took about one half of the turns tallied over the six 7-minute segments analyzed. These proportions contrast sharply with other groups where facilitators' talk amounted to less than 10% of the talk, and where facilitators took about 10% of the total turns.

The facilitator's participatory patterns of questioning and challenging also varied from other groups. Here again, the facilitator assumed a more active role, asking nine times as many questions as combined group members (45 to 5). In the other three groups, this pattern was reversed where students asked three to six times as many questions as facilitators. Group 1's facilitator also tended to recognize individual student's contributions to the ongoing discussion more than other facilitators; however, when compared with his challenging or questioning remarks these seem rather unbalanced. It is possible that this imbalance was detected by the students who engaged in the recognizing behavior to a much greater degree than other targeted behaviors within the group. The frequency of recognizing behavior was similar to other groups.

Among student members of the group, no differences were detected in terms of gender; that is, males and females participated in equal proportions. There was, however, one female who participated in only 6 out of 127 turns. Nonetheless, 3 of these turns were relatively extensive (i.e., more than 5 seconds in length), where in each situation she was explaining a process to group members. Regarding questioning or challenging and recognizing, again, there were no gender differences demonstrated.

Overall, the patterns of talk that occurred over the six analyzed segments were topic related and interactive, although the preponderance of talk was directed by or directed toward the facilitator. At one point after members discussed the possible significance of a specific patient symptom, a female group member asked the facilitator, "Could you enlighten us?" to which he responded, "My job is not to enlighten; it's to stimulate." This interchange was followed by laughter that appeared to signal tacit acceptance of the Socratic role for the facilitator. In another segment, the facilitator initiated a sort of question–answer structure for the students when he said, "Let me give you the medication; you tell me what the mechanism is." In the final segment, the facilitator related a clinical "story" about a patient presenting with an enlarged prostate, complicated by hypoglycemia. This story ran over 4 minutes of the 7-minute segment. Finally, twice over the analyzed segments, it was noted that the facilitator interrupted students in the midst of giving explanations.

In short, Group 1 might best be characterized as "teacher dominant." The teaching method observed could be interpreted as more Socratic than didactic. One third of the turns were questions or challenges posed by the facilitator, who, like Socrates' nettlefish, said his main task was to stimulate. In addition, the lengthy, clinical anecdote told to the students was meant both to raise questions about the reasoning in which they had been engaged and to serve as a parable, warning of the dangers of jumping to conclusions in the practice of medicine.

Subscale scores on the LTS indicate moderate satisfaction, with somewhat higher perceptions of effective performance. Responses to two items might reflect a perceived lack of support among group members. In particular, for Item 17 that stated, "Team members provide helpful feedback to each other," 100% of the group members marked a 4. Indeed, all items that might fall under the heading of recognizing, or providing encouragement and support to each other, received average responses of 3 or 4. On the other hand, performance scores tended to be higher. For example, Item 1 stated, "Our team identifies problems very well." Five of the six respondents rated this item 6 (almost always), and one rated it 5 (most of the time). In short, it appears that group members perceived their group as not particularly cooperative but, nonetheless, highly functional. When the question was posed regarding who might be contributing to the smooth functioning, the most apparent response, based on observation, was the facilitator.

Group 2: Student Negotiated or Transmission. Group 2 was composed of one facilitator, three female students, and two male students. Group 2 was distinguishable from the other groups in terms of its interactive style. In five of the six segments observed, one person assumed the role of "lecturer," providing for the group an example of a mechanism, a synopsis of symptoms, or an overview of causes and effects of the diagnosed condition. These minilectures ran from 1 to 4 minutes; they were usually conducted at the whiteboard accompanied by notations. Twice, each male member of the group served as lecturer, and once, one female assumed such a role. The facilitator talked around 10% of the time, usually posing questions or asking for clarification on a specific point. The two group members, both females, who were not observed presenting material, showed different participatory patterns. One took almost as many turns as other group members, although her total participation time was significantly lower. The other, however, was mostly silent, taking only four turns during two segments.

A notable feature of this group was its ongoing negotiations or procedural member checks. No one simply took over talking. Rather, each lengthy rendition was preceded by language that solicited group consensus. For example, one female asked, "Are we going to finish this before we get the next page?" Another asked, "Someone want to start us off?" There was also evidence that group members were sensitive to issues of dominance. During a recitation, one male asked, "Shall I keep going? Somebody else want to say something?" to which the response came, "Go for it." This anticipation of exceeding limits also occurred before a recitation. One female commented, "I don't know if you want to hear about this. Just cut me off if . . ." Students were also observed to weigh alternatives for discussion. One female posited, "So, do we want to talk about how they screen for prostate cancer or do we want to move on with the case and how this patient should be evaluated?" There was some evidence that this was normal operating procedure for this group. A female commented at two points, "That's what we usually do," whereas a male joked that he would now do his "usual dog and pony show."

The same deferential style was detected in the language of the facilitator. He asked, "What else could we talk about?" and later, "Would someone like to summarize?" Even his suggestions allowed for options: "It might be useful if . . ." or "Do you think you need some help with this, like from a urologist on staff?" In a similar manner, his interruptions took on a conciliatory air: "Could I ask for a time-out here? I'm having a hard time understanding where you're going. Are you focusing on learning objectives or are you following the case?"

We describe the interactions of this group as "student negotiated," but we describe the pedagogical mode as "lecturelike." These students apparently decided that the best way to deal with the information relevant to the case and related to the learning objectives was to "deliver" or "transmit" it from one student to the others. This model has been the most prevalent in Western education and, indeed, represents the "traditional" curriculum from which these students opted out. The difference, of course, is that in PBL the information is relayed from student to student rather than from teacher to student. Typically, a transmission model results in less interaction. In this group, we observed the fewest number of total turns (143), and the fewest number of questions or challenges (27).

The group, however, engaged in recognizing other members' remarks about as frequently as other groups. Much of this behavior was related to the "lectures" delivered or was embedded in the transitions from topic to topic. For example, one female noted, "Cindy had said that . . . do we want to hold off on talking about . . . ?" In another case, the facilitator said, "Marty has kind of done that already, do we want to . . . ?"

Results on the LTS lead one to conclude that Group 2 was the most content. Members perceived little conflict and believed that they performed well as a group. One person's responses on a few items, however, imply somewhat less satisfaction. This person marked a 4, a middle level of satisfaction, with effort put forth (Item 28). Another rating of 4 described one person's level of motivation (Item 29). In addition, one person believed that "helpful feedback" was not sufficient (Item 17). It is impossible to know if this was one respondent. It should be remembered, however, that one female member of this group was virtually silent through most of the segments and was not observed participating in any of the negotiation or lecture structures salient in this group.

Group 3: Single-Student Dominant or Cautiously Interactive. In reviewing the observational findings from Group 3, nothing stands out as particularly striking. If anything, the group, which consisted of three female students, two male students, and one facilitator, appeared to be more interactive than most other groups, having engaged in more turns and reflecting more evenness in turn taking. The facilitator, not unlike those in Groups 2 and 4, participated about 10% of the time. A closer look, however, reveals an interesting pattern.

First, when participation was gauged in terms of time, it was discovered that one female tended to dominate. Indeed, her talk comprised 25% of the total time. Unlike persons who tended to lecture in Group 2, this person's contributions were more interactive, but, at the same time, directive. She was responsible, more than the others, in leading members toward the topic of discussion. For example, at one point she noted, "We haven't done this (normal organ function) for a while. We did it for some of the other cases." In addition, many of the questions regarding what to discuss were directed toward this female group member, and this was particularly evident in the behavior of the two male members. Both males asked questions like "Should we do a normal prostate function?" "Should we do natural history signs, unless you want to do clinical science?" and "So we're saving treatment?" Each of these queries was directed toward and responded to by the same female member of the group.

We interpret this group's dynamics as interactive, but decidedly "led" by one member. We also infer what might be a gender issue here. The males in the group appeared particularly sensitive to the implicit leadership role of the dominant female member and took cautious, tentative steps in shifting topics. The two remaining female group members contributed liberally to the discussion but were never observed to either initiate or negotiate a topic.

LTS results for this group reveal the most disparity among group members. This is obvious on the graph reflecting individual satisfaction scores (Fig. 5.1). Although three members appeared to be very satisfied, two remained quite dissatisfied. Even more noteworthy, and interesting to explore, are perceptions concerning group performance. One person assigned the lowest possible score, a 1, to two performance items: "My team performs well" (Item 30) and "My team is very effective at getting things done" (Item 31). On the other hand, two members are critical of their own performance in the group, maintaining that they do not "put forth a lot of effort to complete team work" (Item 28) and that they are not "very motivated to do well on team tasks" (Item 29). Hence, the mean performance score of 4.8 reflects the diverse perspectives of two particularly dissatisfied members. Again, it is impossible to infer which of the group members provided these responses, but we think it interesting to consider that they might be coming from the male members of the group, in which case this group might be experiencing a serious gender-related problem. On the other hand, they might be the responses of the two non-dominant, less active females who could possibly have felt left out or undervalued by the more active members of the group.

Group 4: Male Dominant or Aggresively Interactive.   As with Group 3, the observational results do not reveal any notable behaviors in this group. Again, we have a facilitator who seemed to play a minor role in the overall discussion. Unlike the other groups, Group 4 was obviously unbalanced in terms of gender (3 males and 1 female); however, the ratio of time engaged in discussion is 3 to 1, which is consistent with the actual gender difference. When looking at questioning or challenging behavior, this group is somewhat distinguishable. Analyses revealed 60 instances of this behavior, which is only slightly higher than Group 1. The difference between these groups is evidenced in the opposite facilitator to student ratio: in Group 1 it was 5 to 1; in Group 4 it was 1 to 4. In other words, it was the students, not the facilitator, who generally asked questions or posed challenges in this group. Finally, recognition results were consistent with all other groups.

There was, nonetheless, a salient dynamic occurring in this group. Much of the back-and-forth discussion involved two male group members who seemed to be at personal odds with each other. We'll call these persons Art and Ben. Tensions became apparent in the first segment where, in response to Art's query about the male patient's condition, Ben quipped, "He could have an endometrial problem." Although there was some group laughter, there was none from Art. The facilitator pointed out that it was time to get on with the case, but Ben had the last word: "There's always time for a 5-second joke." In the third segment, Ben was digressing from the specifics of the case when Art regained the focus by asserting, "We haven't really talked about the pathology."

It was clear that Art wanted answers. After a question was raised concerning the structure of a glandular system, Art appeared frustrated as he exclaimed, "I thought someone could clear this up. Is there or is there not a capsule?" At another point, he attempted to shut down a discussion by stating, "I think we've gotten to the point where we've exhausted our knowledge."

Ben, on the other hand, appeared to like to keep a discussion going. He was more likely to bring in issues raised in previous cases or to speculate about mechanisms and processes. His discursive style was also more linguistically aggressive than those of other persons in this group, or for that matter, in other groups. On a number of occasions he explicitly disagreed, stating things like, "I don't agree with that," or the somewhat mollified "I'm not giving you a hard time, but . . ."

The reactions of other group members were interesting. Again, it should be remembered that the remaining male and female members did participate extensively, but in a notably different manner. The female member tended to end every statement with a raised inflection, as if she was unsure of her knowledge or perhaps was uncertain about how it would be accepted. The remaining male member voiced confusion, discontent, and plans to return to topics at later times (presumably after group meeting hours).

The facilitator seemed to have some awareness of the tension in the group. At one point, after a resolved interchange between Art and Ben, he pointedly asked the two remaining students, "Do you agree with that?" Both nodded. At another point, after a similar situation, the female member turned to the facilitator and asked, "Is that true?" but the facilitator was unable (or unwilling) to answer.

LTS scores portray Group 4 as the most dissatisfied group, although the degree of dissatisfaction varied among members. Interestingly, the greatest degree of agreement occurred in the perception of team performance. In the two items that deal with individual performance, group members assigned moderate to high ratings. For example, Item 28 reads, "I put forth a lot of effort to complete team work," whereas Item 29 states, "I am very motivated to do well on team tasks." The average response ratings on these items are 5.0 and 5.3, respectively, with scores ranging from 4 to 6. By contrast, items related to group performance received low ratings. Item 30, "My team performs well," and Item 31, "My team is very effective at getting things done," scored an average of 2.3 and 2.0 with the range spanning between 1 and 3. Members also agreed that this team compared poorly with other teams in which they have participated. Item 32, which assesses this perception, averages to 1.5 with half of the respondents assigning a 1 and the other half assigning a 2.

In comparing the LTS results with the observed results, we conclude that it might be the tension created by the conflict between the two dominant male members of the group that contributed to dissatisfaction with the process.

Substantive Behaviors Observed in Video Segments. Our second level of coding involved what were defined as "substantive codes" of the observation survey. Results of coding are reported in Table 5.5. The raw scores reported in the table do not reveal any striking differences. It is evident that the more interactive groups (Group 3 and Group 4) hypothesized more than facilitator or student-led groups. What is also notable is the dearth of generation of learning objectives within three of the groups. Of

TABLE 5.5
Substantive Behaviors: Total Raw Scores by Group for Students and (Facilitators)

Behavior	Group			
	1	*2*	*3*	*4*
Connecting basic science to case	22 (3)	22	32	25 (2)
Identifying learning objective	1	2	8	2
Hypothesizing	8 (1)	9 (2)	18	20

course, it needs to be remembered that the introductory session to the case was not subjected to analysis because of lack of variability among groups. Indeed, relatively equal numbers of learning objectives were identified in each group during the first session. Only Group 3 appeared to continue to define areas that required further study as information was discussed. Group 3 also connected more information to basic science than did other groups. Yet this group was split in their perceptions of group performance. It might be that some members of this group valued different types of substantive behaviors than other members or facilitators.

Observed Postcase Group Discussion Results

Because our observations spanned the entire case, we were able to observe the portion of the session devoted to analyses of the case and group processing. As with the groups in the study conducted by Evensen (1999) and Tipping and colleagues (1995), we observed a most cursory evaluation in Groups 1 and 2. In both cases, the facilitator asked the question, "Well, how'd we do?" to which immediate responses of "Fine," "Good," and head noddings followed. Group 3 never addressed their performance; rather, they limited their reflection to evaluating the quality of the case itself. Again, heads nodded and sounds of affirmation were heard as the facilitator read through a checklist that accompanied his case materials.

In contrast, Group 4 spent some 15 minutes on the topic of group processing. The discussion was prompted by the facilitator, who opened the session by saying that he was "not very happy," that he found this and previous group sessions as "really frustrating," and that, as a practiced PBL facilitator, he had "never felt this way" before. He proposed to the group that the processing problems might be his fault. Ben replied that he sometimes got the impression that the facilitator was pushing his own agenda and admitted that "I spend most of my energy (in group) asking myself, 'Should I interrupt; shouldn't I interrupt?'" Ben also suggested that it might be the constraints imposed by the materials that might be the problem, to which Art quickly interjected that "we're not being fair to ourselves if we blame the material and not look to group dynamics." Talk then moved to evaluating their own liabilities: Chris, the only female member, suggested that the group was inefficient because "people are trying not to step on each other's toes." She proposed that learning objectives might be divided and delegated to one person to present (the technique used by Group 2). Ben, however, said that allowing controversy and different perspectives toward topics was important; he saw efficiency not as how topics were treated but as which topics were covered, and he suggested that group members probably hold different philosophies on how groups should work. Art then admitted that he would value more tolerance of "silent time" in the group, time for some reflection before others jumped in. The session ended with Art admitting that he personally disliked being aggressive, to which Ben retorted, "How about excited?" The facilitator thanked them for their honesty.

DISCUSSION

The aim of this pilot study was to explore whether two forms of assessment—the easy-to-administer LTS and the more time-intensive observational checklist—might prove to be viable means through which to gain group processing data on PBL groups. We believe that the previously discussed analyses provide compelling evidence that both of these assessments are worth investigating further. For those who conduct research in PBL environments, these assessments can provide access to factors that might relate to outcome variables such as various forms of achievement. For practitioners, these assessments can achieve the objective outlined by Barrows (1988), that is, to bring aspects of group processing (whether they be perceived as problems or strengths) out in the open so groups can better manage their interpersonal dynamics. We propose that data from these assessments can serve as the impetus for more informed and, therefore, more efficacious postsession discussions.

Similar to the respondents in the Tipping and colleagues (1995) study, three out of four groups in our study provided positive, if not enthusiastic, remarks about group processing during the reflective portion of the group meeting. However, given the more anonymous tool, the LTS, they reported that all might not be well. Members indicated specific concerns that could very well be taken up as points from which the group as a whole could undertake a more focused examination of group processing: "Why is it that some of us see decision-making as a problem?" "What is it that we do that could be contributing to the perception that helpful feedback is not readily available in this group?" "Why is it that most of us would rather be in another group?" "What would that group be like?" Once issues are identified, it becomes incumbent on the group to employ means of deeper reflection and to devise corrective action.

Furthermore, the results of this study demonstrate that the degrees of satisfaction or of dissatisfaction, one aspect of group processing, revealed through the survey instrument might be explained through observed group processing behaviors. Equal participatory patterns, in particular, seem to contribute to positive perceptions of performance. The way in which members of groups participate, however, probably is related to consensus about the type of group they wish to have: one in which "teaching" involves the delivery of information, one in which the expert, or facilitator, knows best, or one in which information is challenged or ideas are extended to areas beyond the scope of the present case.

Curriculum coordinators of PBL programs might wish to probe into this area more deeply to assess whether students' notions of engaging in PBL concur with theirs. Another study that investigated the relations among types of groups, students' satisfaction with group performance, and, additionally, self-regulated learning was conducted by Hadwin (1996). Through inductive analyses of interview data, Hadwin discerned three different types of group interactions. Some groups reported dividing learning objectives among group members who would then individually research topics and report findings to the group. Other groups required all members to research the same learning objectives and to be prepared to discuss findings within the group. Finally, there were groups that prioritized learning objectives, deciding which ones would be researched by all and which "peripheral issues" would be taken up by particular group members.

Hadwin (1996) found that the highest degree of satisfaction was in the third type of group but also found much support for the other models. She concluded that the first model reflected a minilecture format that assumed learning as the transmission of information. Such a model would be unlikely to foster the self-regulation on the part of the "receivers" of the information or to engage them in the critical problem solving strategies central to a PBL curriculum. The second type was more likely to engage students in self-regulated strategies and to position them in an arena where knowledge could be elaborated on through social interaction, but it failed to recognize individual interests and expertise. Only the third form allowed for a balance between self-regulation, informed coparticipation, and distributed expertise.

PBL curriculum coordinators might consider the learning implications of each of these models. If the goals of a program are to produce physicians with an ability to work collaboratively to analyze clinical problems, to build skills for lifelong learning, and to show sensitivity to illness from a patients' perspective, then the desired students' conceptualizations of appropriate group practices would best align with these ideals.

Our results suggest many questions. If learning groups such as the ones observed in this study are to realize the benefits of collaboration, then theories, research, and a new discourse are needed within which to critique performance. We find the typologies proposed by Hadwin (1996) useful as a way to facilitate critical inquiry, and they might serve as the basis of future research projects. In the present study, it was interesting to note that two of the four groups reflected pedagogical patterns associated with more traditional curricular models: the didactic and the Socratic. Yet, the student-led, didactic Group 2 displayed the highest levels of satisfaction and agreement. The teacher-led, Socratic Group 1 appeared less satisfied but perceived their performance as effective. It is possible that these two models addressed individual needs, and that members either made assumptions that individual and group needs are synonymous, or chose to bracket group needs as secondary to the primary personal achievement goal. Studies that investigate the relation of pedagogical models to group performance variables could provide valuable information of what students expect of PBL groups and how expectations might be revised.

If the aim of the PBL program, however, is simply to offer an alternate, perhaps more engaging way of enabling students to acquire the biomedical knowledge foundational to medical practice, then the type of group—didactic, Socratic, or learner centered—might not really matter. However, coordinators should be aware that if this is their aim, then PBL might be perceived as a "weird" rather than an "optimal" way of learning, and that this perception might jeopardize motivations to learn both within the group and among its individual members.

Another topic that warrants more study is the role of controversy in learning groups. In this study, we see the group with the highest level of controversy (both self-assessed and other-assessed) as the most dissatisfied. Group 4, however, was the only group where it was clear that at least one member asserted his right to investigate personally interesting topics in self-selected ways. This practice ran in opposition to another member who appeared intolerant of ambiguity and preferred to stay focused on previously identified learning objectives. This group most closely resembled Hadwin's (1996) third type of group, yet our results did not support her finding that this type of group was indeed the most desirable. Studies that query the relation between the negotiations of individual and group needs and performance factors could provide more insight into how controversy might be addressed and used constructively in the process of group learning activity.

Finally, our observational data suggest the importance of the facilitator to the group processing effort. The only group that demonstrated a positive collaborative process was Group 2, where students and the facilitator appeared to employ a negotiating discourse to move along their procedural repertoire. In Group 4, the facilitator attempted to open a discursive space in which to find solutions to negative group dynamics; however, he did not demonstrate ways for the students to move beyond an identification of the problems toward solutions to them. Group 1's dynamics appeared far removed from collaborative goals because of the facilitator's success at co-opting group control. Likewise, Group 3 appeared somewhat inclined to allow one person to direct, or facilitate, procedures. Our limited exposure to these groups in operation precludes us from generalizing our findings to other situations. It may be that with this particular case these groups performed differently than they usually do; however, we did detect some talk about typical behavior, especially from Groups 2 and 4.

We feel confident that our results indicate a compelling relation between perceptions and observations of group processing behaviors; however, our measures of substantive behaviors were probably too unrefined to assess whether a group was achieving substantive curricular objectives. In other words, the question is not about how many hypotheses are generated in a given segment, but whether hypothesizing leads to topics that will contribute to an understanding of the case or an identification of new and relevant learning objectives. Phenomenological inquiries would provide a way to evaluate the overall performance of these groups and indeed might be investigated through future research.

An impression with which we are left after having completed this inquiry is that collaborative learning does not result from simply meeting in a group, even when the task for the group is carefully constructed and the operations of the group are facilitated by a person holding full membership in a professional community. We contend, with Bruffee (1993), that a pedagogogy of collaboration that sets "interdependence" as its goal needs to be developed. Bruffee succinctly concludes that

> College and university teachers . . . have to find ways in which students, who aspire to join the knowledge communities that their teachers represent, can take an active part in the intellectual negotiation by which beliefs are socially justified in those communities. . . . They have to help students acquire a sense of the authority of their own knowledge by exercising the *craft of interdependence* among themselves as student-peers. They have to help students develop the ability to interact socially over complex, intellectually demanding issues, thus integrating social and intellectual maturity . . . [They have] to *lead them* to collaborative learning. (pp. 188–189, emphasis added)

Recent research has focused on testing whether group learning is indeed more effective, but we are still far away from knowing how group operations lead to increased group effectiveness, and what can be done to increase the effectiveness of groups. Studies that begin with the perceptions of those who constitute the group seem logical places to start since, in the long run, the group will always be the sum of its members. Hence, we need to develop tools through which group members can reflect on and evaluate present practices and work to enhance future practices.

REFERENCES

Abercrombie, M. L. J. (1960). *The anatomy of judgment*. New York: Basic Books.

Barrows, H. (1988). *The tutorial process*. Springfield, IL: Southern Illinois University Press.

Blumenfeld, P. C., Marx, R. W., Soloway, E., & Krajcik, J. S. (1996). Learning with peers: From small group cooperation to collaborative communities. *Educational Researcher, 25*(8), 37–40.

Bossert, S. (1988–1989). Cooperative activities in the classroom. In E. Rothkopf (Ed.), *Review of research in education* (Vol. 15, pp. 225–250). Washington, DC: American Educational Research Association.

Brown, A. L. (1995). The advancement of learning. *Educational Researcher, 23*(8), 4–12.

Brown, J. S., Collins, A., & Duguid, P. (1989). Situated cognition and the culture of learning. *Educational Researcher, 18*(2), 33–42.

Bruffee, K. A. (1993). *Collaborative learning: Higher education, interdependence, and the authority of knowledge.* Baltimore, MD: The Johns Hopkins University Press.

Bruner, J. S. (1977). *The process of education.* Cambridge, MA: Harvard University Press.

Connolly, P. M., & Wilson, C. L. (1992). *Learning team survey: University edition form A.* New York: Clark Wilson Publishing Co.

Eraut, M. (1994). *Developing professional knowledge and competence.* London: The Falmer Press.

Evensen, D. H. (April, 1999). A qualitative study of self-directed learning in a problem-based context. Paper presented at the annual meeting of the American Education Research Association, Montreal, Canada.

Hadwin, A. F. (1996, April). *Promoting self-regulation: Examining the relatioships between problem-based learning in medicine and the strategic content learning approach.* Paper presented at the annual meeting of the American Educational Research Association, New York.

Hmelo, C. E., & Ferrari, M. (1997). The problem-based learning tutorial: Cultivating higher order thinking skills. *Journal for the Education of the Gifted, 20*, 401–422.

Lave, J., & Wenger, E. (1991). *Situated learning: Legitimate peripheral participation.* New York: Cambridge University Press.

Lawshe, C. H. (1975). A quantitative approach to content validity. *Personnel Psychology, 28*, 563–575.

Lincoln, Y. S., & Guba, E. G. (1985). *Naturalistic inquiry.* Newbury Park, CA: Sage.

Pea, R. D. (1993). Practices of distributed intelligence and designs for education. In G. Salomon & D. Perkins (Eds.), *Distributed cognitions* (pp. 47–87). New York: Cambridge University Press.

Salomon, G. (1993). No distribution without individual cognition: A dynamic interactional view. In G. Salomon & D. Perkins (Eds.), *Distributed cognitions* (pp. 111–138). New York: Cambridge University Press.

Salomon, G., & Perkins, D. N. (1989). Rocky roads to transfer: Rethinking mechanisms of a neglected phenomenon. *Educational Psychologist, 24*, 113–142.

Schön, D. (1983). *The reflective practitioner: How professionals think in action.* New York: Basic Books.

Schunk, D. H. (1992). Theory and research on student perceptions in the classroom. In D. H. Schunk & J. L. Meece (Eds.), *Student perceptions in the classroom* (pp. 3–23). Hillsdale, NJ: Lawrence Erlbaum Associates.

Tipping, J., Freeman, R. F., & Rachlis, A. R. (1995). Using faculty and student perceptions of group dynmaics to develop recommendations for PBL training. *Academic Medicine, 70*, 1050–1052.

Vye, N. J., Goldman, S. R., Voss, J. F., Hmelo, C., & Williams, S. (1997). Complex math problem-solving by individuals and dyads: When and why are two heads better than one? *Cognition and Instruction, 15*, 435–484.

Webb, N. M., & Palincsar, A. S. (1996). Group processes in the classroom. In D. C. Berliner & R. C. Calfee (Eds.), *Handbook of educational psychology* (pp. 841–873). New York: Macmillan.

Wilson, C. L. (1995, May). Structure and consideration plus one. Paper presented at meeting of Society for Industrial and Organizational Psychologists, Orlando, FL.

Yager, S., Johnson, R. T., Johnson, D. W., & Snider, B. (1986). The impact of group processing on achievement in cooperative learning groups. *Journal of Social Psychology, 126*, 389–397.

APPENDIX

Factors and item prompts for the LTS[4] (responses to each survey question: from 1 = *Never* to 7 = *Always*).

A. *Commitment to Purpose*
  1. Team members have a clear sense of purpose.
  2. Team members have a shared, meaningful purpose.
  3. Team members have a clear understanding of how performance objectives will be measured.
  4. Team members have a clear idea of "team deliverables."
  5. Our team has distributed the workload fairly.

B. *Commitment to a Common Approach*
  6. Our team has distributed the workload fairly.
  7. Our team stays on schedule.
  8. Our team has the capability to address a problem area.
  9. Team members encourage each other to develop new skills which are important to the team.
  10. Team members seek new ways to solve team problems.

C. *Complementary Skills*
  11. Team members represent a balance of required technical and functional skills.
  12. Our team identifies problems very well.
  13. Our team evaluates alternatives very well.
  14. Our team makes decisions very well.
  15. Our team provides support to each other.
  16. Team members listen very well to each other.
  17. Team members provide helpful feedback to each other.
  18. Team members allow every other member of the team a chance to speak.

D. *Accountability*
  19. Team members trust one another to keep commitments.
  20. Team members hold each other accountable
  21. Team members view accountability for performance as a team (versus individual) responsibility.

---

[4]Used with permission.

E. *Team Conflict*

22. There is a lot of friction in my team.
23. There is a lot of emotional conflict in my team.
24. There are a lot of differences of opinion in my team regarding our work.
25. There are frequent disagreements in my team about opinions regarding the work being done.
26. There are frequent disagreements about who should do what in my team.
27. People in my team often argue about who should do what.

F. *Team Performance*

28. I put forth a lot of effort to complete team work.
29. I am very motivated to do well on team tasks.
30. My team performs well.
31. My team is very effective at getting things done.
32. Compared to other work groups I've been in, this learning team works well together.
33. The members of this learning team encourage each other to work as a team.

G. *Overall Team Satisfaction*

34. If I were to do it over again, I would like to be in the same learning team.
35. This learning team has helped me achieve my personal goals for this course.
36. This team is characterized by open and effective communication among its members.
37. I am satisfied working with this team.
38. I feel fairly well satisfied with the job I do on this team.

Chapter 6

Five Readings of a Single Text: Transcript of a Videoanalysis Session

Edited by
Timothy Koschmann
Southern Illinois University

Dorothy H. Evensen
The Pennsylvania State University

with contributions by
Phillip Glenn, Rogers Hall, Carl Frederiksen,
Annemarie Palincsar, and Jay Lemke

This chapter reports on a special panel presentation at the 1996 Annual Meeting of the American Educational Research Association (AERA) that aptly illustrates the theme of applying multiple methods of inquiry to the task of understanding learning interactions in problem-based learning (PBL). The panel, entitled "Science Discourse in a PBL Meeting," was specifically organized to make visible the diversity of possible perspectives for understanding meaning making in a collaborative learning situation. Five researchers with different analytic interests were invited to view and comment on a single 6-minute segment of video from a PBL meeting. One of the authors (Koschmann) was the organizer and chair for this session, the other (Evensen) videotaped and transcribed the session for this report.

The 1996 session was a follow-up to a similar session organized and presented at the 1994 AERA meeting. The earlier session, entitled "Looking and Listening: Understanding Small Group Process in a Problem-Based Learning Meeting" involved four researchers from the medical education research community. The later session (and the one on which we will report here) involved workers from the broader educational research community outside of adult and professional education. Among the panelists were Phillip Glenn (Southern Illinois University), Rogers Hall (the University of California at Berkeley), Carl Frederiksen (McGill University), Annemarie

Palincsar (University of Michigan), and Jay Lemke (City University of New York). Each of these distinguished researchers has devoted a significant portion of their academic lives to the study of group learning situations. Their perspectives, however, are diverse, and they range from inquiries into the cognitive processes used by individuals in groups, to the sociocultural roles adopted by group members, to the knowledge-constructing collaborative events that take place during group meetings. Each of the panelists was provided with a copy of the videotape prior to the conference and each was asked to prepare a description of how they would analyze the segment. Expanded versions of these five analyses are published in a special issue of *Discourse Processes* (Koschmann, 1999).

The 6-minute data segment features a group of second-year medical students and a faculty tutor (Coach) exploring a clinical case. The case involves an elderly male patient who presents with complaints of clumsiness in one of his legs and difficulty in verbally expressing himself. The interaction captured on the video occurs about 20 minutes into their second meeting on this case, and after a period of self-directed study in which the members of the group independently researched a set of learning issues developed in their first meeting. It opens with one of the students, Betty, offering an hypothesis to account for the patient's symptoms. Her "theory" implicates a particular structure in the brain (the hippocampal region), and a side-sequence unfolds in which the students, at the tutor's (Coach's) bidding, seek to fix its location in the brain. Betty then proposes a second theory. Thereafter, the group engages in a concerted attempt to coordinate what is known about the case with respect to the two theories. A transcript of the 6-minute segment is available in Appendix B of this chapter. A digitized copy of the video segment will be distributed on compact disc in a special issue of *Discourse Processes*.

Hereafter we present an edited transcript of the five presentations and the discussion that followed.

THE SESSION

Phillip Glenn:

Sometimes panels like this remind one of the story of the six blind men of Hindustan who each feel different parts of an elephant and report that it's very different things. The beauty of this session is that we are all using the same bit of data, so maybe at least we're feeling the same part of the elephant.

My work in conversation analysis is informed by ethnomethodology. I attempt to describe how people organize their interactions. I've done most of my work on ordinary conversation, and I've been intrigued by the interactions of these medical students trying to learn and trying to solve problems.

The part of the segment I want to talk about is bracketed by the coach through language not included on the published transcript. It occurs right before Betty says, "My theory . . ." I'll just read it for you. Coach ends a prior segment by saying, "So he's got speech involvement and right leg involvement." Here, the coach summarizes two symptoms. Then he says, "So whatever his problem is, we're pretty confident it's on the left side." Coach is giving a formulation here, a summary of what's been understood to that point and is preparing the group to move forward.

Now, I would invite you to notice on your transcript (line 124) where he performs another of these moves: "So if it's vascular . . ." This one sets up a conditional—if it's—; he then goes on to pose a question, "Did he have a stroke or is he having TIAs, and what's the difference between those two things anyway?"

The part I'm going to focus on is bracketed by those two moves by Coach. In between those we get Betty presenting one theory, then another theory, and the group returning to her first theory. My interest is what is this interactional structure about?

If you go back to the beginning of your transcript, we have Betty saying, "See what it said here, my theory . . ." She does two things here which structurally set up extended turns of talk for her. First, she says, "What it said here" and she's looking down at a book in front of her. So she's bidding for an extended turn space to do some reading from the book. She abandons that momentarily, however, and introduces a theory, "My theory." The possessive pronoun is quite interesting. Two things have been set up. She then comes back to "amnesiac dysnomic aphasia," then she begins to read: "It says the cause of lesion is usually deep in temporal lobe." She stops reading, and looks up at Maria to say, "just like Maria was saying." So there's some involving of prior talk. She then returns to reading. Then, if you notice the pause in line 10, she stops reading, looks up to the group and says, "and I think the hippocampus is like a lot more medial. So if it was affecting that area it might be the anterior cerebral circulation." That is her theory, and she marks that as a shift from reading by the pause, and by looking up to the other group members. Notice also the use of "I think" in line 11. She marks her knowledge of the location of the hippocampus as tentative, not absolutely certain.

Now, one might think that the group would immediately treat the theory, that is, assess it as right or wrong, critiqueable or supportable. One bit of support for it is evidenced in line 15 by Norman's repeating the word "anterior." He doesn't say it after she says it. He says it at the same moment she does. This is a device in conversation to show that we understand someone's message to the extent that we can collaboratively complete the utterance. So that may be taken as a bit of implicit alignment by Norman to Betty's theory.

Nevertheless, at line 16, Coach steers the talk to finding the location of the hippocampus, and they spend about the next minute looking at the charts and dealing with that. There are lots of interesting issues there, but I'm going to bracket those out and return to Betty's theory. If you would move with me to line 68 where Coach says "That's it." That need not necessarily be the end of the hippocampus sequence, but Betty treats it as the end.

Betty now introduces her "other theory." This is interesting. Why go to a second theory if the first theory hasn't been treated yet? She gives us information about the second theory by saying, "if it's not a vascular lesion but a space occupying lesion." What she seems to be doing is invoking a domain of theories; that is, a domain of possibilities where it's got to be one or the other—voicing the second possibility is in some ways relevant to the processing of the first possibility.

She brings up a second possibility of a space-occupying lesion. Now, whereas the first theory didn't get a lot of assessing, this one does. There are two kinds of responses that occur, both of which can be construed as disaffiliative to the theory. Maria, at lines 79, 82, and 85, asks a question which carries in it a criticism of or a difference with the theory. At the same time Norman laughs. Now, we don't have Norman's face on video, so we don't have all of the information available, but structurally in talk it's common that laughs refer to the thing that immediately precedes them, and it is certainly possible that the laughter is in some way engendered by Betty's second theory. Coach, at line 81 gives a long, stretched-out, comic, an exaggerated "ohhhkaaaay." So there's some comic treatment, laughter, and critical questioning of the second theory.

Betty defends it in lines 86 to 100. Coach asks a question at 104: "Why do the leg findings go away?" This brings up a piece of evidence that the second theory should be able to account for. Betty assesses his question, which is an interesting thing for a student to do to a teacher: "That's a good question." She then argues against her second theory—that the symptoms provide evidence against the idea that the problem involves a space-occupting lesion. In other words, it opens critical space for the group members, who indeed jump in. By line 119, Betty says, "it's more likely to be vascular."

So she's introduced theory number one, they've gone off to the hippocampus, she's introduced theory two, they've treated it fairly critically, and have returned to conclude that theory one is more probable. Coach then asks his question, "So if it's vascular . . ." By doing this, he treats that theory not as necessarily correct, but at least as the one to continue to talk about. So for the moment there's some sort of implicit endorsement of that theory as at least treatable.

Rogers Hall:

Phil's description provides a nice lead into my own since I want to spend some time inside the stretch that was bracketed out in the prior account, namely, the section (lines 16–68) that begins with the query, "Where is the hippocampus?" My interests lie in the activities that make up episodes of representation, so I would like to raise some questions about what is taking place in this section.

The first question is, how do these people find their way around "the Brain" given that there is no actual brain or patient available in this setting? I want to read to you the spatial terms: "down there," "bottom of this thing," "in here," "and then in parallel, under that," "inside, under that?" "inside," "on the middle," "middle top." Then there's this interesting stretch by Maria, "if you lift up on the other side" (I think she says "other side" not "inside"). Then after that section the coach comes in: "You can point to it." The group continues: "on the middle top," "middle top?" "that's it." The coach goes on: "go over one more gyrus." "In the temporal lobe," "on the frontal," "left, second row," "left," "in that section." One of Lily's only contributions to this, "In here?" "In that crevice." Then Norman comes back with his own directive which, in an interesting way, parallels what the coach has been up to: "Go to the crevice there." The coach produces the end of the sequence, saying "That's it." What we see here is a demonstration of way finding in this jointly constructed brain.

I want to go back and look a little more deeply into what's going on here. In lines 19 through 68, Norman, Maria, and Jenny are trying to unpack what I would see as a single display in a 3-by-3 array up on a chart. That's where the comments are directed: "in there," "up there." Then Coach (line 28) recommends another location within that array by leading them to the "middle" and "middle top." So he stipulates another thing to look at. Then Maria, at line 29, manually dissects something. If you look at the gesture, what happens is that her right hand comes to the center of her head, grabs or hooks something, lifts, and then rolls back. Her arm leans against her forehead for a moment, and she holds it there as she finishes the part of the exchange and then says, "it's on the inside." Coach then directs the activity back to another display on the chart.

My argument is that there are two different discursive practices that are intersecting here. One has something to do with pulling pieces of the body apart in order to get at an occluded structure. This is what Maria is doing. The other involves historically complex representational artifacts that present standard, or canonical section views of the brain as an ideal type. This is the function of the chart. While "the brain" constitutes the topic under discussion, there is no brain here!

So the question, in general, about these kinds of stretches is how can we follow narrative agents in something as complicated as PBL as they make use of language, gesture, intonation, and kinesthetics to construct representations of phenomena under investigation?

The second question, and the one I find particularly interesting, is how often do people do "having a theory" in this collective, prospective way? That is, they're doing something together, and a theory is proposed that becomes the impetus for what is going forward. It's not like you're finished with a discussion and said, "Well, I have a theory." This is the kind of rhetoric we usually hear about theories, but is it really the case?

One possibility is that doing having a theory is rare, limited to networks of scientists and technologists. The other possibility is that doing having a theory is common, within the discursive practices of ordinary people, agents-in-the-world, and I'm reminded of Eleanor Ochs' analysis of theory building and dinner table conversations (Ochs, Taylor, Rudolph, & Smith, 1992).

So this is a nice paradox that, from a sociology of science perspective, we see scientists being deflated and made ordinary, and, from the sociolinguistics of everyday conversation, we see ordinary people being made scientific. But there's also somewhere in the middle, somewhere where ordinary resources and language are conserved within highly evolved technical, discursive practices. In this space, everyone can look the same. Yet they are not the same. In this case, these students are "ordinary people" becoming "scientists." Learning how scientists manage to convert discourse into something more specialized is important to study.

Carl Frederiksen:

I'm going to look at this from the point of view of a cognitive psychologist. The study of discourse processing from a cognitive perspective has focused on studying the comprehension or production of written text. These studies have tended to imply that multilayered representations are involved in the processing of text or discourse. I find it very interesting to look at examples of interactive discourse such as occurs in tutorial interaction, or, in this case, the situation of problem-based learning. I'm going to ask what kind of questions would a discourse processing analysis of problem-based learning lead you to ask? I want to highlight aspects of the analysis of discourse which focus on the *content* of the discourse, at the level of the local structure, or the propositional content. Next, on the manner in which propositions are pulled together into *conceptual structures*, or mental models. Then, ultimately on the macrostructure of the text as it may reflect aspects of the frame knowledge that's being brought to bear on understanding and producing this text.

Now if you want to look at this problem from the point of view of a discourse processing theory, you first have to recognize that instead of having a single text, you have a transaction space, a rich situational context, in which discourse, action, and representation are all occurring together and evolving over time. Second, you have the notion that the discourse is taking place, and is understood in terms of a constructed mental model or conceptual structure. And third, this construction reflects the prior knowledge of the participants, both in terms of shared and individual knowledge.

First, I looked at this text in terms of the macrostructure as it might reflect the procedural frame (see Fig. 6.1). If you take the entire 6-minute segment, with the exception of the section dealing with the location of the hippocampus, there is an inquiry process, and the discourse as I analyzed it is broken down into stretches of discourse which correspond to parts of this frame. The high-level structure deals with establishing the type of lesion and establishing the diagnosis. There's also a side sequence of going into the anatomical discussion about where the hippocampus is. From the point of view of diagnosis, this is totally off-task. But from the point of view of learning activity it is quite relevant. From this perspective you can see why the coach took them into that space and why nobody objected.

But going back to the main structures, establishing the type of lesion breaks down into three main components: presenting alternative hypotheses, considering hypotheses in relation to clinical evidence, and then selecting the most likely hypothesis. These then break down into the specifics of this particular case: the vascular lesion and the space-occupying lesion. The space-occupying lesion is taken up, then the most likely hypothesis is considered.

The group proceeds to establish a more precise diagnosis with a similar kind of process: preparing diagnostic alternatives—stroke or TIA, stating the diagnostic problems, stating the alternative hypothesis, reviewing clinical evidence, and so on. Now, the interesting thing about this is you can keep track of this locally in terms of the analysis of the propositional content—you can look at the mental models that are created at each stage. At the same time, you can keep track of who initiated each stretch of discourse. It's interesting to look at the correlations between the concepts and who is doing the initiating. I've indicated who the participants in each stretch were, and I've underlined the person who initiated that stretch of conversation.

You'll notice that Betty initiates the vascular segment, and Betty initiates the second hypothesis. There's a break when Coach takes them off into what seems to be another task. Notice that the coach initiates the major shifts that take place in this frame. So you have Coach initiating the evaluation, or criticism, of the space-occupying lesion. The coach also ini-

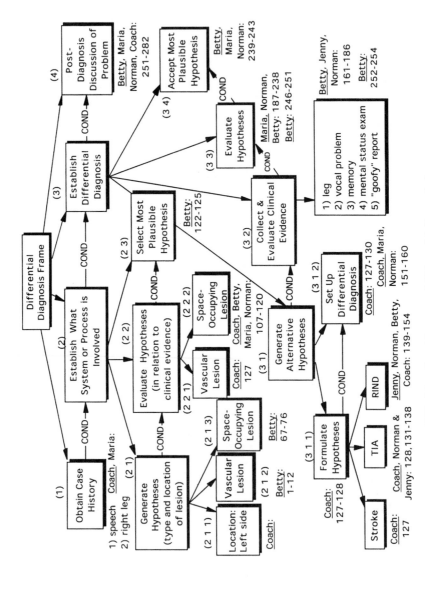

FIG. 6.1. Cognitive map of differential diagnosis frame.

tiates the comparison of diagnostic alternatives, and Coach states the diagnostic problem which is then picked up by the students. This move goes very smoothly, which seems to indicate that the activity going on is constructed through a shared understanding of what the structure of the diagnostic inquiry activity consists of, and you can take this frame as a kind of model of that.

Figure 6.2 represents a conceptual analysis of the discourse. This shows Betty's first theory. Essentially, what you could do is analyze the propositions and represent them using the formalism of conceptual graphs, which means you make them look simpler by linking things together. You can now see a process in which mental models become shared because they are placed outside publicly in language. And you see that the participants are each adding some pieces to this mental model. Sometimes they challenge it, sometimes someone else adjusts it.

The impression that you get as you do this analysis is that you are really seeing a collective cognitive activity involved in constructing local mental models that are not the product of one individual. Where they end up cannot be accounted for on the basis of a single individual. To summarize, I would say that this kind of content analysis complements a conversational analysis in which you end up with a picture of a procedurally guided inquiry activity that the participants share, and that in the process of following, or being guided by that activity, which is largely steered by the coach, they are building, in effect, common mental models that reflect a reasoning process.

Annemarie Palincsar:

We were invited here as "outsiders" to medical education, so I was curious to find out what an insider thinks about the issues raised here today. I found a delightful book by M. L. Johnson Abercrombie (1960) called *The Anatomy of Judgment*, in which the following observation was made: "Discussion in a group does for thinking, what testing on reality does for seeing. We become aware of discrepancies between different people's interpretations of the same stimulus and are driven to weigh the evidence in favor of alternative interpretations" (p. 62). She continued, "The aim of free group discussion is to help the individual participant reach a better understanding of the factors that affect judgment in order to secure better control over them, so they can make sounder judgments" (p. 81). In this text, what Professor Abercrombie is describing are her experiences in the Department of Anatomy at University College, London, where she participated in the preparation of medical students. Her decision to depart from didactic pedagogy in favor of group discussions was influenced by some observations regarding problems that were experienced by

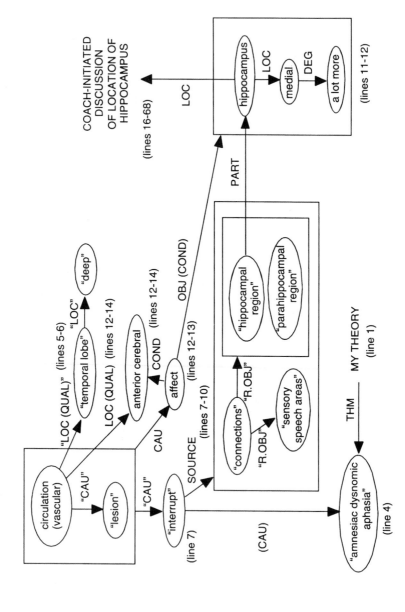

FIG. 6.2.   Betty's modification of textbook theory.

recent graduates. For example, the Royal College of Physicians concluded, "The average medical graduate tends to lack generosity and initiative, his (sic) powers of observation are relatively underdeveloped, his ability to arrange and interpret facts is poor, he lacks precision in the use of words" (pp. 15–16). Although Abercrombie did her work in the 1950s, she clearly shares contemporary interest in thinking of the purposes and the processes of education as the establishment of discourse communities in which individuals can acquire a language, way of reasoning, thinking, problem solving, and the tools of this new community to which they aspire. Kenneth Bruffee (1993) has suggested that we think about these communities that are made up of people who are becoming enculturated to new knowledge communities as "transition communities."

I'd like to focus on what the video excerpts reveal about two features of transition communities. I want to mention that my thinking about transition communities has been very much influenced by the research and writing that I've done with my colleague Charles Anderson from Michigan State on collaborative problem solving within sixth graders in science classes.

The first characteristic that I'd like to attend to regarding the transition community is that they are first, human communities, bound by their own mores, norms, and histories of interpersonal relationships. I'd like to draw an example of this from Betty's presentation of her second theory beginning at line 69. Betty makes a 57-word utterance which is actually quite long in comparison with the mean length of the utterances of her colleagues. I found the group reaction to be very interesting at this point. There is laughter, a clear ripple in the group, and the coach says, "oooohkaaay." What I found especially interesting is that in her next utterance, beginning on line 86, Betty seems to wane in her fluency. In uncharacteristic fashion, she falters: "somatographic, whatever that word was." It struck me as a move that would prevent her from straying too far from the conventions and discourse patterns of the group, and as a move that would affirm her solidarity with group members. Interactions among people are occasions when they have to pursue dual agendas. We all need a sense of power and status on the one hand, and a sense of solidarity or interpersonal connection on the other. These dual agendas are always present within transition communities. On the one hand, the community must experience the kind of social coherence, trust, and interdependence that will give rise to the types of interactions that are important to promote learning in these contexts; on the other hand, individual community members must feel free to challenge others' ideas or present evidence that would build on others' arguments. These are very different types of interactions, and the latter could threaten or erode the sense of trust or coherence of the group. So the challenge is to attend to both the intellectual as well as the interpersonal dimensions of the group activity. The risk, however, is that students' interpersonal agendas might usurp the nature of the problem-solving activity. Examples would be when the conversation becomes explicitly personal rather than driven by the kinds of observations or data in which the students are working.

The second characteristic of the transition community that I thought was nicely illustrated in this excerpt demonstrates the fact that all members are not in the same place in the transition community. This can be described and explained in numerous ways. For example, the knowledge of discourse communities in which participants have previously participated is going to position them differently in this transition community. As I watched the tape, I became intrigued with a possible role that identity played in positioning members of this particular community. Lave and Wenger (1991) remind us that learning involves the whole person. Learning implies not only a relation to specific activities, but a relationship to social communities. Learning is becoming a different person with respect to the possibilities enabled by these systems of relations. And they warn us that if we ignore this aspect of learning, we overlook the fact that learning involves the construction of identity, ways of understanding, viewing oneself, and being viewed by others. This means that in addition to the cognitive, linguistic, and interpersonal challenges that are being faced by these members, there are also the challenges inherent in giving up the identity with which one has been comfortable, and negotiating a different identity. My colleague Jean McPhail (1996) has studied this phenomenon among medical students from underrepresented groups and she has illustrated the powerful role that identity issues play in explaining both the success as well as the failure of these medical students.

For some of the participants in this particular transition community, their identity as a member of the community of medical practice seems quite emergent, and for others it seems more well developed. For example, in response to Coach's question regarding the differences between TIA and stroke, Jenny tentatively quotes from the medical text, and she concludes with "I don't know." Notice too that there is a lot of laughter as she is reading. Betty, in contrast, seems more ready to assume the identity of the discourse community to which she aspires. She's comfortable claiming twice that she has a theory. There's even a point where Betty quotes the patient's wife (lines 179–181 and 245–248) as though it were a person that they had actually interviewed, so alive is this case for her. But what about the young woman at the end of the table who makes neither verbal or nonverbal contributions? What is that nature of her participation in this community? I wonder what she thought might be possible for her? How clearly was she able to imagine a possible self in which she was a productive, well-received member in the community of medical practice?

Identity strikes me as a particularly interesting and important lens with which to examine transition communities because these communities work when all members productively engage in the discourse, and, as Bahktin (1981) has sugested, active engagement occurs only if the individual can populate the discourse with his or her own interests, desires, and purposes.

Jay Lemke:

I've been looking at this episode through the lenses of my own recent research interest—multimedia semiotics. This concerns looking at how people make meaning by codeploying or coordinating different kinds of representations: primarily verbal, linguistic, semantic representations, and visual, diagrammatical, graphical, and, to some extent, mathematical symbolic representations. A semiotic analysis of this episode requires us to look at the kinds of meanings being constructed, their functions, and the linguistic, kinesic, and other means by which they are being made.

Most of the action in the episode is talk, and therefore a linguistic–semantic analysis is most revealing for what meanings are being made through this talk and how they are being made. But there is also significant use of gesture and of the visual semiotic resource of the "chart." My focus here is mainly on the tension I perceive in the episode between the norms and strategies of medical diagnostic discourse as practiced by these students, and encouraged by the coach, and the nature of the phenomena as they are constructed.

The diagnostic approach, and the underlying medical terminology for events, conditions, and anatomical objects is fundamentally, in semantic terms, a "typological" one. That is, it contrasts one diagnostic category with another in either–or terms, imposes a discrete terminology on continuously varying phenomena, and divides even the continuous topography of the brain into bordered regions as seemingly definite as those of nation–states. But natural phenomena, and both natural languages and their technical extensions, require us to be able to also take a more "topological" approach to making meaning. We need to be able to speak of qualitative and continuous variation, of multiple simultaneous, nonexclusive, descriptive features—of overlaps and in-betweens, of matters of degree and instability. In our dominant intellectual culture, however, a privileged position is reserved for classical logic with its narrow view of propositions as either true or false, which in turn requires typological semantic approaches to both reasoning and formal logic. Such dichotomizing runs contrary to the bulk of human historical experience, which shows that this is an excessively limited way to view the world.

Natural languages have also been extended into linguistic registers that have to deal critically with continuous variation and complex quantification. These extensions are found in integrations of mathematical and verbal reasoning. But, far older than mathematics as a means of expressing topological meanings, is visual semiotics. We humans make meaning with depictional semiotic resources ranging from conventionalized pictorial resources to more abstract diagrammatic and graphical ones. Quantitative reasoning in the sciences represents perhaps the most elaborate case of integrated visual, verbal, and mathematical resources being deployed in meaning making. In addition, natural language also coevolved with human gestural and postural systems for communication and is naturally integrated with them in face-to-face communication. Gesture allows us greater latitude and subtlety in making topological meaning relations. In this episode we see two prime instances of the tension between typological norms of medical diagnostic discourse and the topological nature of the phenomena being discussed and constructed. One is the imposition of typologically discrete terminology on the continuous tissue manifold of the human cortex. The other is the imposition of typological disjunctions in the mutually exclusive categories of medical diagnosis for the patient. In both cases, some more topological natural language resources, and the topological power of spatializing gestures, are used by students to help bridge the contradiction and resolve the tension. That is what I want to examine more closely.

Locating the Hippocampus.   Let's consider the first part of the episode in which, after Betty's suggestion that the lesion causing the symptoms may be near the hippocampus, Coach asks the students, "Where is the hippocampus?" What is worth noting here is, first of all, that Betty's immediate reaction is not to begin a verbal answer, but to orient to the need for "a picture" (line 17). Verbal language by itself is pretty powerless to answer the question because its preponderantly typological resources may be very good at saying what things are, but very limited in establishing spatial relations, especially in three dimensions and for spatial regions of irregular shape and/or not readily visible.

Norman first points to the chart from his seat, then gets up and walks a considerable way to be able to point, and finally puts his finger on, or almost on the chart. He "traces' the spatial region corresponding to the hippocampus.

This procedure is then repeated by Lill for a different sectional view of the three-dimensional cortex. Semantic typology is used during the coconstruction of Lill's gestural identification: "go to the crevice," "That's white matter," "That little loop;" but these work "indexically" together with the visual–kinesic–spatial resources being deployed here by the group. At one point Coach says, "That's it. That's the hippocampus, then you go over one more gyrus and you're in the temporal lobe." His contrastive stress on "temporal" presumes the typological approach of medical scientific terminologies. In fact, no sharp boundaries can be drawn for a gyrus or a lobe. The cortex is a quasi-continuous tissue manifold. Even at the microanatomical level, there would not be such boundaries, but rather different cell types intermixing and overlapping in space. I am not even sure if it is absolutely possible to say for any given cell whether it belongs to the hippocampus or not in absolute terms; nor would it necessarily be useful medically to do so.

Between True and False. Let's turn now to a more central concern of the episode, to medical diagnostic reasoning. We will see that it is related to the same basic tension described in the first part of the episode. It is not just spatial continua that are not well represented by typological semantic strategies, it is also conditions and events. When typological categories are imposed to represent phenomena, propositions made about these phenomena in terms of such categories become problematic. But natural language recognizes this by offering us a number of interpolations between truth and falsity. One of these is probability. The warrantability of a proposition is a matter of degree and of polarity, which are normally combinable. We can assert or warrant a proposition both as more or less certain, and as more or less uncertain. Another interpolation is that of frequency. The usuality of a proposition is a semantic attribute we can construct for it, telling the speaker's view of how frequent, normal, usual, or expected something is. Finally, a not very well understood, but fairly common extension of the semantics of usuality is that of stability or temporariness. What is not usual may also be something newly arisen, or something changed from what it has been; it may not be usual because it is only temporarily or recently the case.

In lines 142 to 143, Jenny says that the condition called RIND is "somewhere in between a completed stroke and TIA," and she makes a complex gesture coordinating right hand with "completed stroke" and left hand with "TIA," creating a gestural space which stands here, metaphorically, for the topological space of possible meanings in between the typological categories of the diagnosis. Betty then quips, "like . . . unstable angina of the mind!" making a semantic connection between the issue of stability or temporariness and the continuum of possible conditions under discussion. These conditions differ from each other by a "quantitative" difference in how long symptoms persist. That quantitative difference can be represented spatially in contrast with the discreteness of the typological diagnostic categories, and the instability of the symptoms or condition contrasts with the implicit stability of the notion of that patient "having a condition." The students laugh here over the tension between a norm of clear-cut, right or wrong diagnosis, and the fuzzy nature of the categories they must deal with.

Coach then presses a typological view: "Which one did he have?" and the responses begin with Maria's, ". . . he's progressing to a stroke," which emphasizes instability. Norman comments, "A little bit of both," thus implicitly challenging the either–or semantics of typological categories.

Betty then begins a long discussion that turns on the stability of the patient's condition and symptoms.

In the course of this (line 202 sequence), Norman rather forcefully frames the instability with a contrast between "we're seeing an acute leg deficit" but "now we're seeing five-over-five strength," and he makes hand movements to accentuate this instability and temporariness. (Note that the issue of temporariness and change had been introduced initially by Coach in line 104: "So why do the leg findings go away?").

In lines 214 to 217, Norman argues that the patient's speech is "screwed up," and Betty challenges this in a polar, typological way: "Is it screwed up?" Norman qualifies with "somehow," and Betty concedes only in topological terms: "a little bit" and makes a gesture with her fingers held extremely close together. "It is" versus "it isn't" has been converted again to a matter of in between. But this is not the end of the discussion. In her follow-up, Betty invokes a host of usuality resources ("occasionally," "rarely," "often") and a construction of instability (one part of the mental status exam vs. "the rest" of it). By the time she gets to her conclusion, the resources of warrant-by-degree are in full sway: "I don't know" (i.e., no polar assertion, no high degree of warrantability), "I think," "would probably lean more towards" (lower degrees of probability and warrant), together with the associated instability, "something transient that comes and goes."

Betty's final argument turns on instability (line 245 sequence), that things must have been worse at one time than they are "right now." Again her hands seem to move to show the dynamics she is trying to construct, as opposed to a more static or synoptic view of a patient's definitive condition.

What I take from all of this as a general point is that this is an interesting lens through which to look at medical education and perhaps technical and scientific education. The typological, categorical approach is so dominant in our picture of things that we do not give official status to the topological way of looking at things. We know that professionals "do their magic" precisely by coordinating their topological, continuous variation sense of things—the in-between and the maybes—with the categorical certainties of our official theories about the world.

DISCUSSION WITH THE AUDIENCE

Audience Member #1:

I think that the participants' foci on different aspects of the PBL interaction is related to the fact that they're not necessarily from the same discourse community. Once we look more closely at the conceptual bases of their analyses, we might see more overlap. For example, Jay mentioned the "topological features," and I see that as related to what Rogers talked about concerning cognition in terms of "agent-in-the world." These two concepts are very tightly interconnected once we start pushing out of our respective frameworks.

Audience Member #2:

My particular interest is children and teachers in k–12 settings. I was particularly curious about remarks made about coparticipation because many of the teachers I work with struggle to be more of a "coach" than an "information giver." I'm interested in what you thought about when Coach redirected the group, especially in the segment concerning the hippocampus. Do you think it was helpful to what students needed to know to solve this problem? What was the importance of stopping and doing that? I'm curious about how teachers can make those kind of value decisions.

Jay Lemke:

I think it's important to bear in mind that there are multiple agendas going on here. This is not a kind of pure activity. That's why the task of working out a goal analysis of these sessions is extremely daunting. Coach's intervention in terms of going off to locate the hippocampus has to do with his wondering if everybody there actually knows just where the hippocampus is. This, he believes, is important in terms of the standards that are being set for what one ought to know to participate in a clinical discussion at this level. Another key thing that Coach does is to ask why the leg findings went away. Notice that that gets echoed in a way by Norman asking why his speech is "screwed up." It turns out that Coach is, in effect, leading the group down the garden path, leading them, in fact, away from a route that would have taken them to the correct diagnosis. He is basically challenging them to see if they can explain something that doesn't seem to fit with the proposed theory. But the agenda here is to get them not to the correct diagnosis, but to a consideration of different theories in order to gain more medical knowledge. So Coach's number one goal is for students to get the most practice at diagnostic reasoning. This is exactly the kind of double bind that many teachers find themselves in. On the one hand, we have a goal that we want students to get the right answer or come to some conclusion; on the other hand, we want them to get practice at reasoning and thinking processes. And sometimes those two goals are contradictory.

Phil Glenn:

We should note too that when Betty includes the hippocampus in her explanation, she marks its location as uncertain. It seems that throughout this excerpt students are quite willing to show partial knowledge, incomplete knowledge, tentative knowledge, and that's really important to the process of doing PBL. You might imagine other environments where students would feel constrained about doing that.

Carl Frederiksen:

Typically in tutorial dialogs where students have very little knowledge, the tutor will do a lot of initiation, a lot of modeling, explaining principles, and working through problems. Then, at a point when the students have sufficient knowledge to be able to undertake, with assistance, the problem solving or reasoning themselves, the tutor shifts into a supporting role and gradually fades as the students take on more of the responsibility. What we've seen in this tutorial dialogue is that Coach provides this sort of high-level guidance. If you analyze it in terms of the structure of the procedure that governs their activity, Coach is coming in at identifiable points. I think this is connected with the idea of the transition communities. They're transitional in a number of senses: they're transitioning into the language and also into developing a level of expertise.

Timothy Koschmann:

The use of the term "tutor" produces a lot of confusion. Some people think of the Cambridge tutor, the font of all knowledge, who brings students along through a very labor-intensive and transmissive form of instruction. But in PBL, the role of the tutor is very different. They are there primarily to guide the inquiry and encourage student participation. They may, now and then, step out of the role of tutor, and assume the role of teacher. But they typically mark such departures from their usual role by making it clear that they are doing something very different. At Southern Illinois University we tried to introduce the term "Coach," but with 25 years of past usage, it's difficult to change.

Audience Member #3:

Here's my question: Can we make any cuts in this space and say there are some things that are stable and, therefore, push them into the background? And are there some things that are really important to the learning that we can pull into the foreground? Or is it the case that we're really dealing with a massive process of enculturation where everything is potentially problematic? If everything in these people's experiences is potentially a resource, then in fact, it's just radical contingency. And if that's the case, what are the prospects for this field?

Jay Lemke:

I take the view that it is all radical contingency, but that's not a bad thing nor is it an obstacle to our inquiry into it. For example, ethnomethodology and conversation analysis began with that premise, and both have done wonderful things at the micro level in terms of showing how larger structures emerge out of simple relationships at smaller scales. What we're seeing here is a kind of multilayered approach in which we have multiple kinds of contingencies. Contingencies of interpersonal relationships, contingencies in terms of lines of argumentation and reasoning, contingencies in terms of the kinds of external resources that are used and how they are coordinated, contingencies in terms of whether people wind up leaning more toward using typological or topological resources for one purpose or another purpose. I am a great believer in the self-organization paradigm of human interactive behavior, which basically says that when you put all of these things together and they interact, that structure emerges. The structure is not prebuilt, it's not fixed, and it's not predictable. But that doesn't mean that once it's all worked out, there isn't structure there.

Audience Member #4:

I was struck in the presentations by the absence of discussion about the substance of what these students were talking about. I kept waiting for somebody to tell me, "What is a TIA?" or "Is Betty's idea reasonable?" I find myself unable to judge without understanding the content. It would seem from my perspective that this would be a pretty important aspect of your analysis. So I'd like to ask the panelists, how do you decide what to ignore in doing your analyses?

Timothy Koschmann:

Jay was telling me that when he was doing the analysis he had a medical dictionary by his side. It can obviously be a real barrier to doing research in this area given the amount of special language that is used. One must develop a fluency in that language or it is very difficult to make any sense of these discussions.

Jay Lemke:

I think it's a very important point. I've always chosen to study areas in which I knew how the discourse worked substantively in terms of content or what I call "thematic structures" for insiders. When you come to a new field, you get a very sharp sense of what you're missing. This sends you in the direction of saying this is the thing I need to find out. That might send you to a CD-ROM medical dictionary or to another person. This is actually a special case of a general point related to one Carl was making earlier, namely when you know that these multiple layers or aspects of the interaction exist then knowing what is happening in one point stimulates inquiry into what you need to know in order to understand what is happening in another. That, in itself, is a kind of progress in this analytical technique. When you can realize what it is you need to know in order to get a more accurate analysis of something you're looking at, then you're headed in the right direction.

Audience Member #5:

This is a question for Carl. You talked about procedurally guiding the process of reaching a diagnosis through a shared model of diagnostic process. I was wondering if we can assume that the model of the diagnostic process is shared because it is visible in the analysis? In other words, does the fact that somebody displays a particular structure that has been guided indicate that they really have the structure? What else could be going on, and how would we know?

Carl Frederiksen:

That's a darn good question. Sessions such as this could provide an incredibly rich database. I would want to look across groups and across other instances in that database to see what aspects of the diagnostic frame actually stand up. This was just an exercise; it can be regarded as an hypothesis. But it could be tested across many situations. So this would destroy the myth that this kind of work has to always be case studied. It can be hypothesis-testing research.

In our tutorial studies (at McGill), we always get external data to test our models. In this case, we had only 5 minutes to work with. But the other part of your question is really interesting, that these mental models and procedural structures are made public through talk and action. But that doesn't necessarily mean that it is part of the cognition of any individual. You might infer that because individuals are adding pieces in the appropriate places, it would seem that they have acquired some mental structure that enables them to bring in an appropriate piece or challenge it or evaluate it; but that might not be the case. To know each participant's mental model would require some follow-up techniques to assess what the individual has, in effect, learned from this experience.

Audience Member #6:

I would like to applaud this format. I've seen a lot of different panel discussions where everyone comes in with his or her theory and own personal data to defend that theory. I often find that at the end of those sessions, I'm not sure what people disagreed about, and I'm not sure that I get a whole lot out of it. When I see these people, and I know many of you, I can imagine you all getting into incredible debates in the panel over theory. But when, instead, we focus on a set of data, we see that the approach that everyone brings is incredibly rich, and you come away with this feeling of complement rather than conflict. I think that's really beneficial.

DISCUSSION

It is our intent that the excerpts from the panel discussion provide illustrations of what can be done with the highly complex, rich data that emerges from the phenomenon of the PBL group meeting. Each panelist viewed the event from his or her self-selected window and, through each person's analytic tool kit, fashioned for the attendants (and subsequent readers) a unique interpretation. Yet, as pointed out by an audience member, the interpretations cohere or overlap to create a multidimensional picture that, in retrospect, would be diminished if any perspective were deleted.

Of Babies and Bathwater

There are a number of standard complaints leveled against the types of "fragment-based discourse analysis" (Wegerif & Mercer, 1997) exemplified here. These would include concerns about how data is selected and interpreted (Chi, 1997; Edwards & Westgate, 1994; Wegerif & Mercer, 1997), the absence of controls for extraneous variables (Chi, 1997), and, finally, issues of generalizability (Wegerif & Mercer, 1997). There have been recent proposals (Chi, 1997; Wegerif & Mercer, 1997) that seek to redress these perceived limitations through use of more quantitative approaches.

We must take care, therefore, that our object of study does not become lost in our method of analysis; that would be to cast out the proverbial baby with the bath water. As Crook (1994) has argued:

> There is certainly something missing from accounts of collaboration that dwell only upon inventories of utterances—coded and categorized for their pragmatic content. What, in particular, is not captured is any sense of participants having used language to construct an achievement of shared knowledge (p. 150).

As Jay Lemke notes in the later discussion, the organization of learning in collaborative settings is radically contingent. What structure there is to be seen is an emergent product of the moment—locally organized and interactively achieved. Such forms of organization can not be understood in the aggregate using pre-formulated catgories.

Further, unlike methods that reduce interaction to a table of frequency data from which the original interaction is no longer recoverable, the collection of analyses presented here has the structure of an 'open book' in that the raw data, both in the form of the transcript and the actual video record, are made available to the reader as an interpretive resource. The reader is, therefore, invited to join into the analysis, not as a passive recipient of a given set of findings, but as a full and active participant.

By presenting these five analyses side-by-side along with the data upon which they were based, an interesting form of reflexivity is made possible. We see how the different accounts bring different aspects of the taped interaction to light. We can see in the work of the five analysts yet another example of joint sense making, in this case, in their collaborative efforts of making sense of what is being undertaken and accomplished in the interactions of the PBL group. As a consequence, the project undertaken by the five panelists was more than a simple, practical demonstration of different analytic methods; it was an elucidation of the recursive process of meaning making itself. The presented analyses, therefore, become the grist for another level of inquiry, providing further insights into the processes by which we all make sense of the social world around us.

These sense-making processes are a fundamental component of methods of instruction, such as Problem-Based Learning, in which people learn in the context of joint problem solving. Exercises, such as the one undertaken by this panel, are crucial both for stimulating a discussion on how to better understand sense making and in providing a foundation for future research in Problem-Based Learning.

REFERENCES

Abercrombie, M. L. J. (1960). *The anatomy of judgment*. London: Hutchinson.

Bakhtin, M. (1981). *The dialogic imagination*. Austin, TX: University of Texas.

Bruffee, K. A. (1993). *Collaborative learning: Higher education, interdependence and the authority of knowledge*. Baltimore, MD: Johns Hopkins University Press.

Chi, M. (1997). Quantifying qualitative analyses of verbal data: A practical guide. *Journal of the Learning Sciences, 6*, 271–315.

Crook, C. (1994). *Computers and the collaborative experience of learning*. London & New York: Routledge.

Edwards, A., & Westgate, D. (1994). *Investigating classroom talk*. London: Falmer Press.

Lave, J., & Wenger, E. (1991). *Situated learning: Legitimate peripheral participation*. Cambridge: Cambridge University Press.

Koschmann, T. (Ed.; 1999). Special issue on meaning making [Monograph]. *Discourse Processes, 28*(2).

McPhail, J. (1996, April). *Genuine interest in becoming a physician: Two stories, two lives*. Paper presented at the annual meeting of the American Educational Research Association, New York.

Ochs, E., Taylor, C., Rudolph, D., & Smith, R. (1992). Storytelling as a theory-building activity. *Discourse Processes*, *15*, 37–72.

Wegerif, R., & Mercer, N. (1997). Using computer-based text analysis to integrate qualitative and quantitative methods in research on collaborative learning. *Language and Education*, *11*, 1997.

APPENDIX A

Transcription Conventions

The notational scheme employed in this data was originally developed by Jefferson.[1] All symbols used in the representation of the data are defined below.

Symbol	Name	Function
[ ]	Brackets	Marks the beginning and end of overlapping utterances
=	Equal sign	Indicates the end and beginning of two "latched" utterances that continue without a pause
(1.8)	Timed Pause	Measured in seconds, this symbol indicates intervals of silence occurring within and between same or different speaker's utterances
(.)	Micropause	A brief pause of less than (0.2 seconds)
.	Period	Indicates a falling pitch or intonation
?	Question Mark	Rising vocal pitch or intonation
,	Comma	Indicates a continuing intonation; with slight upward or downward contour
-	Hyphen	An abrupt halt of sound, syllable, or word
< >	Greater than/less than signs	Portions of an utterance delivered at a noticeably quicker (> <) or slower (< >) pace than surrounding talk
° °	Degree signs	Marks texts spoken at a lower volume than surrounding talk
	Capitalized text	Represents speech delivered more loudly than surrounding talk
__	Underscore	Underlined word or syllable indicates stress
↑↓	Arrows	Marks a rise or fall in intonation
:::	Colon(s)	Prolongation of previously indicated sound, syllable, or word
(hhh)		Audible exhalation (linguistic aspiration)
(.hhh)		Audible inhalation
( )	Parentheses	Spoken text in which the transcription is in doubt
(( ))	Double parentheses	Annotations describing nonverbal aspects of the interaction (text italicized)

[1] Jefferson, G. (1984). Transcription notation. In Atkinson, J. & Heritage, J. (Eds.), *Structures of Social Action* (pp. ix–xvi). New York: Cambridge University Press.

APPENDIX B

Segment: My Theory
Tape: #91-002 (0:20:12:20 to 0:26:10:00)

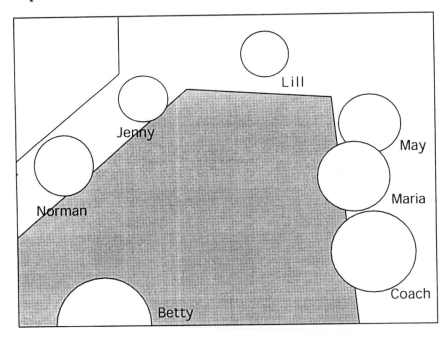

1	|0:20:12:20|	Betty:	See, what it said in here n-<u>my</u> theory
2			⌐about this
3	|0:20:15:00|	(?):	└khu-(.hhhh)
4	|0:20:15:00|	Betty:	amnesic (.) dysnomic aphasia? (0.6) um
5			it says the cause of lesion is usually
6			deep in temporal lobe just like Maria
7			was saying pre<u>sum</u>ably interrupting
8			connections of <u>sen</u>sory speech areas with
9			the <u>hipp</u>ocampal and <u>par</u>ahippocampal
10			regions. (1.0)
11			and I think the <u>hipp</u>ocampus
12			is like a lot more <u>me</u>dial so if it was
13			affecting th<u>at</u> area it m<u>igh</u>t be the
14			⌐anterior cerebral circulation.
15	|0:20:33:00|	Norman:	└Anterior.
16	|0:20:35:00|	Coach:	Where <u>is</u> the hippocampus.
17	|0:20:37:00|	Betty:	I don-do we have a picture up there

18			on ⌐the
19	|0:20:38:00|	Norman:	It'Ls right down there, it's the bottom of
20			this thing.
21			(2.5) ((*Walks over to chart, points*))
22			Right in here
23			(1.2)
24	|0:20:45:00|	Maria:	⌐I think it's un:der that.
25	|0:20:45:00|	(Jenny):	L(I can't remember)
26	|0:20:47:00|	Norman:	It's under that?
27	|0:20:48:00|	Maria:	I think it's on the inside.
28	|0:20:49:00|	Coach:	It's on the middle, (0.7) middle top.
29	|0:20:52:00|	Maria:	Sts-lk-if you lift (("*lifting*" *gesture with*
30			*right arm, elbow out*) up that little
31			temporal lobe ⌐it's on the inside.
32	|0:20:55:00|	Coach:	LYou can you can point it
33			on the middle top.
34			(1.1)
35	|0:20:57:00|	Maria:	Middle top?
36	|0:20:58:00|	Coach:	Mm-mmm.
37			(1.5)
38	|0:21:01:00|	Maria:	°Ye:ah its,°
39			(3.5)
40	|0:21:04:00|	Lill:	In here? ((*points to chart*))=
41	|0:21:05:00|	Maria:	=Yeah, ⌐yeah
42	|0:21:05:00|	Norman:	⌐yeah
43	|0:21:06:00|	Coach:	LThat's it (0.2) tha:t's the
44			hippocampus, then you go over one more
45			gyrus and you're in the temporal lobe.
46	|0:21:10:00|	Maria:	°Ri:ght°
47	|0:21:11:00|	Coach:	So you can also see it on the (0.6)
48			frontal.
49			(1.5)
50	|0:21:15:00|	Coach:	No (you can find it) on the second row left
51			from there
52			(3.3)
53	|0:21:21:00|	Norman:	(hh hh hh)
54			(1.5)
55	|0:21:24:00|	Coach:	Where would it be in that section.
56			(1.5)
57	|0:21:26:00|	Lill:	°Somewhere in here?° ((*pointing*))
58			(1.5)

```
59  |0:21:29:00|   Coach:   Th:at's white matter.
60                          (2.2)
61  |0:21:31:20|   Maria:   °In that cre┌vice?
62  |0:21:33:00|   Norman:          └Go to the crevice there.
63                          (1.0)
64  |0:21:34:00|   Norman:  That little loop?
65                          (1.0)
66  |0:21:36:00|   Norman:  Yeah.
67                          (1.0)
68  |0:21:37:00|   Coach:   That's it.
69  |0:21:38:00|   Betty:   My other theory is that if it was- i- i-
70                          if it's not a vascular lesion but a space
71                          occupying lesion if it was (.) right
72                          there ((points to chart)) in the area we
73                          were pointing to it would be like in a
74                          posterior limb of the internal capsule
75                          which would be where (.) the
76                          corticospinals to the leg would be going
77                          through that part.
78                          (1.0)
79  |0:21:53:00|   Maria:   Wouldn't you expect to ┌see a lot=
80  |0:21:53:00|   Norman:                     └(khh hh huh hh)
81  |0:21:53:00|   Coach:   ┌Whoa ┌kay
82  |0:21:53:00|   Maria:   └    └greater in┌volvement if you got
83  |0:21:55:00|   Norman:                └(hh hh)
84  |0:21:58:00|   Norman:  Yeah
85  |0:21:59:00|   Maria:   internal capsule?=
86  |0:22:02:00|   Betty:   =If it's small. >I mean if< it's
87                          in the very posterior li:mb,(.)
88                          posterior part of the posterior
89                          li:mb.(1.0) Because there's a-the-
90                          (2.0) somato:graphic whatever
91                          that word was,(.) arrangement of the
92                          corticospinals as they go
93  |0:22:13:00|   (?):     ┌°right°
94  |0:22:13:00|   Betty:   └through the (internal) ┌capsule.
95  |0:22:14:00|   Norman:                       └Yeah
96  |0:22:16:00|   Betty:   If you get way to the posterior ↑part of
97                          the internal capsule the only thing that's
98                          there is motor ┌and it's
99  |0:22:18:00|   Norman:              └motor
```

100	|0:22:18:00|	Betty:	going t⌐o be the le:g.
101	|0:22:19:00|	Norman:	⌊motor
102	|0:22:21:00|	Norman:	That's true
103			(3.0)
104	|0:22:24:00|	Coach:	So <u>why</u> do the leg findings go away?
105			(1.0)
106	|0:22:27:00|	Betty:	That's a good question that kind of goes
107			aga<u>i</u>nst it being some kind of a space
108			occupying lesion because you would expect
109			it to get prog<u>ress</u>ive and then (you want
110			it) to involve more <u>a</u>reas.
111			(0.4)
112	|0:22:34:00|	Betty:	So then it's ⌐<u>prob</u>ably more likely
113	|0:22:35:00|	Maria:	⌊<u>Head</u>aches,=
114	|0:22:36:00|	Maria:	=you would expect
115	|0:22:36:15|	Norman:	You'd exp<u>ect</u> to have headaches
116	|0:22:37:00|	Betty:	°Maybe, yeah.°
117	|0:22:38:00|	Maria:	Seizures.
118			(0.7)
119	|0:22:41:00|	Betty:	Um (0.8) it's more likely to be vascular.
120			(2.5)
121	|0:22:45:00|	Coach:	°Oka⌐y°
122	|0:22:46:00|	Maria:	⌊°With his history an⌐d social°
123	|0:22:46:15|	Coach:	⌊So
124	|0:22:48:00|	Coach:	So if it's <u>vas</u>cular did he have a ↑stroke
125			or is he having a TIA. What <u>is</u> the
126			difference between those two things
127			<u>any</u>way.
128	|0:22:53:00|	Norman:	With TIAs, it's like twenty-four
129			hour⌐s
130	|0:22:55:00|	Jenny:	⌊TIAs well, a↑ccording to <u>Harrison's</u> TIAs
131			um shows some neurological <u>dam</u>age but
132			it's all better in twenty-four hours.
133			According to <u>Cec</u>il's it's all better in
134			<u>one</u> hour um a ⌐(hh hh hh)
135	|0:23:09:00|	Lill:	⌊(<u>one</u> of 'em)
136	|0:23:11:00|	Jenny:	and <u>Cec</u>il's also talked about something
137			called <u>RI:ND</u> (.) which is a re<u>vers</u>ible
138			icschemic (1.6)
139			⌐neurological deficits?=
140	|0:23:16:00|	Norman:	⌊⌐neurological deficits
141	|0:23:16:00|	Coach:	⌊⌊neurological deficits

142	|0:23:19:20|	Jenny:	=which is somewhere in be<u>tween</u> a
143			completed stroke and a TIA. Which,
144			(hh huh huh)=
145	|0:23:25:00|	Betty:	Sorta like angina or ⌐unstable angina of
146	|0:23:26:00|	Jenny:	⌊(hh huh huh huh)
147	|0:23:27:00|	Betty:	the <u>mind</u>.
148	|0:23:29:00|	Jenny:	=which um (.) gets better within twenty-
149			four to thirty-↑six hours, um,
150			(1.2) ((*Lips smack then mouths something*
151			*like "I don't know"*))
152	|0:23:38:00|	Coach:	So which one did he ha:ve?
153			(1.0)
154	|0:23:40:00|	Jenny:	°Mm.°
155	|0:23:41:00|	Maria:	I think he's ⌐(.)pro<u>gress</u>ing to a
156	|0:23:41:10|	Norman:	⌊>A little bit of both.<
157	|0:23:43:00|	Maria:	stroke.
158	|0:23:43:20|	Betty:	I think it's really hard to say because I
159			don't think we have a very good history
160			↓about <u>exactly</u> what's happened in the
161			last three weeks. And I don't know how
162			we can im↑prove that.
163	|0:23:50:00|	Jenny:	We don't know h<u>ow</u> <u>long</u> his ↓leg was
164			clumsy
165			(0.5)
166	|0:23:53:00|	Betty:	The leg was ⌐(clum)
167	|0:23:54:00|	Norman:	⌊ We don't know how long it was
168			clumsy? It's <u>gone</u> now yet he still has
169			the ↑verbal problem.
170			(1.5)
171	|0:23:59:00|	Betty:	⌐He doesn't have⌐ ↑<u>any memory</u>
172	|0:23:59:00|	Norman:	⌊(so)⌋
173	|0:24:00:00|	Betty:	problem right now.=
174	|0:24:01:00|	Norman:	=Yeah, which is very o⌐:dd.
175	|0:24:02:00|	Betty:	⌊Based on our mental
176			↑status exam,
177			(0.3)
178	|0:24:04:00|	Coach:	°Hm mm°
179	|0:24:05:00|	Betty:	But yet his wife says that he's
180			periodically gets <u>goo</u>fy or >whatever it
181			was that she said<
182			(3.8)
183	|0:24:11:00|	Betty:	So,

```
184   |0:24:13:00|   Maria:    See a stroke can develop over a period of
185                             several ↓days usually progressing in a
186                             step like fashion=
187   |0:24:18:00|   Norman:   =(Unless it's   )
188   |0:24:19:00|   Maria:    With a deficit being added from time to
189                             time.
190                             (1.0)
191   |0:24:23:00|   Norman:   But then you would think the leg would be
192                             getting worse.
193                             (0.5)
194   |0:24:25:00|   Norman:   °I would think.°
195   |0:24:26:00|   Maria:    We:↓ll it could- I mean usually strokes
196                             are preceded by TIAs.
197                             (0.5)
198   |0:24:32:00|   Norman:   Yeah
199   |0:24:32:10|   Maria:    So then ⌜it could've just been you know⌝
200   |0:24:32:20|   Norman:           ⌞Well I mean that's a yeah⌟    =
201                             =that's a risk factor ↑for 'em. (0.7)
202   |0:24:35:20|   Norman:   The thing is that (1.0) we're seeing an-
203                             an acute leg deficit and now (.) we're
204                             seeing five over five strength.
205   |0:24:43:00|   Maria:    Hm-mm
206                             (1.5).
207   |0:24:43:20|   Norman:   ⌜What ↑happened to it
208   |0:24:45:00|   Betty:    ⌞obviously ⌜there's no-
209   |0:24:45:00|   Maria:               ⌞TI↑A
210   |0:24:47:00|   Betty:    Uh it's most likely there was no
211                             permanent dam⌜age from what=
212   |0:24:49:00|   Maria:                   ⌞Right.
213   |0:24:50:10|   Betty:    ⌜had happened.
214   |0:24:50:22|   Norman:   ⌞But wh:y is his ↑speech now screwed up.
215                             (0.7)
216   |0:24:53:00|   Betty:    Is it screwed up
217   |0:24:54:00|   Norman:   It's screwed up ↑somehow
218   |0:24:55:00|   Betty:    °a little bit° ((hand gesture))
219   |0:24:56:00|   Norman:   =<like it wasn't ⌜before>
220   |0:24:57:00|   Maria:                     ⌞ He says it's gotten
221                             worse in the last couple of days=
222   |0:24:59:00|   Norman:   =Ye:ah.
223   |0:24:59:00|   Maria:    Some:thing's gotten worse I assume it's
224   |0:24:59:00|   Betty:    ⌜But yet when we-
225   |0:24:59:00|   Maria:    ⌞↓his speech.
```

226 |0:25:02:00| Betty: But yet when we actually examine him
227   I mean occasionally not even very <u>often</u> >he
228   has trouble finding the right word and we
229   do a mental status exam< (1.3) <u>rarely</u>
230   >does he have trouble finding the right
231   word and he can complete the ↑rest of the
232   mental status exam with no problems<
233   (1.0)
234 |0:25:17:00| Betty: So I don't kno:w.
235   (7.0) ((*Norman and Jenny looking at board*))
236 |0:25:23:00| Betty: I think I would prob'ly lean more towards
237   (1.0) trans- something transient that
238   comes'n goes 'n we're catching him at a
239   fairly <u>good</u> moment.
240   (1.5)
241 |0:25:31:00| Maria: Uhh ⌈
242 |0:25:32:00| Norman: ⌊Un⌈h: : : : : : : : : : : : : ⌉ ((*"doubt" noise*))
243 |0:25:32:00| Betty: ⌊But I don't know. ⌋
244   (5.0)
245 |0:25:38:00| Betty: An' it seems like to me that for (.) for:
246   his wife to have been concerned about
247   whatever was going on it has to be worse
248   than it is right now. 'Cause it's just-
249   (.) unless we just (.) don't have a very
250   clear picture of what he's really like.
251   Things just don't seem very ba:d.
252   (1.0)
253 |0:25:51:00| Maria: Yeah see I don't t⌈hink we do have a clear-
254 |0:25:53:00| Norman: ⌊I don't see it either.
255 |0:25:54:00| Betty: And I don't know how we can fix that.
256   (5.0)
257 |0:26:01:00| Betty: Except if we asked every single question
258   ⌈in the book.
259 |0:26:02:00| Coach: ⌊Hmm ((*smile*))
260 |0:26:02:00| Norman: ((*smile*))
261 |0:26:03:00| Betty: (hu huh huh hh)
262 |0:26:04:00| Coach: Some patients are vague,
263 |0:26:06:00| Betty: Yep.
264   (1.5)
265 |0:26:08:00| Coach: Just don't give you the answers you wanna
266   hear.

Chapter 7

Groups in Problem-Based Learning (PBL): Essential Elements in Theory and Practice

Ann C. Myers Kelson
Linda H. Distlehorst
Southern Illinois University
School of Medicine

INTRODUCTION

Groups are created for many reasons. The most common reasons, according to Bretcher (1994) are to achieve individual change, to enhance learning in educational settings, to facilitate residential living, and to provide mutual support. Belonging to a group assumes that members share common interests or characteristics. Yet, common sense and personal experience tell us that people often find themselves in groups with highly dissimilar individuals or working on problems far removed from individual purposes or expertise. Of interest in this chapter is one type of education group, the problem-based learning (PBL) group as it operates within medical education. In this chapter we discuss the role that the structure and function of groups play in achieving the outcomes of PBL. Using the Barrows model (1992), we show that the group process models the projected outcomes of PBL, and that elements of group structure and function work together to produce these outcomes. We then look at data from a survey of North American medical schools that show that rarely are all these elements in place. The chapter concludes with a suggestion that a line of research be initiated that would begin to verify hypotheses as to the essential elements of PBL and the consequences of eliminating some of them.

THE SURVEY

In 1997, a two-step survey of North American medical colleges with respect to the use of PBL in their curricula was undertaken by the authors. In step one, a questionnaire was sent to the Associate Deans for Education (or their equivalents) in every medical school on the roster of the Association of American Medical College (AAMC; $N = 124$). This questionnaire asked two primary questions: "Does your institution do problem-based learning?" and "If so, who would be in the best position to respond to a survey about the particular structure of your problem-based program?" Of the 124 institutions queried, 85 (68.5%) responded that they had at least some element of PBL in their curriculum and supplied the name of the individual most qualified to respond to questions regarding it. To these 85, and to the 24 institutions that failed to respond to the initial survey, a detailed follow-up survey was sent. There was no response to either questionnaire from the 24. Of the 85 who responded to the initial survey, 68 returned the detailed survey for a response rate of 80%; however, not all of these completed every item. Numbers for specific items are included as data are presented.

The purpose of the detailed survey was to sort out the range of educational practices that are labeled PBL. Most of the items were forced choice, asking respondents to select the option that best described their curriculum. Among the items in the survey were queries concerning the power of the PBL group process to effect the outcomes for which PBL is generally instituted. Results of this survey are reported throughout the chapter.

THE MODEL TUTORIAL GROUP

For this chapter we adopt the PBL group model as described by Barrows (1992), in which the PBL tutorial group is central to the PBL process. The ideal tutorial group, according to this model, consists of five to seven students and a group facilitator commonly referred to as a "tutor." The group meets to address problems that form the core of the PBL curriculum. In the ideal implementation, these problems are actual, real-world problems,[1] unfolding just as they do in the real world. The problems engender multiple hypotheses and require the application of knowledge and skills for their resolution. Students, aided by a tutor or a group facil-

---

[1]The meaning of the term "problem" throughout this chapter is not restricted to "problematic situation." Rather, consistent with its use throughout cognitive psychology, it is used to denote any situation that inspires a goal for which there is no clear path to reach it. Within this context, the term problem can refer to creative challenges as well as difficulties to be resolved.

itator, approach the problem as a collaborative team, generating hypotheses and inquiring against them using appropriate strategies and sources. As they work through the hypothetico–deductive process, group members, again aided by the tutor's strategic probing, note the knowledge and skills that the problem demands, assess their own competency with respect to these, and identify as "learning issues" that about which they need to learn more. The group plans and implements procedures for acquiring the needed knowledge and skills, each member agreeing to develop functional "expertise" in one or more of the learning issues. After a period of self-directed learning, group members return to the problem armed with their increased competency in the knowledge and skill afforded by the problem. Within a single problem, this process continues until the problem is resolved and explained, with decisions justified based on the underlying explanatory principles and mechanisms. After the resolution of each problem, the group reflects on its work, both collectively and individually. Each member assesses himself and is likewise assessed by peers and the tutor with respect to the four performance outcomes of the PBL process. These outcomes include excellence in knowledge, in problem solving, in self-directed learning, and in collaboration.

Because the tutorial process is the primary shaper of outcomes in the PBL curriculum, the following elements have been abstracted from the previous description. Relevant survey information is presented with each element. For purposes of reporting these data, the Barrows (1992) model is used as a standard for comparison. The responses indicated include all schools that reported some PBL in their program.

- The ideal group size is five to seven students. Of the 62 schools that responded, 25 (40%) reported tutor group sizes of four to seven students; one school reported not using tutor groups; 3 of 62 (5%) reported groups fewer than four students. The majority, 33 of 62 (53%), reported group sizes of seven or more. The highest number of students reported in any group was 20.

- The group is lead by a tutor who acts as a facilitator, not as a deliverer of information. Of 58 schools that responded to this item, 41 (71%) indicated that their tutors do not serve as content experts and are specifically trained to refrain from imparting content knowledge. The remaining 17 of 58 (29%) described their tutors as content experts, trained to impart or use the content in some sort of didactic sessions with the students.

- PBL problems form the core of the curriculum. Only 17 of 57 (30%) of those schools responding to this item indicated "problems/cases in our curriculum are the sole focus of instruction." The remainder preceded or followed problem sessions with faculty-planned and delivered didactic sessions.

- Problems that the group addresses require inquiry rather than presenting as complete cases or as sequential disclosure cases (cases in which information is disclosed in stages). Only 10 of 53 or 18% of the schools responding indicated that students must strategically inquire for information about the case. The majority, 39 of 53 (74%), used sequential disclosure paper cases. Only 4 out of 53 (8%) distributed complete cases to students.

- Group members are responsible for identifying the knowledge and skill demands of the problem, assessing their own competency with respect to these, identifying learning issues about which more must be learned, and locating and using effective resources to address their identified deficiencies. This process is referred to as self-directed learning. Of 61 schools responding 44 (72%) indicated that learning issues were generated solely by the students. Of 63 of them, 37 (59%) indicated that students are given no list of references or readings relevant to the cases they are studying.

- After self-directed learning, newly acquired knowledge and skills are applied back to the problem. This was assessed by a forced-choice item asking whether tutors encouraged giving free-standing reports on learning issue topics or discouraged giving such reports. Of 53 schools responding 46 (87%) indicated that tutors encouraged free-standing reports on learning issues whereas 7 of 53 (13%) discouraged such reports. One respondent indicated that neither was the case.

- Active reflection in the form of self, peer, and tutor assessment is a significant tool in building the team and in individual progress toward curricular outcomes. Of 68 schools responding, 26 (38%) reported counting self-peer-tutor assessment of at least one of the outcomes toward promotion decisions, and another 9 (13%) reported such assessment but not counting it toward promotion.

OUTCOMES OF PBL

The pedagogical appeal of PBL is its perceived capacity to enable the following four student outcomes:

- A flexible, useable knowledge base. This includes a repertoire of concepts and skills seen as essential for effective action in situations students are likely to encounter in future practice.

- Skill at problem solving or reasoning. Here we are specifically referring to the hypothetico–deductive reasoning process where an encounter with the problem suggests hypotheses that guide further inquiry into the problem. Data from the inquiry process is used to strengthen or to weaken hypotheses until a reasoned resolution is reached. This process occurs with problems that seem to have a single solution as well as projects that may suggest a number of possible outcomes. Problem solving around ill-structured problems also carries with it the ambiguity factors: reasoning from uncertainty and decision making in the absence of complete knowledge.

• Skills in self-directed learning including recognizing the knowledge and skill demands of the problem; assessing one's own competence with respect to these; calling on a repertoire of strategies, sources and skills to address the deficiencies; and developing new strategies, sources, and skills when those in the repertoire prove inadequate or require increased efficiency and effectiveness.

• Collaboration as a member of a team working toward three common goals: learning collaboratively, problem solving collaboratively, and achieving individual curricular outcomes collaboratively. Bruffee (1993) described the collaborative learning group as a "transitional community" in which knowledge becomes something that a group of knowledgeable peers construct by negotiation and consensus. The PBL group as collaborative learners is a variant of this definition. They are a group becoming knowledgeable; they are both constructing knowledge as contextualized by the problem and arriving at meaning common to the scientific or other scholarly community (Roschelle, 1996). By extension, we can describe the PBL group as both constructing problem solutions and arriving at a problem-solving process that is common to the professional community. Finally, members of the group are supporting one another's efforts in achieving individual outcomes, and all three of these are working in tandem.

Bruffee (1993) also maintained that to gain access to various communities, the learning group members must reacculturate themselves so they can acquire the special characteristics of the community members, the most important of which is fluency in the language that is the common property of the community. Medical education tutorial group activities are designed to specifically engage students in the discourse of the medical community. Each time they work together, they are expected to translate their understandings of the underlying basic science mechanisms responsible for the patient's problem into an emerging clinical picture described within the requisite language of clinical practice.

These four outcomes we label as *knowledge, problem solving, self-directed learning,* and *collaboration* (cf. Barrows, 1992; Barrows & Kelson, 1990). The majority of schools surveyed (52/68; 76%) considered all four of these outcomes as expected student outcomes for their PBL programs. Only 5 out of 68 (7%) included all except basic or clinical science knowledge as an expected student outcome. The same number, 5 out of 68 (7%) included all except clinical reasoning or problem solving as an outcome. Of the

68, 6 (9%) included all except collaboration as an expected outcome. Clearly the vast majority of PBL programs have expectations that the program will impact these four dimensions of students' performance.

PARAMETERS OF THE PBL GROUP

The function of the PBL tutor group can be described as having three overlapping parameters. They include the group as collaborative learners, the group as collaborative problem solvers, and the group as collaboratively working toward individual outcomes. Not coincidentally, these parameters map onto the major outcomes: knowledge, problem solving, self-directed learning, and collaboration. Clearly the mapping is not a one-to-one correspondence. Self-directed learning is the primary mechanism for knowledge building. Knowledge needs emanate from the problem, and newly acquired knowledge and skills are brought back to the problem, making knowledge and problem solving intertwined. Collaboration defines the learning process, defines the problem-solving process, and contributes to the achievement of individual outcomes. By looking at these three parameters, however, we can see how the PBL group process works to produce the individual outcomes.

The PBL Group as Collaborative Learners

The term *collaborative learning* suggests a wide variety of definitions, ranging from mutual problem solving to enculturation into a community of learners (Koschmann, Kelson, Feltovich, & Barrows, 1996). For purposes of this discussion, it is useful to distinguish collaborative learning from collaborative problem solving. Although in some sense all learning is a form of problem solving, we will reserve the term problem solving for the hypothetico–deductive reasoning process leading to the resolution of a challenge to which there is no clear path. Collaborative learning will be used to refer to the process by which individuals, working from differing perspectives, come to an understanding of rich, complex concepts.

What are the benefits of collaborative learning? P. J. Feltovich, Spiro, Coulson, and Feltovich (1996) argued, based on cognitive flexibility theory (Spiro, Vispoel, Schmitz, Samarapungavan, & Boerger, 1987), that collaborative learning environments provide the multiple perspectives that enable the acquisition of complex concepts and the avoidance of overly simplistic reductions that characterize novice understanding. They argued further that working within the collaborative environment can enable the individual to adopt multiple perspectives when encountering complexity in the absence of a group. Finally, they contended that this internalization of multiple perspectives by the individual comes full circle in that it increases the individual's effectiveness in future collaborative settings.

A similar argument is put forward by Roschelle (1996). Addressing findings that document the unusually strong tendencies of students to construct nonstandard meanings for scientific concepts (Confey, 1990; Eylon & Linn, 1988; McDermott, 1984), he argued that students working collaboratively are able to construct increasingly sophisticated approximations of scientific concepts through the process of gradual refinement of ambiguous, figurative, and partial meanings. He proposed that through an iterative cycle of displaying, confirming, and repairing shared meanings, students collaborating in learning can move from idiosyncratic commonsense notions about the meanings of concepts to meanings and understandings shared by the scientific community.

Problem-Centeredness of the Curriculum. There are at least two principles that are important for understanding the interrelationship between the PBL problem and learning as advocated in a PBL curriculum. First, problems are viewed as central to the curriculum (Barrows, 1992). Curricular knowledge and skills are determined by the selection of problems. The students' need to know is stimulated by the problem, and an important test of knowing is the ability to apply knowledge back to the problem. Second, the responsibility for recognizing the need to know, acquiring the necessary knowledge and skills, and applying this back to the problem must be given to the student.

It is almost axiomatic to say that real problems, in the cognitive science sense, require knowledge and skill for their optimal resolution. These are learning and problem solving or *affordances*[2] of the problems. Reaching optimal resolution of a problem demands that the problem solver be attuned to the problem's affordances, assess his or her own competence with respect to these affordances, resolve any competence deficiencies, and readdress the problem newly armed with the necessary knowledge and skills.

Whether or not problems form the core of the curriculum plays a key role in defining students' goals for learning. When problems are central to the curriculum, affordances of the collection of problems forming the PBL curriculum constitute the content objectives of that curriculum—the flexible, useable knowledge base. Recognizing and addressing these affordances shapes the students' goals for learning. The need to know is stimulated by the problem; an important test for learning is the ability to

---

[2]See Epilogue, this volume, for a discussion of affordances as applied to problems. Also see Bransford, Sherwood, Vye, and Rieser, 1986; E. J. Gibson, 1982; and J. J. Gibson, 1977, for a discussion of affordances and attunement with respect to comprehending.

apply newly acquired knowledge and skills back to the problem. Thus, learning is undertaken in a manner compatible with future practice. On the other hand, when problems are adjunct to a faculty-generated, independent set of knowledge and skills, this independent set constitutes the content outcomes of the curriculum. Addressing this institutional curriculum shapes the students' goals for learning. The need to know is stimulated by faculty demand, and the test for learning is the ability to meet those demands. In this case, learning is likely to be seen as a schooling activity, unrelated to future practice (cf. Bereiter & Scardamalia, 1989, 1993).

Students as Responsible for Attuning to the Problem's Affordances. It is essential that students learn to attune to the affordances of the problem. That is what will make them lifelong learners. We hypothesized that this "bonding" with the problem affordances is less likely to occur if students are told what they must learn to resolve the problem. The intrusion of learning demands outside of or independent of the problem may interfere with the students' developing capacity for attuning. Learning goals shift from recognizing and addressing the affordances of the problem to addressing the prescribed demands of the curriculum.

It is this set of principles—that the problem is at the center of the curriculum and that students are given absolute responsibility for recognizing and addressing the problem's affordances—that forms the basis for what is often referred to as the "student-centered" nature of the ideal PBL curriculum. Given this relation between problem affordances and students' attuning, however, it is more accurately stated that the ideal problem-based program is neither student-centered, with students having free reign as to what they will learn, nor is it faculty-centered, with faculty dictating the content that must be acquired. Rather, it is problem-centered. Knowledge and skills that must be learned are dictated by the affordances of the problems encountered. Faculty input is evidenced in the selection and design of these problems and in the tutor's action in facilitating recognition of the problem's affordances. Hence, knowledge building commences from the problem addressed collaboratively.

The Survey: Collaboratively Learning Depends on Problem-Centeredness

The term *problem-centered* refers to the extent to which the PBL program has problems as the focus of the curriculum and the extent to which students are given the responsibility for attuning to the problem solving and learning affordances of the problem. The survey directly asked whether problems were the sole focus of the curriculum, whether they preceded didactic instruction, or whether they followed it. Of the 57 schools responding to this item, only 30% (17) indicated that problems were the sole focus of the curriculum. Approximately 46% (26) used problems at the beginning of an instructional unit with didactic sessions following, and 25% (14) used problems following didactic sessions. These data suggest that for many reported problem-based curricula, faculty-imposed didactic sessions may be interfering with the students' goals for learning and with their developing ability to respond to problem affordances.

To determine the extent to which students were given responsibility for attuning to and addressing the affordances of the problem, several items of the survey addressed how learning issues are handled. In one such item, respondents were asked to specify whether students or faculty were responsible for generating learning objectives or issues around a problem. Of the 61 respondents, 44 (72%) said that learning issues were generated solely by the students. Of those remaining, 13% (8/61) said that students were given faculty-generated learning objectives prior to receiving the case; 7/51 (14%) said that students were given faculty-generated learning objectives after they had worked up the case, but prior to self-directed learning; 2/61 (3%) said that students were given faculty-developed study questions prior to self-directed learning. Aggregated, the majority of those programs (71%) do hold students solely responsible for attuning to the affordances of the problem, whereas approximately 29% of those programs have faculty-determined objectives or direction associated with the problem. In a related item, schools were asked whether students were given assigned readings related to the problem. Of the 63 that responded, 37 (59%) indicated that students are given no list of references or readings relevant to the cases they are studying. The remaining schools (41%) provided students with related readings or references.

PBL Groups as Collaborative Problem Solvers

Why Groups?   Most problems that challenge the interrelation of reasoning, knowledge, and skills are complex. They have multiple dimensions: they present with insufficient data and consequently demand strategic inquiry for their resolution, and they require that decisions be made in the absence of certainty (cf. Barrows & Felotvich, 1987; Spiro et al., 1987). The complexity of multiple affordances, the complexity of the hypothetical–deductive process, the uncertainty of multiple solution pathways, and the uncertainty of making decisions on incomplete knowledge can be overwhelming. It can easily trigger a natural tendency toward reductivism (Feltovich, Spiro, Coulson, & Myers Kelson, 1995) that is antithetical to the development of the reasoning process and the skill of attuning to and addressing the problem's multiple affordances. Put simply, for most of us acting individually, problem complexity triggers a tendency to come to simplistic resolutions out of our present state of ignorance. The more novice the problem solver, the greater this tendency. The collaborative problem-solving group, however, provides the ideal situation for remedying this, while developing expertise in problem solving through the interaction between reasoning and attuning to problem affordances.

Individuals bring varying expertise to the group. They see different facets of a complex problem and bring unique needs for completeness and tolerance for ambiguity. A group of such individuals, committed to a common goal—the problem's optimal resolution—can collectively enlighten each other regarding multiple perspectives, complex affordances, and reasonable versus reckless uncertainty.

The Hypothetico–Deductive Process.   The PBL tutor group is probably most commonly thought of as a group of problem solvers. Problem solving refers here to the hypothetico–deductive reasoning method: the process of generating hypotheses, inquiring against these hypotheses, and using the data gathered to rule in and rule out hypotheses until an optimal decision can be reached. Inquiring against hypotheses may take many forms and may have many sources. In medicine, the primary, and often exclusive, inquiry source is the patient. The inquiry forms are fairly standard: the patient interview, the physical exam, and a defined set of laboratory tests and procedures. In areas other than medicine, the inquiry sources may vary widely: people, files, models, artifacts, water, soil or air samples, and so on. Equally varied are the forms: interviewing witnesses, reviewing personnel files, creating models, synthesizing a variety of reports, and chemical qualitative analysis, just to name a few. Regardless of the source and the variety of inquiry forms, the cognitive processes across all forms of problem solving are similar: the problem initially presents itself and hypotheses spring to mind or a cognitive search for hypotheses is initiated. In rapid synchronicity, questions or strategies that will test the hypotheses also spring to mind, or the cognitive search for such questions or strategies is initiated. Inquiry addresses these questions, and a rather systematic, but distinctly nonlinear process of testing the hypotheses against the accumulating data takes place. As the process continues, hypotheses may be ruled out, new ones may be generated, and new questions or strategies to further test the hypotheses may suggest themselves, calling for further inquiry. This iterative process continues until something constrains it. Sometimes the process exhausts itself with a firm conclusion. At other times, and perhaps most often, a need for action demands that a best possible decision be made based on the evidence at hand, incomplete and ambiguous though it may be. Deadlines must be met; conditions require immediate intervention; resources are exhausted.

It has been argued that this is not the process an expert follows, but rather the expert is more likely to arrive at conclusions rapidly through pattern recognition (cf. Patel & Groen, 1986, 1991). In our opinion, this argument has been effectively countered with a clarification of semantics. Experts functioning within their comfort zones do engage in pattern recognition. And to a certain extent, the ability to recognize patterns defines their expertise (Chi, Feltovich, & Glaser, 1980; Chi, Glaser, & Rees, 1982). However, when they meet a challenge to their expertise, experts too engage in hypothetico–deductive reasoning, a process at which they also excel (Barrows, Norman, Neufeld, & Feightner, 1982; Elstein, 1994; Elstein, Shulman, & Sprafka, 1978, 1990). Problems as defined for this discussion are those situations that challenge expertise and invoke the hypothetico–deductive process. There are obviously levels of expertise in the hypothetico–deductive process. There are ranges of insight and creativity in generating hypotheses, inquiring against them, determining the significance of emerging data, testing hypotheses against these data, and arriving at an optimal resolution in the absence of complete knowledge. As with all expertise, increased facility in this process emerges with experience. Providing experience in this process is one of the rationales for a PBL curriculum. The extent to which this experience is actually provided depends largely on the nature or structure of the problems in the curriculum.

One controversial aspect of problem-based learning is whether or not a specific algorithm for problem solving should be taught and whether students should be held to it. Barrows (1992) argued that the hypothetico–deductive process is a naturally occurring one—that students merely need to be given free reign with a problem to engage with this process. The advocates of this view would do no more than record the group's hypotheses, facts, and learning issues and provide opportunity for reviewing the hypotheses as new data about the problem are gathered. There are those, however, who hold that students profit from being taught a problem-solving algorithm. Some insist on making linear the hypothetico–deductive process: first, all data for the problem are gathered; only then are hypotheses entertained. This linearization is countered with the observation that it is the spontaneous generation of hypotheses that separates signal from noise in incoming data and that guides the questioning or the implementation of other information-gathering strategies. Others advocate teaching and restricting students to a specific 7-step or 10-step model.

The Survey: The Approach to Problem-Solving in PBL Groups

Two items in the survey addressed the issue of how PBL groups approached problem solving. One looked at the extent to which the problems being used in a curriculum lend themselves to experiencing the hypothetico–deductive process by demanding inquiry for the gathering of data about the problem. Of the 63 schools responding to this item, only 11 (17%) presented problems in such a way that students could fully inquire against hypotheses. Of the 63, 45 (71%) used sequential disclosure problems in which data for the problem are presented in segments: history, then physical examination, then laboratory tests and procedures, and so on. These data allow students to generate questions, but because significant data have been abstracted from that which is insignificant, they are limited in the extent to which they allow students to face the full challenge of the hypothetico–deductive process. Seven out of 63 (11%) of schools responding present students with complete cases which include diagnoses, allowing little, if any, experience in this process.

The other item related to how PBL groups approach problem solving asked whether or not students were explicitly taught and held to a problem-solving algorithm. In 27 of the 64 (43%) schools responding, students were neither taught nor directed to use a particular problem-solving algorithm. The group's deliberations were tracked by a representation that is created on a board, an overhead, or another display device. In nearly as many, 24 of 64 (38%), students were explicitly taught a problem-solving algorithm to which they were held in the problem-solving process. In 6 of 64 (9%), tutors directed students to follow a specific algorithm, but students were not made explicitly aware of it. The remaining 7 out of 64 (11%) used no structure at all in discussing cases.

Although 63 of the 68 (92%) schools responding indicated that problem solving or clinical reasoning was an expected student outcome of their programs, only 17% presented problems in such a way that students could fully exercise the hypothetico–deductive process. The respondents were almost evenly divided on the issue of whether or not students should be taught and held to an explicit problem-solving algorithm.

The PBL Group as Collaboratively Working Toward Common Individual Outcomes

We discuss one final parameter that defines the function of PBL groups: the development of the individual within the group. Though their learning experiences and problem solving are largely situated within the group, PBL students are expected to develop individually as learners and as problem solvers. The group can facilitate this if each individual assumes mutual responsibility for the others' excellence. According to the Barrows (1992) model, each problem ends with a period of reflection on individual performance. Each student assesses himself or herself with respect to each outcome of the curriculum. This is followed by input from every other student in the group as well as from the tutor. Barrows recommended that this procedure be formalized regularly, providing data that "count" for student progress. In our experience, this self- and peer-assessment process can be a powerful agent in developing outcomes in individuals. Students are instructed to cite specific evidence for evaluative statements both in their self-assessment and in the assessment of their peers. They are encouraged to state goals for future improvement and the group is encouraged to enter into planning for reaching these goals as well as for monitoring progress toward them. Every student in the group is entitled to this level of formative evaluation, even those who are "doing well." If any of them has a problem, it becomes the group's problem. This climate of mutual support enables students to be very precise and honest both in their self-assessment and in their assessments of others in the group. As one student said upon being asked whether students avoid giving honest feedback,

> Avoid it? Why would we avoid it? We're responsible for each other. If I know that one of my colleagues could really improve if he addressed some issue and I don't bring it up, it would be like malpractice. In the same way, I'm trusting that my fellow group members are committed to my becoming the best I can possibly be. That means I need their feedback.

In the Barrows (1992) model tutors contribute to the group's assessment but do not assess students privately. All evaluative comments from tutor to student are made in the group. This allows the tutor to model appropriate and constructive ways of giving feedback. It avoids putting the tutor in the untenable position of being, on the one hand, a facilitator who encourages open thinking and risk taking, and, on the other, an independent evaluator who makes private judgments about quality based on these contributions. Such a split role can inhibit if not destroy students' openness. Further, when tutor assessment is brought into the group process, these judgments, along with the criteria for making them and the evidence cited to support them, belong to the common pool. All students profit from each other's assessment. In the final analysis, although tutors do not assess students privately, they are ultimately responsible for the quality of the group's assessment. If group members do not identify issues in members that the tutor recognizes, it is the tutor's responsibility to address them in the group context. Finally, the group is ultimately responsible for its own climate and functioning. The tutor, as manager of the process, must stimulate the kind of group reflection that allows this to happen.

The Survey: PBL Groups as Mutual Supporters of Individual Development

The survey addressed this issue directly by asking schools to indicate the extent to which self- and peer assessment was involved in evaluating students' performance in each of the four curricular objectives. The survey also asked whether tutors submitted assessments independent of the group. From a checklist of 12 possible assessment methods, respondents were asked to indicate all forms used to assess each of the four student outcomes of PBL. Most schools indicated use of more than one method for any given outcome.

Basic Knowledge. Of the 68 schools reporting, 58 (85%) assessed knowledge in their PBL programs. Of these, 23 of 58 (40%) used self- and peer assessment. Of the 68, 20 (34%) asked the tutor to assess each student's knowledge independent of the group.

Clinical Reasoning or Problem Solving. Of the 68 schools reporting, 54 (79%) assessed clinical reasoning or problem solving in their PBL programs. Of these, 28 of 54 (52%) used self- and peer assessment. Of the 54, 21 (39%) asked the tutor to assess each student's clinical reasoning ability independent of the group.

Self-Directed Learning. Of the 68 schools reporting, 53 (78%) assessed self-directed learning within their PBL program. Of these, 33 of 53 (62%) used self- and peer assessment. Of the 53, 24 (45%) asked the tutor to assess each student's self-directed learning skills independent of the group.

Collaboration. Of the 68 schools reporting, 52 (76%) assessed collaboration. Of these, 35 of 52 (67%) used self- and peer assessment and 23 out of 52 (44%) asked the tutor to assess each student's collaboration independent of the group.

These data suggest that only in about 40% of PBL programs the group took responsibility for the individual's knowledge development. In a little over half of the programs the group took responsibility for the individual's problem solving. In about 45% of the programs the group took responsibility for the individual's self-directed learning. Finally, in 67% of the programs the group assesses collaboration, though the data do not tell us whether assessment is of the individual or of the group as a whole. The extent to which even these groups take ownership of this responsibility may be inhibited by the fact that the tutor may be submitting private assessments.

CONCLUSIONS AND DISCUSSION

If the survey data suggest anything, it is that PBL in medical schools has become a generic category encompassing almost any teaching approach that incorporates a patient problem in any format. Yet virtually every program that has adopted the PBL label, no matter what its structure, length, or place in the curriculum, expects the full range of student outcomes: knowledge, problem solving, self-directed learning, and collaboration. It is almost as if the PBL label itself is meant to magically confer the results.

Closer scrutiny of the data from the survey suggests just how unrealistic such a notion is. The combination and permutation of features addressed in the survey creates an incredible number of PBL variants. Adaptations are made for many reasons. Sometimes PBL gets started in a single course or a single course segment, and discipline-related limitations are imposed on what is essentially a multidisciplinary approach. Sometimes adaptations are made because interest in PBL has started in a small group of faculty and there is not enough institutional support (time and resources) to make the structural changes that a full PBL approach would require. There are other reasons, but sometimes adaptations are made because faculty do not trust the PBL process to actually produce the expected student outcomes. They do not trust that well-chosen and well-designed problems and a well-trained tutor can bring them about or that the student can be engaged by the problem and by the knowledge underlying it. Most such adaptations seem designed to protect the knowledge outcome with little attention as to how such adaptation may affect the achievement of the other three outcomes.

Reflecting on the survey data, they also suggest that medical educators are guilty of the same error as that inherent in studies designed to address the efficacy of PBL. Such studies look at apples and generalize to the entire fruit bowl. All PBL is declared effective or ineffective based on data about one of the variants; often the variant is not even fully described. Meta-analyses are uninterpretable under such circumstances.

This leaves the medical education community (and other communities using PBL) with a huge research challenge. We can theorize as to essential elements of a PBL model, and we can theorize as to the consequences of specific adaptations, but we have little empirical data in support or refutation of such theories. Although there are data that show that the Barrows (1992) model of PBL "does no harm" with respect to Step I of United States Medical Licensing Examination (USMLE) scores, the basic science segment of the national licensing examination, and that students from such PBL programs perform significantly better than standard curriculum students in clinical clerkships and in USMLE Step II, the clinical segment of the national licensing examination (Distlehorst & Robbs, 1998), there may be no extant PBL program that can produce sound empirical evidence that its students are achieving the expected outcomes for the long haul. We conclude by suggesting a few areas of research that look at the efficacy of variants of PBL, identify the essential elements which will produce the expected student outcomes, or do both (see also Blumberg, this volume):

1. In theory, providing faculty-designed didactic sessions, learning objectives, references, or relevant readings could influence students' developing ability to respond to problem affordances and consequently their ability to become independent in recognizing and responding to learning demands. Empirical evidence is needed to evaluate these claims.

2. In theory, providing faculty-designed didactic sessions, learning objectives, references, or relevant readings could change the student's goal for learning from one that is problem centered to one that is assignment centered, with the assumption that the latter contributes less to retention and usability. Again, evidence is needed to test the problem-centeredness of the PBL model.

3. There are data to support the conclusion that expertise in the hypothetico–deductive process can be developed through experience (Elstein et al., 1978). In theory, problems that demand full inquiry can provide such experience. However, there is a great economy of time, in both curriculum development and in delivery, to be gained through the use of sequential disclosure problems. Empirically, however, little is known about trade-offs with such adaptations.

4. The Barrows (1992) model holds that the hypothetico–deductive reasoning process is a natural response to problem challenges; one, however, that improves with experience. Consequently, students should merely be guided in this natural process rather than having a process imposed on them. Other models hold that teaching and holding students to specific algorithms produces the more efficient and effective problem solver. Studies are needed to compare the two models.

5. Not all groups develop a climate of mutual responsibility for each other's excellence. We would hypothesize that the absence of grades contributes to such a positive climate. Having the tutor's evaluation directed openly within the group rather than privately is also important. Finally, making the development of this climate the group's responsibility, with the tutor initiating group evaluation of its status, would seem to be critical. Empirical evidence is needed to test these notions.

In conclusion, in the rush to "prove" or to "disprove" the efficacy of PBL, we have failed to define its essential elements. The next generation of research efforts requires open collaboration among the various practitioners of PBL in defining these essential elements and in determining what is lost in terms of expected student outcomes when such elements are reduced, transformed, or removed.

REFERENCES

Barrows, H. S. (1992). *The tutorial process* (2nd ed.). Springfield, IL: Southern Illinois University School of Medicine.

Barrows, H. S., & Feltovich, P. J. (1987). The clinical reasoning process. *Journal of Medical Education, 21*, 86–91.

Barrows, H. S., & Kelson, A. M. (1995). *Problem-based learning: A total approach to education.* Springfield, IL: Southern Illinois University School of Medicine.

Barrows, H. S., Norman, G. R., Neufeld, V. R., & Feightner, J. W. (1982). The clinical reasoning process of randomly selected physicians in general practice. *Clinical and Investigative Medicine, 5,* 49–56.

Bereiter, C., & Scardamalia, M. (1989). Intentional learning as a goal for instruction. In L. B. Resnick (Ed.), *Knowing, learning and instruction: Essays in honor of Robert Glaser* (pp. 361–392). Hillsdale, NJ: Lawrence Erlbaum Associates.

Bereiter, C., & Scardamalia, M. (1993). *Surpassing ourselves.* Chicago, IL: Open Court.

Bransford, J. D., Sherwood, R., Vye, N. J., & Rieser, J. (1986). Teaching thinking and problem-solving: Suggestions from research. *American Psychologist, 41,* 1078–1089.

Bretcher, H. S. (1994). *Group participation: Techniques for leaders and members.* Thousand Oaks, CA: Sage.

Bruffee, K. A. (1993). *Collaborative learning: Higher education, interdependence, and the authority of knowledge.* Baltimore, MD: The Johns Hopkins University Press.

Chi, M. T. H., Feltovich, P. J., & Glaser, R. (1980). Categorization and representation of physics problems by novices and experts. *Cognitive Science, 5,* 121–152.

Chi, M. T. H., Glaser, R., & Rees, E. (1982). Expertise in problem solving. In R. Sternberg (Ed.), *Advances in the psycholgoy of human intelligence* (pp. 7–75). Hillsdale, NJ: Lawrence Erlbaum Associates.

Confey, J. (1990). A review of research on student misconceptions in mathematics, science and programming. In C. Cazden (Ed.), *Review of research in education* (Vol. 16, pp. 3–55). Washington, DC: American Educational Research Association.

Distlehorst, L. H., & Robbs, R. (1998). A comparison of problem-based learning and standard curriculum students: Three years of retrospective data. *Teaching and Learning in Medicine: An International Journal, 10*(3), 131–137.

Elstein, A. S. (1994). What goes around comes around: Return of the hypothetico–deductive strategy. *Teaching and Learning in Medicine, 6*(2), 121–123.

Elstein, A. S., Shulman, L. S., & Sprafka, S. A. (1978). *Medical problem solving: Analysis of clinical reasoning.* Cambridge, MA: Harvard University Press.

Elstein, A. S., Shulman, L. S., & Sprafka, S. A. (1990). Medical problem solving: Ten-year retrospective. *Evaluation and the Health Professions, 13,* 5–36.

Eylon, B., & Linn, M. C. (1988). Learning and instruction: An examination of four research perspectives in science education. *Review of Educational Research, 5,* 251–301.

Feltovich, P. J., Spiro, R. J., Coulson, R. L., & Feltovich, J. (1996). Collaboration within and among minds: Mastering complexity, individually and in groups. In T. Koschman (Ed.), *CSCL: Theory and practice of an emerging paradigm* (pp. 25–44). Mahwah, NJ: Lawrence Erlbaum Associates.

Feltovich, P. J., Spiro, R. J., Coulson, R. L., & Myers Kelson, A. (1995). The reductive bias and the crisis of text (in the law). *Journal of Contemporary Legal Issues, 6,* 187–212.

Gibson, E. J. (1982). The concept of affordances in development: The renaissance of functionalism. In W. A. Collings (Ed.), *The concept of development: The Minnesota symposium on child psychology* (Vol. 15, pp. 55–81). Hillsdale, NJ: Lawrence Erlbaum Associates.

Gibson, J. J. (1977). The theory of affordances. In R. F. Shaw & J. D. Bransford (Eds.), *Perceiving, acting and knowing: Toward an ecological psychology* (pp. 67–82). Hillsdale, NJ: Lawrence Erlbaum Associates.

Koschmann, T., Kelson, A., Feltovich, P. J., & Barrows, H. S. (1996). Computer-supported problem-based learning: A principled approach to the use of computers in collaborative learning. In T. Koschmann (Ed.), *CSCL: Theory and practice of an emerging paradigm* (pp. 83–124). Mahwah, NJ: Lawrence Erlbaum Associates.

McDermott, L. C. (1984). Research on conceptual understanding in mechanics. *Physics Today, 37,* 24–32.

Patel, V. L., & Groen, G. (1986). Knowledge-based solution strategies in medical reasoning. *Cognitive Science, 10,* 91–116.

Patel, V. L., & Groen, G. J. (1991). The general and specific nature of medical expertise: A critical look. In A. Rescission & J. Smith (Eds.), *Toward a general theory of expertise: Prospects and limits* (pp. 93–125). New York: Cambridge University Press.

Roschelle, J. (1996). Learning by collaborating: Convergent conceptual change. In T. Koschman (Ed.), *CSCL: Theory and practice of an emerging paradigm* (pp. 209–248). Mahwah, NJ: Lawrence Erlbaum Associates.

Spiro, R. J., Vispoel, W. L., Schmitz, J., Samarapungavan, A., & Boerger, A. (1987). Knowledge acquisition for application: Cognitive flexibility and transfer in complex content domains. In B. C. Britton & S. Glynn (Eds.), *Executive control processes* (pp. 177–200). Hillsdale, NJ: Lawrence Erlbaum Associates.

Chapter 8

Commentary on Part I: Process and Product in Problem-Based Learning (PBL) Research

Carl Bereiter
Marlene Scardamalia
Ontario Institute for Studies in Education
of the University of Toronto

Let us begin by distinguishing PBL (uppercase) from pbl (lowercase). PBL is a distinctive, well-documented instructional approach that originated in medical education. Although there are variations, and although it has been applied in other disciplines, practitioners of PBL acknowledge its medical school origins and tend to adhere to the structure and procedures systematized by Barrows (1986). Lowercase pbl refers to an indefinite range of educational approaches that give problems a central place in learning activity. Mathematics and physics have traditionally done this, but most other disciplines have not. A problem-based literature course, for instance, would be a novelty even today. However, case-based education, as practiced in law schools and in business schools, would count as lowercase pbl, insofar as the cases are treated as problems to be solved, much like the cases that typically figure in medical PBL.

Lest everything be counted as pbl, however, it is worthwhile to distinguish between exercises and problems. Elementary school mathematics, for instance, is full of exercises that are often glorified as problems. This, however, is a far cry from the kind of mathematics education that Lampert (1990) has pioneered, where the problems with which students wrestle are problems of method and justification, or the kinds of mathematics problems presented in the Jasper Woodbury adventures (Cognition and Technology Group at Vanderbilt, 1997), which are complex, realistic problems much more like medical cases than like typical schoolbook word problems. Uppercase PBL entails more than a focus on problems, however. It also entails a collaborative group process, and it is mainly this aspect of PBL that is treated in the chapters on which we comment. Collaborative group work, certainly a pedagogical novelty in the early days of PBL, has caught on much more widely and is now to be found associated with many forms of lowercase pbl as well.

Our own work, which provides the vantage point from which we write this commentary, is lowercase rather than uppercase pbl. The label we attach to it is *collaborative knowledge building* (Scardamalia & Bereiter, 1994; Scardamalia, Bereiter, & Lamon, 1994). Although our work has been mainly with elementary and middle school students and with graduate students in education, there are notable similarities to PBL as practiced in medical schools:

1. Everything starts with and keeps returning to a problem.
2. Dialog is central to the problem-solving process.
3. An important part of work on a problem is identifying what needs to be found out in order to advance.
4. Small groups work collaboratively on solving the problem.
5. Information search and other tasks are distributed among group members instead of having everyone do the same things.
6. The focus is on achieving a cognitive outcome rather than on producing an artifact or a presentation, thus distinguishing it from much of what is called "project-based learning" (Marx, Blumenfeld, Krajcik, & Soloway, 1997).

However, there are also notable differences:

1. The problems are usually at the level of principles rather than cases; for instance, "How does heat affect matter?" rather than "Why doesn't the ball go through the ring?"
2. The focus is on understanding rather than on reaching a conclusion or achieving a practical result.
3. Problems themselves are expected to undergo transformation in the course of inquiry, as they do in science. Thus, it is not expected that problems will be solved but that the state of collective knowledge will be advanced.
4. The teacher functions as a coinvestigator—moreso than seems to be typical of tutors in PBL.
5. Much of the collaborative problem-solving work is computer mediated and asynchronous in addition to being conducted face-to-face. It uses technology generically known as Computer Supported Intentional Learning Environments, or CSILE™ (Scardamalia & Bereiter, 1994), the most current version of which is Knowledge Forum™.

    6. The software environment supports and structures interactions in ways that would be the responsibility of the tutor in PBL.

These differences raise several points for discussion in light of the research reported in preceding chapters.

THEORY BUILDING: GENERAL THEORIES AND THEORIES OF THE CASE

It is interesting that in several of the excerpts from PBL discussions, students speak of what they are doing as advancing and testing theories. This struck some of the participants in the American Educational Research Association (AERA) discussion (chapter 6) as curious, and they took it as indicating one student's recognition of the tentative character of her ideas. That is no doubt true, but calling something a theory implies more than uncertainty. Some might regard it as a bit pompous. However, if we take a theory to be a coherent explanation of a body of facts, then theory building is precisely what students are supposed to be doing in PBL. We wonder if it would not be helpful to both students and to tutors to make this more explicit.

    Theories are commonly thought of as general in nature, like Newtonian or Darwinian theory. However, there are theories of dinosaur extinction, and they are explanations of a particular case, albeit a very large one. That is, they don't explain species extinction in general but rather a one-time-only event. However, as Thagard (1989) has shown, the same kind of explanation is involved, subject to the same standards of judgment. It is "argument to the best explanation." The best explanation is one that explains all of the facts and that does not imply anything contrary to them. What constitutes the facts needing explaining is a major issue in its own right, but one that we need not go into for the present purposes. It is, however, relevant to note that in the typical case-based PBL session the facts to be explained are all laid out for the students, whereas in collaborative knowledge building, the domain of facts in need of explanation is not constrained and tends to grow as the problem deepens (Bereiter, Scardamalia, Cassels, & Hewitt, 1997). This is characteristic of science, where powerful theoretical principles, such as Newton's laws, turn out to explain facts quite remote from those that initially motivated theory building. Studies of expertise in medical diagnosis make it clear that argument to the best explanation is the expert's way, whereas the novice's way is to reason backward from a tentative diagnosis (Patel & Groen, 1991). Experts are not content with a diagnosis (read here "a theory of the case") that fits the main symptoms. They want to "tie up loose ends" to account for all the facts. Accordingly, learning to pursue argument to the best explanation would seem to be an important part of professional education in medicine. There are indications throughout the chapters under review that tutors recognize this. They are continually trying to nudge students in this direction, pointing out facts that their theories do not explain or pointing out implications that are incompatible with facts. What is worrisome to us is that this high-level monitoring of theory construction may remain in the hands of the tutor; there does not seem to be any organized effort to turn it over to the students. Until that is done, there would seem to be little reason for students to abandon the labor-saving novice strategy: Stick with a diagnosis until somebody shows you what is wrong with it.

In collaborative knowledge building, problem-centered theory construction is singled out as one of the major activities students may engage in. Scaffolds are provided that signal "my theory," "I need to understand," "new information," and "what we have learned." Teachers are encouraged to shift the focus of work from finding answers to improving theories. This has, first of all, the effect of raising the quality of the problems that students formulate. Students have been found to formulate quite different kinds of questions, depending on whether they anticipate that they will be expected to find answers to them (Scardamalia & Bereiter, 1992). When they are expected to find answers, they tend to ask what we call "text-based" questions, questions of the kind that routinely accompany textbooks and for which the answers are to be found in the text. When freed of the obligation to find answers, they ask what we call "knowledge-based" questions, questions that arise from their own puzzlement or perceived lack of understanding. These are questions that teachers and independent raters judge to be of considerably greater educational potential than text-based questions. We have found that shifting the emphasis from finding answers to improving theories encourages students to formulate knowledge-based problems (Scardamalia, Bereiter, Hewitt, & Webb, 1996). Having posed a problem, students next advance their initial theories as solutions. Then, as they acquire additional information by whatever means, they work to improve their theories. This is always possible, whereas finding an answer to a knowledge-based question often is not. The second advantage of shifting from finding answers to improving theories is that it engages students in a process much more like real science, where practitioners seldom expect to discover final answers but rather work to improve on existing knowledge (Bereiter et al., 1997).

BUILDING DISPOSITIONS TOWARD LIFELONG LEARNING

Is PBL merely an alternate way of covering subject matter or is it supposed to produce a different kind of educated person? The expressed intent, of course, is the latter, with the emphasis being on producing people able and willing to solve problems in their fields. Another sort of whole-person out-come that is receiving attention these days, however, is that of producing people who will remain able and willing throughout life to pursue new learning. The need for this is highlighted by technological changes that alter job requirements. In scientifically grounded professions like medi-cine, there is not only the need to master new technology but also the need to continually revise practice in light of advances in knowledge.

Standard PBL practice sends students out in search of knowledge required to solve the immediate problem. To the extent that this experi-ence has long-term effects on dispositions, it should promote one kind of lifelong learning. You could call it a lifelong disposition to do web search-es. That is not a trivial development. The way things are heading, we may see a widening divide between those who utilize web searches in dealing with life's problems and those who do not. Those who do not will most likely be making poorer decisions, receiving poorer services, and paying more money for inferior goods.

However, there is another side to lifelong learning, which is not a mat-ter of obtaining information relevant to immediate action. It is exploiting the potentialities of new knowledge—revising one's beliefs and practices in light of it, building more powerful conceptual frameworks, and coming up with new ideas. This second kind of lifelong learning is problem based as well, but the problems are of a different kind. They are not means–end problems with new knowledge providing the means. Rather, they concern the knowledge itself—its meaning, validity, and implications, its relation to other knowledge, and its possibilities of application.

Both kinds of learning are of obvious lifelong importance. Both are essential to staying on top of one's field. When professional journals arrive we are likely to read them with a knowledge-building purpose. Then we put them on the shelf where, if they are ever taken down again, it is like-ly to be with a means–end purpose in mind. Our work in schools could be criticized for slighting the means–end kind of learning. PBL could be crit-icized for slighting the more open-ended, knowledge-centered kind of learning.

FULLER AND MORE BALANCED PARTICIPATION

Several of the studies reported in the preceding chapters indicate wide individual differences in level of participation by students in the PBL process. There are also some reports of whole groups exhibiting a low level of engagement. None of this is peculiar to PBL, of course, but it is a matter of particular concern because of the expectation that PBL should produce fuller and deeper involvement in the learning. In the next section we consider the role that technology might play in achieving this result, but here we want to consider a more fundamental issue. What are the motivators in PBL? What are students trying to get out of it? Lacking empirical answers to these questions, we can only speculate on the basis of adaptationist assumptions (Anderson, 1990).

Educators tend to be process people and to believe that if they can get the process right it will be intrinsically rewarding. That is the faith that has given rise to most educational innovations of the 1900s—the activity method, the English infant school, open education, learning by discovery, and project-based learning, not to mention a host of more specific inventions such as the microsociety school (Richmond, 1973). PBL clearly reflects the same faith. The inevitable finding is that any given process will be much more engaging for some students than for others. Looking critically at their own lowercase pbl innovations, Lampert, Rittenhouse, and Crumbaugh (1996) discovered a number of students who found the public airing, criticizing, and defending of ideas aversive. Of course, everyone is likely to find these painful at times. We persist, however, because there are other rewards, which come from achievement rather than from process.

Apart from the variable pleasures of participating in the process, the rewards coming from PBL would seem to be the following, in likely order of importance to the student: good grades, awareness of having learned things of future professional value, and a sense of achievement from solving a problem. In principle, the order should be reversed, but it is easy to see why this would not be the case in reality. The presented problems in PBL are not real problems. They are actually puzzles. Real problems are such that when you solve them your situation in the world improves; you can now do something that you couldn't do before or you can understand something that you didn't understand before. To the extent that real problems arise in PBL, they are likely to arise as "learning issues" incidental to solving the puzzle. Solving a puzzle can be rewarding to many people, as evidenced by the popularity of puzzles in newspapers. However, for most people it is a fairly weak attraction, easily overridden by other concerns, such as anxiety over making it through medical school. As for the rewards of acquiring useful knowledge, the evidence is pretty clear. The payoff from PBL comes later than from traditional instruction. On measures of immediate learning traditional instruction does better, whereas PBL does better on long-term retention (chapter 2, this volume). That is fine as far as cognitive outcomes are concerned, but in terms of motivation it means that students in traditional classes are more likely to have a sense that they are gaining knowledge of value.

That brings us to grades, whose motivational importance typically transcends instructional method. Instructional designers can do little to influence the importance of grades, but they do a lot to determine on what grades are based. If grades are based on measures of individual learning, as they evidently usually are in PBL, it is natural for students to opt for any strategy that will enhance their mastery of testable subject matter. Active participation in collaborative problem solving may not figure prominently in such strategies. If grades are based on performance and on participation in the PBL process itself, a grade-maximizing strategy may well call for the kinds of "overparticipation" identified by Duek (chapter 4, this volume). Basing grades on a combination of learning and participation may encourage some to dominate the process while others withdraw and hit the books.

The research on levels of participation would suggest follow-up with experiments to alter reward structures and conditions of adaptation. Three suggested directions are replacing puzzles with real problems, preferably problems arising from the students; finding ways to make what is learned more immediately visible and its importance more salient; and basing grades in part on contribution to others' knowledge advancement.

ROLES FOR TECHNOLOGY IN PBL

Because the focus of this book is on process, we confine our attention to technology that supports processes and ignore such other potentially important technology as computerized presentation and indexing of cases and use of web resources for researching learning issues. The technology we have been developing is of the process-supporting kind, suggested by its generic name, Computer Supported Intentional Learning Environments. Other, more limited kinds of process supports are bulletin boards, chat rooms, and threaded conferencing software, all of which have found some use in versions of PBL. There is also software that supports specific social or cognitive processes. One that could be especially relevant to PBL is Convince Me (Schank, Ranney, & Hoadley, 1995), which provides a way of evaluating argument to the best explanation, as discussed earlier.

The most comprehensive effort that we know of to create a computer-supported environment for PBL is the one reported by Koschmann, Kelson, Feltovich, and Barrows (1996). Koschmann and colleagues have taken each of six phases of PBL and looked for ways that technology could support each of the processes, from problem presentation to reflection. They suggested that use of technological supports should subtlely change pedagogy—and presumably the communicative process through which it is mediated—although they do not specify in what ways. They indicated that only three kinds of communication are to be mediated by computer: transfer of raw data, candidate contributions to an electronic "blackboard," and polling.

The research reported in preceding sections suggests, however, that a more "problem-based" approach to technology for PBL might be justified. Two of the problems that technology might help to solve are the tendency of many tutors to assume too directive a role, complemented by a tendency of students to depend too much on the tutor (chapters 4 and 5, this volume); and disparities in participation and involvement, as noted in the preceding section, resulting in some students dominating the group process while others withdraw.

Any sort of computer conferencing system could be expected to alleviate these problems to some extent. The tutor is no longer at the center of the communication web. Asynchronous communication means that students do not have to capture a conversational turn to contribute to discussions, and so it becomes less likely that a few students will dominate. The more reticent or less verbal student may also benefit from having more time to formulate an utterance. The only drawback to this pretty picture is what Guzdial (1997), in a public address, called "the dirty little secret" of computer-supported collaborative learning: that students don't like computer conferencing very much and that participation is scanty and hard to maintain. We have seen this in CSILE classrooms, where teachers complain that they can't get students to comment, or where discussions peter out after one or two responses. More commonly, however, we see students enthusiastic about carrying out inquiries through CSILE or through Knowledge Forum™ and many instances of sustained collaboration.

The solution, we believe, cannot be through software design alone, but neither can it be through better engineering of social processes. The situation is the same one discussed in the preceding section, whether or not computer support is involved. Computer conferencing is a process, and if participation in the process is the only reward, that will not be sufficient for most people. Indeed, in comparison to face-to-face discussion, computer conferencing probably reduces both the social pains and the social pleasures. If computer support of sociocognitive processes is to be valued by the learners, it has to provide more than an enjoyable experience. It has to pay off in things that students value. In CSILE classes that take on a knowledge-building mission, students report cognitive rewards, not just social ones. They are aware of solving problems that matter to them and achieving important gains in knowledge. That, however, requires designing the whole learning situation so as to produce those yields. When educators set about designing a high-yield environment for building knowledge and for solving real problems, it becomes quickly obvious that technology can help. If, instead, they start with technology and with existing classroom processes, it is often questionable whether the two go together.

We see the kind of research reported in these chapters as providing one important kind of data for further development of PBL. It would be a misuse of the research, however, to start tinkering with participatory structures in the belief that those could be improved without giving serious attention to what makes it worth the students' while to participate at all. For an educational approach with the high aspirations of PBL, that means looking for ways to make participation cognitively more rewarding to the students. That is a large challenge but one that, in our experience, can be met as long as it is kept firmly in view.

DIRECTIONS FOR FUTURE RESEARCH

The authors of the preceding chapters appear to share with us a belief that the point of PBL research is the improvement of practice. On this basis, the reported research must be judged as preliminary, for it is almost all descriptive or correlational. Such research may at times indicate what needs changing, but it cannot be expected to guide invention and experimentation. Still, as Drucker (1985) pointed out in a different context, one of the great spurs to innovation is unexpected findings. Accordingly, it is worth considering further analytic research that holds promise of unexpected findings. The following are a few ideas as to what might lie beyond the current research:

• Research into PBL tutorials as self-organizing systems. The Koschmann, Glenn, and Conlee study (chapter 3, this volume) is a case study that strongly suggests the potential of this approach. What emerges in the tutorial process cannot be explained by the individual actions of tutors and of students, but neither can it be illuminatingly explained by an additive combination of factors, as in the Schmidt and Moust model (chapter 2). Self-organizing systems are characterized by emergent complexity, giving rise to structures that are not predictable from the inputs. Accordingly, they frustrate research of the variable-manipulating kind. However, if, as seems obvious, the definitive task for social research on PBL is to understand emergent behavioral patterns, then it is necessary to bite the bullet.

• Development of proximal outcome measures. Faidley, Evensen, Salisbury-Glennon, Glenn, and Hmelo (chapter 5, this volume), after demonstrating a coherent pattern of relations among students' perceptions and observed group performance, noted that their measures were "probably too unrefined to test for the relation between performance and group effectiveness." Although effectiveness must ultimately be judged by what students have learned, learning measures are too distant from the process to be helpful in improving it. A more immediate result that needs to be evaluated is whether a collaborative problem-solving episode made progress—advanced toward a solution or toward fuller understanding. Assessing the progress of a discourse remains a challenge that discourse analysts have not fully met, but it is a challenge that surely needs to be taken up by PBL researchers.

• Opportunistic research. When graduate students undertake research using transcripts or recordings, they typically strive for exhaustive classification, using some predetermined scheme. They don't want to miss anything. Yet if they find out anything interesting, it almost comes from noticing something that lies outside their classification scheme. Chapter 6 of this volume provides a sampling of approaches to analysis of a single segment of videotaped PBL. The approaches range from "What's interesting here?" to "How can we exhaustively describe the multilayered processes represented here?" The situation does not permit a fair comparison of these approaches, but based on our readings of related research over the years, we would say that the first approach is decidedly superior, provided there is a sufficiently well-developed conceptual framework within which to judge what is interesting. We therefore want to conclude our punditry by urging researchers to be less concerned about coding, to stand back from their data, to ask themselves "What's interesting here?" and then to pursue those interesting observations until they begin to yield insight.

If the ultimate objective is improvement of PBL, however, then at some point there needs to be a shift to design experiments (Brown, 1992), where results are fed back into further cycles of design. In earlier sections we have suggested innovations such as moving away from exclusively case-based problems and making theory construction a more salient aspect of the process. Of course, there are already many variations in practice, creating quite a fuzzy boundary between uppercase PBL and lowercase pbl. Those who think that there is something special about the pure version that should not be lost are rightly suspicious of innovations that threaten to obliterate its identity so that it becomes lost amid the host of educational approaches that are in some sense problem based. However, few people, we assume, want PBL to be a cult. The only alternative that we can see is for PBL to become a principled program of ongoing instructional design, and it is in sympathy with that conception that we offer this commentary.

REFERENCES

Anderson, J. R. (1990). *The adaptive character of thought*. Hillsdale, NJ: Lawrence Erlbaum Associates.

Barrows, H. S. (1986). A taxonomy of problem-based learning methods. *Medical Education, 20*, 481–486.

Bereiter, C., Scardamalia, M., Cassels, C., & Hewitt, J. (1997). Postmodernism, knowledge-building, and elementary science. *Elementary School Journal, 97,* 329–340.

Brown, A. L. (1992). Design experiments: Theoretical and methodological challenges in creating complex interventions in classroom settings. *The Journal of the Learning Sciences, 2*(2), 141–178.

Cognition and Technology Group at Vanderbilt (1997). *The Jasper project: Lessons in curriculum, instruction, assessment, and professional development.* Mahwah, NJ: Lawrence Erlbaum Associates.

Diehl, C., & Schank, R. C. (1995, April). *Multiple representations for improving scientific thinking.* Paper presented at the meeting of the American Education Research Association, San Francisco, CA.

Drucker, P. (1985). *Innovation and entrepreneurship.* New York: Harper & Row.

Guzdial, M. (1997). Information ecology of collaborations in educational settings: Influence of tool. In R. Hall, N. Miyake, & N. Enyedy (Eds.), *CSCL '97* (pp. 83–90). Toronto: CSCL.

Koschmann, T. D., Kelson, A. C., Feltovich, P. J., & Barrows, H. S. (1996). Computer-supported problem-based learning: A principled approach to the use of computers in collaborative learning. In T. D. Koschmann (Ed.), *CSCL: Theory and practice of an emerging paradigm* (pp. 83–124). Hillsdale, NJ: Lawrence Erlbaum Associates.

Koschmann, T. D., Myers, A. C., Feltovich, P. J., & Barrows, H. S. (1994). Using technology to assist in realizing effective learning and instruction: A principled approach to the use of computers in collaborative learning. *The Journal of the Learning Sciences, 3,* 227–264.

Lampert, M. (1990). When the problem is not the question and the solution is not the answer: Mathematical knowing and teaching. *American Educational Research Journal, 27*(1), 29–64.

Lampert, M., Rittenhouse, P., & Crumbaugh, C. (1996). Agreeing to disagree: Developing sociable mathematical discourse. In D. Olson &. N. Torrance (Eds.), *Handbook of education and human development: New models of learning, teaching and schooling* (pp. 731–764). Cambridge, MA: Basil Blackwell.

Marx, R. W., Blumenfeld, P. C., Krajcik, J. S., & Soloway, E. (1997). Enacting project-based science. *Elementary School Journal, 97,* 341–358.

Patel, V. L., & Groen, G. J. (1991). The general and specific nature of medical expertise: A critical look. In K. A. Ericsson & J. Smith (Eds.), *Toward a general theory of expertise: Prospects and limits* (pp. 93–125). Cambridge: Cambridge University Press.

Richmond, G. H. (1973). *The micro-society school: A real world in miniature.* New York: Harper & Row.

Scardamalia, M., & Bereiter, C. (1992). Text-based and knowledge-based questioning by children. *Cognition and Instruction, 9*(3), 177–199.

Scardamalia, M., & Bereiter, C. (1994). Computer support for knowledge-building communities. *The Journal of the Learning Sciences, 3*(3), 265–283.

Scardamalia, M., Bereiter, C., Hewitt, J., & Webb, J. (1996). Constructive learning from texts in biology. In K. M. Fischer & M. Kirby (Eds.), *Relations and biology learning: The acquisition and use of knowledge structures in biology* (pp. 44–64). Berlin: Springer-Verlag.

Scardamalia, M., Bereiter, C., & Lamon, M. (1994). The CSILE project: Trying to bring the classroom into World 3. In K. McGilley (Eds.), *Classroom lessons: Integrating cognitive theory and classroom practice* (pp. 201–228). Cambridge, MA: MIT Press.

Schank, P., Ranney, M., & Hoadley, C. (1995). Convince Me [Computer program and manual]. In J. R. Jungck, N. Peterson, & J. N. Calley (Eds.), *The BioQUEST library.* College Park, MD: Academic Software Development Group, University of Maryland.

Thagard, P. (1989). Explanatory coherence. *Behavioral and Brain Sciences, 12,* 435–502.

Part II

Self-Directed Learning

Evaluating the Evidence That Problem-Based Learners Are Self-Directed Learners: A Review of the Literature

Phyllis Blumberg
University of the Sciences in Philadelphia

Through an analysis of research evidence, this chapter supports the hypothesis that students participating in problem-based learning (PBL) curricula demonstrate self-directed learning skills. Various types of self-directed learning research is reviewed. In addition to that which compares students and graduates of PBL programs with their counterparts in traditional, lecture-based curricula, the review also focuses on research that assesses PBL students and graduates themselves. In particular, the literature on students' and teachers' perceptions is considered. The conceptual framework directing this review evolves from Candy's (1991) model of self-directed learning (SDL). Candy organized this model along three dimensions: the process of learning itself, learning strategies, and performance outcomes of SDL.

ORGANIZING FRAMEWORK

To provide a concise way in which to think about SDL research, I developed a 3 (dimensions) × 2 (levels of breadth) framework to organize studies reviewed in this chapter (Table 9.1). The three dimensions, as stated previously, are learning processes, learning strategies, and performance outcomes. The first dimension, learning processes, relates to abilities to define what to learn; plan and operationalize learning, specifically through time management; seek, use, and evaluate the effectiveness of

TABLE 9.1
Organizing Framework for Research Reviewed

Dimension	Learning Process	Learning Strategies	Outcomes: Short Term & Long Term
Breadth			
Component	See Table 9.2 for specific studies	See Table 9.4 for specific studies	See Table 9.5 for specific studies
Holistic	See Table 9.2 for specific studies	Not applicable	See Table 9.5 specific studies

resources; and evaluate SDL skills. Along the second dimension, learning strategies refer to the methods students use to study material or process information. The performance outcomes, the variables along the third dimension, are classified as either short term (immediate) or long term (years after students completed the PBL program). The breadth of each dimension of the framework is conceptualized as either component or holistic skills and forms the other axis of the organizing matrix. This distinction is made between studies that investigate SDL skills as discrete entities or those that look at SDL skills more globally.

All of the reviewed research is classified in an appropriate cell of the framework (Table 9.1), with each cell further delineated in Tables 9.2, 9.4 and 9.5 (see later in text). Many different research methodologies are appropriate for examining SDL (as discussed in the next section). Hence, each of the studies is classified into three types of research methods: self-report, faculty report, or performance data. Some studies collected more than one type of data and thus are placed in several cells on the summary tables. These summary tables also show empty cells indicating areas where no work has been done or areas where it would not be logical to do such research. In light of this absence of research, this chapter concludes with a proposed research agenda outlining areas where further study is needed.

Rationale for Research Methods Considered

Although the underpinnings of PBL are clearly derived from social learning theories, learning is still largely an individual phenomenon. Individual learners, therefore, need to be considered key informants in any research on learning processes. This acceptance of the primacy of the learner-in-context becomes even more relevant when SDL is studied (Candy, 1991). Hence, self-report data are crucial to understanding and evaluating the SDL process. These data will include the person's direct perceptions of himself or of herself. In addition, self-report data can be used to help in the process of data triangulation needed to draw inferences about the processes underlying students' work and achievement. The ability to accurately evaluate oneself is often included in definitions of SDL (Candy, 1991; Jennett, 1992). Thus, self-evaluations become an essential aspect to be included in a comprehensive review of research on PBL programs. Studies on students' developing abilities to self-evaluate, to introspect, or to think about their skills need to be considered in studies of SDL.

In addition to the learner's perspective, those who assist the learners in this process are also relevant informants (Candy, 1991). For PBL, the planners of the curriculum and those who facilitate the small-group discussions of cases or problems are key informants to understanding learning processes. Those who assist students or trainees should evaluate learners on adequacy and accuracy of knowledge, appropriateness of resources used, and the type and amount of assistance given in relation to the students' ability to learn in a self-directed fashion. In short, faculty who facilitate the small-group discussions should evaluate their students on their progress toward becoming self-directed learners. Likewise, people who teach advanced students coming from problem-based programs or those who supervise these graduates are important evaluators to assess long-term SDL skills.

Both the processes of learning and performance outcomes are relevant subjects for SDL research and need to be documented. Performance outcomes should be measured both during the learning phase as well as over a longer term. An important outcome to measure is the ability of the learner to apply and use what is learned in new situations; this can be both in the short term and in the long term. Highly competent practitioners see the need to continuously acquire new knowledge that is application-driven and to reflect before taking actions in new situations (Schön, 1987). Therefore, the ability to be a reflective practitioner is also a key element to be evaluated in self-directed learners. One of the most important long-term outcomes is for the learner to remain a lifelong learner. Thus, SDL is an ongoing process that is essential to remaining professionally current.

LEARNING PROCESSES

Table 9.2 summarizes the research discussed relating to learning processes. Component skills that have been studied include the ability to define what to learn; the ability to plan and operationalize learning, specifically time management skills; and the ability to seek out, use, and evaluate resources. More holistic studies examine these SDL skills in combination.

TABLE 9.2
Summary of Research Reviewed on Learning Process

	Type of Data Collected		
Category	Self-Report	Faculty Report	Performance
Component Skills			
Ability to define what to learn	Rosenfeld (1995)	Blumberg, Michael, & Zeitz (1990)	Schmidt et al. (1993)
Ability to plan, operationalize learning: time management	Blumberg & Michael (1992) Gijselaers & Schmidt (1992) Williams, Saarinen-Rahikka, & Norman (1995)		
Ability to seek, use, and evaluate the effectiveness of resources	Watkins (1993) Blumberg & Michael (1992) Saunders, Northup, & Mennin (1985) Rankin (1992) Marshall et al. (1993) Friden (1994) Blumberg (1997)		Blumberg & Sparks (1999)
Holistic			
Ability to evaluate self-directed learning skills	Blumberg & Michael (1992) Ryan (1993) Blumberg & Daugherty (1994)	Blumberg & Michael (1992) Blumberg & Daugherty (1994)	Blumberg, Michael, & Zeitz (1990) Blumberg, Cohen, Ryan, & Sullivan (1994)

Component Skills

Ability to Define What to Learn. Candy (1991) argued that a self-directed learner should be able to define what needs to be learned. The process of defining and using student-generated learning issues may be an essential element in the development of SDL skills. PBL programs differ in the importance that they place on students' defining what needs to be learned. In the more student-centered programs, students are expected to develop their own learning issues, which emerge from the discussions of cases. These student-generated learning issues play a central role in defining the content to be learned and the focus of the discussions of the cases. Two studies relating to the ability to define what to learn are listed on the first row of Table 9.2. Faculty-reported research is discussed before self-report research because the former sets the context for the latter.

Blumberg, Michael, and Zeitz (1990) reviewed the seven extant PBL medical curricula in North America in the late 1980s to compare their use of student-generated learning issues. Using a structured interview, key informants from each of these programs were asked questions regarding the use of student-generated learning issues at their medical schools. Informants were asked to describe the common practice. In five of the seven programs, student-generated learning issues played a major role in defining the content to be learned. In most of these PBL programs, however, students had access to faculty-generated objectives. Only the medical students in the Primary Care Curriculum at the University of New Mexico did not have access to faculty objectives. Students in four of these programs (McMaster Faculty of Health Sciences, the Alternative Curriculum of Rush Medical College, the PBL curriculum of the Bowman Gray School of Medicine, and the New Pathway at Harvard University School of Medicine) measured their own issues against faculty objectives that were made available at different times in the discussion of the case. In some of these student-centered programs, the student-generated learning issues played a role in program evaluation in that they were used as a tool to review the curriculum (Blumberg et al., 1990).

In more faculty-centered programs, the students were given learning objectives that they were expected to master (Blumberg et al., 1990). Student-generated learning issues played a secondary role in the faculty-centered programs, such as the Track II program at Michigan State University and Mercer College of Medicine, where student-generated learning issues were deemphasized in favor of faculty objectives and required reading lists. The study found that students in these programs rarely selected additional material to read and librarians had little contact with problem-based curriculum students. In contrast, librarians from the problem-based programs that relied heavily on student-generated learning issues reported extensive contact with students. The two faculty-centered programs did not evaluate their students on their ability to develop student-generated learning issues. Interestingly, faculty from these two schools reported that their students had a decreased motivation to become self-directed learners (Blumberg et al., 1990).

This last study demonstrates that PBL and SDL may not be synonymous; rather, SDL results from PBL programs that are more student-centered. In the remainder of this chapter, research is reviewed from the more student-centered PBL programs because little research on SDL has been conducted at the faculty-centered programs. PBL programs are cited without reference to the student–faculty–centered continuum.[1]

Faculty expect that their learning objectives at least partially direct students' learning even in student-centered PBL programs. However, this may not always be the case. Rosenfeld (1995) asked second-year PBL medical students at McMaster University to describe how and how often they used faculty learning objectives. Although these students had very specific faculty-generated learning objectives available to them at the beginning of the unit, most of them reported that they did not consult these lists prior to the discussion of the cases. Students reported that they most frequently used the faculty objectives as a checklist at the end of the case to ensure that they had covered all of the relevant topics. The majority of the students either collectively referred to these faculty objectives at the end of their group discussions of a specific case or individually used the list to check the completeness of their content knowledge. When students found they had not covered an objective, they learned this material independently or made it a group learning issue (Rosenfeld).

Rosenfeld (1995) explained that the confidence these students have in their ability to define what they should learn relates to the philosophy of this educational program. The entire Faculty of Health Sciences at McMaster University is PBL, thus the medical students cannot compare what they learn to what lecture-based students learn. Exams are not directly related to cases but evaluate students on broad knowledge and understanding. It appeared that these students were comfortable with PBL and had no reason to believe that they were not mastering the relevant material. In a school where two tracks coexist, PBL students may be more motivated to compare their learning to faculty-generated objectives to be sure they are covering the same content as the traditional students.

Ability to Plan and Operationalize Learning. Self-directed learners need to understand what is required in order to learn. This includes time

---

[1]Unless otherwise indicated, the research comes from entire PBL curricula and not from hybrid lecture–PBL programs.

management, the strategies learners used to acquire resources, efficient access and use of resources, the type of assistance sought, and the learner's evaluation of the effectiveness of resources. The studies discussed in this section are listed in the second and third rows of Table 9.2. Only self-report studies are relevant here because only the students have access to their planning processes and can be aware of how they reached their learning endpoints.

Time management is an appropriate measure because self-directed learners need to be able to make efficient use of their time. Students who spend too much time on one activity, such as searching for materials, and do not leave adequate time for organization or synthesis may not be good self-directed learners or productive members of the group discussing the problem. Self-reported time spent in independent study is generally considered an appropriate measure of effort (Schmidt, Van Der Arend, Moust, Kokx, & Boon, 1993). Self-reported estimates from traditional and from PBL medical students indicated that both types of students spend about the same amount of time per week in educational activities, but that PBL students spent more time in nonscheduled, or SDL activities (Blumberg & Michael, 1992). Increasing instructional and other scheduled time, as is the case for traditional students, generally led to less independent study time (Gijselaers & Schmidt, 1992). Diaries of occupational and physical therapy problem-based students indicated that they spent between 32 and 49 hours per week in nonscheduled educational activities. During their academic weeks, the grand ratios of nonscheduled to scheduled time were 2.85 to 1 for both types of rehabilitative science students. As the students progressed through their programs, they spent less time in both scheduled and unscheduled educational activities. Authors have attributed the decrease in self-directed or unscheduled activities to greater efficiency (Williams, Saarinen-Rahikka, & Norman, 1995).

Informal interviews with medical students at two different problem-based programs, rehabilitative sciences students at one university, and public health students at another, offer some explanations for why experience leads to greater time efficiency for PBL students. Novice PBL students reported that they are overwhelmed with their learning tasks. As they progress through the program, they are better able to determine the depth of the information they are required to know, they become very familiar with using the library and human resources effectively, and they can gain information more efficiently.

Schmidt and colleagues (1993) compared the self-reported study time and achievement of 1,120 undergraduate health sciences students at the University of Maastricht in seven different problem-based undergraduate programs in a cross-sectional study of all four years. These researchers found that as students get more proficient at PBL, they spend more time engaged in self-study if they have content-expert group facilitators. This finding did not hold for first- and for second-year students. Schmidt and colleagues explained that early PBL students relied more heavily on their facilitators for content knowledge and direction regardless of their level of expertise as facilitators, and performance indicators revealed that these students performed better when they relied more on the facilitator. Thus, these novice students reported spending relatively equal amounts of time in independent study. By contrast, upper level students showed an effect for tutor expertise. Third-year students reported spending 15% more time, and fourth-year students reported spending 47% more time in self-study when they had expert tutors. There were small, but still significant differences in achievement in the last 2 years depending on the expertise of the facilitators.

One possible explanation of these complex results with advanced problem-based learners is that an expert facilitator uses the subject matter in such a way as to ask more difficult or stimulating questions. This leads the students to spend more time in self-study pushing the frontiers of their knowledge. However, both groups of advanced students are good enough self-directed learners that they learn what they need to learn to do well on their tests. Perhaps the tests do not ask enough advanced questions to be able to distinguish the levels of learning among the advanced students.

Resources Sought. The research on resource use is reviewed in this section and is listed in the third row of Table 9.2. Resources can be classified as either self-directed or as teacher directed. Materials developed for a specific class, such as course syllabi or cooperative lecture notes generated by the students, are teacher directed. Resources intended for a more general audience, and especially those not assigned, are self-directed because the learners have to decide what they want to learn from these resources. Textbooks may be both teacher directed or self-directed depending on the stimulus and the motivation for using them. Because most PBL courses do not have assigned texts, PBL medical students often consult as many as 7 to 15 different texts. Watkins (1993) found that this practice of consulting many different books encourages the development of personal libraries early in students' medical education careers.

At the end of each of the 2 years of the preclinical curricula at Rush Medical College, students in both the traditional lecture-based and in the PBL tracks were asked to indicate on a five point scale, from 1 (*never*) to 5 (*always*), how frequently they used eight study resources and five types of library resources and how they used these resources (Blumberg & Michael, 1992). There were highly significant differences in the ratings of these resources between the two groups of students. The three resources used most frequently by the PBL students were textbooks (4.74), informal discussions with faculty or with peers (3.42), and journals or other books

(3.06). The authors classified these resources as self-directed resources because specific reading assignments were not given in the PBL track. The traditional track students most frequently used faculty-prepared course syllabi (4.80) and cooperative lecture notes (4.21), which the authors classified as teacher directed, and textbooks (3.26). Because these traditional students reported that they read specific, teacher-generated assignments, textbooks here were classified as teacher directed. Further, these students rated the frequency of their use of each library resource. The traditional curriculum students reported using all types of library resources less than four times a year, whereas the PBL students reported using all library resources weekly. The PBL students reported using computer bibliographic searches two to three times a month (Blumberg & Michael, 1992).

The results of the study just described were further confirmed by several independent surveys of library usage among many PBL and among traditional medical students (Friden, 1994; Marshall, Fitzgerald, Busby, & Heaton, 1993; Rankin, 1992; Saunders, Northup, & Mennin, 1985). Compared to the traditional students, the PBL students made significantly greater use of the library, of library services, and of student-directed and self-selected (as opposed to faculty-selected) reading materials. They also spent more time in the library at each visit and frequently felt competent in information-seeking skills. These findings have been replicated in so many different settings that it should be concluded that PBL students use libraries and library collections and services more often and more comprehensively than traditional students.

Blumberg and Sparks (1999) found that the type of self-directed resources consulted is probably dependent on the discipline being studied as well as the learning requirements of the case. For example, the School of Public Health at Allegheny University of the Health Sciences has a PBL Master of Public Health program. The disciplines emphasized in the first semester of this integrated curriculum are epidemiology, natural history of disease process, and bio-statistics. To have a comprehensive understanding of the issues in the cases, students were frequently required to obtain current statistics on the incidence and prevalence of diseases and the causes of morbidity and mortality in American populations. This type of information is found easily on the Internet. In the middle of the fall 1996 semester these students were asked to list the resources they found most helpful and useful. Of 25 students in the class, 24 (96%) stated that the Internet was the most helpful and most used resource, and 72% found computer bibliographic information-searching resources useful. Both textbooks and human resources were very useful for 44% of the class. Textbooks were seen as less useful because they did not contain the type of material the students needed and the textbooks did not explain the material clearly enough for the students. Journals were a very useful resource for 36% of the class.

These same students were asked this question again during the following spring 1997 semester that emphasized the behavioral sciences such as developmental and health psychology. In contrast to their earlier responses, none of the students found the Internet to be their most useful resource. Instead they preferred their textbooks and journal articles (Blumberg & Sparks, 1999). In short, students found the information required for their epidemiology course, such as the number of White women who died of breast cancer in 1990, on the Internet, but they were not able to find critical evaluations of behavioral theories there. This may also have reflected the state of the Internet during its early years of development, especially before many journals were available through the World Wide Web.

Evaluating the Effectiveness of Resources. Professionals need to make decisions based on accurate information or from empirical research. Health professionals are expected to use evidence-based practice to remain competent and current professionals. This type of practice implies that professionals assimilate current research findings into their knowledge base and use the findings to help in making decisions. One of the basic tenets of evidence-based practice is that one must evaluate the accuracy and validity of information gained (Evidence Based Working Group, 1992). Yet, many students do not know how to evaluate the accuracy of resources. There appears to be almost blind trust that what is written, especially in textbooks or in journals, or spoken by a human resource, such as a faculty member, practitioner, or community resource person, is true. However, this ability to evaluate evidence to inform decisions is often associated with the type of SDL that PBL attempts to foster.

Eight weeks into the first semester of the Allegheny University Master's in Public Health program, 24 students were given a take-home examination (Blumberg & Sparks, 1999). One of the questions on this exam asked students to list their most helpful resources, to justify why they were most useful, and to critically evaluate these resources. Six months later, at the midpoint of the second semester on another take-home examination, 23 remaining students were asked to answer the same question about their use of resources. Table 9.3 summarizes the students' level of critical evaluation in their first and second semesters. The students changed their perceptions of the usefulness of their resources. They started with an unquestioning acceptance of their resources and became selective and critical as the year progressed. One explanation for these differences in the way the students answered the question relates to their developing abilities to evaluate their resources and their own SDL. The students who appeared to lack insights regarding the use of resources may not have realized the importance of evaluating and reflecting, or they may not have

TABLE 9.3
Evaluation of Resources Used by PBL Students

Level of Critical Evaluation Criteria	Midpoint 1st Semester	Midpoint 2nd Semester
Merely listed resource: no explanation	6/24 (25%)	3/23 (13%)
Justified usefulness without critical evaluation	12/24 (50%)	2/23 (9%)
Evaluated strengths only	4/24 (17%)	1/23 (4%)
Evaluated strengths and weakness	2/24 (8%)	17/23 (74%)

taken the question seriously enough on the examination (Blumberg & Sparks, 1999).

Quotes from the more reflective answers discussing their critical evaluations show the students' understandings of their own learning. (Blumberg, 1997 unpublished data):

The Internet

Student A: There is a wealth of resources on the Internet. While it does not replace the books and journals in the university library, it is very useful in obtaining most recent federal documents in the fastest and most convenient way. One must, however, be very careful in selecting the articles on the Internet since anyone can write anything even if he or she is not an expert on the field. There is no quality assurance on the Internet. The following sites were useful: Cancer Statistics Page. It was very useful in providing graphs and figures on various cancer incidence, prevalence, survival rates and mortality rates. It does not go beyond 1980 so if the trend is needed, Health 1995 is still the resource for this.

Student B: Although the Internet seems to be a good beginning source of information, I have found most of the sites to contain only summary information, and therefore supplementation is usually necessary. The other major problem with the Internet for me has been believability. Information that is in print always suggests to me that it is somehow authoritative, but because the Internet is not really filtered for accuracy, I have had to learn to become more skeptical when I am not familiar with the source of the information.

Journal Articles

Student C: One example is the way I am learning to read journal articles. I previously accepted the conclusion put forth by the authors of a study simply because the study appeared in a journal. Although my newfound grasp of data interpretation is quite rudimentary, I have learned that data can be manipulated, seen how sample size can effect outcome and how confounding factors can introduce bias.

Student D: This is still, in my mind, the best way to find new, specific, respected research on a topic. You still have to be a critical reader and read more than one article to be sure you are getting a good understanding.

Student E: Journal articles have been the most consistent source of information for me. I find them useful because they are generally well structured, they rarely have extraneous information, and they can be relied on to be up-to-date. The drawbacks of journal articles are that they can often be slanted, they are sometimes too specific, and they require more critical evaluation to accept their validity.

The previous quotes are examples of different students learning to engage in evidence-based practice and learning how to evaluate the appropriateness of various resources. These students are clearly demonstrating an understanding of the limitations of the Internet rather than just seeing the strengths of the resource, suggesting that they are learning to be more critical in their use of resources. They are also showing an understanding of how evidence in journal articles can be slanted toward a particular point of view.

Reference Books

Student F: The Vital Statistics of the United States of America volumes are useful because they offer actual numbers telling how many people died, in a specific population, geographical region, state or province, the demographics behind the deaths and the causes of deaths. I liked being able to search past statistics and compare to more recent statistics. I did not like the possibility of inaccurate numbers when researching causes of death. Also, I would have liked the causes of death broken down more specifically (into different population subgroups).

This comment probably reflects the specific learning issues that students generated from the cases on morbidity. They researched how causes of death are recorded and found them to be subject to the doctor's knowledge of the patient. The students also found the classifying categories of White, African-American, Asian and two types of Hispanic populations to be lacking. For example, in the named source all Hispanic people are considered alike, whereas, according to other sources, each nationality has different risks for diseases.

Students develop conditional knowledge as they become more self-directed. In the next example, students show an understanding of when human resources are appropriate and helpful.

Human Resources

> Student G: I have recently learned to call organizations throughout the city to locate information . . . In general these resources are great because they are focused on community outreach and they seem anxious to share information. However, in some cases I felt that the information might have been inaccurate because my call had been directed to someone who was not really knowledgeable about the question I was asking.

> Student H: One great method I have learned this block is that one need not turn to a written source of information. It is beneficial to seek out individuals from organizations and ask them about their work. The answers received may be biased but so can any journal article. It is important to keep an open mind when gathering information.

> Student I: Perhaps the most beneficial resources I utilized this block were the contributions of other students . . . In critically assessing their contributions, however, I must remember that each person's experience is just that—one person's experience.

Professionals rely heavily on human resources and yet traditional students often do not learn to how to call on experts in their field. These early problem-based learners have developed the self-directed skill of knowing whom to call, what information to expect from experts, and how to evaluate the information learned. This last quote illustrates the power of collaborative learning that has been practiced through a PBL curriculum.

The ability to use a wide variety of resources and to use them appropriately and effectively are characteristics of self-directed learners. The evidence obtained from diverse types of health-professional students indicates that PBL fosters these skills.

Holistic Skills

The research on the holistic evaluation of SDL skills is listed on the bottom row of Table 9.2. Recall that studies of holistic skills involve all of the SDL skills combined.

Evaluation of Students' SDL Skills. Many PBL curricula evaluate students on their SDL skills within the small-group tutorial discussions. Inherent in the PBL process within the more student-centered curricula are students' definition of learning issues. Between sessions, students either acquire the necessary resources on their own or read from assigned or recommended assignments. At the beginning of the follow-up session students describe what resources they used, discuss how helpful they were, and share particularly good ones with the other students if they have not done so before class. This brief discussion helps students to develop a working knowledge of useful resources for different types of objectives, as well as to practice evaluating their search strategies. At the end of each session students are expected to evaluate their own and their peers' performance. This self-evaluation ability is theorized to be an essential characteristic of self-directed learners (Candy, 1991).

Throughout the PBL program at the School of Public Health at Allegheny University of the Health Sciences, students are evaluated on learning skills along with other dimensions. Students and faculty have checklists for each of these dimensions to guide their self-, peer, and facilitator evaluations of students' performance in their small-group PBL sessions. Eleven characteristics are listed for learning skills including many that have already been discussed. Some additional characteristics include the following: prioritizing learning objectives, focusing study questions, identifying group and personal areas of knowledge deficit, gathering relevant information from primary sources, searching information broadly, integrating material effectively to evaluate the quality of the information, and demonstrating a commitment to quality learning (Allegheny University of the Health Sciences, 1996).

The PBL programs that value the students' developing SDL skills, such as their ability to define their own learning objectives and to obtain their own resources, usually also have formal evaluation mechanisms that are intended, among other things, to assess SDL more holistically. For many programs, evaluations take the form of the "triple jump" or "Individual Process Assessment" (Blumberg et al., 1990). These types of exercises require individual students to simulate what they usually do in a group; however, both the content to be learned and the time to complete the case are reduced. These evaluation tools require individual students to generate hypotheses that attempt to explain the scenario and to generate learning issues that follow from these hypotheses and the case. Students then seek out resources, appraise the information, synthesize their knowledge related to their self-generated learning issues, and finally demonstrate their mastery of the content. Although many PBL health professional schools employ such examinations, research has not documented how differential performance on these measures relates to the development of SDL, nor have empirical comparisons of PBL and traditional students been attempted using these measures.

As part of a program evaluation for accreditation, medical students and faculty associated with both traditional and with problem-based tracks at Rush Medical College were asked to describe perceived advantages and disadvantages of their own track (Blumberg & Michael, 1992). SDL skills were not mentioned by students or faculty in relation to the traditional curriculum. On the other hand, the PBL students reported that one of the strong benefits of their curriculum was that they learned to be good self-directed learners. They reported an increased ability to define what they needed to learn independently, to find the relevant resources, and to see gaps in their own mastery of the material. The self-study document reported that faculty noted a consistent difference in students in the two tracks in their self-directed learning skills. Faculty felt that the PBL students possessed skills that included their willingness to admit a lack of understanding and to consequently pursue relevant resources to remediate their deficiencies and an ability to obtain information on their own. Also, PBL students asked more questions. These differences continued to be noted by respondents into the clinical years.

Registered nurses taking their first university-level course to upgrade their credentials participated in a study that explored the relation between the importance they placed on developing SDL skills and perceptions of their own abilities (Ryan, 1993). Three times during a PBL course on nursing practice, these part-time students rated their competency as self-directed learners and their perceived importance of SDL. The students perceived SDL to be important from the beginning, but they valued this attribute significantly more as the semester continued. The scores for perceived ability changed significantly from low to moderate in the beginning of the semester through moderate to high by the end of the semester. Ryan hypothesized that it was a highly supportive environment that overtly assisted these students to develop and successfully use their SDL abilities. The group facilitators encouraged the development of SDL skills and students received regular feedback on their progress. In addition, students were asked to critically reflect on their learning processes periodically throughout the semester (Ryan).

The ability to evaluate the usefulness of one's learning is a characteristic of SDL (Candy, 1991). Research, therefore, should also look at the students' view of their acquired learning. The approach that a learner uses in any educational endeavor is influenced by the purpose that the learner has in mind. The student's interest in the content to be learned, personal commitment to the discipline, previous knowledge, and perceptions of competence all relate to the learner's perceptions of the learning task at hand (Marton & Saljo, 1976a).

Medical students, because of the keen competition for admissions and for residency positions in North America, are highly motivated and generally do well on exams. However, students often complain that their traditional preclinical courses and examinations are not professionally relevant because they require mastery of highly technical and specialized knowledge areas that do not reflect medical practice. Even examination items that appear to involve problem solving often simply require students to call on memorized material in applying basic science knowledge to a practiced problem. Thus, medical students in traditional curricula often place their preclinical education into the category of "learning for school." One of the reasons PBL has become popular is because it appears to have high face validity—students discuss medical cases throughout their preclinical education. It is more likely that PBL medical students would classify their learning more as "learning for life."

Medical faculty and students in PBL or in traditional first- and second-year preclinical curricula from Rush Medical College were asked to rate 17 educational activities according to how effective this activity was for passing an examination and how effective this activity was for becoming a good physician (Blumberg & Daugherty, 1994). Within each curriculum, correlations were computed for the relation between perceptions for passing examinations and for becoming a good physician for both faculty and for students. The PBL students perceived that activities that were effective for passing exams were also effective for becoming a good physician ($r = .83$). On the other hand, the traditional curriculum students felt that there was almost no relation between their activities that were effective for passing examinations and those for becoming good physicians ($r = .07$). This could be seen as learning for the short-term goals of their education. The activities most valued most by the students from each curricula, passing an examination for traditionals, and becoming a good physician for PBL students, received parallel ratings of importance from faculty in each curricular track. Seeking out information on their own and improving and updating their knowledge were two of the SDL skills rated most highly by PBL students. These activities were seen as useful for both passing examinations and for professional practice.

A review of 632 end-of-curricular-unit summative evaluations, representing the whole range of McMaster PBL medical students from those "not making satisfactory progress" through those deemed "entirely satisfactory," revealed 243 specific concerns or worries about learning (Blumberg, Cohen, Ryan, & Sullivan, 1994). Throughout the program the students were evaluated on six dimensions, including self-directed skills. Evaluations from the first curricular unit had significantly more concerns than any other preclerkship unit. Almost 65% of the concerns detected in the first unit were related to three dimensions: personal qualities, clinical skills, and learning skills. The number of concerns, especially for learning skills, decreased markedly throughout the rest of the preclerkship units. In several preclerkship and clerkship units, no concerns were raised in learning skills (Blumberg, Cohen, Ryan, & Sullivan, 1994).

LEARNING STRATEGIES

Learning strategies refer to the methods students use to study and process information (Table 9.4). In this section, I examine studies of the component processes of learning strategies. Learning is often classified either as

TABLE 9.4
Summary of Research Reviewed on Learning Strategies

Type of Component Data Collected		
Self-Report	*Faculty Report*	*Performance*
Newble & Clark (1986)	Not appropriate	Hmelo, Gotterer, &
Coles (1985)		Bransford (1997)
Camp et al. (1992)		Hmelo & Lin (this volume)

superficial or rote learning or conceptual learning (learning for under-standing and meaning; Candy, 1991). In school-learning situations, students frequently adjust their learning to the demands of the teachers or the tests, thus relinquishing ownership over learning objectives. This lack of ownership is the opposite of what is characteristic of self-directed learners. Saljo (1979) made the distinction between "learning for or in school" and "learning for life" after asking 90 people to describe their conceptions of learning. "Learning for life is relevant, meaningful, viable, and significant" (Candy, 1991, p. 409). The aim of SDL, especially in professional learning contexts, is to conjoin school and life learning.

SDL also involves the learners' ways of engaging with learning activities. Different types of learning approaches or processes can lead to qualitative differences in learning outcomes. For example, surface-level processing, usually involving rote memorization strategies, often leads to superficial understanding, whereas deep-level processing, involving translations and syntheses of information into new knowledge structures, often leads to a conceptual understanding of the material (Marton & Saljo, 1976a, 1976b). Newble and Entwistle (1986) incorporated these two learning approaches into their strategic model of learning. Their model includes the process of learning, the motivation, the intention, and the outcome. Students who showed a deep level of processing, or critical thinking (Ramsden, 1979), were interested in the subject matter, were motivated due to its relevance, and learned by connecting ideas. These strategic learners used whatever learning style was necessary to achieve high performance (Newble & Entwistle). Likewise, self-directed learners actively choose what they learn because they take on greater responsibilities for their learning and have personal control over how they learn. It is hypothesized that they would prefer to use deep-level processing (Candy, 1991).

Self-Report Measures

Preclinical and clinical PBL medical students at the University of Newcastle and traditional medical students at the University of Adelaide completed a 64-item self-report questionnaire that assessed their learning strategies (Newble & Clarke, 1986). The items on this questionnaire were grouped into 16 subscales. The PBL students rated themselves higher on the items relating to deep-level processing than the traditional students in all years. The traditional curriculum students, however, rated themselves significantly higher on deep-level processing as they progressed through medical school. Also, the traditional curriculum students rated themselves significantly higher in all years on the items relating to surface level of processing. Further, PBL students rated themselves higher on the items relating to deep-level processing and lower on the surface-level items than any other group of students previously tested at other, non-PBL institutions (Newble & Clarke). These self-reported strategy scores for the PBL students closely reflect the aims of most medical schools in relation to SDL.

Coles (1985) used the same learning strategy inventory with European traditional and PBL medical students and found similar results. Upon entry, the students in the two schools involved in the study rated themselves similarly in their study approaches. However, by the end of the first year, the traditional curriculum students showed a significant shift to poorer approaches, using more surface-level and less deep-level and strategic processing.

Mitchell (1994) developed a questionnaire to measure different areas of cognitive behavior—learning behaviors and learning experiences. Learning behaviors included the cognitive processes of learning, cognitive representations of information, approaches to studying, and estimates of the amount of information learned and retained. In the questionnaire, students were asked about their memorization (using rote-learning techniques), conceptualization (constructing a knowledge base in an active way, such as model building), and reflection behaviors (thinking about what one has learned as well as how one learns). Five medical schools, three with a traditional and a PBL curricula (University of New Mexico, Rush Medical College, and Bowman Gray School of Medicine) and two with entirely PBL programs (McMaster University and Harvard University) administered this questionnaire to their preclinical students. The results were remarkably similar across the schools. The traditional students used memorization the most; the PBL students used conceptualization the most. The PBL students, regardless of the school, often used visualization and model building as a strategy to help them master the material. In addition, PBL students rated their learning experience more positively than the traditional students (Camp, Mitchell, Blumberg, Kalishman, & Zeitz, 1992).

Evidence from different PBL programs in Australia (Newble & Clark, 1986), Europe (Coles, 1985), and North American (Camp et al., 1992) shows that PBL supports the development of deep-level processing in students. Various components of PBL might explain these findings. Because students are not given the material in lectures, they must study in a more active way to make meaning out of information. Simply reading textbooks or journal articles may not provide the information in the way the students want it. Rather, they often have to transform the material as presented to answer their specific learning issues. This transformation process to make meaning out of the information is an active learning process. The discussions of the cases themselves, as well as the preparation for the discussions, also stimulate deep-level processing. Examinations within PBL programs often require students to apply their knowledge to clinical situations. Further research is needed to understand what specifically within the PBL process contributes to this development of more meaningful learning.

Performance Measures

In an experimental situation, Hmelo, Gotterer, and Bransford (1997) compared the types of student-generated learning issues developed by traditional students who participated in a PBL elective with traditional students who had not participated in this elective. Those students with limited exposure to PBL were more likely to use disease-driven learning issues. Disease-driven learning issues result from hypotheses that attempt to explain the data on the basis of disease mechanisms. The non-PBL students were more likely to generate data-driven learning issues that assumed that the pattern of data should determine the cause. This study implies that students who have learned to use some PBL are transferring the kinds of strategies being modeled during the PBL component. Hmelo and Lin (this volume) replicated this result comparing students in full-time PBL and in traditional tracks.

PERFORMANCE OUTCOMES

Table 9.5 summarizes the research on performance outcomes. Short-term studies are usually conducted during or at the end of the course. Long-term studies are follow-up research pursued months or years after the students complete the problem-based curriculum. Due to these definitions, the holistic evaluation of performance of SDL, process skills (as discussed earlier and summarized in the cell represented by the last column, last row of Table 9.2) may be the same as short-term performance outcomes.

Short-Term Component Outcomes

Circulation data of all books, bound journals, and reserved readings from the library confirm the self-reported data that PBL students used the library

TABLE 9.5
Summary of Research Reviewed on Self-Directed Learning Performance Outcomes

Category	Short Term	Long Term
Component		
Use of library	Blumberg & Michael (1992)	Blumberg & Michael (1992)
New management		Shin, Haynes, & Johnston
regimens		(1991)
Continuing education		Tolnai (1991)
participation		
Holistic	Blumberg, Michael, & Zeitz	
	(1990)	
	Blumberg, Cohen, Ryan,	
	& Sullivan (1994)	

more frequently than traditional students. PBL students, while in the PBL preclinical track at Rush Medical College, borrowed significantly more material from the library ($M = 66.98$ circulated materials/student/year) than did the traditional curriculum preclerkship students ($M = 43.33$, $t(236) = 16.43$, $p < .001$; Blumberg & Michael, 1992).

Long-Term Component Outcomes

One goal of PBL programs is to develop lifelong learners among their graduates. SDL is a characteristic often associated with lifelong learners (Candy, 1991). If self-directed learners can define their own learning needs, assess the information independently, and finally evaluate the adequacy of their learning, then they should be able to effectively function as lifelong learners. Professionals also have to maintain their motivation to remain current. Unfortunately, few research studies have looked at the long-term effects of PBL in terms of SDL.

Significant differences in library borrowing practices continued into the clerkship when the PBL and traditional students were in the same curriculum at Rush Medical College ($t(236) = 18.87$, $p < .001$; Blumberg & Michael, 1992). The graduates of the PBL curriculum borrowed a mean of 43.33 materials per student per year; the graduates of the traditional curriculum borrowed a mean of 11.38. These numbers are most likely underestimates for both groups because clinical students frequently used libraries at other schools or hospitals. As preclinical students, the PBL students reported reading unassigned research literature for the purposes of being aware of medical advances one to two times a week, whereas the traditional curriculum students did this type of reading a few times a year. It is hoped that the habit that the PBL students acquired of reading medical journals for the purpose of staying current in the field (which continued through the clerkship) persists throughout their careers (Blumberg & Michael, 1992).

Primary care physicians who had graduated 5 to 10 years earlier from a PBL school (McMaster University) were compared to traditional medical school graduates (University of Toronto) of the same era. The PBL graduates were more familiar with new developments in the management of hypertension than the traditional school graduates (Shin, Haynes, & Johnston, 1991). Because this study was limited to one area of practice, one cannot generalize to all medical practice. In addition, the interpretation is complex because, in general, the graduates of this PBL program were more involved with educating medical trainees than were their counterparts from traditional schools (Ferrier & Woodward, 1987). In a review of this study, Woodward (1992) questioned that even if they are more up-to-date than a comparison group, is being up-to-date a direct result of enhanced lifelong learning skill or is it an indirect effect, mediated by being more involved in teaching? Perhaps there is a relation between learning in a PBL format and wanting to be involved as teachers in one's profession that also relates to lifelong learning. Further investigation is needed to untangle the relation between PBL and postgraduate knowledge seeking.

Participating in continuing education activities may be one way to stay current in one's professional field. No differences were found in the amount of formal continuing medical education activities in which PBL graduates (McMaster University) and traditional school graduates (University of Ottawa) engaged (Tolnai, 1991). It is questionable whether formal continuing education activities are actually a good way to operationally define lifelong learners. It could be argued that lifelong learners may engage in either more or less continuing education courses (Woodward, 1993). It may also be true that physicians engage in formal continuing education activities for many different reasons, including the requirement to attend formal continuing education programs to remain certified or to take advantage of various professional incentives.

PROPOSAL FOR A RESEARCH AGENDA

This section raises relevant questions and outlines areas where future research might be directed. Possible research on the learning process is discussed prior to those on learning strategies. This is followed by a discussion of long-term outcomes or performance. Possible research methodologies or valid comparison groups are briefly mentioned. Finally a summary of evidence-based conclusions is offered.

Learning Process Studies

Most of the work reported in this chapter was with medical students and, to a lesser extent, other health professional students. This type of research needs to be extended to students in other professions, such as engineering, business, or law. Also, as PBL is spreading to other type of learning, we need to study nonprofessional and younger students. For example, do PBL students who are neither as motivated to learn nor as competitive as medical students also develop SDL skills?

The independent learning components of the PBL process have not been well researched. For example, what do PBL students do after they have identified their learning issues? How do they actually develop a learning plan? How much does this plan dictate their actions? Are PBL students efficient in their access and study of material? How do PBL students use previously learned knowledge? Are they good time managers when left on their own? A hypothesis might be that one of the reasons that students feel less overwhelmed as they progress through a PBL program is that they learn efficient and effective study strategies. To test this hypothesis, comparisons among novice, intermediate, and advanced PBL students would appear warranted. Also, studies that compare outstanding PBL students with weaker ones might give us a better understanding of the SDL process. Analyzing students' journal entries would be one possible way of looking at independent learning processes.

We also do not know enough about how human resources are used and why. Why do PBL students seek assistance? Research in this area might investigate the purposes of students seeking assistance. Two possible explanations might be that they cannot understand some material on their own (need further clarification) or because they find human resources a good way to access material (learning style preference). Are there more individual differences in seeking assistance or can similarities among PBL students be noted? Are their differences in the types of human resources that novice and advanced PBL students seek?

What elements of PBL are essential in order to foster self-directed learning? The comparison of early PBL programs (Blumberg, Michael, & Zeitz, 1990) indicated students in faculty-centered PBL programs did not develop SDL skills. In the more student-centered programs, the students developed more SDL skills. A possible explanation for these differences involves the actual learning process employed by these students. For SDL skills to develop, students must be able to define what they will learn and must be allowed to access material on their own. A further essential characteristic is that SDL is valued enough in the program for students to be evaluated on these skills. Assessing material itself may lead to efficient library users who have good computer searching and retrieving skills. This could be empirically tested.

Another way to determine the essential elements for fostering SDL would be in controlled experiments with traditional students. Does the examination format also relate to the development of SDL? For example, if problem-based and traditional students had to take identical tests, would there be as much deep-level processing among the PBL students, or would they rely more on rote learning?

As many schools are implementing hybrid programs that combine PBL and lecture formats, the question of essential characteristics needed to foster SDL—for example, how much PBL—becomes more relevant. Do students in these hybrid curricula still develop SDL skills, and to the same extent that students in the purer, student-centered PBL programs do? To answer these questions, one would need to systematically classify programs according to the extent to which they require their students to attain the characteristics of SDL and to compare and contrast these programs.

Learning Strategies

Because few studies have investigated performance measures on learning strategies, this field has many fertile areas for research. Studies on learning strategies will lead to a better understanding of how PBL students learn. Being a reflective learner or a reflective practitioner are often associated with being a self-directed learner (Candy, 1991). How does PBL foster the development of these skills, if it does? Are PBL students or graduates more reflective than traditional students? To answer that question we would need to evaluate these students on their ability to think before they act, assess their ability to develop plans of action, and examine their plans before implementation.

Although we have enough evidence to conclude that PBL students use deep-level processing and learn for understanding, we do not know if this skill is maintained once the students are no longer in school. Do professionals continue to build models and to conceptualize when they read to solve practical problems, or is this just a study skill that is used to succeed as students?

Long-Term Performance Outcomes

Very little research exists on the long-term effects of PBL as related to SDL. Although PBL students become very good at defining their own learning needs in academic settings with defined parameters, we do not know how well graduates can define their own learning needs in nonacademic or in practice settings. In these settings, cases or problems can be more poorly defined or much broader than those faculty-developed cases experienced by students. Also in professional practice, faculty do not guide them through the case. Therefore, we need to test the assumption that graduates of PBL programs are good at defining their own learning needs in professional practice. We also need to ask the following questions: Do graduates of PBL programs apply new knowledge, or use their knowledge in new situations well? Are PBL graduates "better" practitioners than traditional graduates? Are PBL graduates good time managers, or do they seriously delay decision-making by oversampling resources?

The research evidence presented in this chapter indicates that students in PBL programs can define their own learning needs, learn for meaning and understanding, and feel positive about their learning and about their SDL skills. Therefore, a reasonable hypothesis is that graduates of PBL curricula will become effective lifelong learners, a long-term goal of most PBL programs. Lifelong learners are probably better practitioners because they remain current in their fields. Still, these hypotheses about PBL graduates, lifelong learning, and being effective practitioners have yet to be adequately tested.

One attribute of lifelong learners is that they remain current or up-to-date in their professional practice. This requires critically reading the discipline's scholarly literature on a regular basis. There are many possible ways to determine whether professionals are remaining current. One could ask a large group of professionals from PBL and from traditional schools what professional literature, especially journals, they regularly read. Further, they could be asked why they read what they read. Or, quasi-experimental studies could be devised in which professional problems, which are not easily addressed or are very rare, are used in tasks that require practitioners to consult resources, check the resource, and judge its usefulness.

Day, Norcini, Webster, Viner, and Chiraco (1988) studied physicians' performance on recertification examinations. These physicians came from traditional programs. Questions were classified as old, new, or changing knowledge. The decline in performance that was noted in relation to time since graduation was found to be due to a relative inability to acquire new or changing knowledge, not to forgetting previously learned knowledge (Day et al., 1988). This study provides a clear example of traditional physicians failing to be lifelong learners. A follow-up to this study could replicate the methodology and classify the physicians as graduates of traditional and PBL programs. If the PBL graduates knew more of the new or changing knowledge, then we would have good evidence that PBL leads to lifelong learning.

A further way to study whether PBL graduates become lifelong learners in terms of remaining current would be to study situations of patient management where the accepted management regimen has changed over time, such as in the use of steroids in the treatment of asthma. We need more studies like the one done by Shin and colleagues (1991) that compared graduates of PBL and of traditional programs to see whether they adjusted their treatment to remain current with the latest practices. A more ecologically valid study design would compare actual practice behaviors such as prescription writing, rather than comparing behaviors simulated by experimental situations.

As new resources become available, lifelong learners need to learn how to use them efficiently and effectively. Computers and the information highway are new tools that professionals need to use more and more for accessing and storing data. Do PBL graduates learn to use new resources sooner or more effectively than traditional graduates?

Many questions remain unanswered about the long-term effects of PBL. Many of these studies are complex, requiring sophisticated and perhaps novel methodologies. In addition, several of the suggested research studies, such as those on maintaining current knowledge or remaining professionally competent, can only be conducted when there are sufficient numbers of PBL graduates to have an adequate population to sample. However, the more we can focus on the long-term outcomes of PBL, the better we will be able to evaluate this instructional methodology.

Possible Research Methods

Specific investigative approaches follow from the assertion that the learner, per se, and the learning process are key to research on the evaluation of SDL within PBL. Given the individualistic nature of the research, naturalistic and interpretive approaches become as useful as normative, statistics-based studies. When such naturalistic, interpretive approaches are used, the conventional standards of research and evaluation, including internal and external validity, reliability, and objectivity give way to interpretive criteria such as credibility, transferability, dependability, and confirmability (Lincoln & Guba, 1985). One way to achieve these standards and to address the issue of small sample size is through the triangulation of data from different sources. When several studies with different students in different PBL programs find similar results, then we can trust that we have met the criteria.

Naturalistic, interpretive approaches can help document what learners know, how they know it, what their concerns are about their learning, and what they understand of their own learning knowledge bases. These research approaches often present "slice-of-life" episodes during the learning process and afterward in the application and use of the knowledge. This type of evaluation can assess how well students know the material, the processes used in learning, and how confident they feel about their knowledge (Wolf and Tymitz, 1976–1977). These studies are usually conducted in authentic contexts or in learning situations. Some examples of this type of research are given in other chapters in this volume. Researchers need to develop approaches that reflect the dynamic, constantly changing nature of learning endeavors. Self-evaluation to determine whether the material was learned adequately is also an appropriate method for research into the effectiveness of PBL curricula.

SUMMARY OF THE RESEARCH RESULTS

The research evidence is becoming strong enough to reach the following conclusions about PBL students and their SDL skills:

1. A perceived advantage of PBL is that it fosters the development of SDL. This is well recognized by the students themselves, by the faculty who participate in these programs, and by medical school accreditation boards (Blumberg & Deveau, 1995). This may be one reason why so many professional schools, especially medical schools, are moving in the direction of PBL.

2. PBL students are active library users. They seek and use a variety of library resources, including electronic bibliographic searching tools, books, journals, and online data sources. These students use them appropriately and often. PBL students use the library resources in a self-directed fashion. These students have superior library skills compared to traditional curriculum students. Although there is less evidence on this point after completion of PBL programs, these PBL graduates appear to continue to be good library users.

3. PBL students employ study strategies that result in deep-level processing. They learn to understand and apply knowledge to novel tasks rather than just to repeat it back in the same format on a test. This learning for meaning contrasts with the learning-for-recitation characteristic of medical students in the first two years of traditional curricula.

4. Students engaged in PBL perceive themselves as continuing to improve their own SDL abilities. Others, including their teachers, confirm this skill development. Specific SDL skills develop including the ability to define what is to be learned, to access material, and to actively study the material.

The long-term SDL effects of PBL are not as well researched. However, it can be hypothesized that students who acquire good SDL skills should continue to apply these skills throughout their professional lives. The main conclusion of this review is that we have need for much more research to better understand how, when, and why PBL fosters the development of SDL.

REFERENCES

Allegheny University of the Health Sciences, School of Public Health. (1996). *Student handbook* (School of Public Health, Allegheny University of the Health Sciences, 1505 Race St., Philadelphia, PA 19102).

Blumberg, P. (1997). [Graduate students' perceptions of the usefulness of resources]. Unpublished raw data.

Blumberg, P., Cohen, G. S., Ryan, N. C., & Sullivan, P. L. (1994). Analysis of academic problems encountered by medical students. *Teaching and Learning in Medicine, 6*, 96–101.

Blumberg, P., & Daugherty, S. R. (1994). A comparison of the perceived effectiveness of two educational methods in achieving school-related and practice-related goals. *Teaching and Learning in Medicine, 6*, 86–90.

Blumberg, P., & Deveau, E. J. (1995). Using a practical program evaluation model to chart the outcomes of an educational initiative: Problem-based learning. *Medical Teacher, 17*, 205–214.

Blumberg, P., & Michael, J. A. (1992). Development of self-directed learning behaviors in a partially teacher-directed problem-based learning curriculum. *Teaching and Learning in Medicine, 4*, 3–8.

Blumberg, P., Michael, J. A., & Zeitz, H. (1990). Roles of student-generated learning issues in problem-based learning. *Teaching and Learning in Medicine, 2*, 149–154.

Blumberg, P., & Sparks, J. A. (1999). Tracing the evolution of critical evaluation skills in students' use of the Internet. *Bulletin of Medical Library Association, 87*, 200–204.

Camp, M. G., Mitchell, R., Blumberg, P., Kalishman, S., & Zeitz, H. J. (1992, April). *Students' perceptions of the learning environments in problem-based and traditional medical school curricula: Exploring the implications for educational planning.* Symposium presented at the annual meeting of the American Educational Research Association, San Francisco, CA.

Candy, P. C. (1991). *Self-direction for lifelong learning.* San Francisco: Jossey-Bass.

Coles, C. R. (1985). Differences between conventional and problem-based curricula in their students' approaches to studying. *Medical Education, 19*, 308–309.

Day, S. C., Norcini, J. J., Webster, G. D., Viner, E. D., & Chiraco, A. M. (1988). The effect of changes in medical knowledge on examination performance at the time of recertification. In *Proceedings of the Twenty-seventh Annual Conference, Research in Medical Education* (pp. 139–144). Washington, DC: Association of American Medical Colleges.

Evidence Based Working Group. (1992). Evidence based medicine: A new approach. *Journal of the American Medical Association, 268*(17), 2420–2425.

Ferrier, B. M., & Woodward, C. A. (1987). Career choices of McMaster University medical graduates and contemporary Canadian medical graduates. *Canadian Medical Association Journal, 136*, 39–44.

Friden, K. (1994). Library use and information seeking skills: A study of two Swedish student populations [Abstract]. *Proceedings of the Faculty of Health Sciences McMaster University Conference on Problem-Based Learning in the Health Sciences: The State of the Art* (p. 26). (Available from McMaster University, 1200 Main St. West, Hamilton, Ontario L8N325, Canada)

Gijselaers, W. H., & Schmidt, H. G. (1992, April). *Exploring a model of study time allocation in a problem-based medical curriculum.* Paper presented at the annual meeting of the American Educational Research Association, San Francisco, CA.

Hmelo, C. E., Gotterer, G. S., & Bransford, J. D. (1997). A theory-driven approach to assessing the cognitive effects of PBL. *Instructional Science, 25*, 387–408.

Jennett, P. A. (1992). Self-directed learning: A pragmatic view. *Journal of Continuing Education in the Health Professions, 12*(2), 99–104.

Lincoln, Y. S., & Guba, E. G. (1985). *Naturalistic inquiry.* Newbury Park, CA: Sage.

Marshall, J. G., Fitzgerald, D., Busby, L., & Heaton, G. (1993). Study of library use in problem-based and traditional medical curricula. *Bulletin of Medical Library Association, 81*, 299–305.

Marton, F., & Saljo, R. (1976a). On qualitative differences in learning: I. Outcome and process. *British Journal of Educational Psychology, 46*, 4–11.

Marton, F., & Saljo, R. (1976b). On qualitative differences in learning: II. Outcome as a function of the learner's conception of the task. *British Journal of Educational Psychology, 46*, 115–127.

Mitchell, R. (1994). The development of the cognitive behavior survey to assess medical student learning. *Teaching and Learning in Medicine, 6*, 161–167.

Newble, D. I., & Clarke, R. M. (1986). The approaches to learning of students in a traditional and in an innovative problem-based medical school. *Medical Education, 20*, 267–273.

Newble, D. I., & Entwistle, N. J. (1986). Learning styles and approaches: Implications for medical education. *Medical Education, 20*, 162–175.

Ramsden, P. (1979). Student learning and perceptions of the academic environment. *Higher Education, 8*, 411–427.

Rankin, J. A. (1992). Problem-based medical education: Effect on library use. *Bulletin of Medical Library Association, 80*, 36–43.

Rosenfeld, J. (1995). *Students' use of learning objectives in a PBL program.* Unpublished manuscript, McMaster University, Hamilton, Ontario, Canada.

Ryan, G. (1993). Student perceptions about self-directed learning in a professional course implementing problem-based learning. *Studies in Higher Education, 18*, 53–63.

Saljo, R. (1979). Learning about learning. *Higher Education, 8*, 443–451.

Saunders, K., Northup, D. E., & Mennin, S. P. (1985). The library in a problem-based curriculum. In A. Kaufman (Ed.), *Implementing problem-based medical education* (pp. 71–88). New York: Springer.

Schmidt, H. G., Van Der Arend, A., Moust, J. H., Kokx, I., & Boon, L. (1993). Influence of tutors' subject-matter expertise on student effort and achievement in problem-based learning. *Academic Medicine, 68*, 784–791.

Schön, D. A. (1987). *Educating the reflective practitioner: Toward a new design for teaching and learning in the professions.* San Francisco, CA: Jossey-Bass.

Shin, J. H., Haynes, R. B., & Johnston, M. (1991). The effect of a problem-based self-directed undergraduate education on life-long learning. *Clinical Investigative Medicine, 14*, A82.

Tolnai, S. (1991). Continuing medical education and career choice among graduates of problem-based and traditional curricula. *Medical Education, 25*, 414–420.

Watkins, M. C. (1993). Characteristics of services and educational programs in libraries serving problem-based curricula: A group self-study. *Bulletin of Medical Library Association, 81*(3), 306–309.

Williams, R., Saarinen-Rahikka, H., & Norman, G. R. (1995). Self-directed learning in problem-based health sciences education. *Academic Medicine, 70*, 161–163.

Wolf, R. L., & Tymitz, B. L. (1976–1977). Ethnography and reading: Matching inquiry modes to process. *Reading Research Quarterly, 12*(1), 5–11.

Woodward, C. A. (1993). Some reflections on evaluation of outcomes of innovative medical education programmes during the practice period. *Annals of Community-Oriented Education, 5*, 181–191.

Chapter 10

Becoming Self-Directed Learners: Strategy Development in Problem-Based Learning

Cindy E. Hmelo
Rutgers University

Xiaodong Lin
Vanderbilt University

INTRODUCTION

A patient presents in the emergency room with an unusual set of signs and symptoms. A new piece of life-support equipment is in the intensive care unit but none of the night shift personnel know how to use it to aid a critically ill patient. An elderly patient in a nursing home develops an infection that is resistant to all of the usual broad-spectrum antibiotics. In all of these situations, competent physicians need to know how to go beyond what they already know to deal with new problems successfully. In order to go beyond what is known and to create new knowledge for novel situations, they need to know what they need to learn about a particular situation, what particular medical procedures and resources are appropriate for the situation, how to formulate questions to seek the specific information needed, and how the knowledge (new or old) can be applied in practice. Collectively, these abilities define what has been referred to as expertise in self-directed learning (SDL) skills or metacognitive learning abilities (see Brown, Bransford, Ferrara, & Campione, 1983; Brown & Campione, 1990). These abilities help people to grow intellectually by adapting and applying knowledge to new situations, as well as by recognizing the need to move beyond one's current knowledge state to a new level of understanding. Learning experiences that support the development of SDL skills are important in enabling the practicing physician to be a lifelong learner and a competent problem solver.

However, even students in professional learning contexts often leave school without the SDL skills needed for lifelong learning. This is particularly problematic in fields such as medicine where the knowledge is continually changing and advancing and in which dealing with novelty will be an important aspect of work (Eden, Eisenberg, Fischer, & Repenning, 1996). To prepare students for the lifelong learning required for success in such fields, they need to have experience in SDL while in school (Bereiter & Scardamalia, 1989).

There are many ways to scaffold students' SDL activities. The approach that is discussed in this chapter is to provide students with opportunities to learn specific medical knowledge and skills in the context of solving complex problems. This approach to training is referred to as Problem-Based Learning (PBL; Barrows, 1985). The term PBL means different things at different institutions, leading to considerable confusion in the literature about what it is and how one should go about it. In order to understand the real value and potential that PBL may have to offer to learning and instruction, we need to clarify the particular PBL activities that are associated with SDL and the specific learning effects that result from engaging learners in these activities. Examining PBL and its effects on SDL in a detailed and specific manner enables us to take a closer look at the nature of these activities in relation to successful learning. In this chapter, we discuss and analyze a long-term study conducted to compare and contrast PBL curricula with traditional medical curricula and their effects on learning.

Toward a Model of SDL in PBL

PBL is being used at many medical schools to help students learn basic science integrated with clinical knowledge, clinical reasoning skills, and SDL skills (Barrows, 1985; Williams, 1993). Because the problems used are complex, students work in groups, where they pool their expertise and experience and together grapple with the complexities of the issues that must be considered. As they work through the problems, they have opportunities to identify gaps in their knowledge and then set their learning goals and conduct research to reduce these gaps. Facilitators guide students' reflection on these experiences, facilitating learning of the cognitive and social skills needed for problem solving and for SDL. Because of the discovery nature of learning in PBL, skills needed for SDL are acquired as students manage their learning goals while coping with the problems they are trying to solve (Barrows, 1985).

There are several features of PBL that specifically support the development of SDL skills:

1. the student-centered nature of PBL;
2. having students attempt to identify and solve a problem with their existing knowledge;
3. identifying knowledge deficits and generating appropriate learning issues;
4. the independent research effort;
5. critiquing the resources used for research;
6. applying the new knowledge to the problem;
7. collaborative reflection on SDL.

Each of these features has an important function in supporting the development of SDL skills. Figure 10.1 summarizes those SDL activities that occur during the problem solving itself.

First, the degree to which PBL is student-centered is important in determining the opportunities for SDL. In traditional curricula, the teacher determines the type and sequence of information to be learned by the students. In the PBL curricula that we studied, learning was student-centered with faculty facilitation, meaning that the students took much of the responsibility for their own learning. This was accomplished through

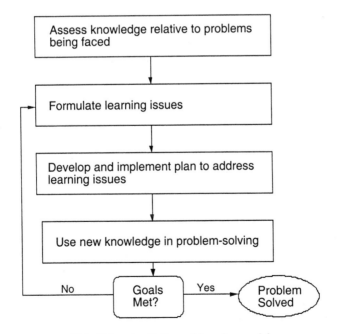

FIG. 10.1.   A self-directed learning model.

careful design and sequencing of problems and through training faculty in facilitatory skills (Barrows, 1986). The facilitator performs the role of a coach by modeling and scaffolding the kinds of self-assessment questions that the students need to ask themselves to be self-directed learners. For example, the instructor may ask questions, such as "Why did you request that information?" "What do you specifically hope to learn?" or "What more do you need to know?" Using these kinds of questions to facilitate student learning in PBL helps gradually transfer the agency of assessment to students. Eventually, the students internalize these questions and pose them to themselves in a metacognitive fashion (Collins, Brown, & Newman, 1989). This enables them to go further in self-assessing and understanding themselves on their lifelong journey of learning and knowledge building (Bereiter & Scardamalia, 1989). Second, students are encouraged to attempt problem solving when they have a knowledge base that is inadequate to deal with the problems posed, as indicated in Fig. 10.1. This helps students to realize the inadequacies of their existing knowledge as well as to develop skills such as self-assessment. This experience sets the stage for students to generate their own personally relevant learning needs and to plan for further learning (Lin & Bielaczyc, 1997). Through recognizing what they do not know, students are able to create opportunities for learning and inquiry (Bransford & Nitsch, 1978). This also serves to motivate the students and to activate their prior knowledge, making it easier for them to understand new information (Schmidt, De Grave, DeVolder, Moust, & Patel, 1989).

Third, as students try to use their existing knowledge to solve a problem, they identify their knowledge deficiencies as learning issues. Generating learning issues gives the students experience with setting their own learning goals relative to a problem being faced. This enables students to develop the skills and goal orientation that they need to be mindful self-directed learners (Bereiter & Scardamalia, 1989; Ng & Bereiter, 1991).

Fourth, and perhaps what is most obvious, is the factor related to the students' independent research efforts. The students in the PBL groups divide the learning issues and independently research their topic(s). Students become proficient in locating appropriate information resources and in posing questions to experts when necessary. Because they have the opportunity to use these information-seeking skills and the knowledge gained on a variety of problems, they construct conceptual knowledge as well as procedures for solving problems. This prepares students to become flexible and adaptive learners who can use their expertise in learning in a range of novel situations (Hatano & Inagaki, 1992).

Fifth, as part of the independent research effort, students need to critically evaluate the resources they have used. They need to consider the reliability of the resources and how those resources contribute to knowledge construction. Students might consider the date of a publication, whether it was from a respected source that underwent an appropriate review process, and how useful that resource might be for a future problem.

Sixth, students need to actually apply the fruits of their research to solving the problem. A key feature of the PBL methodology is that students are learning in order to apply their knowledge. Students learn to distinguish what is relevant from what is not and how knowledge can be used as a tool. According to numerous studies conducted by Bransford and colleagues, students who learn in ways that facilitate an understanding of the relevance of information are more likely to develop contextualized knowledge structures that connect isolated pieces of information. Building such knowledge will facilitate access when relevant problems arise (Bransford, Sherwood, Vye, & Rieser, 1986; Bransford & Stein, 1993). Furthermore, contextualized knowledge is important in problem recognition and in monitoring problem solving (Bransford & Stein, 1993).

Finally, students frequently reflect on their SDL experience throughout the PBL process, not just at the completion of the problem solving. Reflective self-assessment is an important learning tool that scaffolds students' inquiry in PBL settings. Students reflect on the usefulness of the knowledge they construct as a result of their SDL and on the processes in which they engage to achieve their learning goals. In addition, they consider how effective their strategies are and how they might improve in the future. Reflection is a critical component of the SDL process if students are to transfer their strategies and knowledge to new situations (Salomon & Perkins, 1989). Different types of reflection will lead to different types of learning and transfer (Lin & Lehman, 1999). For example, having students simply reflect on procedures to solve problems is not nearly as effective as having them monitor and evaluate the quality of the processes they went through to learn in PBL contexts. Such process-oriented reflection engages students in metacognitive monitoring and regulation of their own learning. Reflecting on the PBL process will help students identify what they need to understand, build connections between the procedures and concepts, and identify the causal mechanisms underlying a wide range of problems (Berardi-Coletta, Buyer, Dominowski, & Relinger, 1995; Lin & Bielaczyc, 1997; Lin & Lehman, 1999). Moreover, the collaborative discussions in the PBL group support reflection as students share and compare their thinking with others in the group.

Theoretical Basis for PBL

Theoretical support for the effectiveness of PBL in the development of SDL skills is drawn from information-processing theories of transfer as well as sociocultural theories such as cognitive apprenticeship. Information-processing theories of transfer-appropriate processing suggest that, in order for knowledge and strategies to be used in problem-solving situations, they must be learned in such contexts (Adams et al., 1988; Needham & Begg, 1991; Perfetto, Bransford, & Franks, 1983). In PBL, students continually apply their knowledge and practice their SDL strategies in problem-solving contexts, so this theory predicts that there should be transfer to novel problems. Because the students in a problem-based curriculum have opportunities to use their knowledge in a large variety of cases (100 or more during the first two years of medical school), they should be able to flexibly apply their SDL strategies to new situations. Moreover, the reflective activities in the tutorial groups enhance the likelihood that the students will be able to apply their SDL strategies in a range of situations (Salomon & Perkins, 1989).

Sociocultural theories offer additional support for the development of SDL skills in PBL. Cognitive apprenticeship models of instruction note the importance of situating learning in authentic tasks such as the medical cases used in PBL. Because the problems are complex, the students need various supports, also called scaffolding, to help them deal with the complexity of the problems. Scaffolding may take the form of modeling of expert thinking and coaching provided to learners as they try to apply new strategies (Collins et al., 1989). Sociocultural theorists suggest that through participation in the tutorial discourse, students internalize the thinking processes that are initially made external through the group's discussion (Wertsch & Bivens, 1993).

Because the thinking required is more difficult than any one student can handle, the cognitive load needs to be distributed among a collaborative group. The knowledge required to complete the whole puzzle does not reside in any one individual and needs to be distributed among such a group. In addition, the problems are rich enough to provide opportunities for all learners to explore and contribute to solutions. Ideas generated by the group are needed to reach a deeper understanding of the problem. Moreover, by collecting ideas contributed by everyone in the tutorial group, multiple perspectives about the problems are generated. Learners are engaged in knowledge coconstruction processes. According to Schwartz (1999), learners usually feel most motivated to participate and contribute in collaborative learning situations when they feel themselves to be an idea "contributor" rather than just a "borrower," especially when they see that their ideas are adapted and used in problem-solving situations. An opportunity to contribute may be a key motive for students to collaborate.

We find many of the features of cognitive apprenticeship in the PBL methodology. The facilitators provide models of expert SDL as they model their thinking and ask the students the questions that will eventually need to be internalized. Good self-directed learners set their learning goals, proactively select information, and self-evaluate the effectiveness of their learning strategies and determine whether or not there is a need to iterate through the SDL cycle again (Zimmerman, 1996). The facilitator models the SDL cycle and coaches the students by the types of questions the students are asked. For example, the facilitator may ask the students if an obvious point of confusion needs to be listed as a learning issue or how helpful their resources were in their learning. Eventually, the PBL students start asking each other these questions and the facilitator is able to fade back the scaffolding. This type of coaching model is important because it allows students to gradually take control of their own learning processes, which is crucial to the development of students' metacognitive learning abilities (Brown, 1997; Collins et al., 1989). In these instances, the facilitator helps students make their thinking visible so they can apply the feedback from the peers and instructors to address their knowledge deficits (Carpenter, Fennema, Peterson, Chiang, & Loef, 1989).

Empirical Studies of SDL

Prior research provides some limited support for the SDL model shown in Fig. 10.1. Hmelo, Gotterer, and Bransford (1997) found that PBL students have developed strategies for setting learning goals and for seeking information that are consistent with their problem-solving strategies. These students tended to take a hypothesis-driven approach to both their problem solving and their learning, choosing learning issues that are tied to their hypotheses, whereas non-PBL students are more likely to use clinical findings to guide their research. Dolmans (1994) noted, however, that once PBL students initially construct learning plans, other factors may subsequently influence their information-seeking behavior. Blumberg and Michael (1992) found that the PBL students were more likely to use self-chosen learning resources, whereas students in the conventional curriculum used faculty-chosen resources. PBL students were more likely to report selecting the material to study themselves, whereas conventional curriculum students reported reading specific teacher-generated assignments.

Strategies for SDL

Although the model in Fig. 10.1 describes the stages of SDL, it does not describe the nature of an effective strategy for generating learning objectives and for identifying resources. The empirical research suggests that PBL students take different approaches to SDL, but it is not clear that these approaches are better than what traditional students do. Cognitive science theory does, however, support the notion that hypothesis-driven learning may be superior to data-driven learning when the goal is conceptual understanding, as it is in the first two years of medical school (Bassok & Holyoak, 1993). Bassok and Holyoak suggested that SDL which proceeds in a hypothesis-driven manner, should lead to more flexible knowledge as compared with a data-driven strategy.

Data-driven learning requires that students make generalizations from multiple examples. The learners do not engage in deep analysis of principles and may end up knowing sets of correlated features (including some that are irrelevant). A search that proceeds by investigating the significance of isolated data (e.g., symptoms) may also not effectively limit the search space, causing the learner to examine many irrelevant concepts. In contrast, when one has a hypothesis, choosing to search for information in the context of that hypothesis may be more efficient than a search that is data-driven. Hypothesis-driven learning depends on prior knowledge of the domain coupled with active learning strategies that allow the learner to make principled judgments about the importance of features to the learner's goals. To the extent that hypothesis-driven learning enables learners to successfully identify relevant but nonobvious features of a problem, more flexible transfer will be promoted (Bassok & Holyoak, 1993; Patel & Kaufman, 1993).

In the PBL curriculum implemented in medical schools, the students are encouraged to think about the patient problems with the underlying scientific principles in mind rather than just collecting sets of features; thus, they are being coached to take a hypothesis-driven approach to their learning. As cases are connected to domain principles, the learner can begin to understand how knowledge can be applied to solving problems (Chi, Bassok, Lewis, Reimann, & Glaser, 1989).

Examining SDL in PBL

In this study, we examine the extent to which the predicted advantages of PBL for SDL are realized by comparing SDL processes for students participating in PBL experiences with those in traditional medical education. In particular, we investigate the development of strategies for identifying learning issues and constructing plans to remedy knowledge deficits as well as the degree to which students were able to integrate new information into their problem solving. In addition, we examine the students' perceptions of how successful their learning has been.

We made several predictions regarding the differences in SDL between PBL and non-PBL students. Because of the strong focus on making the connections between hypotheses and the clinical information, we expected that the PBL students would become more likely to define their learning issues in terms of relevant hypotheses than the non-PBL students. We also expected differences in the types of learning resources that students from different curricula would plan to use. Earlier work suggested that the PBL students would have a better specified starting point for their SDL because of the extended amount of practice and reflection (Hmelo et al., 1997). One concern of PBL students is that they may not be learning the science as well as the non-PBL students, so we anticipated that the PBL students' confidence in their science knowledge would be lower than that of the non-PBL students but because the PBL students gained experience with clinical cases, they would be more confident in their clinical knowledge. Finally, we expected the PBL students to be better at integrating new knowledge into their explanations of the clinical case and that the type of information that was integrated would be related to their hypotheses. We made this last prediction because in PBL, students are encouraged to apply the new information to the problem rather than lecturing each other on their chosen learning issues; thus their educational experience prepares them to use new knowledge as a tool for problem solving.

METHOD

Participants

Students from two medical schools participated in this study. At School A, a midwestern medical school, 35 first-year students participated. Of the 35, 16 students were from the school's traditional curriculum and 19 were from the PBL curriculum. At School B, a southern medical school, 39 first-year students participated. Of these, 19 students were in a PBL elective and 20 students were in a different (non-problem-based) elective. Students were paid for participating in three 2-hour sessions during their first year of medical school. The sessions took place before the start of classes, after 3 months, and after 7 months of medical school.

Instruction

At School A, the students in the traditional curriculum spent approximately 40 hours a week in lecture and laboratory courses in the basic biomedical sciences, whereas the PBL students had two 3-hour sessions for their PBL group meetings and a third optional 1-hour session a week where resource faculty were available to answer questions. In School B, the PBL and non-PBL electives were taken in addition to a traditional curriculum. The actual PBL group meetings were very similar at the two schools except that the School A students had a much more intense PBL experience than the School B group.

Assessment Task

The students' task was to generate pathophysiological explanations, in writing, for the mechanisms underlying a medical problem. At the end of each problem, the students were asked to identify additional knowledge that they needed to understand the patient's problem (the learning issues), and to develop a plan to address those learning issues. They were also asked to rate their scientific and clinical knowledge relative to the problem using a Likert scale. Six different problems were used that covered a variety of body systems and disease processes. At the completion of the second case in each session, the students were provided with four paragraphs to read. A separate set of paragraphs was constructed for each case. One paragraph was a summary of the features of the disease. The second paragraph discussed the important science concepts associated with the patients' clinical problem. The third and fourth paragraphs each discussed a particular clinical finding. For example, for a patient with myasthenia gravis, a neuromuscular disorder, the disease passage presented an overview of the disease, including its clinical features and treatment, the science passage presented a discussion of the neuromuscular junction, and the third and fourth paragraphs discussed two of the clinical findings, muscle weakness and lung function tests. Earlier work indicated that student learning issues fell into either hypothesis-related or data-related categories (Hmelo et al., 1997) so these paragraphs were chosen to examine whether the students' self-reported learning issues coincided with what they actually did while engaged in SDL. Students were randomly assigned to six different orders of presentations of materials that were counterbalanced across conditions.

At each session, the subject received two problems. The problems were presented in a format similar to those used in the PBL classes. Although the non-PBL students had not seen this problem format, they had been exposed to patient cases used to illustrate various biomedical concepts.

All analyses were coded from the students' protocols (as described in the Results section) by a rater who was blind to the conditions. A random sample of 20% of the protocols was scored by a second independent rater who was also blind to the conditions. Interrater agreement was 96%.

RESULTS

Learning Issues

The learning issues (LIs) the students identified fell into two categories: hypothesis-related or data-related. Hypothesis-related learning issues included issues related both to diseases and to basic science mechanisms.

TABLE 10.1
Examples of Learning Issues

Category	Example
Hypothesis-related	
Basic Science	". . . the physiology of the adrenal gland: what are the compounds which it synthesizes, and what are the systemic effects of their release into blood in abnormally elevated levels?"
Disease	"What are the risk factors which disposed Rosie for disseminated Mycobacterial infection?"
Data-related	"What were those crystals in his ankle, where do they come from and what do they do?"

An example of a disease-driven hypothesis-related LI is the student needing to know more about "complications of diabetes." A basic science driven hypothesis-related LI might be learning about "acid–base physiology." An example from the second category, a data-driven LI, is needing to learn about the significance of an elevated respiratory rate. Additional examples from the students' protocols are displayed in Table 10.1. If the students' SDL strategies are consistent with their reasoning strategies, the PBL students should generate more disease-driven and basic science LIs because the PBL students tend to learn hypothesis-driven reasoning strategies (Hmelo, 1998). In other work, we have found that this distinction between data and hypothesis-related SDL strategies discriminated between PBL and non-PBL students (Hmelo et al., 1997). For analytical purposes, the subjects' responses were classified into three patterns of learning issues: those that involved only vague issues or none at all; those that involved strictly hypothesis-related LIs; and those in which the LI referred to data. Because the differences between the schools were minimal and were not related to the hypotheses being tested, the data reported here are collapsed across the two schools.

The LIs that the students generated after working through each case were counted and classified in terms of their content, as shown in Fig. 10.2. The PBL students initially generated more learning issues, as shown in Table 10.2, than the non-PBL students but they decreased the number of LIs generated over the course of the year so that at the end of the year, there was very little difference in the number of LIs between the two groups, $F(1, 68) = 14.11, p < .001, MSE = 1.40$.[1] This puzzling result can

---

[1]These results as well as subsequent analyses were either ANOVAs (or log-linear analyses for the categorical variables) with two levels of the between-subject factor (condition) and three levels of the within-subject factor (time) but, unless otherwise noted, we report only the condition by time interaction as that was the hypothesis being studied as we examined relative change over time for the PBL and the non-PBL students.

TABLE 10.2
Means and Standard Deviations for Learning Issues

	Time 1	Time 2	Time 3
PBL			
M	3.34	3.00	2.25
SD	1.84	1.69	1.00
non-PBL			
M	2.03	1.93	2.01
SD	1.15	0.94	1.04

be better understood by examining the subjects' qualitative patterns of LIs. Initially the PBL students started out by having many data-related LIs but over the course of the year they switched to more hypothesis-related LIs, as indicated in Fig. 10.2, $\chi^2(4) = 16.82, p < .005$. The qualitative patterns of LIs for the non-PBL students did not change much over the year. They generated a large proportion of hypothesis-related LIs. The reasons for this may be related to their expectation that they will be learning about scientific mechanisms at this stage of their medical education. The initial high number of hypothesis-related LIs for the PBL students may reflect the expectations that they had about using patient cases. It is likely that they expected an emphasis on clinical issues as part of PBL. It may also be that over the course of the year, the PBL students realized that researching isolated data (i.e., signs and symptoms) is less efficient than using their hypotheses as the context for their search. As we show in the following section, the qualitative results from the students' learning plans suggest that the latter explanation is more likely.

Learning Plans

Generating LIs is only a part of the SDL process. As Fig. 10.1 shows, the students also need to determine what resources they will use. We predicted that given their experience, the PBL students would be more facile with choosing the learning resources for this task. However, the non-PBL students also had considerable experience in writing papers and using the library. Thus, we made no predictions about which group would use more resources, but we did expect them to use different ones. The learning resources that the students used were counted and categorized into basic science textbooks, clinical textbooks, unspecified textbooks, and the use of expert consultants.

The PBL students (across all time periods) used more resources than the non-PBL students (PBL: $M = 2.96$, non-PBL: $M = 2.53$), $F(1, 68) = 4.95, p < .05; MSE = 3.85$, but there was no differential change over time.

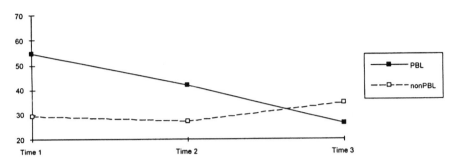

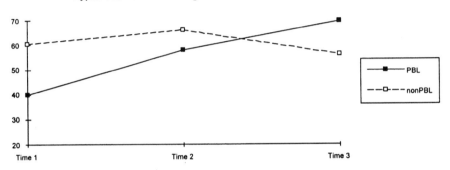

FIG. 10.2.   Distribution of learning issues.

The qualitative results are again more informative in understanding how the students' learning plans changed over time.

Although the students' learning plans clearly differed at the beginning of the year, there were differing trends for the two groups (see Table 10.3). At the beginning of the year, the PBL students were more likely to use science texts and experts. A substantial number of them used unspecified texts, although not as many as the non-PBL students. Over the course of the year, the PBL students became more likely to use clinical and science texts and less likely to use experts and unspecified texts, whereas the non-PBL students remained more likely to use experts and unspecified texts: clinical texts: $\chi^2(4) = 11.54, p < .05$; science texts: $\chi^2(4) = 9.38, p = .05$; experts: $\chi^2(4) = 10.05, p < .05$; unspecified texts: $\chi^2(2) = 15.30, p < .001$. This suggests that the PBL students developed a better understanding of the range of resources available. Although the students' goal for the first year of medical school was to learn science, given a patient case, many PBL students wanted to first look in a clinical textbook such as *Harrison's Internal Medicine*. Such a textbook, although emphasizing clinical infor-

TABLE 10.3
Percentage of Students Using Different Learning Resources

	Time 1				Time 2				Time 3			
	Clin	Sci	Expert	Unsp	Clin	Sci	Expert	Unsp	Clin	Sci	Expert	Unsp
PBL	24%	46%	55%	27%	61%	61%	40%	16%	57%	59%	37%	9%
Non-PBL	21%	24%	57%	41%	18%	27%	83%	46%	24%	38%	57%	31%

Note: "Clin" refers to clinical texts, "Sci" refers to basic science textbooks, "Expert" refers to human consultants, "Unsp" refers to textbooks that did not have any descriptors that would allow it to be classified.

mation, may contain some information about the causal mechanisms of the illness as well. In contrast, the non-PBL students only seemed to have undifferentiated plans about how to get started.

Success at SDL

The students' success at their SDL was indirectly measured by their knowledge ratings following each case. Both the PBL and the non-PBL students increased in their self-perceived science knowledge over the course of the year (overall mean rating at Time 1: 2.22 out of a possible 5, Time 2: 2.82, Time 3: 3.29), $F(1, 68) = 72.87$, $p < .001$, $MSE = 1.19$, but only the PBL students grew significantly in their self-perceived clinical knowledge (Means: PBL Time 1: $M = 1.75$, Time 2: $M = 2.82$, Time 3: $M = 3.10$; non-PBL Time 1: $M = 1.74$, Time 2: $M = 2.00$, Time 3: $M = 2.49$), $F(1, 68) = 9.06$, $p < .005$; $MSE = .62$. Although the evidence is indirect, a possible explanation for the PBL students' greater growth in self-perceived clinical knowledge is that, in the problem-based environment, students learned to integrate basic science with clinical information. For example, they may have been more likely to learn about the contexts in which particular scientific concepts are likely to be relevant and the symptoms through which they are manifested. We discuss a more direct examination of students' success at learning in the next section in which we examine how well students integrated new information with their prior knowledge.

Integrating Information

To examine the last stage of the SDL model, information integration, we examined two sources of data. First, if the students were using different sources of information, we might have expected this to be reflected in different percentages of time spent reading the different paragraphs. This was not the case. Both the PBL students and the non-PBL students divided their time evenly among the four paragraphs. Because the students were asked to read all of the paragraphs, it is likely that they did just that without focusing attention on the particular paragraphs that contained information for which they asked. Second, if the students were differentially utilizing different kinds of information, this might have been reflected in their problem solutions. For this in-depth analysis, we examined only the Time 3 data where we expected the group differences to be the greatest.

The paragraphs for these cases were parsed into idea-units and the students' explanations were examined to see whether they integrated the new information and from which paragraph it came. Table 10.4 shows an

TABLE 10.4
Integrating Information: Example of Idea Units

Myasthenia Gravis: Disease Passage

D1.1	Myasthenia Gravis (MG) is a disease
D1.2	characterized by muscle weakness.
D1.3	episodic
D2.1	The muscle weakness is due to the inability
D2.2	of the neuromuscular junction to transmit signals
D2.3	from nerves to muscles.
D3.1	MG is believed to be an autoimmune disease
D3.2	in which patients have developed antibodies
D3.3	to the acetylcholine receptor in the neuromuscular junction.
D4.1	The most common symptoms are
D4.2	drooping eyelids,
D4.3	double vision,
D4.4	and muscle fatigue after exercise.
D5.1	Difficulty swallowing and
D5.2	limb weakness are
D5.3	common.
D6.1	The clinical effects vary in degree
D6.2	over the course of hours to days.
D7.1	Life-threatening respiratory involvement
D7.2	(myasthenic crisis)
D7.3	occurs in about 10% of patients.
D8.1	The diagnosis of MG is confirmed by
D8.2	improvement with a drug
D8.3	anticholinesterase.
D9.1	Anticholinesterase drugs are used to treat current symptoms.
D10.1	Steroids,
D10.2	immunosuppressive drugs, and
D10.3	surgical removal of the thymus
D10.4	change the disease course
D10.5	by interfering with autoimmune processes.

example of the parsed disease passage in the case of a woman with myasthenia gravis.

As shown in Fig. 10.3, the PBL students integrated more information into their explanations than the non-PBL students, $F(1, 65) = 10.68$, $p < .005$. Note that this analysis excludes five of the PBL students who included all of the important causal ideas in their explanation prior to reading the passages and so had no need to use the information contained in the paragraphs. However, even if these students are included, the PBL students still incorporated reliably more ideas from the passages (PBL students' $M = 5.08$), $F(1, 68) = 4.80$, $p < .05$. For those students who integrated any ideas from the texts into their explanations, the percentage of hypothesis-related ideas was higher than that of data-related ideas

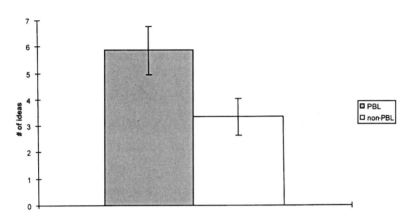

FIG. 10.3.   Number of ideas integrated into problem solving.

for both groups as shown in Fig. 10.4, $F(1, 58) = 51.03; p < .001$. There was a marginal trend for the PBL students to incorporate more hypothesis-related ideas than the non-PBL students, $F(1, 58) = 3.34; p < .08$, consistent with the types of LIs that they generated.

To understand how the students differ, it is useful to examine the protocols of two students more closely. Table 10.5 shows an example of a PBL student (S #46) and a non-PBL student (S #72) who integrated some information. Both students were trying to explain the cause of a patient's illness. The patient had drooping eyes (*ptosis*) and difficulty breathing and swallowing. The cause ultimately turned out to be myasthenia gravis, which is conclusively demonstrated by observing a response to a drug. The problem in this disease is that the chemical transmitter (acetylcholine, often abbreviated as ACh) between the nerves and muscles is degraded too quickly, causing weakness in various muscles (see Table 10.4). To understand how the students used the text, we also present their last attempt at solving the problem prior to reading the passages.

Both of these students had at least partially correct explanations prior to integrating the new information. They both noted that there seemed to be some problem localized to the ACh transmission. In addition, subject 46 was trying to explain the clinical data but she did not connect many of the symptoms to her first hypothesis. Both students integrated some information from the paragraphs, but the PBL student made clear connections between the scientific mechanisms and the clinical signs. Specifically, she has noted which of the clinical signs identified in the disease passage were consistent with the patients' symptoms (e.g., D4.2, D5.1, and D7.1). She also pointed out that the diagnosis was definitive

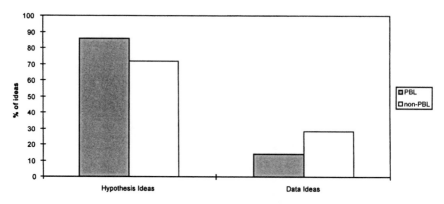

FIG. 10.4.   Types of ideas integrated into problem solving.

TABLE 10.5
Examples of Student Protocols

Curriculum	Explanation Before Passages	Explanation After Passages
PBL S #46	Well, it seems her problem may be partially caused by ACh problems, maybe myasthenia gravis. Her throat problems may then be the result of thymus problems, and the drooping eyelids could be explained by this diagnosis as well. I am still unsure of the role of the increases in WBC types in this patient's difficulties.	If Ms. Dupree does indeed have MG (and she did improve with anti-cholinesterase, which is used to determine a diagnosis of MG), most of her symptoms are characteristic of this disease, including ptosis, difficulty swallowing, and respiratory distress. The patho-physiological process that accounts for her symptoms is that insufficient amounts of ACh are binding to neural receptors.
Non-PBL S #72	apparently there is a process in which the cholinesterases are overactive or the acetylcholine release is too low, therefore causing the weakness.	impairment of the neuromuscular communication at the neuromuscular junction can account for the symptoms in this case. I must admit MG crossed my mind but I did not know the extent of its clinical effects beyond muscle weakness. But, in general, there is inadequate muscle response to signals from the CNS.

based on one of the tests, again, something that she learned from D8.1 to D8.3 in the disease paragraph. Subject 72 noted the pathophysiological mechanism but did not use that to account for the clinical signs other than the muscle weakness (D2.1–D2.3). Besides these differences in how the two students used the information, the PBL student used nine ideas from the passages in solving the problem whereas the non-PBL student used three ideas. These results provide further support for the notion that the PBL students are better at using new information to help them in their problem solving.

DISCUSSION

In this chapter we provided evidence that PBL can be effective in facilitating the development of SDL strategies. Specifically, we have shown that

1. PBL students are more likely to identify hypothesis-related learning issues.
2. PBL students are more likely to develop a well-specified starting point for their SDL in the plans they generate.
3. PBL students are more likely to integrate new information into their problem solving, and this information tends to be hypothesis related.

These outcomes are consistent with the features of PBL that have been implemented in the schools that we studied. The facilitators model and coach the students to consider their hypotheses as the students generate LIs. The students discuss the resources that they use for their SDL. Moreover, the students do not just present the information they have found; they put their knowledge to use as a tool for problem solving. What we have found in this study may only be part of the SDL story. Dolmans (1994) suggested that there may be additional dynamics involved in SDL. She found that what students planned to do was not necessarily related to what they actually did while pursuing independent study. This suggests that the model in Fig. 10.1 is incomplete and that there may be additional cognitive activity between developing a plan, implementing it, and using the new knowledge—and that the linear model may be an oversimplification. There is a complex relation between student-generated learning issues and the subsequent activities and resources used. Utilization of learning resources may be a dynamic phenomenon and, while perusing the literature and having discussions with experts, additional issues may arise that receive the learners' attention. This still suggests that where students start their learning (i.e., what resources they initially use) will influence subsequent learning. We have noted that the students' initial learning plans are likely to evolve from the starting point they actively identify. Clearly, further research needs to be done to test this last hypothesis as well as to examine whether a hypothesis-related strategy for directing one's learning is more effective. Examining the dynamic nature of effective SDL strategies is important in order to understand how to facilitate the development of effective strategies. These are important issues both for cognitive science and for education.

There are many varieties of instruction that are being called PBL and that are being used in practice (Barrows, 1986). However, not all these "PBL" learning environments afford SDL to the same degree. For example, in a lecture-based case, the teacher presents the students with information in a case vignette to illustrate an important point in the lecture and to show its relevance. The case is not problematized in this approach as the teacher has already done the analysis and identified the relevant problem features. The students do not have to deal with a problem in its full complexity so they do not learn to notice what it important (Bransford, Franks, Vye, & Sherwood, 1989). There is no opportunity for them to engage in any SDL because the teacher has already identified the learning objectives and tried to transmit them to the students. The reiterative PBL model that we describe here presents a problem in its full complexity, as in the cognitive apprenticeship model (Collins et al., 1989) and uses the facilitator and the PBL methodology to provide a form of scaffolding that supports the SDL process. In this method, the students also get feedback on the effectiveness of their SDL as they put the knowledge to use when they iterate back through solving the problem.

Other features of the PBL method are important to consider in understanding the SDL outcomes. For example, an individual dealing with a problem is certainly one type of PBL environment, but it does not afford enriched discussions and shared knowledge and ideas. In addition, when working alone, a student may not be able to view the same problem from multiple perspectives. Important features of a problem may be missed without the monitoring and feedback of the other group members. It is also unlikely that individual learning will promote the skills of asking good questions and generating explanatory feedback.

Merely embedding a problem in a social environment may not necessarily promote SDL because the culture of the social environment may not promote active participation, exploration, reflection, and revision. A number of studies have shown that different ways of organizing problem-centered learning environments can affect the degree of participation and learning through joint problem solving and knowledge coconstruction (Brown & Campione, 1994; Collins, Hawkins, & Carver, 1991). In contrast, if the social environment supports SDL, students will be able to choose what and how to investigate issues about which they need to learn to solve the problem. Information obtained from students' choices in a socially supported inquiry may serve as a dynamic assessment to inform both students and teachers of the emergent learning competence achieved throughout the process (Brown, 1992). Therefore, it is important for us to understand the social mechanisms that may affect SDL in PBL settings.

Another key feature of PBL is the student-centered nature of the tutorial group. If PBL is accomplished with the teacher providing the learning objectives, students do not have the opportunities to set and satisfy their learning goals. At another extreme, PBL that does not provide any guidance or support will not be optimal either. In a PBL environment that does not provide any support, students may get lost in tangential inquiry, similar to the perils of unguided discovery learning (Brown & Campione, 1994). Thus, the problems need to be structured to constrain the search space. The guidance of the facilitator is critical as well. A good facilitator will not prevent the students from exploring any possible blind alley but will gently guide them toward key aspects of the problem space to help students take advantage of the problem affordances.

Similarly, the role of reflection may vary in PBL. Reflection helps students make their thinking visible, allows them to observe the thinking of others and refine their strategies. Also, it helps the student consider the range of circumstances in which the strategies might be used. This reflection component is thus critically important for the development of SDL skills. In our research, we have seen the reflection component dropped due to time constraints, which will likely place limits on the learning that will occur. As discussed earlier, the specific types of reflections in which students engage affect the degree and quality of learning and performance.

These are just a few examples, but given the wide range of variables associated with PBL, the effects of specific instructional components, and their effects on SDL, these are important issues for further research if PBL is to reach its potential. Helping physicians learn to go beyond what they already know is critical if they are to become adaptive problem solvers under conditions of rapidly changing knowledge.

ACKNOWLEDGMENTS

The research reported here and the preparation of this paper were supported by a Vanderbilt University Dissertation Enhancement Award, an American Psychological Association Dissertation Research Award, a grant from the Rush Medical College Alternative Curriculum project to the first author, and Vanderbilt University Research Council grant to the second author. There are many people whose help and advice are greatly appreciated: John Bransford and Gerald Gotterer for many thoughtful discussions as this study was being conducted and analyzed; Howard Zeitz for his support and encouragement; Nathalie Coté and Katherine Lestock for doing the reliability coding; and Susan Goldman for her helpful advice in constructing the materials used in this study. We also thank Howard Barrows and Tom Duffy for their comments on an earlier draft of this chapter.

REFERENCES

Adams, L., Kasserman, J., Yearwood, A., Perfetto, G., Bransford, J., & Franks, J. (1988). The effect of fact versus problem oriented acquisition. *Memory & Cognition, 16*, 167–175.

Barrows, H. S. (1985). *How to design a problem-based curriculum for the preclinical years*. New York: Springer.

Barrows, H. S. (1986). A taxonomy of problem-based learning methods. *Medical Education, 20*, 481–486.

Bassok, M., & Holyoak, K. J. (1993). Pragmatic knowledge and conceptual structure: Determinants of transfer between quantitative domains. In D. K. Detterman & R. J. Sternberg (Eds.), *Transfer on trial: Intelligence, cognition, and instruction* (pp. 68–98). Norwood, NJ: Ablex.

Berardi-Coletta, B., Buyer, L. S., Dominowski, R. L., & Rellinger, E. R. (1995). Metacognition and problem solving: A process-oriented approach. *Journal of Experimental Psychology, 21*, 205–223.

Bereiter, C., & Scardamalia, M. (1989). Intentional learning as a goal of instruction. In L. B. Resnick (Ed.), *Knowing, learning, and instruction: Essays in honor of Robert Glaser* (pp. 361–392). Hillsdale, NJ: Lawrence Erlbaum Associates.

Blumberg, P., & Michael, J. A. (1992). Development of self-directed learning behaviors in a partially teacher-directed problem-based learning curriculum. *Teaching and Learning in Medicine, 4*, 3–8.

Bransford, J. D., Franks, J. J., Vye, N. J., & Sherwood, R. D. (1989). New approaches to instruction: Because wisdom can't be told. In S. Vosniadou & A. Ortony (Eds.), *Similarity and analogical reasoning* (pp. 470–497). New York: Cambridge University Press.

Bransford, J. D., & Nitsch, K. E. (1978). Coming to understand things we could not previously understand. In J. F. Kavanaugh & W. Strange (Eds.), *Speech and language in the laboratory, school, and clinic* (pp. 267–307). Cambridge, MA: MIT Press.

Bransford, J. D., Sherwood, R., Vye, N. J., & Rieser, J. J. (1986). Teaching thinking and problem solving. *American Psychologist, 41*, 1078–1089.

Bransford, J. D., & Stein, B. S. (1993). *The IDEAL problem solver*. New York: Freeman.

Brown, A. L. (1992). Design experiments: Theoretical and methodological challenges in creating complex interventions in classroom settings. *Journal of the Learning Sciences, 2*, 41–178.

Brown, A. L. (1997). Transforming schools into communities of thinking and learning about serious matters. *American Psychologist, 52*(4), 399–413.

Brown, A. L., Bransford, J. D., Ferrara, R. A., & Campione, J. C. (1983). Learning, remembering, and understanding. In J. H. Flavell & E. H. Markman (Eds.), *Handbook of child psychology: Cognitive development* (Vol. 3). New York: Wiley.

Brown, A. L., & Campione, J. C. (1990). Interactive learning environments and the teaching of science and mathematics. In M. Gardner, J. G. Greeno, R. Reif, A. H. Schoenfeld, A.

Disessa, & E. Stage (Eds.), *Toward a scientific practice of science education* (pp. 112–139). Hillsdale, NJ: Lawrence Erlbaum Associates.

Brown, A. L., & Campione, J. C. (1994). Guided discovery in a community of learners. In K. McGilly (Eds.), *Classroom lessons: Integrating cognitive theory and classroom practice* (pp. 229–270). Cambridge, MA: MIT Press/Bradford Books.

Carpenter, T. P., Fennema, E., Peterson, P. L., Chiang, C. P., & Loef, M. (1989). Using knowledge of children's mathematics thinking in classroom teaching: An experimental study. *American Educational Research Journal, 26*, 499–532.

Chi, M. T. H., Bassok, M., Lewis, M. W., Reimann, P., & Glaser, R. (1989). Self-explanations: How students study and use examples in learning to solve problems. *Cognitive Science, 13*, 145–182.

Collins, A., Brown, J. S., & Newman, S. E. (1989). Cognitive apprenticeship: Teaching the crafts of reading, writing and mathematics. In L. B. Resnick (Ed.), *Knowing, learning and instruction: Essays in honor of Robert Glaser* (pp. 453–494). Hillsdale, NJ: Lawrence Erlbaum Associates.

Collins, A., Hawkins, J., & Carver, S. M. (1991). A cognitive apprenticeship for disadvantaged students. In B. Means, C. Chelemer, & M. S. Knapp (Eds.), *Teaching advanced skills to at-risk students* (pp. 216–243). San Francisco: Jossey-Bass.

Dolmans, D. (1994). *How students learn in a problem-based curriculum.* University of Limburg, Maastricht, The Netherlands: University Pers Maastricht.

Eden, H., Eisenberg, M., Fischer, G., & Repenning, A. (1996). Making learning a part of life. *Communications of the ACM, 39*, 40–42.

Hatano, G., & Inagaki, K. (1992). Desituating cognition through the construction of conceptual knowledge. In P. Light & G. Butterworth (Eds.), *Context and cognition: Ways of learning and knowing* (pp. 115–134). Hillsdale, NJ: Lawrence Erlbaum Associates.

Hmelo, C. E. (1998). Problem-based learning: Effects on the early acquisition of cognitive skill in medicine. *Journal of the Learning Sciences, 7*, 173–208.

Hmelo, C. E., Gotterer, G. S., & Bransford, J. D. (1997). A theory-driven approach to assessing the cognitive effects of PBL. *Instructional Science, 25*, 387–408.

Lin, X. D., & Bielaczyc, K. (1997). Supporting metacognition: Context, forms and functions. Manuscript under review.

Lin, X. D., & Lehman (1999). Supporting learning of variable control in a computer-based biology environment: Effects of prompting college students to reflect on their own thinking. *Journal of Research in Science Teaching, 36*(7), 1–22.

Needham, D. R., & Begg, I. M. (1991). Problem-oriented training promotes spontaneous analogical transfer. Memory-oriented training promotes memory for training. *Memory and Cognition, 19*, 543–557.

Ng, E., & Bereiter, C. (1991). Three levels of goal orientation in learning. *Journal of the Learning Sciences, 1*, 243–271.

Patel, V. L., & Kaufman, D. R. (1993). *Development of knowledge-based reasoning strategies with medical training* (TR CME93–CS3): Cognitive Studies in Medicine: Centre for Medical Education.

Perfetto, G. A., Bransford, J. D., & Franks, J. J. (1983). Constraints on access in a problem solving context. *Memory & Cognition, 11*, 24–31.

Salomon, G., & Perkins, D. N. (1989). Rocky roads to transfer: Rethinking mechanisms of a neglected phenomenon. *Educational Psychologist, 24*, 113–142.

Schmidt, H. G., DeGrave, W. S., DeVolder, M. L., Moust, J. H. C., & Patel, V. L. (1989). Explanatory models in the processing of science text: The role of prior knowledge activation through small group discussion. *Journal of Educational Psychology, 81*, 610–619.

Schwartz, D. L. (1999). The productive agency that drives collaborative learning. In P. Dillenbourg (Ed.), *Collaborative learning: Cognitive and computational approaches* (pp. 198–219). New York: Elsevier.

Wertsch, J. V., & Bivens, J. A. (1993). The social origins of individual mental function: Alternatives and perspectives. In R. Cocking & K. A. Renninger (Eds.), *The development and meaning of psychological distance* (pp. 203–218). Hillsdale, NJ: Lawrence Erlbaum Associates.

Williams, S. M. (1993). Putting case based learning into context: Examples from legal, business, and medical education. *Journal of the Learning Sciences, 2,* 367–427.

Zimmerman, B. J. (1996). Enhancing student academic and health functioning: A self-regulatory perspective. *School Psychology Quarterly, 11,* 47–66.

Chapter 11

What Directs Self-Directed Learning in a Problem-Based Curriculum?

Diana H. J. M. Dolmans
Henk G. Schmidt
University of Maastricht

Many studies on learning and cognition indicate that learning is an active process of constructing knowledge, rather than a passive process of memorizing information (Bruning, Schraw, & Ronning, 1995; Glaser, 1991). Information is stored in memory in meaningful, dynamic structures (Anderson, 1990), and adding new information to a meaningful structure results in a richer structure in which many relations exist among the concepts included in the structure. The richer a structure is, the more can be done with the information. This theory implies that educational programs should be developed that encourage students to develop rich knowledge structures. Problem-based learning (PBL), an instructional approach consistent with such research findings on learning and cognition, sets out to do just that.

In PBL, students are actively involved in their own learning. Problems play a key role in this process. Preliminary discussion in the small group will help students mobilize whatever knowledge is already available. Based on this prior knowledge, learners actively construct explanatory models, which in turn facilitate the processing and comprehension of new information. In addition, the new information is better understood because students are stimulated to elaborate on it. Elaboration in the tutorial group takes place through discussion and through answering questions. These activities help students to construct rich cognitive models of the problems presented to them (Schmidt, 1993) because both conditions, activation of prior knowledge and elaboration, facilitate students' learning. Illustrative evidence for these claims comes from two experiments conducted by Schmidt, De Volder, De Grave, Moust, and Patel (1989) and by Schmidt (1984). In these experiments, participants were asked to discuss a problem and elaborate on possible explanations. Subsequently, these participants were required to study a problem-relevant text. The participants who had discussed the problem recalled much more information from the text than the control group. These data suggest that problem-based analysis is indeed an effective knowledge activation and knowledge elaboration procedure facilitating comprehension of and access to relevant new information.

Research has also shown that educational strategies in which learning is seen as a passive process of transmitting information into memory, usually characterized by a high level of external regulation by instruction, encourage students merely to memorize information. On the contrary, educational strategies in which learning is seen as an active constructive process, usually characterized by a high level of internal regulation by students, encourage students to relate and structure information (Vermunt, 1989). It is the learner's actions that accomplish constructive activities. Educational programs should be developed in which students are encouraged to become architects of their own knowledge and to eventually take full responsibility for their own learning (Bereiter & Scardamalia, 1989).

PBL is an educational strategy in which students are encouraged to take responsibility for their own learning. In PBL students "learn to learn," so that they can make their learning relevant to their own educational needs (Barrows & Tamblyn, 1980). By means of analyzing and discussing problems, students learn how to deal with problems in the future, preparing themselves to become independent, self-directed, lifelong learners. In addition, Barrows and Tamblyn claimed that students learn to see gaps in their own knowledge and learn to evaluate their own strengths and weaknesses. Students learn to reflect on and control their own learning and develop self-regulatory skills (Glaser, 1991). Moreover, because students conduct literature searches themselves, they learn to find the necessary materials independently and acquire the ability to continue their education after they graduate (Barrows & Tamblyn). In other words, the emphasis on selfdirected learning should promote an inquisitive learning style. The active learning emphasized in PBL promotes the self-directed learning strategies needed for lifelong learning (Bereiter & Scardamalia, 1989).

Although the emphasis on self-directed learning in PBL promotes an inquisitive learning style conducive to lifelong learning, some teachers are concerned that students might lack skills to work independently. They argue that students cannot know what they ought to study and are unable to identify all of the "required" knowledge. On the one hand, teachers expect students to become self-directed learners, which requires that student are given some freedom, but on the other hand, teachers feel a need to ensure that students possess a sufficient knowledge base and cover the intended curriculum content to a sufficient degree. The dilemma of students' responsibility for their own learning and faculty's responsibility to ensure that students acquire sufficient knowledge to be qualified physicians has led to the development of a PBL curriculum at the Medical School of the University of Maastricht. This curriculum includes elements that provide students with guidelines for their individual study.

The problem-based curriculum at the Medical School of the University of Maastricht is divided into courses. Each course is usually 6 weeks long and addresses a particular interdisciplinary theme, for example, fatigue or blood loss. Central to the course are the problems discussed by students in the tutorial group meetings. The problems cover multiple disciplines related to the theme of the course. Traditional lectures are also part of the curriculum. They are used to introduce a curriculum course, to help students understand difficult topics, and to provide unique information (e.g., from an invited speaker in the field). On average, approximately two lectures are held per week. In addition, a skills training program is offered to students from the beginning of the first year. Different practical skills are taught: specific examination skills (e.g., neurological, physiological, etc.), attitude skills, and communication skills. Moreover, health-practice contacts are scheduled for students. The intention of the skills training program and the health-practice contacts is to integrate theory and practice as tightly as possible. Finally, an amount of time per week is scheduled for individual study. The learning issues generated in the tutorial groups serve as a guide for studying the literature relevant to the problem at hand. To facilitate individual study, students are provided with many facilities. Next to a library, a "study landscape" has been created, with multiple copies of all current handbooks, a video and slide library, space to sit for studying, and computer facilities. Computer facilities include computer-assisted learning programs, simulation programs, word processing, the Internet, statistical facilities, and e-mail facilities. For each course, students can make use of a coursebook containing the problems to be discussed in the tutorial groups during the 6-week period, a short description of the global course objectives, and the lectures and skills training program. In addition, suggestions for learning resources are listed and a self-assessment test is included.

From this description of the curriculum, it should become clear that students are not only confronted with problems in a particular course but also with global course objectives, a limited number of lectures, reference literature, and test items. This degree of external regulation may result in subverting the development of student's self-directed learning skills. For example, students, while filling out a self-assessment test, may tune their learning activities to the content that is tested instead of the learning issues generated for a particular problem. The same holds for providing students with reference literature. If students confine themselves to the immediately available literature, they may not conduct literature searches themselves. In both situations, the development of student's self-directed learning skills may be subverted.

Blumberg and Michael (1992) examined whether student-generated learning issues are a driving force in self-directed learning skills, even when the curriculum is partially teacher directed. They compared the use of library resources among students in a traditional curriculum and students in a PBL curriculum in which they were required to determine their own learning issues, but could also compare their learning issues with faculty-generated objectives. The data showed that students in the PBL curriculum acquired behaviors that reflected continued and self-directed learning skills. Blumberg and Michael concluded that the availability of teacher-generated learning objectives does not subvert the development of self-directed learning skills.

The aim of this study was to investigate to what extent curricular elements, such as tests, course objectives, lectures and references, affect students' individual study and the development of students' self-directed learning skills.

METHOD

Participants

The study was conducted at the Medical School of the University of Maastricht, the Netherlands. Students from four different curricular years were included. About 150 students participated in each of four curricular years. These students were randomly assigned to 18 tutorial groups, each comprised of 8 to 10 students. Each tutorial group was guided by a tutor. A total of 407 students (68%) filled out the questionnaire distributed by the investigators. The response rate was 77% ($N = 115$) in the first year, 77% ($N = 115$) in the second year, 49% ($N = 73$) in the third year, and 69% ($N = 104$) in the fourth year. The low response rate in the third year was attributed to the fact that many of the third-year students had left for elective studies abroad shortly after the questionnaire was distributed among them.

Materials

A questionnaire was developed that was aimed at identifying to what extent several elements of the curriculum influenced students' decisions on what to study. It was divided into themes reflecting aspects that might influence students' learning activities during self-study, and it contained 20 statements: 4 about the influence of the discussion in the tutorial group, 6 about the influence of content tested, 3 about the influence of course objectives, 2 about the role of lectures, 3 about the influence of the tutor, and 2 about the selection of reading materials (see the Appendix for complete survey items). Some examples of statements are "I do not spend time on studying particular issues, if I am convinced that these issues will not be tested" and "I usually confine myself to the reference literature cited in the course book when searching for relevant literature." Students were asked to indicate on a 5-point Likert-type scale whether they (1) *totally disagree*, (2) disagree, (3) are neutral, (4) agree, or (5) *totally agree* with each statement. While judging these statements they were requested to keep in mind their learning activities for self-study during the previous academic year.

A confirmatory factor analysis model was carried out to assess the adequacy of the six elements influencing students' decisions on what to study: (1) discussion, (2) content tested, (3) course objectives, (4) lectures, (5) tutor and (6) reference literature. The 6-factor model showed a reasonable fit with the data. Coefficients alpha—an index of internal consistency—were computed to estimate the reliability of each factor. The coefficient alpha for each factor varied between 0.51 and 0.82. Analysis of variance was used to compare the average scores for each factor within different curricular years.

RESULTS AND DISCUSSION

Table 11.1 provides an overview of the mean scores and standard deviations for each factor for curricular years 1 to 4 together and for each year separately, as well as the corresponding p values to test whether the average scores for each factor differ across the 4 curricular years. A p value lower than .05 is assumed to be significant.

The mean scores for curricular years 1–4 in Table 11.1 indicate that all factors have an impact on students' decisions on what to study. Factor 3, the influence of course objectives, received the highest average score on a scale from 1 (*totally disagree*) to 5 (*totally agree*). Factor 1, the influence of the discussion in the tutorial group, also scored relatively high. Factor 2, the influence of content tested, and Factor 4, lectures, received the lowest average scores. As can be seen in Table 11.1, significant differences between the curricular Years 1 to 4 were found for Factor 2, the influence of content tested, Factor 4, the influence of lectures, and Factor 6, the impact of reference literature on students' decisions on what to study. In the following section, each factor is discussed separately.

TABLE 11.1
Mean scores (scale 1 'totally disagree' to 5 'totally agree'), with standard
deviations within parentheses, for curriculum years 1 to 4 together (average) and 1
to 4 separately. *P* values are also included to test whether the average scores
per factor differ significantly across the 4 curriculum years.

Factors'	1–4	1	2	3	4	P
1. Discussion	3.36	3.28	3.30	3.39	3.50	0.084
(4 items)	(0.69)	(0.69)	(0.74)	(0.67)	(0.64)	
2. Content tested	2.86	3.08	2.89	2.62	2.74	0.000
(6 items)	(0.71)	(0.68)	(0.62)	(0.68)	(0.78)	
3. Course objectives	3.48	3.56	2.55	3.43	3.35	0.363
(3 items)	(0.99)	(0.96)	(0.99)	(0.98)	(1.05)	
4. Lectures	2.99	3.32	2.79	2.90	2.89	0.001
(2 items)	(1.04)	(0.91)	(1.03)	(1.18)	(1.01)	
5. Tutor	3.12	3.22	3.12	3.10	3.04	0.321
(3 items)	(0.73)	(0.67)	(0.71)	(0.79)	(0.78)	
6. Reference literature	3.15	3.60	3.21	3.22	2.55	0.000
(2 items)	(0.92)	(0.83)	(0.80)	(0.88)	(0.87)	

The Influence of the Discussion in the Tutorial Group

It may be obvious that the discussion preceding the generation of learning issues and the learning issues that are eventually listed contain important information about the direction of students' self-study. The initial
problem discussion provides students with clues that they use when
searching for relevant information. This assumption is corroborated by
the data presented in Table 11.1. As can be seen in Table 11.1, the influence of the tutorial group on what students will study is higher in curricular Years 3 and 4 than in curricular Years 1 and 2 (albeit not
significantly). This finding might be explained by an increase in experience of students in generating learning issues that provide clear guidelines regarding what content should be studied. Thus, students might
become better self-directed learners as a result of being in the curriculum
for a longer time.

The Influence of Content Tested

In each coursebook, a self-assessment test was included to provide students
with formative feedback about their performances. At the end of each
course an achievement test was administered to the students, which is also
aimed at providing students with formative feedback. The results in Table
11.1 demonstrate that the influence of content tested on students' self-study
is highest in curricular Year 1, decreases in the curricular Years 2 and 3, and
shows a slight increase in curricular Year 4. A disadvantage of including a

self-assessment test in the coursebook is that students may tune their learning activities to the content that is tested. This would imply that students' learning activities are not guided by the learning issues generated in the tutorial group, which hence, would be detrimental to the development of self-directed learning skills. The results indicate that students in the first and second curricular years are more test driven than students in the third and fourth curricular years. Thus, test-directed studying seems to diminish over the curricular years. This implies that less value is attributed to the momentary knowledge needed to answer a test and the focus shifts to functional knowledge over the curricular years.

Course Objectives

In each coursebook, global course objectives were listed. These objectives provided students with information about the subject matter dealt with in the course and gave students information about what they were expected to study during a course. As such, course objectives were assumed to influence students' self-study. Three questions were included in the questionnaire about this aspect of a problem-based curriculum. The results in Table 11.1 indicate that the influence of the course objectives on students' learning activities was strong in each curricular year and did not differ significantly across the four curricular years. Guidelines about what subject matter students are assumed to deal with during self-study in each course seem to play an important role in all four curricular years.

Lectures

In each course, a limited number of lectures were included. The questionnaire contained two items about the influence of these lectures on students' self-study. The results in Table 11.1 indicate that the influence of topics covered during lectures on students' self-study was strongest in curricular Year 1. A possible explanation for the finding that first-year students tend to rely more on content covered in lectures than students in the other 3 years is that first-year students are less experienced self-directed learners. The content covered in a lecture gives students an idea of the topics that receive attention and, as a consequence, are seen as important topics to study. It is likely that as students become more experienced self-directed learners, they tend to rely less on the content covered in lectures.

The Influence of the Tutor

The tutor also influences what students will study, because he or she guides the tutorial group process and uses his or her expert knowledge—

if any—when discussing the problem. As can be seen in Table 11.1, no significant differences were found among the four curricular years. This finding might be explained by the well structuredness of the curriculum; that is, clearly presented problems and clearly defined course objectives. Due to this well structuredness, a tutor's level of expertise is less likely to be actually "used" by students or is seen as having less surplus value. Students relied on the curriculum or allowed the curriculum do its work instead of the tutor in the Medical School of the University of Maastricht (Dolmans, Wolfhagen, & Schmidt, 1996).

The Selection of Reading Materials

Students in a problem-based curriculum are encouraged to consult different resources. In each coursebook, suggestions for learning resources were listed at a rather global level. Two items were included in the questionnaire about the use of different resources and the influence of the list of resources on students' self-study. The results in Table 11.1 demonstrate that students, in particular during the first year, largely confined themselves to the reference literature cited in the coursebook when searching for relevant literature. During the fourth curricular year, students made less use of the reference literature cited in the course book. In the first year of their study students have no previous experiences with the usefulness and readability of books so they rely on the literature cited, whereas in later years, they seem to select books based on their own preferences and experiences. Making less use of reference literature during the four years again provides evidence for the assumption that students become better self-directed learners.

CONCLUSION

In a problem-based medical curriculum, faculty feel a need to ensure that their students possess sufficient knowledge and that no large gaps in their knowledge exist. On the other hand, students are supposed to be responsible for their own learning and should be given the freedom to decide which learning issues should be generated. This dilemma makes curricular design in a PBL curriculum a painstaking activity. Although these responsibilities seem to be contradictory, this study has shown that the two requirements can be, and in fact have been, successfully combined in the PBL curriculum under study.

The present study was aimed at identifying to what extent several elements of a problem-based curriculum influence the nature of students' self-study. The results demonstrate that the availability of a reference list, course objectives, lectures, tests, and the tutor all have an impact on students' learning activities during self-study. First-year students tend to rely more on the literature cited in the reference list and on content covered in tests and lectures than students in the other three curricular years. In general, the influence of these elements diminishes over the 4 curricular years. The influence of the discussion in the tutorial group, on the contrary, seems to increase over the 4 curricular years (this increase, however, is not significant). These findings provide evidence to support the assumption that students in a problem-based curriculum become better self-directed learners. Increased experience of students in generating learning issues that provide clear guidelines regarding what content should be studied may explain these findings. A recent study, investigating the use of student-generated learning issues, found that first-year students confined themselves more strictly to the learning issues generated, whereas in later years students were more likely to study beyond the learning issues generated (van den Hurk, Wolfhagen, Dolmans, & van der Vleuten, 1998). First-year students used learning issues as a tool to demarcate the literature, whereas in later years, students tailored their studying more according to their own needs and interests. Thus, students in a problem-based curriculum seem to become better self-directed learners as a result of being in the curriculum for a longer time even though they are provided with many clues that may play a role in their decisions on what to study. Hence, experience is an important factor.

In this study, it was shown that development of self-directed learning skills and subject matter coverage are not necessarily incompatible goals of PBL, but can coexist and in fact were successfully combined in the PBL curriculum under study. This finding is in agreement with the results of the study of Blumberg and Michael (1992) who also concluded that the availability of teacher-generated learning objectives does not subvert the development of self-directed learning skills. They argued that the key to encouraging self-directed learning skills lies in consistency among all aspects of the curriculum, such as the student-generated learning issues, faculty objectives, the material covered in resource sessions, and the material that is tested. Thus, a curriculum should be developed in which all aspects consistently stimulate students to take responsibility for their own learning.

Since this study was not a longitudinal study, the results could also be explained by differences between students in different curricular years. A longitudinal study is needed to find out whether students indeed become better self-directed learners and whether this behavior is continued in professional practice.

ACKNOWLEDGMENTS

The results of this study have been previously published in *Medical Education* (1994), *28*, pp. 372–380 and in *Bulletin Medisch Onderwijs* (1994), *13*, pp. 73–79, a Dutch journal on medical education.

REFERENCES

Anderson, J. R. (1990). *Cognitive psychology and its implications*. New York: Freeman.

Barrows, H. S., & Tamblyn, R. M. (1980). *Problem-based learning. An approach to medical education*. New York: Springer.

Bereiter, C., & Scardamalia, M. (1989). Intentional learning as a goal of instruction. In L. B. Resnick (Ed.), *Knowing, learning and instruction: Essays in honor of Robert Glaser* (pp. 361–392). Hillsdale, NJ: Lawrence Erlbaum Associates.

Bereiter, C., & Scardamalia, M. (1992). Cognition and curriculum. In P. W. Jackson (Ed.), *Handbook of research on curriculum*. New York: MacMillan.

Blumberg, P., & Michael, J. A. (1992). Development of self-directed learning behaviors in a partially teacher-directed problem-based learning curriculum. *Teaching and Learning in Medicine, 4*(1), 3–8.

Bruning, R. H. Schraw, G. J., & Ronning, R. R. (1995). *Cognitive psychology and instruction*. Englewood Cliffs, NJ: Prentice Hall.

Dolmans, D. H. J. M., Wolfhagen, H. A. P., & Schmidt, H. G. (1996). Effects of tutor expertise on student performance in relation to prior knowledge and level of curricular structure. *Academic Medicine, 71*, 1008–1011.

Glaser, R. (1991). The maturing of the relationship between the science of learning and cognition and educational practice. *Learning and Instruction, 1*, 129–144.

Schmidt, H. G. (1984). Activatie van voorkennis en tekstverwerking. [Activation of prior knowledge and text processing]. *Nederlands Tijdschrift voor de Psychologie, 39*, 335–347.

Schmidt, H. G. (1993). Foundations of problem-based learning: Some explanatory notes. *Medical Education, 27*, 422–432.

Schmidt, H. G., De Volder, M. L., De Grave, W. S., Moust, J. H. C., & Patel, V. L. (1989). Explanatory models in the processing of science text: The role of prior knowledge activation through small-group discussion. *Journal of Educational Psychology, 81*, 610–619.

van den Hurk, M. M., Wolfhagen, H. A. P., Dolmans, D. H. J. M., & van der Vleuten, C. P. M. (1998, April). *The impact of student-generated learning issues on individual study and academic achievement*. Paper presented at the Annual Meeting of the American Educational Research Association in San Diego, CA.

Vermunt, J. D. H. M. (1989, September). *The interplay between internal and external regulation of learning, and the design of process-oriented instruction*. Paper presented at the third conference of the European Association of Research on Learning and Instruction, Madrid.

APPENDIX

Items Included in the Questionnaire and Their Related Factors

Discussion

1. The discussion in the tutorial group determines to a large extent what I will study.

2. The tutorial group discussion is an important stimulus for my learning activities during individual study.
3. The learning issues generated are the most important starting point for my learning activities during individual study.
4. I study to a large extent independently from the learning issues generated.

Content Tested

5. I do not spend any time on studying particular issues, if I am convinced that these issues will not be tested.
6. I take a look at the questions included in the tests to get an idea of how deeply I should study particular subject matter.
7. The questions that are included in the tests to a large extent determine what I will study.
8. The closer the date the test will be administered, the more time I spend on test preparation.
9. The closer the date the test will be administered, the less time I spend on studying the learning issues generated in the tutorial group.
10. The learning issues generated in the tutorial group are tuned to the subject matter expected to be tested.

Course Objectives

11. At the start of a course, I consult the course objectives stated in the coursebook.
12. At the end of the course, I consult the course objectives to check whether I covered all subject matter I was expected to cover.
13. During the course, the course objectives influence what kind of learning activities I am going to conduct.

Lectures

14. Topics covered during lectures influence which topics I select for individual study.
15. Lectures are an important source of information to decide which topics I will study more extensively.

Tutor

16. In general, tutors stimulate my learning activities.

17. In general, tutors stimulate students to make use of different sources of information.
18. In general, tutors have an important influence on the selection of learning issues.

Reference Literature

19. I usually confine myself to the reference literature cited in the course book when searching for relevant literature.
20. I hardly review literature beyond the sources that are included in the course book.

Chapter 12

Observing Self-Directed Learners in a Problem-Based Learning Context: Two Case Studies

Dorothy H. Evensen, Ph.D.
The Pennsylvania State University

What we presently know about self-directed learning[1] in educational contexts is mostly inferred from surveys and from structured, decontextualized learning tasks (Blumberg & Michael, 1992; Dolmans & Schmidt, 1994; Hmelo, Gotterer, & Bransford, 1997; Newble & Clarke, 1986). In the necessary methodological step of aggregating data, what is often masked in these studies is the entity central to the construct: the self.

Candy (1991) argued that "If ever there were a topic that lent itself to, or even demanded, an ideographic or case study approach, it must be the phenomenon of self-directed learning" (p. 452). In other words, to understand this construct more fully, we need to be able to see what self-directed learning looks like as it is practiced by individual learners in particular educational environments.

In medical education, self-directed learning stands as a principal component of problem-based learning (PBL) curricula (Barrows & Tamblyn, 1980; Schmidt, 1993). Blumberg (this volume) has reviewed the literature on self-directed learning and concludes that we have evidence attesting to what self-directed learners do, but we still lack information about what factors might contribute to or constrain their actions. She advocates that

---

[1]Within the field of adult education, there has been much theorizing on the dimensions of self-directed learning. Most theories hypothesize interactions among sociological, pedagogical, and psychological dimensions. Because the present study takes place within a particular educational institution, it is assumed that self-directed learning is the "degree to which the learner, or the self, maintains active control of the learning process" (Long, 1989, p. 3).

researchers adopt "naturalistic, interpretive approaches" that attempt to discover perceptions, concerns, and motives of learners in PBL curricula.

This chapter presents two cases taken from a larger study (Evensen, 1999) of six first-year medical students enrolled in a PBL program. The larger study employed a grounded approach (Strauss & Corbin, 1990) to inductively identify factors that contribute to self-directed learning strategies (both cognitive and motivational) and to discover how such factors interact. The study yielded a model that closely corresponds to social cognitive theoretical models of what is known in the educational psychology literature as "self-regulated learning" (Bandura, 1986; Winne, 1997; Zimmerman, 1989). These theories maintain that personal, environmental, and behavioral factors operate interactively and reciprocally in constituting the degree of self-regulated learning.

The two case studies have been selected from the larger study because of their intrinsic and comparative value (Stake, 1995). Individually, each one presents a picture of how one learner selected particular strategies based on personal attributes and interpretations of the learning environment. Hence, each provides a unique picture of the self-directed learner. Together, the two cases invite speculation on characteristics of self-directed learning that might be useful to the study of learning in other contexts, particularly within adult populations in higher education or in professional training contexts.

In the sections that follow, I first describe the context of learning for the two persons featured in this chapter. Next, I present each case, chronologically punctuating it into phases where shifts in the degree of self-directed learning were discerned. I use the cases to infer characteristics of self-directed learning in this context, and I connect these inferences to those found in the literature on self-directed and self-regulated learning. Finally, I conclude with a discussion of some implications for the continued study of professional education and lifelong learning.

THE CONTEXT

The First Year of the First-Year Program

Beth and Kyle[2] were among 24 first-year medical students who opted to participate in a PBL curricular track at the medical college affiliated with a large, northeastern research university. The "traditional" track featured a curriculum organized into basic science disciplinary units that were delivered largely through lecture. This traditional curriculum was select-

---

[2]The names of the students have been changed to help assure anonymity.

ed by the majority of students, 81 in number. Problem-based curricula had been offered to approximately 20% of the second-year class for the two previous years; this was the first year that it was being offered to first-year students who then would be compelled to continue in PBL during the second year.

Barrows (1986) has identified variations of problem-based curricula from "pure" to "hybrid." The curriculum at this medical college is described by one coordinator as "case based." Students meet in groups of five or six with one or two facilitators who are usually faculty members from both the M.D. and the Ph.D. ranks but can also be nonfaculty, staff physicians, or, occasionally, fourth-year students who have been identified as having been particularly successful in previous PBL work. These groups meet three times per week (Monday, Wednesday, and Friday) for 3 hours in the morning. The meetings center on a paper case that presents a medical problem. The information embedded in the case unfolds incrementally over the course of two or three sessions.

One of the first things students learn is the framework for analyzing the case and for directing their own learning. One student usually assumes the role of "reader"; another acts as "scribe." As the case is read aloud, group members begin by isolating "facts" from the case scenario while the scribe lists these in a column on a large whiteboard. Once completed, students venture to hypothesize by combining facts to form differential diagnoses or to speculate about pathways and processes. Next, students determine further questions they might ask to or about this "patient" or about the discrete processes or conditions. Finally, and most pedagogically important, students determine "learning objectives"—what they need to know to understand this case. Students are then expected to direct their own learning experiences around these learning objectives, deciding either collectively, individually, or both, what resources to consult, how deeply to inquire into particular topics, and how to organize study and review materials. In this medical college, topical learning objectives are appended to the "last page" of each case and are usually given on the final day of the group meeting around the case.

The semester is divided into two PBL blocks of approximately 8 weeks. A total of 12 to 15 cases are studied during each block. Students meet within the same randomly formed group with one or two facilitators for the entire block, and groups are reconfigured for subsequent blocks. Over the course of the 2-year PBL program, students can expect to be members of eight different groups.

Besides the group meeting, members of this PBL class are required to participate in some structured curricula. Two courses are taken with "traditionals"—Humanities and Introduction to Medicine: Physical Diagnosis. Each meets for 3 hours per week over the entire semester. PBL students also participate in about 12 hours of MEDLINE training and 6 hours of what is called "Critical Appraisal"—sessions that focus on ways of reading and interpreting the medical literature.

Like most PBL programs, evaluation plays a major role in this context. Besides reflection and self-evaluation, which are designed to be ongoing, students' participation is rated on a daily basis by facilitators and constitutes 40% of the block grade. An equally weighted assessment, the Block Exam, focuses on the learning products of cases. Finally, an Individual Performance Assessment, which simulates the entire PBL case process, accounts for 20% of the grade. Two quizzes are given prior to the first Block Exam, and students are responsible for completing "exercises" (mostly problems in histology, pathology and biochemistry), some written reports, and two informatics problems that require searching the recent MEDLINE literature. In addition, the "boards" or the National Board of Medical Examiners (NBME), Part 1 examination, loom largely for these students even though they will not be facing them until the end of the second year. Below each set of case-specific learning objectives printed on curriculum materials appears a list of NBME objectives that relate to the case.[3]

METHOD

As mentioned previously, Beth and Kyle were two of six students who volunteered to be part of a study that sought to discover what strategies first-year PBL students used to negotiate their way through this new curriculum during their first semester in medical school. Students received a $250 honorarium for participation and agreed to allow me to observe all formal PBL sessions; participate in interviews every other week; keep what were called "oral learning logs" in which they used a minicassette recorder to tape what they were studying, how they were making selection decisions, and outcomes or reflections on study sessions; and make available notes, written materials, and test results. These data sources were transcribed, analyzed, reduced, and compared using methods of grounded theory (Strauss & Corbin, 1990).

---

[3]Because this was the first year of the first-year program, program directors reported that they consciously "started out cautiously," and took such measures as listing NBME objectives in order to avoid experiences encountered in other PBL start-up programs where PBL students' board scores were inferior to "traditionals." Other more "structured" elements of the PBL program, such as quizzes and exercises, were instituted in response to the anticipated disparity in students' basic science knowledge. By the second year, the curriculum became less structured.

During the data collecting and analysis phase of the study, the focus of the research shifted. It became obvious that what was most interesting was not what strategies were being employed, but why particular strategies emerged. Through a constant comparison method and triangulation of observational, interview, and learning log data, it was theorized that the learner's selection of strategies resulted from the interaction of academic self-concept factors (such as goals, background, perception of learning style, and sense of self-efficacy) and perceptions of program affordances (such as the case-based curriculum, the opportunity to make decisions about how and what to study, and the opportunity to meet in a group).[4]

In addition, strategies were found to be affected by feedback regarding program stakes: daily evaluations, quizzes, tests, and the ubiquitous "boards." These stakes, both low and high, were discovered to have the power to significantly disturb the equilibrium of these students to the extent that after each test or evaluative event, a kind of redirection or refocusing could be discerned regarding both perceptions of self, of the environment, and of strategy use. Thus, three "phases" were identified within each data set, each phase serving as a temporal unit of analysis. Finally, in keeping with the analytical scheme of grounded theory, a superordinate code was selected to name the overarching phenomenon discernible from the study. This was selected, in part, by gaining theoretical sensitivity through an ongoing review of the literature. The term that best applied to the phenomenon under study appeared to be "self-directed learning."

The "cases" that follow are narrated, largely through the words of Beth and Kyle, in keeping with the chronologies and categories outlined previously. These narratives are the result of both a deconstructive process wherein data were reduced to categories and concepts and a reconstructive process that selected and drew together quotes that were deemed to best represent relevant ideas. The narratives are designed to allow the reader to follow Beth and Kyle through the three phases of their first semester by attending to salient personal and environmental concerns that could be interpreted as contributing to decisions about the learning and motivational strategies each employs. At the end of each section, conclusions are drawn concerning each student's degree of self-directed learning.

---

[4]The model that emerged provided units and subunits of analysis within which to analyze and interpret data. Evidence that could explain self-directed strategies was sought by analyzing interactions between personal and environmental variables. For example, one student who perceived himself as an autonomous learner saw the group situation as both academically high risk and emotionally disconcerting. After discovering that being silent was a strategy that would incur negative evaluations from both facilitators and peers, he devised a strategy of "making charts." In other words, he would come to the meeting with a chart representing one or more processes relevant to the case and would, at some point in the discussion, offer the chart to the group.

THE CASES

Beth: Phase 1

Beth is a 22-year-old female who graduated from a seven-sister college with a major in theatre arts. Beth's father was a physician and faculty member of the teaching medical college and was instrumental in instituting the existing program in humanities. Tragically, he died in an automobile accident during Beth's freshman year in college. Beth reported that she had thought about becoming a doctor on and off since grade school but with parental support chose to focus on drama through high school and college, believing that she would miss opportunities in theatre (especially to direct) if they were not taken in school and that she could always pick up the study of medicine in later years. Beth did, however, take a science minor as an undergraduate and worked as a teaching assistant in an introductory biology course. Beth prepared herself for the Medical College Admission Test (MCAT) by buying a review book and setting up a study schedule for herself. She reported,

> I was working totally independently. All I had was this big, fat paperback book and my textbooks. I would make an outline and would say, "I'm going to look at these four topics tonight. I'm going to master them." And I would. And then I would check them off on the outline. I could sit there after 4 weeks of work and look at all those little check marks and I'd say, "Good, I'm doing really well. I'm a third of the way through." (LL 2.11)[5]

I'm Counting on That Happening. Beth began the semester with definite goals and preferences. She admitted to being idealistic in focusing on being the best doctor she could be, and attributed this to her remembered experiences with her father:

> When we were little I remember we used to come in here with my father and just watch. He was very involved in a team approach—a group of people trying to help this person. And the whole concept really appealed to me as a way to spend most of my time, which is the way I tend to view a job—what you're going to do for 12 hours of your day. (I 1.12)

Beth appeared to know herself as a learner and demonstrated a high degree of self-efficacy.[6] She offered an anecdote to illustrate her prefer-

---

[5]Quotes are taken from interviews (I) and learning logs (LL). These are furthermore sequentially numbered.

[6]The term "self-efficacy" is used in the broad sense suggested by Bandura (1986): individuals' "judgment of their capabilities to organize and execute courses of action required to attain designated types of performance" (p. 391).

ence for "learning by doing," telling of her early adventures in play production.

> We just did it—and floundered and flailed—trial and error and error and error. We had a good advisor. I would go and I could formulate a specific question for him, but he was standing off in the sidelines. (I 1.4)

It is the opportunity to engage in decision-making activities as a member of a group that drew Beth to PBL. Not exactly freewheeling, Beth admitted to a need for structure, but gave examples of instances where she was able to construct her own frameworks when she found them institutionally lacking. Participation, improvisation, and catching up had, up to now, been behaviors she could count on. While she was "counting on" these kicking in here in medical school, she was "concerned" that her lack of background knowledge, at least in comparison to other members of her group, would make this previously comfortable and dependable process more difficult. She stated, "I feel like I know so much less than they do" (LL 2.3); "I feel like I have nothing to say" (I 1.2).

Covering All of the Bases. Two aspects of PBL strongly appealed to Beth: the opportunity for self-study and the group meeting. Her only concerns related to time (she saw the "light" caseload early on as fostering habits of taking things at a slow pace), and participation. She maintained, "Listening to everyone's expertise at the beginning of a case is very scary. And at the beginning of a case I have nothing to say" (I 2.10).

Beth perceived these issues as relatively minor, but voiced serious concern about problems she detected in the curriculum. First, she worried that the practice of immersing students in the case method could place too much emphasis on the process and detract attention from the substantive content issues of the case. She also detected an unevenness and inconsistency in some of the tasks required of students:

> This program is a bizarre mixture sometimes of very demanding, intense work that you can do or not do independently . . . and then they have these exercises and it's like work that I did in like phonics. It's confusing. I guess they're trying to cover all of their bases. (LL 2.14)

Covering bases is what Beth set as a goal for herself regarding the stakes—especially regarding the NBME. She looked forward to her first quiz mostly as an indicator of the amount of learning that had taken place, but at the same time worried that she might have been missing content required for the boards, or was perhaps learning it in a way that was inconsistent with the priorities inherent in that test. She intimated:

I have this kind of concept like I'm in some guy's clown act where he starts dropping all of his cigarettes and everytime he bends down to pick one up, he drops another. And I'm just afraid I'm going to do that, and 2 years from now I'm not going to have a hold of anything. (LL 2.12)

Take Action. With risk areas defined, Beth set out to use her strengths— a proclivity for experimentation, an ability to create structure, and a desire to take action and learn by doing—to devise strategies for learning. Her first concern was her lack of background in many areas of science. This she addressed by employing easy texts from undergraduate days, one dubbed "baby bio," to serve as a basis for more difficult reading. She related:

Since hormones is one of my least favorite and most poorly understood topics, I'm going to start out with my baby bio book and read through that chapter, and I'm just trying to get the background so I can read the text that I'm really supposed to read (in the medical textbook; LL 3.3).

She further revealed the questions that served to guide her experimentation with ways of reading and studying:

I think I'm still trying to find out what the best way is for me to learn all this. Is it reading a chapter and taking notes? Is it reading a chapter and writing down what I remember? Going back over it and then taking notes? Is it highlighting? Is it all of these different things? (LL 2.10)

Beth started out by taking notes while reading, but soon saw this as organizationally problematic. In assessing and revising her strategy, she first determined that she must set concrete goals for her reading, which she accomplished by reading through material without taking notes to gain a larger picture of the topic under study. She also found that this procedure allowed her to bypass some of her basic reading as she found background information embedded in more difficult texts. She reserved her notetaking for her second, goal-driven reading. Beth also spoke of a strategy she called "redoing notes." She explained this as taking notes on notes in a reductive fashion. Finally, in search of the relevance of what she was studying, she located primary research articles related to the topic. She reported that this was "one of my favorite aspects. But I do it following the textbook reading and it gives relevance and adds an element of interest to moderately dry material" (LL 3.5). These strategies appeared to serve Beth's need to attend to the present; however, she also kept her eye on the future. Beth purchased an NBME review book and, as she did for the MCAT, used the book as a checklist for topics covered.

Beth adopted an array of motivational strategies during this phase. First, she coached herself to refrain from comparison with fellow students, she cheered herself on recognizing her hard work ("I'm feeling brilliant right now . . . I just picked and axed my way through this text and did really well"; LL 2.2), she "vented" to her boyfriend, and she rewarded herself with a weekend break from her studies. Probably the most significant action taken by Beth was her decision to run for PBL representative to the Curricular Affairs Committee. She stated,

> I am running for the office of PBL rep for the faculty organization because I'm an idiot (laughs)—No, to see if I can make some difference. One big difference is the dean needs to say to these faculty members that they cannot cut up one another's programs in front of students. (LL 2.15)

Beth entered medical school aware of the challenges she was facing, willing to accept the responsibility of filling gaps in her knowledge, anxious to participate in social contexts, and ready to take whatever action was necessary to achieve her goals. What she did not anticipate was what she perceived as inconsistencies between the theoretical principles of the curriculum and the way it was operationalized. Another unexpected tension occurred as she found herself in the context that was so much a part of her father's life:

> I really haven't been here since my father died, and he was a big cheese at the hospital. And I hear about him everywhere. I was down in the library, and I turned around and there was his picture on the wall. And I thought that this certainly messes with your mind. I'm really beginning to understand how stuff like this can get in the way of learning. It takes time to be messed up. (LL 2.9)

But Beth was not so "messed up" that she lost sight of her plans or ceased to devise methods to achieve her goals. She admitted a proclivity to compare, but recognized this as a residual behavior from earlier school days and acted quickly to dispel its influence. In short, Beth's level of self-regulation appeared high during this phase. Her high degree of metacognitive awareness and her conscious use of motivational strategies were impressive. In particular, her clear goals and keen awareness of the high degree of compatibility between her learning style preferences and program affordances might have served as predictors that Beth's transition would be a smooth one in spite of her relatively lesser fund of background information in science.

Beth: Phase 2

If I Didn't Care. The minor disillusionments Beth faced in the first few weeks of medical school began to turn into more deep-seated dissatisfactions in this phase. Beth revised her goal of being the "best possible doctor" to "doing well," and accompanying her diminished ideal were the beginnings of doubt about the appropriateness of medicine as a career. She stated, "I think academically I'll just sort of plod along and I'll be OK. But now it tends to be a large question: Is this really what I want to do?" (I 3.1).

Beth's self-efficacy continued to be challenged as she sat in awe of the displays of knowledge among her group members. In addition, her role as PBL rep brought with it a series of frustrations as she found herself attempting to explain and justify the program to outsiders (traditionals) and supporting practices that she herself found questionable to insiders (fellow PBL students). Her growing sense of frustration is illustrated in the following:

> Sometimes I wish I didn't have to be defender of the faith. But that's a problem with initiating a new program, and I don't want the program to fail, which is why I ran for PBL rep. I'm trying to do what I'm trying to do. If I didn't care, it would be a lot easier. (LL 4.1)

Whom Do You Trust? Beth struggled to retain trust in the PBL program in spite of the incongruities she recognized: the artificiality of the process of receiving successive "pages" of cases while facilitators "hold onto learning objectives," and the potential danger of what she saw as a curriculum and program that was the product of one person's point of view—Dr. Howell, the program coordinator. Beth also faced some disappointments in terms of evaluations. She was "nailed" on exercises for not supplying the level of detail required by the program director. She also earned a relatively low but passing score on the first quiz. In the former case she believed this to be another example of the lack of clarity concerning task expectations. In the latter case, she was satisfied that, given her lack of background, she performed as well as she could have expected.

Beth maintained that, in spite of these conflicts, she remained certain that PBL was better than the traditional curriculum; still, she wished that a few more bugs had been programmed out before implementation:

> There's no way of avoiding the fact that we're the first group through this. Somebody has to be first. But at the same time, I don't think there's been any compensatory response to that. No one said, "You're the first and here's how I'm going to show you it's OK." There's been none of that. (I 4.12)

Beth also began to become skeptical of what self-study might mean in PBL. This tension was exacerbated when viewed in the context of the group.

There was this sort of myth that we were going to be able to go and learn things that we wanted to learn. I'm not seeing a lot of latitude for that. Part of it is that when you get into group, you can't really present stuff other people haven't looked at. People say, "Where did you read that? Was I supposed to have read that?" So you kind of have to keep it to yourself. It's not applicable to the group, and it's not really applicable to a test, but you kind of learned it because you thought it was interesting. But then what do you do with it? And if you don't do anything with it, you're just gonna forget it. (I 4.14)

In general, and opposed to beliefs she held concerning ideal group operations, Beth saw group members reading the "same stuff," using the same books, and becoming text-bound. She supposed that this attitude resulted from the apprehension arising from daily evaluations made by facilitators and from prospective exams that she too admitted were affecting her study decisions. Again, she struggled with the issue of trust concerning the importance of grades:

And Dr. Howell is over here and we're over here (spreads arms)—and we both value different things. Everyone has the vibe that he doesn't care very much about grades, but these are medical students—they've had to care a lot about grades to get here and you can't just ask them to forget that. And you get a grade here and that gets you into a residency program. That's of great importance to me. (I 3.9)

Plod Along. In spite of the emotional turmoil Beth experienced in this phase, she continued to not only "plod along," but also to refine her study strategies. She increased her use of library resources to fill in her knowledge gaps and to provide a "big picture" of topics under study. One strategy she developed was using textbooks devoted exclusively to particular organs, systems, or processes. She explained:

I don't think I've ever read past page 30 in any library book, but the introductory chapters are often really good—that's where the really good stuff is—the best explanations and the best diagrams. These are really what the authors are trying to do—write about the liver, not about the physiology of the whole body. (I 4.3)

Beth maintained at this point that she "knows" her books:

The way I use each different book is unique to each one. I have this shelf of $700 worth of textbooks and I look at it and say, "I use all of those." And that's neat—and you get better at knowing which—like our pathology book—usually at the beginning of each section on diseases they have a nice little section on say the liver—five pages on the liver—very easy to read. (I 3.4)

Beth persisted in her general study and notetaking strategy devised earlier—reading first, taking notes during a second reading—and also engaged in her process of reducing notes as a study tool.

Because self-efficacy remained tenuous in this phase, Beth continued to invoke self-assessment measures to gauge her progress. The NBME checklist remained as did study sessions with Carol, a fellow group member, and Bob, her boyfriend who was not a medical student. During these sessions she reported bringing her reduced notes and "exploding" them verbally as she talked through the details that underlay and exemplified the abstracted topics noted. Beth also began to attend lunchtime talks given by staff physicians that dealt with particular patient concerns. Beth challenged herself to follow these discussions and mentally noted how much she understood and how much eluded her.

The day-to-day operations, especially the more "structured" features of the curriculum were perceived by Beth as encumbrances on self-directed learning and appeared to present a certain degree of risk—at least emotional risk—in this phase. In response to this, Beth tried to put her disappointments in perspective and increased her participation in the politics of PBL through her rep position. She admitted that she would be "dying" in the traditional curriculum and concluded that getting involved" would allow her to face her disappointments. Beth did not, however, appear to deal in any direct way with the problems she perceived in the group in spite of the fact that she voiced awareness of the tension and degree of disapproval she was encountering. Such lack of action seems anomalous, but it might be interpreted as a way to gain time until further assessments could have been made. On the other hand, Beth may have felt intimidated by either individual members of the group or by the group as a whole, especially because they appeared united in their decision to stay close to textbooks and remained directed almost exclusively by the learning objectives.

In summary, this phase presented increased dilemmas for Beth and although they seemed to affect her attitude and goals, they did not appear to detract from her study routine. Her degree of self-directed study appeared high although somewhat precarious as it remained to be seen what effect her lack of action concerning the group dynamics had on her practices. In other words, did she compromise her typical ways of interacting in order to placate the evident anxieties of group members or accommodate what she perceived as the preferences of the facilitators? She foresaw that this could be detrimental to her learning when she reported that "everyone looks at you" when you bring in unique material, and furthermore, "I almost feel like our facilitators don't like it when one person is further ahead of the rest. So I feel that I'm not motivated to learn more—and that's not really a 'me' thing to do" (LL 4.5).

Beth: Phase 3

Caring Too Much. Faced with a mediocre but passing grade on the first block exam, Beth once again reframed her goal.

> I intend to pass. I never in my entire life said I just want to pass and 80% of the world thought I was going to be an exception to that, but I don't think that's a really low goal now. (LL 5.4)

Although Beth seemed to be compromising her goals, she was nevertheless holding on to her ideals and realized that "being a doctor" was something she could actualize in PBL through the case-based nature of the study and her proximity to the world of medicine. This means–end transformation was apparent in the remark, "I want to make it through the basic sciences but I want to do it by being a doctor, not just reading textbooks" (I 8.1).

In this, the second block, Beth became a member of a new group. Here she found that her lack of background knowledge was not so obvious. In fact, she worried that in "fooling" the group into thinking she knows more than she knows, she might also have been fooling herself, creating an unnecessary area of risk.

> And I was thinking about that, and it may actually turn into a problem. I tend to say, "I'll get that" or "I know that well enough." Everyone in group says over and over, "Your lack of science background doesn't show up" which is probably true for the group, but not for exams or for the boards. (I 7.3)

Overall, Beth held fast to her learning style through this phase. She needed to go beyond the basics and beyond the texts to find relevance and "adventure" in her learning and in "being a doctor." She recognized, however, that this proclivity blinded her to the need to "play the game." She reflected,

> In my need for relevance, some other parts of my learning style were being directly countered by what I was being asked to do. Some of this is definitely learning how to play the game. That's something that I don't learn as quickly as most people—which hoops you're supposed to jump through the right way. (I 8.9)

Interestingly, Beth's sense of self-efficacy began to improve in this phase as she realized, through the various forms of self-assessments she had devised, that she knew more than she thought she would have known at this point. She seemed certain that her "problems" were not academic but were the emotional results of "caring too much" about the day-to-day operations of the program and its perception among persons in the medical school. She lamented,

> There are times I think that I am one of the least happy people in the program. It's not because of the program, but because I know more about it and I have strong feelings about the way it's set up. (I 8.15)

The Way It Is.   By the end of the first semester, Beth seemed to have accepted the program. She continued to recognize contradictions within the curriculum but was more convinced that what she was learning and the way she was learning was allowing her to live her goal of "being a doctor" while, at the same time, achieving her reframed goal of "passing" in the program. In particular, she produced evidence supporting one of the pedagogical principles of PBL—the idea that revisiting (or spiraling through) information presented in different forms and in different situations results in more efficient learning. She stated:

> It was interesting looking over the cholera case. Sure enough, the spiral has made a big difference in my understanding. At first I really didn't understand it, but now having nailed digestion very hard, and with all the work I did with the vitamins and all, I was looking over the learning objectives for cholera and I was thinking, "Oh, no problem." So that was kind of exciting. So that boosted my morale. (LL 6.6)

She also came to realize during this phase that trust and patience would be key to participating in this program. She affirmed that "there are no shortcuts" (LL 5.7) and admitted to sometimes wishing that she was in a program where students were told, "This is what you need to know; read these chapters and you'll do well" (LL 5.7). Beth's reaction to her undistinguished score on the first block exam also reflects this attitude of acceptance. She stated: "I think it really reflected the fact that I have a long way to go. If I had really done well, I would have had to think that it sort of magically happened" (I 7.3).

Finally, Beth's reassessment of the context of learning extended to her perceptions of the group. She saw that being "too different" or "shining" is incompatible with the culture.

What Works.   Having worked through the disappointments encountered in Phase 2, Beth engaged in strategies that were aimed at extending practices that had proven effective, and ameliorating the tensions that resulted when self-directed learning was perceived as at-risk. It was in the area of self-study where Beth seemed most assured about what she had been doing. She no longer talked in terms of experimentation, but continued to rely on her method of overviewing multiple texts before taking notes around identified learning objectives. She adopted three additional strategies for review and for self-assessment in this phase. First, she checked and reinforced her knowledge by challenging her understanding through a novel text:

> I study from my notes and then go and read something that I haven't read before. They almost always end up saying the same thing, but I go back and read a book on alcoholism just to hear it restated. Maybe they'll say something that will help me remember it better, or it's like, "Oh, I knew that!" and that makes me happy. (I 7.8)

Second, she reported discovering that "review articles" can serve to organize previously studied material and can function as outlines for essays that might appear on an exam. Third, Beth used human resources as a way to check on the status of her knowledge and pull information together: "I'm going to the internal medicine seminars and they talk about procedures, and all this provides a framework on which to hang all of this information I'm studying" (I 6.7).

Beth was convinced that what works is hard work. She spoke about trying to take shortcuts and their lack of success:

> I got a bunch of neat articles but I didn't have time to take notes on them and highlighted them instead because that's obviously faster. But when I got into group, I couldn't say anything about them because I hadn't organized them. So that was kind of useless. (LL 6.4)

Beth continued to follow her own lengthy process of reading and rereading, cyclically reducing text through successive notetaking sessions, then engaging in study sessions—mostly alone, but occasionally with another person—where she "exploded" terms and concepts to include details and elaborations of processes. In addition, she adopted a strategy strongly suggested by program coordinators of actually writing out essays from learning objectives in preparation for the block exam.

Regarding day-to-day interactions and maintaining an emotional equilibrium in the face of disappointments, Beth devised reactive, or coping strategies. She made inquiries into what steps would need to be taken to change directions and pursue a Master of Fine Arts. This, however, became overshadowed when she sought the advice of some doctors to whom she had access and reflected on "where I may or may not fit into this whole scheme." She concluded that she "can choose to do it in a different way" (LL 6.1).

Beth also revealed examples of "playing the game." Her discomfort with group interactions, barely mentioned during the last phase, were clearly recognized in this one. She realized that she could rub some people the wrong way and needed to tread lightly. When speaking about bringing in some non-textbook sources to the group she stated: "I'm going to bring it up, but I'll try not to be obnoxious" (I 5.6). Later in this phase she intimated, "I just know when not to say stuff" (I 7.3). She also took precautions to ensure that she was not engaging in a practice identified by one group member as "showcasing," but was contributing something useful to the group in the most efficient way: "If I have something that I know that no one else is going to look up, I make sure that I have it in its own little outline and it's all ready, so that when I bring it up, it's very clear" (I 6.3).

Beth continued to find the group work the most enjoyable part of the program, was willing to be an active member (if not a leader) of the group, but interpreted others' lack of participation or strict adherence to materials presented in textbooks as unfortunate. She "campaigned" for her own strategies to be adopted, and delighted in reporting, "I think that I managed to encourage some of the people in my group to go and look up some things when I ended up finding the best thing on malnutrition in a book on tropical diseases" (LL 5.8).

Beth also confessed to "playing the game" during her first block exam when she spent an extra half hour rewriting an essay, adding what she called "itsy-bitsy details," because she expected the section to be scored by Dr. Howell.

In summary, Beth seems to have adopted a pragmatic stance in the final phase of the first semester. She was convinced that she had learned how she needed to learn in this environment. Privately, she was highly self-directed, discovering new ways to assess learning and new resources to enhance learning, but publicly, she tempered her idiosyncratic strategies and generally played within what she perceived as the boundaries of the culture. Beth ended this phase with a generally accepting attitude. She accepted, for example, the "spiral" model offered by the program coordinators after some initial skepticism. She stated,

> I know that I'm not failing, and I know that I'm not getting a high pass this block. So it has got to be just for me—what I'm learning is for my own good. I'm beginning to learn how to study for exams. I'm doing better and feeling better about it. So whatever it is that I'm doing is working. (I 9.15)

CASE 2: KYLE

Kyle is 21 years old and has just completed a bachelor of science degree at a large research university. His major was premed, and he distinguished himself academically throughout his undergraduate studies. Kyle served as a teaching assistant in many laboratory-related courses. Kyle reported wanting initially to be a veterinarian, but because of severe allergies, he switched his career ambition to medicine. Both of Kyle's parents are high school teachers and have consistently supported and encouraged him. Kyle remembered always having done well in school, but recalled not performing up to expectations on the verbal portion of the Preliminary Scholastic Aptitude Test (PSAT). He related:

> My father just sat there and said, "I can't believe this. Where does the discrepancy come from?" (Kyle had scored 800 on the quantitative section, and thought he scored in the high 400s on the verbal section) and he gave me the New York Times every day for the next 2 years and said read the front page and the editorial, and any words you don't know, look up and write the words down in a little book. I have a little book full of definitions. If you opened it up and asked me any of them, I couldn't tell you. And I would understand the articles—there might be 20 unfamiliar words, but I'd understand them all from context . . . but I brought my score up to a 680 I think, but that was a struggle. (I 1.9)

Kyle: Phase 1

If It's in the Book . . .   Kyle began medical school with clear goals: to learn it all, to do well, and to become a good doctor. The "it" was the objectives of the curriculum. Kyle perceived the achievement of these goals as necessary results of each other. He seemed to possess much understanding of and confidence in himself as a learner. His experiences in the premed program coupled with the fact that he elected to take many advanced courses at the graduate level served as the basis for this confidence. He stated, "They said you pick up physiology as you go, and biochemistry. I've already taken those courses. I've had a good background, so it shouldn't be that difficult" (I 2.7).

Kyle was very definite about how he learns—through reading. He told a story from junior high school days when, after a relatively long absence due to illness, he returned to school on a day when the class was facing a major science test. The teacher assured him that he could take the test at a later date, but because he had "read ahead" while home convalescing, he opted to take the exam. Not surprisingly to him, but, he reported, to the teacher's dismay, he "aced" the test. He reported, "I thought if the information is in the book, I can learn it" (I 1.1). Kyle continued to rely on books. He confessed that he rarely attended lectures as an undergraduate. "I'd start off in the lectures and find them just not worth the time. I'd be much better off just getting up and reading for the hour" (I 1.1).

Kyle believed that the proof of learning was the ability to use what has been learned: "If I haven't learned it, I can't use it" (I 1.6). Learning for Kyle was not memorization, and he affirmed having a tolerance for ambiguity and an acceptance of approximations during the process of learning new things. He recognized early on that this tendency toward lack of certainty might pose interpersonal problems in group. He stated:

> If you give me an equation, say in physics—I can figure out how to plug things into it. I don't need to memorize every single thing. I'm much more likely in group to say "Well, this is probably the way it happens." (I 1.8)

As this first phase proceeded, Kyle based his confidence on his belief that once he had read something, he knew it, and if indeed learning had occurred, he would have no trouble either writing or talking about it. He also believed that medical school would prove more difficult than any other learning context previously encountered. By the end of this phase, however, it is this notion that slightly nudged his sense of self-efficacy. Although he sees people around him struggling with material and running out of time, he finds himself gliding along.

> I still seem to be ahead. I'm not sure that that is true or that I just keep fooling myself into thinking that I'm ahead. With this case I didn't have any difficulty or at least I didn't recognize any difficulty. Everyone else seems to be having trouble with it. (LL 3.4)

It Couldn't Hurt.   Kyle set out almost indifferent to the curriculum. He admitted that PBL had been attractive because it would have allowed him to study on his own without the pretense of learning from lectures. He spoke of enjoying the cases and working through them to identify learning objectives, but was glad that, unlike some PBL programs, this one distributed the case writer's objectives near the end of the study period (usually in the second or third day of the case). Concerning "getting" the learning objectives, he stated, "I'd like to know that I'm not missing something. I like to know that someone has looked to make sure that I'm going to learn everything in my 4 years" (I 1.12).

One aspect of the curriculum became a source of annoyance to Kyle early on. He was bothered by the reintroduction of topics already studied. This resulted in two problems for him. First, it simply "irritated" him to find himself revisiting topics. Second, it instilled doubts that he had sufficiently dealt with topics under study. "I see topics again and I think to myself, 'Am I supposed to be going deeper? And if so, how?' " (I 2.13). Another area of the curriculum that Kyle found distracting was the non-PBL courses such as Humanities, Physical Diagnosis, and Critical Appraisal. He perceived these courses as taking time away from the work he needed to do to study cases.

Kyle admitted that he might have been overdoing things in this phase. Early in the third week he said, "I definitely think I read too many chapters. I read something like 25 to 30 chapters in that (second) week" (I 2.6).

He voiced an interest in experimenting with how much he needed to do, but was not adverse to doing too much. His responses reflected a pragmatism, or an awareness of the consequences of his work. For example,

> I got two chapters of biochemistry out of the way today—both very much review, but nevertheless I need to know them for the boards, if not for the case, and quite possibly for the exam. So reading them certainly couldn't hurt. (LL 1.4)

This attitude of "not hurting" also applied to his perception of his role in the group. Kyle was quite emphatic that he did not need the group for his own learning, and in fact, acknowledged that his speculative style might have been repugnant to one group member in particular. Nonetheless, he accepted the fact that attendance was compulsory and felt a responsibility both to group members and to himself to be prepared. He maintained,

> I don't do very well if I walk into that group unprepared—not unprepared, rather not having read just about everything. I think I'd be at a loss because I have trouble picking up vast amounts of facts just by talking. (I 1.5)

Getting Things Out of the Way. Kyle appeared to be quite comfortable, confident, and highly self-directed in this phase. His major strategy was to rely on his reading to learn. He did devise an organizational system to direct his reading. He constructed a bibliography of sources on each topic before reading, then checked each off after reading. He also streamlined his reading, having disregarded sections of chapters that were not relevant to the particular case at hand. He affirmed relying on his own approaches rather than those proposed by the group. Commenting at the beginning of a study session he stated, "I'm going to read it in the order it's in the book, rather than in the order they suggested in group" (LL 2.1). He continued to be concerned about the depth of his study, but coached himself to trust that the designers of the curriculum had allowed for topics to be revisited in order to gain more depth.

Kyle's main objective was to get things done. His priorities were clearly focused on learning pursuant to the case, but he also "got done" with non-PBL requirements:

> I think of them as a little something I have to do. I try to finish up all this week's readings for those classes before I start in on the case because I think that when I'm working on a case, I want to concentrate. I don't want to think that I have to take off an hour here and read these little things. I thought about reading the whole Humanities book this weekend and just have that one out of the way, but I really can't do that because I'll forget the specifics of poems and things when I get to it. (I 2.11)

Kyle: Phase 2

New Stuff. Kyle remained assured that his style of learning would prove sufficient in this new educational setting. He revealed insights about his own process:

> Ask me after I read about something like cholera. I could sit right down and write about it. I only spent a half hour reading about it, but I could write an essay. I think I do a lot of organizing automatically—unconsciously—putting things together in my head and making those broad overview statements, then understanding how facts fit into them. (I 4.10)

Kyle also provided further clarity about the annoyance he felt when he encountered previously studied material: "I always hope when I first start something that I'm gonna be learning . . . I'm always looking for new stuff because new facts will keep me interested. But a lot of it is just reviewing" (I 4.4).

The nagging question of what was known persisted in this phase, but two incidents occurred that served to bolster Kyle's self-efficacy. One involved a football game. Kyle returned to his Alma Mater for the first big game. Thinking that his friends would be immersed in game activities, he had brought no books or study materials with him. When he arrived, he learned that his friends were facing a major exam that Monday and that they needed to study almost up until game time. Kyle related,

> I thought, "What can I do? I don't have anything here to read and my friends are studying. So I'll sit down and go over the learning objectives (from memory)." You know how they say "Write them out?" I did the first one, I wrote it out—and when I got home I checked, and I had included everything from my notes and the book. (I 3.7)

On another occasion he was driving home with a friend from a reception held by the Dean of the College of Medicine. His friend brought up the problems he was having understanding a particularly difficult case on wound healing. Kyle remembered, "And I described it to him on the whole way home. Probably gave a better answer than I did on the test" (I 3.9). When asked if he had been surprised by his ability to respond so glibly Kyle said, "I wasn't that surprised. It was another confirmation—it made me feel good because I wasn't sure that I was learning things well enough. But when I was able to do that, I knew that I was learning things well" (I 3.9).

The Right Stuff. An incident occurred that threw Kyle in this phase. He related the story of a few points lost on a quiz:

Whoever corrected it—the book that I used had three stages of wound heal-ing, and that's what I divided my paper up into—I figured three nice para-graphs to explain each stage. Well, *his* book had divided them up into five stages, and so he basically wanted five paragraphs. And since I started off mine by stating, "There are three main stages of wound healing," my intro-duction got a zero because there are five main stages. (Laughs). There are probably fifty—it just matters how you subdivide it. (I 4.11)

In the same vein, Kyle began to observe that some of the cases were taken from specific books. Again, he saw this as posing a philosophical incongruity, but more immediately (and importantly) an unnecessary risk in terms of exams. He opined,

You can't say, "Here's the case"—have us study all these other books—when we could have just opened *Harrison's* to a page and there's the whole answer. I'd rather not have it that way, but if it's gonna happen, I'd rather have that than get what is a wrong answer from another text. (I 4.14)

This realization also violated Kyle's belief that learning for tests is learn-ing it all and learning for the future. He continued: "I know that I'm learning it just as well for my future career, but for right now, I'm being tested. I would much rather be tested on my future career" (I 4.14).

In spite of this motivational setback, Kyle continued to delight in his studies. He related, "The first time I sit down, I can get 2 to 3 hours in without even noticing that I'm working that long" (I 3.2). He also saw three benefits in group meetings at this point. He saw the sessions good for get-ting the big picture, for collectively deciding what was important in a case (although he was not always willing to limit his study to identified areas), and what was most important to him, he saw the meeting as a good way to review. He perceived his group as one that got a lot accomplished. When asked if he would mind being in a group that did less, he responded,

I don't think that would be that bad for me since I use the group as a review, but I think it would be taking a review away from me, and the review is def-initely helpful. I don't think I'd be hurt as much because I'm not using the group to understand concepts, but I'm definitely using it to put them together. (I 3.11)

Kyle was, however, somewhat uncomfortable with a role that was being foisted on him in group. He claimed,

According to people in the group, they say that they all use me as an expert and they always ask me questions. I know I understand this stuff, but often they will say, "Kyle, is that right?" And my response is—I open the book and say, "Yeah, it's right here." I don't think I'm the one to be trusted for the final say on things. I think it's better to trust something in the text than to trust my interpretation of the text. (I 4.10)

The riskiness of not studying the right stuff appeared to overshadow the positive feedback Kyle was receiving from both himself and others. He seemed overly occupied in this phase with what "they" wanted him to know. Even his self-evaluation posed a problem for him: "I did my self-evaluation which was not too easy. I had no idea where to rank myself on a lot of the things, but I took guesses and used their (the facilitators') evaluations as a basis" (LL 4.3).

The Best Way.   Having been faced with an increasing number of cases, Kyle created a structure in which to work and began experimenting with ways of studying "the best way." He outlined his typical day:

> I get up 7:30 to 8:00—take my time getting ready and get here (to the PBL meeting room) quarter to nine. Sit, have the discussion. Right after the discussion, go over to the gym until about 1:30 and then by 2:00 I'm home opening a book. I usually work from 2:00 to 5:00 or 6:00—make dinner—usually done by 7:00–7:30—read until 8:30, 9:00. I usually end up watching television for about a half hour, then I read again until about midnight, then go to bed. This sounds terrible, but if we have Physical Diagnosis or Humanities or something that is lighter reading, I will often read it in front of Letterman. (I 3.1)

Kyle continued to use his bibliographic checksheet to direct his reading on a topic, but found that he needed to make a few adjustments to his reading and study routine. First, and reportedly for the first time in his academic life, Kyle was encountering materials that forced him to flip back in the text and to reread sections. Second, Kyle was learning that he did not have the time to retake notes, or for that matter, to reread texts. He recognized that early on he had used notes as the means of getting through material. At this point, he realized that notes needed to be his study tool and the bases for review. In this way, he came to a redefinition of what reviewing was. He connected this new insight with what was touted in the program:

> And Dr. Howell has described his cycling. I just have to remember that I'm cycling over that again, and I just want to review it. And if there's something that I don't remember or don't know, then I relearn it. But most importantly when I see a learning objective which matches an earlier one, I think I just have to review, not reread. (I 3.13)

A final adjustment to his studying process concerned his struggle to decide whether or not to take the suggestion of program coordinators and write out essays for learning objectives. Kyle's two spontaneous "experiments" to gauge what he knew, reported during Phase 1, had seemed to preclude the necessity of adopting this strategy. However, his discovery that information from some sources held a higher value forced him, he reported, to adopt accommodating strategies such as purchasing a copy of *Harrison's* when he already owned a copy of *Cecil's*. Likewise, he reluctantly decided to write out essays to prepare for the first Block exam: "I've tried it before and it just seemed like a waste of time, but I think I'll try it one more time—give it one last shot" (I 4.1).

One more strategy surfaced during this phase. In spite of Kyle's reluctance to play "expert" in the group, he did recognize the edge he sometimes had in having been able to understand concepts. He maintained, however, that this understanding did not result from the group interaction, but from his thorough studying and synthesizing of material accomplished in his self-study sessions. He reported on his new, active role:

> When it looks like somebody sits down and is thinking, I try to make a broad statement about a general concept.
> Q: Are you doing this consciously?
> Yes, I see that people are sitting around confused. I just say then—like in summary, "Is this what we're saying?" and I say it. (I 4.9)

Although it is clear from these data that Kyle continued to self-direct his learning, some motives appeared to be responsive to other forces. What he perceived as the subjective grading of his quiz essay and the fact that some cases could have been traced to certain books resulted in his adopting strategies that compromised his autonomy (e.g., in having selected his own texts) and challenged his self-efficacy (e.g., I can decide what is important). In a more constructive way, Kyle demonstrated an ability to modify his notions of what should have been studied when he consciously redefined what it meant to review. At the end of Phase 2, Kyle's degree of self-directed learning remained high though slightly tempered in this educational context.

Kyle: Phase 3

Is It Enough?   In this final phase, Kyle found himself still struggling to define the relations among his goals: learning "it," doing well, and becoming a good doctor. He worried about the validity of his initial assumption that "it" was connected with future practice. He stated, "Yeah, I'm learning enough according to them, but am I learning enough?" (LL 8.1). Once again in this phase, he showed renewed concern about the repetition of topics and interpreted this as having spent time on the old while having neglected the new. His inability to maintain the reconciliation he devised in Phase 2 was evident in the following: "I feel that if I have overlap, I am not learning. I know that you can't hit every single thing, but I would rather hit many broad topics than cycle back" (I 10.12).

He was more certain, however, that he was quite capable of learning "it," as defined by the program coordinators, on his own. He also knew that this could result in doing well, but only through hard work. Kyle asserted,

> It really didn't surprise me that I did well because I really worked at it. It's been a long, long time since I really, really worked at a test. It just told me that I'm really going to have to work at this to be sure to do well. (I 9.8)

The extent that Kyle was willing to go, or work hard, is exemplified in the following:

> My hand is utterly exhausted from writing out these essays, but I think it's probably a good thing to build up writing endurance for this test because last time I was not putting things in essays simply because my hand was too tired. I don't want that to happen again. (LL 9.1)

Enough Is Enough. Kyle appeared much more assured that the case-based curriculum afforded him the best opportunity to learn albeit in his own way. He stated,

> I don't think the importance is the way you learn it, I think the importance is that you go through the problems (cases) and see the interrelations—the clinical, the physiological, the biochemical. Whether you do it by sitting with a book, by discussing it with a group, or by making up charts—what matters is the fact that this case presents these four ideas and they're tied right into each other. (I 7.5)

Kyle's way remained anchored to independent reading. He trusted that he would learn enough if he read everything. He asserted, "Almost all I do is on my own. There's almost no other place where I learn. I don't learn very much in the groups. I learn it on my own by seeing it in the books" (I 7.1) and "I don't trust myself to go the whole semester without reading every piece of information I have" (I 8.7).

At this point, Kyle seemed to have constructed his own stakes, which went beyond the block exams and the boards. Although he did not delude himself into thinking that this was all he needed to know, he realized that he had to predict beyond the stakes set in medical school. He differentiated these in the following way:

Studying for the grade is entirely different from studying to learn. Just because of the way I can predict that questions are going to be on the test pretty easily (makes me realize that) there's other information you don't need for the grade, but I think you *do* need it for the boards and anything else. (practice; I 8.4)

Balancing. Still facing areas where reconciliation was needed between what he values and what the program demands, Kyle adopted strategies to balance these forces. In the end, Kyle believed that PBL had served his goals well. He persisted in finding repetition "annoying," but had devised ways of spotting topics that could be skimmed rather than studied. He also became more willing to let learning objectives govern his reading rather than following topics as they were presented in textbooks. These strategies resulted in affording him more time, with which he began research using nontextbooks, mostly articles he found through MEDLINE. This he found particularly exciting because it was here that he located the "new" information that he had been seeking throughout the semester.

There is no question that Kyle valued the scientific information that would allow him to understand the workings of the body and the practice of medicine. He was less interested in the social or political aspects of his field, but saw the need to "balance" his study by having included these areas if for no other reason than for performing well on a test. He revealed,

I got together with Jim and Pete and we sat and talked about the essays that we really don't have scientific facts for: the religions in society, the things that affect medical care in Africa, how to communicate Down's Syndrome to parents. We talked about these things and we formulated outlines for these. So if we do have to write an essay, which I'm pretty sure we will, I at least have an outline to write from. Hopefully, that will work. (LL 9.4)

Kyle balanced out his first semester by having devised a review scheme:

I wrote out every learning objective at least once. It took me from Friday afternoon and I was done Monday morning. When I finished, I then went through it Monday afternoon and identified a few essays that I really didn't think were good enough. I used my notes and did a little more research—looked up a couple of topics and went back and did an entirely new essay. And then I spent the rest of the week basically just reviewing those essays, and I spent one day just reviewing all my notes. (I 9.1)

Kyle continued to claim that he used the group for review, not for what he called "learning." Nevertheless, he had shifted his role in this second group from resource to cooperative member. He spoke of the sharing and shared planning that went on in this, his second group:

We spend a lot more time getting articles. We get lit searches together and talk about what books are best. We share a lot of resources. We would go to the library and we would each choose a topic to look up. We would look them up and get the articles, and the best one or two we would copy for everyone. (I 9.4)

Kyle also spoke about how this cooperation extended to the use of text-books:

In the last block we all ended up having the same sets of books. In this block all these people had completely different books. That's good because now when I read a chapter in pathology and I don't think mine is good, they just lend it to me and I read theirs—and that happens a lot. (I 9.4)

Kyle's most challenging balancing act concerned how to negotiate between what was needed for a grade and what he saw as necessary for his future. He regretfully admitted to having completed a MEDLINE assignment in a way that had compromised his autonomy: "I kept trying to make it (the printout) look like theirs (the model), so I spent 2 hours doing something that should have taken me 10 minutes" (LL 8.1).

Kyle's dilemma was also evident in the following:

I'm aware of doing things that are not necessary for my knowledge but I know that they will improve my grade. And that makes it interesting because you have two ways to study—and I have to decide how much in one direction I want to go. I don't want to let down the grade too much—I'm doing well. But if I concentrate on that I might lose the other knowledge—I might not study so much in any of the other areas, and that's not good either. But then again, on a couple of cases where I go crazy studying everything, I lose out on being prepared for the test. So it's kind of interesting to find a balance. (I 8.5)

In the end of the first semester, Kyle seemed to have found that balance. He proved that he could make the grade—he earned high honors, and he also admitted to having more confidence that what he was learning was what he would need both to continue his medical studies and to practice medicine. In short, Kyle adjusted his self-directed learning to meet both personal and environmental requirements.

DISCUSSION

I have been selective in my portrayal of Beth and Kyle, choosing their words purposefully (Patton, 1990). My aim has been to construct a representation of self-directed learners in this specific medical school context.

What these representations mean to particular readers will be determined by the degree of transferability (Eisner, 1988) individually experienced. As Firestone (1993) maintained, the reader must ask, "What conditions are present in this case that would make it applicable to my setting?" I, however, attempt to generalize from case to theory and infer what these narratives might suggest about the more general nature of self-directed learning by noting where generalizations derived from the studies are supported by the literature on self-directed and self-regulated learning.

1. Self-Directed Learning Is Residual

Both Beth and Kyle brought ways of learning with them to medical school. In a sense, Beth remained the "director," orchestrating her learning by way of an array of texts. Kyle relied on his tried and true method of "reading everything" that had its roots in elementary school.

Whether one adheres to perspectives of inherent self-determination (Benn, 1976; Gibbs, 1979) or more social theories of learned self-management (Dittman, 1976; Wang, 1983), it appears obvious that self-direction is, in part, an attribute that contributes to the stance one takes toward particular learning situations. Gagne (1985) identified executive control as the means through which learners choose strategies, and contended that such control follows from expectancies established prior to learning events. Beth and Kyle's current behaviors are clearly generated by beliefs, dispositions, and habits that are connected to their histories as learners.

2. Self-Directed Learning Is Proactive

Both of these students appeared to hit the ground running. They entered this context with goals and methods of achieving them. Both demonstrated proclivities for experimentation in learning and devised systems of testing the effectiveness of their learning experiments: Beth through her conscious challenges to comprehend unfamiliar texts or follow physician-directed seminars; Kyle through his impromptu knowledge dumps sans materials.

The importance of goal orientation to self-regulation has been empirically established (see Ames, 1992, for review) and generally conceptualized as the difference between mastery goals (learning in order to achieve a long-term, comprehensive understanding of a domain), and performance goals (learning in the short-term, particularly aimed at passing tests or at doing better than others). Butler and Winne (1995) described what they call "recursively planned experimentation" whereby goals are converted into plans derived from previous contexts. The interplay between goals and plans can be seen both at the outset and throughout the period of the present study.

3. Self-Directed Learning Is Responsive

Both students remained aware of program requirements and interpersonal dynamics, and they modified their behaviors and strategies accordingly. Beth, for example, realized that her methods might upset members of her group, so she made certain that her presentations were brief and to the point. Kyle perceived the tension between present and future goals and, through this heightened awareness, appeared to be able to balance the substance of his learning. In addition, both students welcomed and sought feedback in order to gauge progress and to adjust attitudes (sometimes negatively) and behaviors.

The dynamic, interactive character of self-directed learning has definitively been supported through research, and the idea that self-directed learning as isolated learning is mostly rejected (Brookfield, 1984). Candy (1991) identified this as "learner control of instruction." Long (1989) referred to it as "pedagogical self-directed learning." Rich (1986) theorized that self-direction involves a negotiation between a learner's freedom from varying degrees of pedagogical control and freedom to pursue learning in individually determined ways. Beth and Kyle encountered both foreseen and unanticipated constraints within the PBL curriculum, and they responded in some circumstances by deferring or adapting to curricular or perceived contextual demands.

4. Self-Directed Learning Seeks Structure

There was nothing haphazard about the systems of learning devised by Beth and Kyle. Chene (1983) noted that self-directed learning "takes more careful planning and structure to support the enhancement and expansion of the learners' control over his or her learning development efforts than is required in more traditional learning context" (p. 35). Even when Beth or Kyle encountered the unexpected, each person's response involved an adaptation of a preexisting form. Social cognitive theorists (Bandura, 1986; Mischel & Peake, 1982; Zimmerman, 1983) have highlighted the crucial role of the environment in self-regulated learning, and research (Marcus, 1988) has confirmed that students who are able to structure time, space, and procedures possess higher degrees of self-regulation.

5. Self-Directed Learning Is Reflective

Although participation in the study demanded that these students reflect on their ways of learning, still it seems unlikely that such a high degree of self-awareness and articulate self-reporting could have been possible without an inherent ability to self-reflect. In addition, the program required continuous self-reflection afforded through daily group evaluations and periodic personal evaluations conducted with facilitators. Brookfield (1986) argued: "Self-directed learning involves an internal change in consciousness that is most complete when instructional processes are combined with critical reflection" (p. 3).

Both Beth and Kyle (to a greater extent than participants in the larger study) used the learning log tool as a means through which to consider past actions, deliberate about alternate actions, and decide on the next course of action. They also turned a mirror on themselves. Beth, perhaps more so than Kyle, was sensitive to the degree to which she was not acting like herself in response to certain environmental circumstances. Kyle's reflections tended to be more "scientific"—results or outcomes of his experiments.

The cognitive, metacognitive, and motivational aspects of self-directed and self-regulated learning have been clearly delineated both theoretically and empirically. Bandura (1986) specified metacognitive awareness of self-regulation as self-observation, self-judgment, and self-reaction. In terms of motivation, self-regulation has been found to be inextricably linked to perceptions of self-efficacy (see Zimmerman, 1989). It follows that perceptions result from reflections. Throughout the case reports, we see Beth and Kyle standing back from themselves, evaluating their status, and electing certain courses of action. Concurrently, we see their sense of self-efficacy variably affected, though in the end, both seem content with themselves as learners.

6. Self-Directed Learning Is Self-Generative

These data indicate that the more one learns or the more aware one becomes regarding self-direction, the more likely one is to engage in maintaining, revising, or inventing new methods of self-direction. In other words, in a learning environment that values self-direction, we could expect that the processes as well as the substance of learning become the "content" of teaching and learning. Neither Beth nor Kyle appeared comfortable with the self-evaluative devices that were part of the PBL curriculum (Kyle, for example, chose to echo the evaluations of the facilitators rather than run the risk of being perceived as overly self-confident; Beth elected to put her method of using alternate texts underground rather than risk the hostility of the group), yet they both privately relied on their self-directed methods throughout the semester.

The tension that exists between the public and private forms of self-direction, that which is officially suggested and sanctioned by the curriculum and that which is invented by the learner, is somewhat like what Winne (1997) calls "bootstrapping." This means that learners, in the absence of instruction in forms of learning, will construct personally new forms of self-regulated learning from forms experimented with earlier. This construct of bootstrapping could explain the wide differences observed in brands and levels of self-regulation.

7. Self-Directed Learning Seeks Recognition

Beth and Kyle appeared to have a need to emphasize the effectiveness of their particular ways of learning to the group. This might be interpreted as an effort to validate their personal learning styles and methods. Beth delighted in her clear demonstration that highly specific texts could provide the most insight into an issue. Kyle was adamant that anything needed was in the book and took every opportunity to point this out to his fellow group members.

Nothing like this generalization could be located in the literature on self-directed or self-regulated learning, but I include it because I find it intriguing and connected to the generalizations offered previously. It is clear that self-regulation demands a high investment. Although no investment is without risk, so is it the case that if successful, the higher the risk, the greater the satisfaction. Future research might inquire into this phenomenon to determine how far learners will go in pursuit of personal learning agendas, and the extent to which they seek to share this information with others.

None of these generalizations operate separately or independently, nor do they stand in contradiction to each other. Rather, they are interwoven into the fabric of lived academic and developing professional lives. The self-directed learner needs to be reflective, proactive, and responsive as he or she pursues his or her goals within the context of educational institutions. Institutions need not unduly constrain self-direction. As Dewey (1938) argued: "Since freedom resides in the operations of intelligent observation and judgment by which a purpose is developed, guidance given by the teacher to the exercise of pupil's intelligence is an aid to freedom, not a restriction upon it" (p. 12).

Likewise the self-directed learner must find his or her own goals and structures in order to embark on the lifetime pursuit of generating learning strategies to meet contextual needs. Again, Dewey (1938) helps us to understand the reciprocal relations between the educational institution and the self. He stated, "If the learning process does not become increasingly self-directed, then it is not genuinely educative" (p. 7).

Learning and Identity

It should be obvious from the preceding discussion that self-directed learning within the context of PBL is more than what the learner does after he or she leaves the group meeting, nor is it exclusively an "in-the-head" experience. The methodological choice to adopt a case approach narrowed the interpretive possibilities of this study. I chose to character-ize rather than to theorize. Yet, the characterizations constructed of Beth and Kyle bring to mind theoretical perspectives of learning that include more than cognitive and motivational factors. Indeed, they suggest a per-spective that would not, as Prawat (1998) maintained, retain dualist dis-tinctions that separate process from content and interest from effort. Beth and Kyle are portrayed here as individuals, as "selves" who are clearly interested and invested in their own learning, but who are also active and responsive to the learning environment in its social, cultural and political aspects. It is this self-interest that promotes learning activity while, at the same time, it shapes identity.

Dewey (1916) defined this process. He stated, "self and interest are two names for the same fact . . . interest means the active or moving identity of the self with a certain object" (p. 352). This identity is evolving and is developed in accordance with aspects of the self in relation to affordances within the environment.

Situated perspectives, such as one known as "legitimate peripheral par-ticipation" (Lave & Wenger, 1991), also address how identity is implicated in learning. Lave and Wenger stated, "Learning and a sense of identity are inseparable: They are aspects of the same phenomenon" (p. 115). They further claimed that learning in this holistic sense is not so much related to instruction, but that it "occurs through centripetal participation in the learning curriculum of the ambient community" (p. 100). They differen-tiated between a "teaching curriculum" and a "learning curriculum"—a distinction that aligns well with foundational principles of PBL where teaching, in its traditional sense, is rejected.

It is interesting to note how Beth and Kyle elected to participate in this learning environment and how the community was structured to confer what it deemed as legitimate participation and to constrain other forms of participation. Beth very quickly jumped into the political arena legitimized by the medical college through the office of program representative. It might also be surmised that she attempted to co-opt power within her first group by bringing in information beyond that targeted through consensus. She "learned," however, that the group did not legitimate her initiatives, and tempered her idiosyncratic tendencies while at the same time realizing that this was not a "me" thing to do. Whereas the former "me" might be the director; Beth's new "me" is the doctor, the identity she seeks.

Kyle entered this learning context with a strong identity that might be characterized as "good student." In line with this image, he saw himself as an isolated learner and seemed to take pride in his history of indepen-dence from teachers. This identity seemed resilient, and it is interesting that Kyle's notion that teaching is superfluous is evident in his rejection of the role (identity) of teacher when the group attempted to confer such a role on him. Yet, we see that a shift occurred in Kyle in his second group when he began to accept the idea that satisfaction in learning can be enhanced when the group collaborates to move beyond the requirements of the learning objectives of a particular case. This change coincided with Kyle's awareness of a distinction between learning for the test and learning for later (to be a doctor). It should be remembered that at the outset of the semester, Kyle saw these two ends of learning as synonymous. It was only after a significant period of participation in the environment that he revised his viewpoint and, it might be argued, appended his identity, now trafficking between being a student and a novice doctor.

The analyses offered in the previous arguments speculate beyond the limits allowed by the research tradition that has been adopted. They may, however, prompt further inquiries that seek to find relations between self-directed learning and the construction of identity.

CONCLUSION

The first semester stories of Beth and Kyle allow us to observe what Spear (1988) has called the "essential elements" for understanding the process of self-directed learning. First, we see "learner expectations" in the form of both shifting goals and variable states of self-efficacy. Second, we see demonstrations of "individual's inventory of skills and knowledge" as they are played out in the day-to-day operations of the medical school context. Third, we come to know the "particular resources present within the environment"—the texts, the groups, the opportunities to participate in the workings of the teaching hospital, and the bases on which these learners make their decisions about which resources to select.

The complex nature of self-direction is evident in the strikingly different approaches adopted by these learners—approaches that allowed them to travel different roads to the same end, that is, successful completion of the program. In the Fall of 1997, Beth and Kyle entered their fourth year of medical school. Each performed well in the PBL program, passed the NBME boards after the second year, and have achieved high ratings in their clinical rotations. Each is applying for residencies: Beth in general medicine, Kyle in pediatrics. Each feels confident that the learning processes practiced in the PBL curriculum and continued during clinical studies will sustain them through professional life, and each has established a heuristic for lifetime learning.

The question that remains about their stories concerns the degree of affective dissonance experienced by both. Orientation to the processes of

PBL was brief and students were not offered a regular critical space in which to question or comment on curricular components. Early in the semester there was a "town meeting" held, but students worried that because it was facilitated by one of the program coordinators, their comments could have an impact on future evaluations. The debriefing session at the end of each group meeting was brief indeed. Typically students voiced only general comments like, "Today went well" or "This was OK." On one occasion there was an "eruption" when one student began to voice serious concerns about the group's operation. By the following day, however, the issues became buried.

Educators involved in PBL programs might respond to some of these issues by keeping the processes used by students in directing their own learning more salient. Students could be asked to keep journals or portfolios that chronicle specific learning tactics and experiences. These could then be shared with group members—compared and contrasted without being evaluated. There is little doubt that self-directed learning is indeed a characteristic of the self—part of the learner's nature. It is likewise true that, especially as learners move on to new pedagogical contexts, for example medical school, self-directed learning needs to be nurtured. Before we can do that, however, we need to better understand what it is, what it looks like, and what difference it makes.

ACKNOWLEDGMENTS

This research was supported by the Spencer Foundation through a National Academy of Education Postdoctoral Fellowship awarded during the 1994–1995 academic year. Additional funding was provided by the Pennsylvania State University College of Medicine at Hershey. In addition, the author wishes to thank Jerry Glenn M.D., Ph.D., co-codirector of the PBL program, and Tanya Heatwole, coordinator of the same program, for their unwavering support and assistance.

REFERENCES

Ames, C. (1992). Classrooms: Goals, structures, and student motivation. *Journal of Educational Psychology, 84*, 261–271.

Bandura, A. (1986). *Social foundations of thought and action: A social cognitive theory*. Englewood Cliffs, NJ: Prentice-Hall.

Barrows, H. S. (1986). A taxonomy of problem-based learning methods. *Medical Education, 20*, 481–486.

Barrows, H. S., & Tamblyn, R. M. (1980). *Problem-based learning*. New York: Springer.

Benn, S. I. (1976). Freedom, autonomy and the concept of the person. *Aristotelian Society Proceedings, 76*, 109–130.

Blumberg, P., & Michael, J. A. (1992). Development of self-directed learning behaviors in a partially teacher-directed problem-based learning curriculum. *Teaching and Learning in Medicine, 4,* 3–8.

Brookfield, S. D. (1984). *Adult learners, adult education and the community.* New York: Teachers College Press.

Brookfield, S. D. (1986). *Understanding and facilitating adult learning.* San Francisco, CA: Jossey-Bass.

Butler, D. L., & Winne, P. H. (1995). Feedback and self-regulated learning: A theoretical synthesis. *Review of Educational Research, 65,* 245–281.

Candy, P. C. (1991). *Self-direction for lifelong learning.* San Francisco, CA: Jossey-Bass.

Chene, A. (1983). The concept of autonomy in adult education: A philosophical discussion. *Adult Education Quarterly, 34,* 38–47.

Dewey, J. (1916). *Democracy and education.* New York: The Free Press.

Dewey, J. (1938). *Experience & education.* New York: Macmillan.

Dittman, J. K. (1976). Individual autonomy: The magnificent obsession. *Educational Leadership, 33,* 463–467.

Dolmans, D. H., & Schmidt, H. G. (1994). What drives the student in problem-based learning? *Medical Education, 28,* 372–380.

Eisner, E. (1988). The primacy of experience and the politics of method. *Educational Researcher, 17*(5), 15–20.

Evensen, D. H. (1999, April). *A qualitative study of self-directed learning in a problem-based context.* Paper presented at the annual meeting of the American Education Research Association, Montreal, Canada.

Firestone, W. A. (1993). Alternative arguments for generalizing from data as applied to qualitative research. *Educational Researcher, 22*(4), 16–23.

Gagne, R. (1985). *The condition of learning and the theory of instruction* (4th ed.). New York: Holt, Rinehart & Winston.

Gibbs, B. (1979). Autonomy and authority in education. *Journal of Philosophy of Education, 13,* 119–132.

Hmelo, C. E., Gotterer, G. S., & Bransford, J. D. (1997). A theory-driven approach to assessing the cognitive effects of PBL. *Instructional Science, 25,* 387–408.

Lave, J., & Wenger, E. (1991). *Situated learning: Legitimate peripheral participation.* New York: Cambridge University Press.

Long, H. B. (1989). *Self-directed learning: Emerging theory and practice.* Oklahoma City: Oklahoma Research Center.

Marcus, M. (1988). *Self-regulation in expository writing.* Unpublished doctoral dissertation, Graduate School of the City University of New York, New York.

Mischel, W., & Peake, P. K. (1982). Beyond deja vu in the search for cross-situational consistency. *Psychological Review, 89,* 730–755.

Newble, D. I., & Clarke, R. M. (1986). The approaches to learning of students in a traditional and in an innovative problem-based medical school. *Medical Education, 20,* 267–273.

Patton, M. Q. (1990). *Qualitative evaluation and research methods, 2nd ed.* Newbury Park, CA: Sage.

Prawat, R. S. (1998). Current self-regulation views of learning and motivation viewed through a Deweyan lens: The problems with dualism. *American Educational Research Journal, 35,* 199–224.

Rich, J. (1986). Student freedom in the classroom. *The Journal of Educational Thought, 20,* 125–133.

Schmidt, H. G. (1993). Foundations of problem-based learing: Some explanatory notes. *Medical Education, 27,* 422–432.

Spear, G. (1988). Beyond the organizing circumstance: A search for methodology for the study of self-directed learning. In H. G. Long (Ed.), *Self-directed learning: Application and theory.* Athens, GA: University of Georgia.

Stake, R. E. (1995). *The art of case study research*. Thousand Oaks, CA: Sage.

Strauss, A., & Corbin, J. (1990). *Basics of qualitative research: Grounded theory procedures and techniques*. Newbury Park, CA: Sage.

Wang, M. C. (1983). Development and consequences of students' sense of person control. In J. J. Levine and M. C. Wang (Eds.), *Teacher and student perceptions: Implications for learning*. Hillsdale, NJ: Lawrence Erlbaum Associates.

Winne, P. H. (1997). Experimenting to bootstrap self-regulated learning. *Journal of Educational Psychology, 89*, 397–410.

Zimmerman, B. J. (1983). Social learning theory: A contextualist account of cognitive functioning. In C. J. Brainerd (Ed.), *Recent advances in cognitive developmental theory* (pp. 1–49). New York: Springer.

Zimmerman, B. J. (1989). A social cognitive view of self-regulated academic learning. *Journal of Educational Psychology, 81*, 329–339.

Chapter 13

A Commentary
on Self-Directed Learning

Barry J. Zimmerman
Graduate School and University Center of the City University of New York

Robert B. Lebeau
Temple University Center for Research in Human Development and Education, Laboratory for Student Success

The final chapters of this volume explore the role of problem-based learning (PBL) in fostering self-directed learning. Definitions of self-directed learning, such as those adopted by the authors of these chapters, are highly similar to what has been termed self-regulated learning in the educational psychology literature (Zimmerman, 1986, 1989, 1994, 1998), and we will draw on parallels between these two literatures in our response to these important chapters. As an instructional technique designed to foster greater self-direction of learning, PBL is distinctive from but overlaps to some degree such techniques as computer-assisted instruction (Winne & Stockley, 1998), strategy instruction (Graham, Harris, & Troia, 1998; Hofer, Yu, & Pintrich, 1998; Pressley, El-Dinary, Wharton-McDonald, & Brown, 1998), academic studying methods (Zimmerman, Bonner, & Kovach, 1996), modeling methods (Schunk, 1998; Schunk & Zimmerman, 1997), tutoring (Butler, 1998), and self-monitoring (Lan, 1998; Zimmerman & Paulsen, 1995). Like PBL, each of these instructional techniques involves social as well as personal teaming components. During this commentary, we first consider the components of PBL and their variations, followed by conceptualizations of self-directed learning processes, findings reported in these chapters and their implications, and finally, unresolved issues and future research directions.

CONCEPTUALIZING PBL AND ITS VARIATIONS

From our perspective, PBL involves three important components in addition to the posed problems for learning: (a) a tutor, facilitator, or coach; (b) cooperative learning groups of peers; and (c) self-directed learning experiences, which are manifested in such forms as library searches, reading, behavioral practice, or written output. The first two components (a and b) are primarily social whereas the last component (c) is mainly personal. Of course, reading also can be construed as social because text is written by experts to convey information to a receptive audience, and hybrid educational programs that use PBL as an adjunct to regular lectures or instruction utilize still another source of social support. Although PBL is described as an educational strategy in which students are encouraged to take responsibility for their own learning (Evensen & Hmelo, this volume), it clearly blends personal discovery with many forms of social support.

The point of this analysis is not to contrast self-direction with external direction as being antithetical forms of learning, but rather to emphasize that PBL differs fundamentally from what has been referred to historically as *discovery learning* because it relies on many social resources. As several of the authors noted, PBL might be better described as a mix of discovery with cooperative learning or distributed cognition because much of this learning is planned and carried out as a shared experience (see Lebeau, 1998). Historically, the literature on self-regulated learning has treated basic social learning processes, such as modeling, explanation, and feedback from others, as potentially self-controllable. Bandura (1986; 1991) and others (Schunk & Zimmerman, 1998) have suggested that causality between self (or personal influences) and social environmental influences is reciprocal, and that initially external social influences are supplanted by self-regulated ones during the course of skill development. However, even at the highest level of functioning, individuals continue to depend on social resources on a self-selective basis (Zimmerman, 2000), such as when an experienced family physician consults with a specialist regarding a difficult case. Indeed, it could be argued that PBL offers a particularly suitable format for inducing social forms of learning and their adaptation to varying problem contexts because it encourages experts and peers to adopt modeling, coaching, and cooperating roles.

CONCEPTUALIZING SELF-DIRECTED LEARNING

There is a fair amount of conceptual agreement about the components of self-directed learning among the authors of the present chapters. Blumberg's (chapter 9, this volume) adaptation of Candy's (1991) model of self-directed learning focuses on six key self-directed learning processes: defining what should be learned, identifying one's own learning needs, developing learning objectives, identifying a learning plan to achieve those objects, successfully implementing the learning plan, and self-evaluating the effectiveness of the learning. Dolmans and Schmidt (chapter 11, this volume) defined students' self-directed learning in terms of their decisions regarding "what to study," which is similar to Blumberg's first process.

Hmelo and Lin (chapter 10, this volume) offer a process model of self-directed learning that substantially overlaps Blumberg's model. The key processes identified by Hmelo and Lin are as follows: assessing knowledge relative to problems being faced, formulating learning issues, developing and implementing plans to address learning issues, using new knowledge in problem solving, and reflecting on meeting the goals of self-directed learning. This model follows the classical tradition in research on self-regulation (Watson & Tharp, 1997) by beginning with the process of self-observation or self-assessment before setting specific goals for learning. In contrast, Blumberg's model posits self-assessment after setting the goal for learning during a second step (i.e., identifying one's own learning needs). This difference in sequential order between these two models perhaps originates in the combination of social and personal components in PBL. Self-assessment can occur during group discussion of what needs to be learned in response to a problem and in subsequent self-directed study. Another attractive feature of Hmelo and Lin's model is its cyclical properties (see Fig. 10.1). Self-directed learning is an inherently cyclical phenomenon because students are seldom successful in their first effort to learn and must adapt their performance in successive attempts on the basis of self-monitored feedback (Zimmerman, 1998).

Evensen (chapter 12, this volume) adopts a social cognitive model from the self-regulation literature (Bandura, 1991, 1997; Zimmerman, 1989) that emphasizes personal, behavioral, and environmental dimensions in students' use of such processes as goal setting, strategy choice, self-monitoring, self-reactions, and forming perceptions of self-efficacy. This formulation focuses on how task and environmental context features constrain students' problem-solving efforts, and how students strategically manage their immediate environmental context as well as their own performance.

Three major classes of self-directed learning processes can be derived from these theoretical accounts that parallel those used in research in self-regulated learning: (a) identifying learning objectives, (b) pursuing learning issues, and (c) self-evaluating learning. These processes correspond to activities in which students engage before, during, and after self-directed learning within each regulatory cycle. For example, Blumberg's (chapter 9, this volume) first four processes would be classified within category (a), her fifth process (implementing the plan) would fall in category (b), and her sixth process (self-evaluating the effectiveness of the learning) would be identical to category (c). Similarly, Hmelo and Lin's (chapter 10, this volume) first two processes would be placed in category (a), their third and fourth processes would be classified in category (b), and the post-process decisions in their flow diagram regarding goal attainment and successful problem solving (see Fig. 10.1) would be classified in category (c). Dolmans and Schmidt's (chapter 11, this volume) self-directed learning process of deciding "what to study" would be placed in category (a).

The three derived classes of self-directed learning processes correspond directly to the major components of self-regulated learning: forethought, performance or volitional control, and self-reflection (Zimmerman, 1998). Forethought involves goal setting, task analysis strategies, and self-motivational beliefs, such as self-efficacy; performance or volitional control concerns strategy use and self-observational processes; self-reflection refers to self-judgments and self-reactions. That cyclical model of self-regulation has revealed that differences in the success of students' self-regulated learning efforts are particularly dependent on the quality of forethought processes, which tend to encourage use of proactive rather than reactive forms of self-regulatory control (Zimmerman, 2000).

RESEARCH ON PROBLEM-BASED LEARNING

Prior research on PBL, as reviewed by Blumberg in this volume (chapter 9) and by others (e.g., Albanese & Mitchell, 1993), has established that these programs differ to the degree that problem-based learning forms an entire curriculum in pure form, or exists as a majority, if not a minority component of an overall hybrid program of PBL coupled with explicit training through lectures, tutorials, and other formats. Furthermore, considerable variation exists among PBL approaches as well, in use of particular combinations of expert-, group-, and individually driven learning. This issue looms large because of conflicts regarding an optimal blend of social and self-directive processes. To guide our commentary, we use these three components in PBL programs along with the three major classes of self-directed learning processes that we discussed previously: identifying learning objectives, pursuing learning issues, and self-evaluating learning. This formulation is presented visually in Fig. 13.1. We turn now to PBL research reported in the present chapters.

IDENTIFYING LEARNING OBJECTIVES

The centrality of generating learning objectives to problem-based learning is stressed by all of the present authors. Both collaborative and indi-

SELF-DIRECTED LEARNING PROCESSES	PBL INFLUENCES		
	Expert-Driven	Group-Driven	Self-Directed
Identifying Learning Objectives			
Pursuing Learning Issues			
Self-Evaluating Learning			

FIG. 13.1. PBL influences on major classes of self-directed learning processes.

vidual determination of learning objectives, in response to a problem, is portrayed as critical to this self-directed learning process. The present chapters reveal that defining what to learn occurs on multiple levels—from faculty-provided objectives to students' individually or collectively created objectives—which allows for varying degrees of self-direction.

Expert-Driven Influences

The impact of faculty, of group leaders, and of other experts on the generation of learning objectives is considerable. Regarding the composition and sequencing of objectives, experts design them so that students can identify gaps in their basic science and clinical knowledge related to the resolution of a particular problem (Hmelo & Lin, chapter 10, this volume). The influence of the group facilitator emerges as he or she monitors and stimulates students' discussion of learning objectives and attempts to ensure that a productive list is achieved. In this way, self-direction is expert constrained and socially supported so that productive self-directed learning processes can follow.

Faculty direction in creating objectives was shown to exert a great influence in the particular programs described in these chapters, especially under conditions where testing is linked directly to the problems studied. For example, Evensen's (chapter 12, this volume) study shows how students develop a sense that a given problem stands for more than itself. Students were described as "playing the game" of taking apart a case to see not only how the case related to general problems that doctors face, but also to see how it indicated basic knowledge on which they will be tested. Learning objectives identified in this fashion emerged from the students' decoding of faculty objectives in light of future practice and of impending, other-directed evaluation. The provision of faculty-generated, topical learning objectives, along with case-specific objectives linked to the National Board of Medical Examiners (NBME) examinations, reinforces this other-directed influence on self-directed generation of learning issues. However, some students, such as Beth, in Evensen's study felt that these objectives detracted from the otherwise "real" process of identifying what needs to be known to address a given medical problem.

Dolmans and Schmidt (chapter 11, this volume) provide some evidence that faculty-generated, global course objectives did not interfere with the development of self-directed learning skills. Faculty course objectives continued to receive the highest average rating by the students regardless of their growth in self-directed learning of skills with increasing PBL experience. An unexpected benefit of faculty-generated objectives was their use by students as a source for evaluating rather than guiding their learning. Blumberg cites a study (Rosenfeld, 1995) in which students used faculty objectives for self-evaluation. The two students in Evensen's (chapter 12, this volume) case studies also used faculty objectives (along with other PBL resources) for self-evaluative purposes.

Group-Driven Influences

The initial identification of learning objectives is also constrained and supported by the group context in which problems are first encountered. As Hmelo and Lin (chapter 10, this volume) describe, the group setting is a critical source for modeling and for scaffolding of the processes by which students can better direct their own learning. Scaffolding refers to introducing conceptual aids temporarily to promote learning. Evensen's (chapter 12, this volume) detailed portrayal of the actual experience of group participation in her case studies reveals that social processes can have counterproductive effects as well as intended ones on students' objectives. Students' acute sensitivity to the perceptions of others in their group can restrict the identification of learning objectives of a given problem to those considered relevant by other group members. For example, Beth conveyed her unwillingness at times to introduce issues she knew other group members would find irrelevant even though she felt them relevant to her own personal context.

Self-Directed Influences

The specific nature of the self-generated learning objectives is addressed by several chapter authors. From her case studies, Evensen (chapter 12, this volume) describes the personal process by which students responded to their perceptions of faculty and group guidance as they identified their own learning needs. Of central importance were the individualized learning agendas that the two students developed. Each personal agenda established a context that gave the problems relevance. For example, Beth described how she identified primary research articles that enhanced the relevance of the textbook in addressing the learning objectives. Neither student pursued the exact learning objectives that were initially generated but did use them as reference points.

Hmelo and Lin's (chapter 10, this volume) study takes a unique approach to determining the role of learning objective generation in the development of overall self-directed learning skills. These authors view the type of learning objectives that PBL students generated as indicators of their subsequent self-directed learning strategies. As they gained learning experience, PBL students generated hypothesis-related learning objectives in response to a problem with increasing frequency. However, there is reason to question whether this type of objective leads to a beneficial self-directed learning strategy. Albanese and Mitchell (1993) reviewed studies indicating that hypothesis-driven reasoning of PBL students was similar to backward reasoning patterns displayed by novices in non-PBL research. In contrast, expert non-PBL reasoners were shown to use forward, data-driven reasoning strategies for problem solving. However, Hmelo and Lin (chapter 10, this volume) have interpreted evidence of backward hypothesis-driven reasoning of PBL students as functional when dealing with the uncertainty of many patients' problems. From their perspective, uncertainty faces medical practitioners of all experience levels when novel problems are encountered. The resolution of this issue must await further research on the effectiveness of each strategic approach to problems of varying novelty by PBL experts as well as by students.

PURSUING LEARNING ISSUES

The impact of PBL on group- and on individually generated learning issues is difficult to unravel at a detailed level. Among the subprocesses that were used by students to pursue learning issues were the following: making plans, using resources, and employing learning strategies. Blumberg's (chapter 9, this volume) review clearly shows differences in resource use between PBL students and their counterparts in conventional programs. Although it is not surprising that medical students tend to seek out learning resources on their own when denied explicit guidance in the form of assigned textbook reading, the findings in these chapters indicate individual differences in patterns in resource use as well as shifts in plans and strategies. These differences are related to students' degree of PBL experience (Dolmans & Schmidt, chapter 11, this volume); self-selected type of instruction (Hmelo & Lin, chapter 10, this volume); and personal goals, expectations, learning style, and experience (Evensen, chapter 12, this volume). These personal differences in patterns and in shifts in methods of learning are common to all PBL programs because of their dependence on and encouragement of self-directed learning processes.

Expert-Driven Influences

Just as students use faculty-provided learning objectives with greater or lesser degrees of self-direction, so too do they make self-directed use of the faculty-provided resources described in these chapters—including reference lists, assigned readings, and implicitly, if not explicitly, favored textbooks. Studies conducted at the University of Maastricht suggest that, as students gain experience with PBL formats, they relied less on lectures, on course-provided reference literature, and on content tests. These results are of interest as an indicator of the possible shift from expert-driven learning to self-directed learning, but these developmental shifts must be interpreted with some caution because the cross-year changes were not linear in trend, and post hoc tests were not conducted regarding the significance of year-to-year changes. These findings, although tentative, do suggest how initial social structuring can promote enhanced self-directed learning skills.

Diverse expert supports were used in the PBL programs to master assigned as well as self-selected learning techniques. For example, Blumberg (chapter 9, this volume) describes how students used the Internet and other resources to fulfill highly directive requests for information as part of a PBL program. The PBL track described by Evensen (chapter 12, this volume) includes selection of resources in preparation for finely-tuned review exercises on which the faculty provided feedback. Although such practices might not find a place in purer forms of PBL, they are common in conventional curricula. The significance of such practices as part of PBL are that students are provided with contextually relevant opportunities to exercise skills for obtaining and exploiting learning resources in increasingly unstructured contexts.

In expert-driven forms of PBL, clashes can occur between students' fidelity to common learning objectives and their self-control of resources. For example, Kyle, in Evensen's (chapter 12, this volume) study, found that the scoring of quizzes in his program delimited his autonomy over textbook selection. He attributed one of his incorrect responses to differences between the textbook description he used and the description in the quiz grader's text. Initially, he did not change his beliefs regarding his efficacy as a learner from medical texts but simply became more conservative in his choice of texts. However, he reversed this course of action by the end of the semester, and he eventually incorporated group research and nontextbook resources into his previously independent pursuit of learning objectives raised by given cases and covered on examinations.

Group-Driven Influences

Evensen's (chapter 12, this volume) case study also captures Kyle's personal reactions to group processes and to case features. Interaction with other group members provided him with a context to broaden the resources that he used. However, Evensen's depiction of Beth's experience demonstrates an opposing trend. Beth found that she was unable to introduce some of the personal resources she used in the group context, finding instead an evolving but restrictive group standard for relevant references. These limitations by the study group were reinforced by the program's testing structure and the presence of the all-important board examination.

Self-Directed Influences

Hmelo and Lin (chapter 10, this volume) address the question of how self-directed learning strategies influence subsequent knowledge integration during problem solving. First-year PBL students displayed increasingly focused use of clinical and basic science texts as a result of their improving resource planning and information integration, two key indicators of self-directed learning. First-year non-PBL students "seemed to only have undifferentiated plans about how to get started." Planning is conceptualized as a continuum with specific texts on one end and expert consultations and nonspecific texts on the other. The former is favored by PBL students, and the latter is favored by non-PBL students. These differences in planning influenced the types of knowledge that students used. PBL students appeared to develop particular facility in using texts to guide problem solving that enhanced their ability to select resources and integrate new information. The Hmelo and Lin study does not, however, directly link learning plans and knowledge integration because the information provided to students was independent of what they wanted to know.

As summarized by Blumberg (chapter 9, this volume), researchers have found that PBL students' study behaviors appear to be oriented more toward meaning and less toward memorization and recall. Elements of self-regulation such as time spent studying, the locations chosen for studying, and resources used while studying appeared to be different for PBL students. Blumberg cites findings by Schmidt, Van Der Arend, Moust, Kokx, and Boon (1993) that indicate self-study time increases for third- and fourth-year PBL students who study with content expert tutors. Schmidt and colleagues did not find such an increase with first- and second-year students, but they did find better test performance on the part of these students when their groups were led by content-expert tutors.

The expert-driven features of the PBL programs described in these chapters created opportunities for personal development of self-directed learning skills that could be applied to ongoing medical education and to anticipated practice. Group discussions also served to reduce the complexity of problems or to highlight problematic aspects of problems for individual study.

Conversely, the absence of prescribed reading materials and the encouragement of personal integration of disparate resources also led to greater self-directed resource use by students in PBL programs. In such impoverished contexts, students appeared to employ deeper learning strategies that increased the personal and professional relevance of material beyond the demands of formal tests. Blumberg (chapter 9, this volume) reviews prior evidence for this, Evensen (chapter 12, this volume) documents such patterns in Kyle and Beth's struggles, and Hmelo and Lin (chapter 10, this volume) link successful learning strategies to the quality of self-generated learning issues and plans.

Evensen's (chapter 12, this volume) case studies also document the dynamic patterns of resource use and learning strategy. For example, Beth remarked on her intimate knowledge of her growing library of textbooks and her targeted use of each volume. Beth's comments paralleled the findings of the study by Watkins (1993), cited by Blumberg (chapter 9, this volume), on how PBL encourages the early development of personal libraries. From one perspective, buying more books and reading more widely is a necessary (albeit a self-selected) response to a deficient task environment. The account by Evensen, however, reveals much more: Students' complex goal setting, group discussions, and re-evaluation were designed to serve well beyond the immediate demands of a case regarding test preparation. Evensen's description of Kyle's response reveals how such self-direction is supported and constrained by the social context in which it occurred. This study was perhaps the first to describe how such self-direction occurred as a result of shifts in personal, environmental, and behavioral interplay of students, faculty, and other PBL group members.

These studies indicate important differences in learning plans and knowledge integration between PBL and non-PBL students, but they raise further questions about conditions when expert help seeking is an appropriate self-directed learning activity and how the students' use of texts evolves in group contexts and ultimately in clinical practice.

SELF-EVALUATING LEARNING

As discussed previously, students' self-directed learning involves a continuing evaluation of the relevance of learning goals and activities in light of the immediate demands of a case; the demands of board examinations, residency requirements, and grading procedures; and shifting personal interests, perception of group concerns, and goals for professional practice. Self-evaluations of each of these demands by students are shown to impel self-directed learning in these chapters. Self-directed influences are not treated separately in the following section for this topic.

Expert-Driven Influences

The testing procedures, review exercises, and faculty feedback in the program provide students with information that, as in Kyle's case, can find its way into students' own self-evaluations. Beth, on the other hand, sought out a variety of ongoing and veridical medical activities to use for self-evaluative purposes. She attended seminars conducted by and for practitioners to see how she was doing and whether she could follow such discussions. As Blumberg (chapter 9, this volume) reports, the facilitators' case discussions and feedback also contribute information that students use to evaluate the relevance of what they are learning and to measure their success in learning.

Group-Driven Influences

Group discussions provide an ongoing source of information for self-evaluation that enable students to compare their progress to that of their peers. Students' identities as learners are influenced by other members of their group. As Evensen (chapter 12, this volume) documents, perceptions of a student as particularly knowledgeable (e.g., Kyle's science proficiency) or as particularly adaptable (e.g., Beth's ability to overcome her weaker science background) are manifestations of other students' judgments of progress. An inability to keep up with the group, or as Beth noted, divergence from the common pace that is forced on a group by facilitators become immediate markers of one's progress. Clearly, students' social milieu has a major impact on the way that they self-evaluate their academic progress.

UNRESOLVED ISSUES AND FUTURE RESEARCH
DIRECTIONS

A central question underlying the present as well as previous PBL research
is how to evaluate the impact of key aspects of this curriculum in terms of
self-directed learning processes and academic outcomes, such as test
scores. Structural variations in PBL programs were discussed in the content and complexity of patient problems, the way students could access
problem information, the nature of problem-based group interaction, and
the type and specificity of the learning resources provided to students.
Evaluating the impact of these structural variations in PBL is complicated
by the intervening role of self-directed learning processes, such as the
time students require to adapt to the PBL format and their self-reactions
to initial problem-solving experiences (Albanese & Mitchell, 1993).
Although the present chapters offer an evaluation of such structuring
through the use of students' self-ratings of the helpfulness of certain features of PBL programs as well as case studies of students' reactions to specific features of their PBL program, it is difficult to determine the validity
of these self-reports in terms of academic outcomes.

An inherent difficulty in evaluating students' use of self-regulatory
processes in PBL is the essential role of their choice and control (Zimmerman, 1994). Under these self-directive conditions, students' personal
beliefs, affect, and motivation influence academic outcomes as much as
their cognitive competence (Garcia & Pintrich, 1994; Schunk, 1994;
Zimmerman, 1998; 2000). In evaluations of other-directed forms of
instruction, such as lecturing, students' choice and sense of control are
restricted experimentally to ensure "treatment fidelity," and as a result,
academic outcomes can be attributed directly to treatment variations.
However, when students are expected to exercise selective use of learning
methods, more complex research designs are necessary.

A number of researchers on academic self-regulation (Schunk &
Zimmerman, 1994) have advocated designs where self processes (SP) are
distinguished from the instructional (I) methods that were used to instill
them and from the academic or professional outcomes (O) they were
expected to enhance. A three-component I–SP–O method of analysis
enables researchers to link specific aspects of PBL instruction conceptually to performance outcomes through a common set of self-directive
processes. These I–SP–O approaches have proven useful in prior experimental self-regulation research (Schunk, 1984) as well as in applied self-
regulation research (Schunk & Zimmerman, 1998; Zimmerman, Bandura,
& Martinez-Pons, 1992). The use of path-analysis statistical models to
assess the mediating role of self-directed learning processes could prove
to be a great benefit in future PBL research as they have in self-regulation

research. The authors of the present chapters on PBL have set the stage for such analyses by identifying a common set of self-directive processes and have begun linking them to PBL experiences and to academic outcomes.

Triadic I–SP–O research designs provide more comprehensive explanations regarding unexpected as well as expected PBL outcomes in varying performance contexts. The findings in the present chapters offer a glimpse of self-directed learning emerging from unanticipated PBL resources, such as when students used faculty objectives for self-evaluation instead of for guidance purposes. In other instances, self-directed learning may have been undermined paradoxically by PBL supports, such as when Beth felt that faculty-devised objectives detracted from solving "real" medical problems. Whether these students' self-directed learning practices or beliefs improved or impeded acquisition of medical knowledge and skill, respectively, is unclear, but a three-component design would enable researchers to separate the effects of PBL from self-directed learning processes and would allow them to examine any potential interactions they might conjointly have on students' academic outcomes.

CONCLUSION

In this commentary, we consider the components of PBL programs as well as conceptualizations of self-directed learning processes that these programs sought to promote. The authors of the present chapters report wide variations in emphases and in approaches among PBL programs in universities in the United States as well as abroad. Although PBL is often conceptualized as a form of discovery learning, it also provides a framework where extensive social or cooperative learning is encouraged through curricular supports, such as faculty- or peer-group-derived course objectives, resource lists, and evaluative criteria. The authors demonstrate that students' use of these supports appeared more-or-less self-directed in relation to varying PBL experiences, such as expert guidance, collaborative group structure, and explicit self-direction.

This edited volume represents a major contribution to research on PBL through the authors' identification of a common set of underlying self-directed learning processes and self-beliefs, which include the identification of learning objectives, the selection of resources and strategies for pursuing those objectives, and efforts made to evaluate progress toward achieving objectives. The importance of these three classes of self-directed learning processes is underscored by their parallelism to three phase processes identified in research on self-regulated learning: forethought, performance or volitional control, and self-reflection. Greater cross-fertilization between these two literatures will prove to be mutually beneficial in future research.

Finally, we discuss unresolved issues and future research directions and suggest that PBL research and theory could benefit from the further development of research designs that assess self-directed learning processes as an intervening variable between PBL experiences and students' academic outcomes. The resulting research could not only provide further clarity regarding the fundamental relation among these variables but could eventually enable faculty to craft PBL programs that enhance those self-directed learning processes leading to selected academic outcomes. Many advocates of PBL would argue, however, that students' attainment of academic self-direction is the primary and most enduring contribution of this important approach to learning.

REFERENCES

Albanese, M. A., & Mitchell, S. (1993). Problem-based learning: A review of literature on its outcomes and implementation issues. *Academic Medicine, 68*, 52–81.

Bandura, A. (1986). *Social foundations of thought and action: A social cognitive theory*. Englewood Cliffs, NJ: Prentice-Hall.

Bandura, A. (1991). Self-regulation of motivation through anticipatory and self-reactive mechanisms. In R. A. Dienstbier (Ed.), *Perspectives on motivation: Nebraska symposium on motivation* (Vol. 38, pp. 69–164). Lincoln, NE: University of Nebraska Press.

Bandura, A. (1997). *Self-efficacy: The exercise of control*. New York: W. H. Freeman & Co.

Butler, D. L. (1998). A strategic content learning approach to promoting self-regulated learning by students with learning disabilities. In D. H. Schunk and B. J. Zimmerman (Eds.), *Self-regulated learning: From teaching to self-reflective practice* (pp. 160–183). New York: Guilford.

Candy, P. C. (1991). *Self-direction for lifelong learning*. San Francisco, CA: Jossey-Bass.

Garcia, T., & Pintrich, P. R. (1994). Regulating motivation and cognition in the classroom: The role of self-schemas and self-regulatory strategies. In D. H. Schunk & B. J. Zimmerman (Eds.), *Self-regulation of learning and performance: Issues and educational application* (pp. 127–154). Hillsdale, NJ: Lawrence Erlbaum Associates.

Graham, S., Harris, K. R., & Troia, G. A. (1998). Writing and self-regulation: Cases from the self-regulated strategy development model. In D. H. Schunk and B. J. Zimmerman (Eds.), *Self-regulated learning: From teaching to self-reflective practice* (pp. 20–41). New York: Guilford.

Hofer, B. K., Yu, S. L., & Pintrich, P. (1998). Teaching college students to be self-regulated learners. In D. H. Schunk and B. J. Zimmerman (Eds.), *Self-regulated learning: From teaching to self-reflective practice* (pp. 57–85). New York: Guilford.

Lan, W. (1998). Teaching self-monitoring skills in statistics. In D. H. Schunk and B. J. Zimmerman (Eds.), *Self-regulated learning: From teaching to self-reflective practice* (pp. 86–105). New York: Guilford.

Lebeau, R. B. (1998). Cognitive tools in a clinical encounter in medicine: Supporting empathy and expertise in distributed systems. *Educational Psychology Review, 10*, 3–24.

Pressley, M., El-Dinary, P. B., Wharton-McDonald, R., & Brown, R. (1998). Transactional instruction of comprehension strategies in the elementary grades. In D. H. Schunk and

B. J. Zimmerman (Eds.), *Self-regulated learning: From teaching to self-reflective practice* (pp. 42–56). New York: Guilford.

Rosenfeld, J. (1995). *Students' use of learning objectives in a PBL program.* Unpublished manuscript, McMaster University, Hamilton, Ontario, Canada.

Schmidt, H. G., Van Der Arend, A., Moust, J. H., Kokx, I., & Boon, L. (1993). Influence of tutors' subject-matter expertise on student effort and achievement in problem-based learning. *Academic Medicine, 68,* 784–791.

Schunk, D. H. (1984). Self-efficacy perspective on achievement behavior. *Educational Psychologist, 12,* 48–58.

Schunk, D. H. (1994). Self-regulation of self-efficacy and attributions in academic settings. In D. H. Schunk & B. J. Zimmerman (Eds.), *Self-regulation of learning and performances: Issues and educational applications* (pp. 75–100). Hillsdale, NJ: Lawrence Erlbaum Associates.

Schunk, D. H. (1998). Teaching elementary students to self-regulate practice of mathematical skills with modeling. In D. H. Schunk and B. J. Zimmerman (Eds.), *Self-regulated learning: From teaching to self-reflective practice* (pp. 137–159). New York: Guilford.

Schunk, D. H., & Zimmerman, B. J. (1994). Social origins of self-regulatory competence. *Educational Psychologist, 22,* 195–208.

Schunk, D. H., & Zimmerman, B. J. (Eds.; 1998). *Self-regulated learning: From teaching to self-reflective practice.* New York: Guilford.

Watkins, M. C. (1993). Characteristics of services and educational programs in libraries serving problem-based curricula: A group self-study. *Bulletin of Medical Library Association, 81*(3), 306–309.

Watson, D. L., & Tharp, R. (1997). *Self-directed behavior: Self modification for personal adjustment* (7th ed., chap. 1–7). Pacific Grove, CA: Brooks/Cole.

Winne, P. H., & Stockley, D. B. (1998). Computing technologies as sites for developing self-regulated learning. In D. H. Schunk and B. J. Zimmerman (Eds.), *Self-regulated learning: From teaching to self-reflective practice* (pp. 106–136). New York: Guilford.

Zimmerman, B. J. (1986). Development of self-regulated learning: Which are the key subprocesses? *Contemporary Educational Psychology, 11,* 307–313.

Zimmerman, B. J. (1989). A social cognitive view of self-regulated academic learning. *Journal of Educational Psychology, 81,* 329–339.

Zimmerman, B. J. (1994). Dimensions of academic self-regulation: A conceptual framework for education. In D. H. Schunk & B. J. Zimmerman (Eds.), *Self-regulation learning and performance: Issues and educational applications* (pp. 3–21). Hillsdale, NJ: Lawrence Erlbaum Associates.

Zimmerman, B. J. (1998). Developing self-fulfilling cycles of academic regulation: An analysis of exemplary instructional models. In D. H. Schunk and B. J. Zimmerman (Eds.), *Self-regulated learning: From teaching to self-reflective practice* (pp. 1–19). New York: Guilford.

Zimmerman, B. J. (2000). Attainment of self-regulation: A social cognitive perspective. In M. Boekaerts, P. Pintrich, & M. Seidner (Eds.), *Self-Regulation: Theory Research and Applications.* Orlando, FL: Academic Press.

Zimmerman, B. J., Bandura, A., & Martinez-Pons, M. (1992). Self-motivation for academic attainment: The role of self-efficacy beliefs and personal goal setting. *American Educational Research Journal, 29,* 663–676.

Zimmerman, B. J., Bonner, S., & Kovach, R. (1996). *Developing self-regulated learners: Beyond achievement to self-efficacy.* Washington, DC: American Psychological Association.

Zimmerman, B. J., & Paulsen, A. S. (1995). Self-monitoring during collegiate studying: An invaluable tool for academic self-regulation. In P. Pintrich (Ed.), *New directions in college teaching and learning: Understanding self-regulated learning* (No. 63, Fall, pp. 13–27). San Francisco, CA: Jossey-Bass.

EPILOGUE
Assessment of Students
for Proactive Lifelong Learning

Ann C. Myers Kelson
SIU School of Medicine

INTRODUCTION

This chapter builds on a very basic premise: Assessment drives learning. I argue that assessment drives learning in at least three ways:

1. Assessment determines the goals students set and the metacognitve and self assessment strategies they use to determine what they will learn, how they will learn, and how they will know that they know.

2. Assessment shapes the curriculum. Assessment results feed back on the curriculum to maximize test results.

3. Over time, assessment shapes the mental model students carry with them as to what it means to know, what it means to learn, and how challenges are approached in the real world.

From these dimensions of the basic premise it follows that for an educational endeavor to achieve its proposed student outcome, not only must the curriculum remain true to this outcome, but the assessment system must also model it.

In this chapter I develop the notion of the "proactive lifelong learner" as a student outcome consistent with goals articulated in current calls for reform in education. The proactive lifelong learner, as is explained in the following sections, is one who habitually responds to challenges by attuning to and addressing the problem's affordances, and is thus positioned for the development of expertise from experience. I postulate that this student outcome is best achieved when both the curriculum and the assessment systems are built on a model in which learning is a response to problem demands integrated as a natural part of the problem-solving process. The Southern Illinois University School of Medicine Problem-Based Learning Curriculum and its assessment system are used to illustrate this approach.

The Premise: Assessment Drives Learning

There is sufficient anecdotal evidence to convince most of us that the nature of learning activity in school is largely determined by the assessment system to which students are held accountable. This has also been theorized and investigated formally (Darling-Hammond & Wise, 1985; Frederiksen & Collins, 1989; Wiggins, 1989). At a very basic level, this premise has been understood to mean that many, if not most, students will essentially be immune to all curricular efforts except those that determine their grades. "How much does it count?" is undoubtedly one of the most commonly asked questions regarding classroom assignments and examinations. For many students the external motivation provided by grades or marks may be the sole determiner of their goals for learning. When grades are determined largely by examinations requiring recall of factual material, then students will focus the majority of their cognitive energy in memorizing factual material. Should, however, assessment be designed to model precisely a different student outcome, then cognitive energy can be expected to be in the direction of that outcome.

Assessment Influences Students' Learning Goals and Metacognitive Strategies. "Assessment drives learning" may be thought of as a special case of goal setting (cf. Bereiter & Scardamalia, 1989; Frederiksen & Collins, 1989; Pellegrino & Glaser, 1982; Scardamalia, Bereiter, & Steinbeck, 1984). Commonly, students set goals in relation to the assessment system—to make a passing mark, to make an "A," to get the highest grade in the class. This goal drives planning and strategizing— "What kind of test is it?" "Is there a penalty for guessing?" "Will we need to know dates?"—and the goal shapes the interplay between metacognitive and cognitive strategies. Metacognitive strategies such as "Highlight what is likely to be on the examination," "Rehearse lists," or "Develop a mnemonic" signal that the cognitive activity "Memorize for recall" is being operationalized. This goal setting, planning, and strategizing are natural and inevitable processes. If, as students are engaged in assessment-driven goal setting, planning, and strategizing, they are engaged in preparing for future performance in the real world, then this power of assessment has been harnessed appropriately. It is detrimental, however, when there is a mismatch between goal setting, planning, and strategizing fostered by the assessment system and that which would lead to the projected student outcome.

Even when students seemingly avoid the "working for grades" trap, their goals may be highly influenced by or subsumed under what Bereiter refers to as a "schoolwork module" (Bereiter, 1990; Bereiter & Scardamalia, 1989). To understand the schoolwork module, it is necessary to look at common happenings in curriculum design. Early on in the curricular planning process, desired outcomes are identified. These are usually a collection of ability and attribute statements that collectively define the "product" of the educational system. A typical set of outcomes emerging from reform initiatives since the mid-1980s includes statements about the students' having a well-rounded, useable base of knowledge and skills, having the ability to solve problems in multiple contexts, and having self-reflection and self-directed learning habits that will enable them to continually gain knowledge. Added to these are statements regarding working collaboratively, producing consistent, high-quality products, communicating effectively in a number of modalities, and functioning as responsible citizens in local and global communities with diverse populations. In the typical curriculum design process, these outcomes are then reduced to a set of observable objectives coupled with assignments and classroom activities constructed to reach those objectives on various levels. Finally, examinations are written to assess whether objectives have been reached.

Students, and teachers as well, focus on the completion of the educational activities, particularly those that "count," and on the achievement of acceptable test scores. These, rather than learning itself, become the objects of educational effort. Having completed the assignment and having scored acceptably on the examination is taken as the equivalent of having achieved the outcomes. It is this reductive substitution of means for end that Bereiter (1990) refers to as the schoolwork module. Although learning certainly may, and does, occur under these conditions, it is incidental to completing the activities. This reductivism is pervasive across all levels of education. For example, it is not uncommon for medical students to bemoan the fact that because they must "do the reading assignments" or "cram for exams" (i.e., complete assignments) they must postpone the gratification of "really understanding" or "seeing how all this interrelates" or "getting the big picture" until some mythical future when there will be more time. They postpone the very cognitive activities essential for achieving the anticipated outcomes. Nevertheless these students believe, as do others, that they are learning and that they are achieving the outcomes promised them as matriculants, because they are covering the assigned material, scoring acceptably on examinations, and getting acceptable grades. The actual learning outcome of this approach is clearly problematic because when the learning that is meant to lead to the expected student outcome is relegated to a secondary position, it alters the outcome. The educational outcome is a function of what is being practiced, and what is being practiced, often for years, is a subroutine of completing assignments and preparing for domain-organized recall examinations.

Assessment Feeds Back on the Curriculum to Maximize Assessment Results.   The schoolwork module is pervasive, in part, because it is self-perpetuating, and assessment plays a significant role in its perpetuation. Assessment acts in symbiosis with the curriculum so that its own results are maximized. In other words, student assessment scores not only influence students' goals, they shape the curriculum (Frederiksen & Collins, 1989). In particular, when students' performance on assignments or examinations fails to meet expectations, there is inevitably an impact on the curriculum. Assignments are made clearer and more doable, or students are given more assistance in completing them. Review sessions are held for exams. When performances do, in fact, meet expectations, there is an equally powerful impact. Educational activities that produced this performance become entrenched. "But our students do very well on the tests" is an effective deterrent to educational reform. As Frederiksen and Collins (1989) pointed out:

> Test scores . . . become the currency of feedback within an adapting educational system. The system adjusts its curricular and instructional practices and students adjust their learning strategies and goals, to maximize the scores on the tests used to evaluate educational outcomes. (p. 27)

Assessment Affects Epistemologies.   That students adjust their learning strategies and goals to maximize test performance (Frederiksen & Collins, 1989), and that long-term practice of the schoolwork module may habituate it as a lifelong approach to learning (Bereiter, 1990; Bereiter & Scardamalia, 1989), allows us to project the assessment drives learning principle one step further. Not only does assessment have an immediate effect on the goals of learning and consequently on the cognitive processes involved, but, over time, consistent assessment actually shapes the mental model students carry with them as to what it means to know, what it means to learn, and how one responds to problems in the real world. If assessment drives learning, and in essence shapes both the hidden and the stated curriculum, then assessment has a powerful impact on long-term outcomes for students in school. Persistent expectations generated by assessment procedures over time become internalized as self-expectations in encountering challenges and in continuing learning. The schoolwork approach to learning, propagated by assessment expectations derived from that approach, does not magically disappear as the student leaves school. There is evidence that for many individuals their approach to learning remains locked in the schoolwork context. Many never think of themselves as learners but continue to think of themselves as completers of assignments, or rather they think of the two as one and the same. (cf. Bereiter, 1990; van Rossum & Schenk, 1984). This suggests a connection to one of the most commonly heard cries from the consumers of the schooling product—employers—that graduates demonstrate little initiative or independence in addressing the challenges of the workplace. They seem to insist on being told precisely what to do, how to do it, and how much or how little is enough. In short, they want assignments to complete.

The Call for Reform

Since the mid-1980s, at least, educational organizations have been calling for educational reform among their constituents. (e.g., *General Professional Education of the Physician (GPEP) Report*, 1984, for the call for reform of medical education; National Commission on Excellence in Education, 1983, for the call for reform of public school education; and the *Secretary's Commission on Achieving Necessary Skills (SCANS) Report*, 1991, for insight into workplace demands of schools.) Concern is expressed that students are engaged primarily in rote learning, which entails the acquisition of facts that have little staying power. Critics note that in schools, students are being asked to absorb greater and greater quantities of factual knowledge but are not being challenged to apply knowledge and skills to novel contexts. They are being asked to complete assignments covering designated curricular objectives but are given far too little experience in problem solving or in critical thinking. These "passive" recipients of instruction show little initiative when encountering challenging situations. Their schooling experience leaves them with neither the propensity nor the skills for lifelong learning. These expressed concerns can be traced to the actual outcomes of curricula and assessment systems that have reduced expected outcomes to sets of educational activities and tests of factual knowledge. Thus, the call for reform demands a radical restructuring of both curriculum and assessment, one in which the actual outcome and the expected outcome are congruent.

Standards currently being produced and distributed by national organizations in response to calls for reform almost universally include both a lifelong learning component and a problem-solving or critical thinking component (GPEP, 1984; SCANS, 1991). Employers across all spectra of the workplace are challenging educational institutions to turn out students who are ready to take on the challenges of a work environment through adaptive problem solving and continuing learning (Feltovich &

Barrows, 1997). True to form, however, the conceptual agreement that lifelong learning is an important goal of education is addressed in a typical schoolwork manner. It is converted into assignments such as making note cards, doing computer searches, or writing reports. The outcome is predictable. Students, and very often teachers, see the completion of the assignment as the educational focus. Any skills acquired that might be useful in another context are acquired incidentally and are likely accessible, if at all, only when someone gives a similar assignment. What is needed is not simply a call for reform, but a way to operationalize lifelong learning as both a pedagogical method and as an outcome.

The Expected Outcome: The Proactive Lifelong Learner

Bereiter and Scardamalia (1989) used the term *lifelong learner* to mean one who expects learning to be a part of life and establishes patterns that make this possible. Here, the basic definition will be expanded to include not only the expectation and development of patterns for learning but also the habituation of learning and problem solving as an orchestrated whole. Such an individual will be referred to as the "proactive lifelong learner." This is not merely the individual with an insatiable, freestanding curiosity about knowledge in general or topics in particular, a curiosity that would take a lifetime to satisfy, though this is certainly an admirable quality. Rather, the term is used to refer to the individual for whom any problem triggers a dual demand: the need to problem-solve and the need to know.

A number of sources have described the characteristics that serve the problem-solver well (Palinscar & Brown, 1984; Salomon & Perkins, 1989; Schoenfeld, 1988). In addition, researchers have described the characteristics that make for effective independent learning (Bereiter & Scardamalia, 1989; Brown, Bransford, Ferrara, & Campione, 1983; Feltovich, Spiro, Coulson & Myers-Kelson, 1995; Perkins, Simmons, & Tishman, 1990; Spiro, Coulson, Feltovich, & Anderson, 1989; Spiro, Vispoel, Schmitz, Samarapungavan, & Boerger, 1987). The proactive lifelong learner, the outcome for our educational endeavor, is more than a combination of problem-solver and independent learner, however. The outcome sought is the individual who, on encountering a challenging situation, as an integral part of problem solving, identifies issues about which he or she needs to know more, skills he or she needs to have, ambiguous knowledge that needs further elucidation, and concepts that he or she needs to rethink. Furthermore, these responses are automatic because they were developed within a system of valued and rewarded practice (cf. Bereiter & Scardamalia, 1989). This "need to know" is afforded by the problem itself, not initiated from some source external to the problem (cf. Bransford,

Sherwood, Vye, & Rieser, 1986; E. J. Gibson, 1982; J. J. Gibson, 1977a, 1977b).

Similarly, this automatically triggered need to know sets in motion a preliminary plan for addressing that need, a plan that interdigitates with the problem-solving process—the plan itself is situated in the problem. For this reason, recognizing the need to know is not met with foreboding but with enthusiasm. The proactive lifelong learner has a repertoire of sources and skills that immediately begin to come together to form an initial, flexible frame of a plan for acquiring the needed knowledge, skills, or both.

For the proactive lifelong learner virtually any challenge can trigger this constellation of cognitive events. Rather than being a passive observer until some extrinsically generated promise of reward or threat of punishment signals a change to an active one, the proactive lifelong learner meets challenges of the world with curiosity, with a need to explain, and with a need to resolve or to improve on it. He or she is primed, because of acquired patterns and habits, to respond to the problem encountered in a proactive way. Specifically, the proactive life-long learner "attunes" to the affordances of the problem.

The term "affordances" is used in the sense first proposed by perceptual psychologist James Gibson (J. J. Gibson, 1977b, 1979; E. J. Gibson, 1982, 1991). J. J. Gibson (1979) described affordances as "what the environment offers to the animal, what it provides or furnishes for good or ill" (p. 127). He illustrates the concept with the following example. If a surface is nearly horizontal as opposed to slanting, nearly flat, sufficiently extended relative to the size of the animal, and rigid relative to the weight of the animal, then the surface *affords* support. Although affordances in this original sense are physical properties, the properties that define the affordance have unity only relative to the animal (1979, p. 127). However, affordances are not invented or read into events by the perceiver. They reside in an objective sense in the environment. They are a function of features of the object, there to be perceived. A lever affords facilitation of moving something even in the case of a small child who is as yet ignorant of its utility. He or she simply does not perceive its affordance (E. J. Gibson, 1991). The Gibsons theorized that learning to perceive affordances in the environment played a significant role in the child's development.

Here the concept of affordances is extended to problems. First, the term "problem" is used to refer to ill-structured problems (Spiro et al., 1987), those which by definition are problematic because they present with less information than is needed to resolve them algorithmically, because there may be more than one viable approach to resolving them, because they must often be resolved in the absence of complete knowledge, and because they often demand decisions in the absence of certainty. Secondly, knowledge and skills here refer to all kinds of knowledge: declarative, procedural and situational.

In extending the concept of affordances to problems, it will be argued that problems afford both resolutions and learning. A problem affords a particular set of resolutions and not others. Just as the object's affordance of support is a function of certain physical features of the object, so the unique set of resolutions is a function of the knowledge and skill demands of the problem. The possible problem resolution(s) only come together as a meaningful unit, however, relative to the problem solver, in particular, relative to the extent to which the problem-solver is able to engage in a dynamic interplay between the features of the problem itself and its knowledge and skill demands. This, in turn, is a function of the problem solver's ability to perceive and respond to the problem's knowledge and skill demands (cf. Bransford, Franks, Vye, & Sherwood, 1989). The knowledge and skill demands, however, are not invented or read into the problem by the problem solver. They reside in the problem itself. Hence different problem solvers may arrive at different resolutions, and these may be of varying quality.

Some knowledge and skill demands of the problem may not represent competencies of the problem solver. When this is the case, the problem has the potential of *affording learning* for that problem solver. If problem solving proceeds in the absence of these competencies, some possible resolutions will not be perceived and other non-viable ones may not be discarded. If, on the other hand, the learner attunes to the problem's knowledge and skill demands, assesses his or her own competence with respect to these, and carries out strategic action to acquire the requisite competencies, and returns to the problem, armed with these newly acquired competencies, then the problem has afforded learning as well as problem solving.

Two examples will serve to instantiate these concepts. First from medicine, a medical problem in which a patient presents with numbness and tingling in the hands and feet may suggest a set of hypotheses that might initially include peripheral blood clots, diabetic neuropathy, tabes dorsales, pernicious anemia, other peripheral neuropathies, toxicity, and spinal injury. There are, no doubt, others. The actual problem itself, however, affords some (or none) of these resolutions and not others. Arriving at an (or the) optimal resolution is a function of the problem solver's ability to engage in dynamic interplay between the features of the actual problem, most of which initially may not be apparent, and the problem's knowledge and skill demands. For this problem, the latter might include neuroanatomical and neurophysiological mechanisms that can produce these sensations. It might include knowledge of peripheral vasculature and blood clots, of diabetic neuropathy, and of the source, of tertiary syphillis, of absorption and metabolism of Vitamin B12. It might include skills in eliciting specific neurological findings and assessing circulation. It would include much more. The problem solver does not impose these knowledge and skill demands. The problem makes the demand. The problem solver who approaches the problem with a deficit in the knowledge and skill demands of the problem will fail to perceive the full range of viable resolutions, will be unable to engage effectively in uncovering the relevant features of the problem, and will consequently be unable to rule in or rule out hypotheses appropriately. However, the problem solver who recognizes his own deficit with respect to the knowledge and skill demands, resolves the deficit and returns to the problem armed with additional knowledge and skill, not only stands in better stead to resolve the problem, but has acquired knowledge in the process.

Can one arrive at a resolution in the absence of extensive knowledge? Absolutely! However, beyond making a lucky guess, the quality of the resolution is a function of the extent to which the problem solver is able to work with the knowledge and skill demands of the problem to uncover the problem's salient features and to reason to a resolution. For example, the problem solver may be armed with only the rather superficial knowledge that "glove and stocking" numbness and tingling are commonly associated with diabetes. A quick diagnosis based on this pattern of clinical correlates may through happenstance correspond with a more thoughtful diagnosis based on deep reasoning. This single hypothesis may trigger a search for a salient problem feature: abnormal glucose indices. The problem solver could happen to hit pay dirt. However, this superficial knowledge alone will not be sufficient to arrive at a resolution should the patient's blood glucose indices be normal.

For a non-medical example, consider the challenge of creating a landscape design for a particular site. The problem—with its geographic, climactic, and access feature, budget, owner preferences, etc.—affords certain resolutions and not others. The problem also demands certain knowledge and skills—knowledge of horticulture, geology, hydrodynamics, skill at lay-out, to name a few. Arriving at an optimal resolution is a function of the problem-solver's ability to work creatively within the problem's knowledge and skill demands and the features of the problem itself. Is it possible to create a landscape design in the absence of knowledge that the problem demands? Most of us can attest to the fact that it certainly is! However, the quality of the design is directly related to the extent to which the problem solver is competent with respect to the knowledge and skill demands of the problem and can use these competencies to address the problem's features. Similarly, the power of the problem to drive further learning is a function of the extent to which the problem-solver is motivated to resolve identified knowledge and skill deficiencies in order to increase the likelihood of an optimal resolution of the problem.

Following the Gibsons (J. J. Gibson, 1977a, 1977b; E. J. Gibson, 1982, 1991) I will hypothesize that learning to perceive and address problem affordances, both resolution affordances and learning affordances, plays a significant role in the development of expertise.

The Proactive Lifelong Learner: Positioned to Develop Expertise

The development of expertise involves many variables (cf. Ericsson, 1996; Sternberg, 1996, 1998). Clearly not all graduates of educational programs will become experts. However, education programs should do everything possible to position their graduates to become experts. Based on what we know now, the greatest potential for the development of expertise may be seen as a combination of knowledge, problem solving, and the propensity to turn experience into learning all orchestrated into a functional whole, a process very similar to the approach of the proactive lifelong learner.

The development of expertise is dependent on learning from or within experience, not just on having experience. There is an old saw that says, "One can have 20 years' experience or the same year's experience 20 times. They are not the same." Bereiter and Scardamalia (1993) hypothesized the following process related to the development of expertise: Initially demanding tasks become automatic or proceduralized (Anderson, 1982), freeing up mental resources. The would-be expert is one who reinvests these freed-up resources in the activity itself. This reallocation may involve consciously refining the process by chunking elements into patterns—enabling proceduralization (Chi, Glaser, & Rees, 1982), or it may involve directing deeper or more creative attention to the problem's affordances. Either has the potential for moving the problem solver farther along the expertise continuum. Bereiter and Scardamalia (1993) suggested that expertise comes not from merely solving many problems in a domain but from extending oneself beyond each of these problems, thus continually adapting to an environment that is constantly changing in ways that require still higher levels of expertise. The proactive lifelong learner is positioned to develop expertise. He or she has acquired an approach to problem solving that actively searches for problem affordances and invests cognitive resources so as to maximize these affordances both in the direction of the problem's optimal resolution and in adding to his or her general repertoire of knowledge and skills.

Again, although many elements contribute to the development of expertise, many beyond an educator's control, the one over which we do have some control is the design of curriculum and assessment systems. Curriculum and assessment systems that model closely this interplay between knowledge acquisition and problem solving have the greatest chance of producing a learner practiced in the behaviors that will sustain learning across a lifetime.

Education Models That Interconnect Knowledge Acquisition and Problem Solving[1]

Expertise in problem solving in any domain does not exist in a knowledge vacuum. Problems demand knowledge for their resolution (Chase & Simon, 1973; Chi et al., 1982; Glaser, 1984; Lesgold et al., 1988). In addition, virtually any real-life problem that is in fact "problematic" is so because the individual encountering the problem recognizes a deficit in the full complement of knowledge and skills essential to its adequate resolution. Otherwise the individuals would engage in algorithmic activity rather than in problem-solving activity. Even when ill-structured problems must be addressed without the benefit of external resources, the initial response of the expert problem solver is an awareness of a deficit in knowledge, in skills, or in both afforded by the problem. In the absence of external resources, the deficit must be made up via reconstructive processes in which the disassembling and reassembling of prior knowledge, skill and experience generate new contextually situated knowledge for the present experience (cf. Brown, Collins, & Duguid, 1989; Spiro et al., 1987). Conversely, when the status of the problem allows for the utilization of external resources, the problem solver will engage in knowledge construction vis-à-vis these resources, be they textual, human, or both. Hence, problem solving, knowledge, and knowledge acquisition are inextricably linked.

Educational approaches that attempt to capture the connection between problem solving, knowledge, and knowledge acquisition generally do so from one of four perspectives. The first three are outlined as follows:

Problem Solving or Reasoning Can Best Be Taught in the Course of Knowledge Acquisition (e.g., The Socratic method; Inquiry approaches). One educational approach, which builds on the interconnectedness of knowledge acquisition and problem solving, looks at knowledge acquisition as appropriately a form of problem solving. Inquiry approaches, after the tradition of Socrates, are within this model (cf. Collins & Stevens, 1982; diSessa, 1982; McDiarmid, 1996). In such approaches the teacher persistently confronts students with cases, with counter examples, with demands for prediction, and with other forms of the Socratic dialogue, repeatedly

---

[1]The meaning of the term "problem" throughout this chapter is not restricted to "problematic situation." Rather, consistent with its use throughout cognitive psychology, it is used to denote any situation that inspires a goal to which there is no clear path. Within this context, the term problem can refer to creative challenges as well as to difficulties to be resolved.

challenging their thinking processes within a content domain. The acquisition of domain knowledge serves to promote the development of sound
reasoning and problem solving.

Knowledge for Future Use Is Best Acquired in Problem-Solving Situations
(e.g., Anchored Instruction). A number of approaches to, or recommendations for instruction have supported the use of problem-solving contexts for knowledge acquisition, theorizing that this will increase the
probability that knowledge and skills acquired in these contexts will be
more useable in others. These approaches specifically address what
Whitehead (1929) has termed "inert" knowledge, knowledge that can be
recalled if it is specifically requested, but that is not spontaneously available for use in problem-solving situations (Bereiter & Scardamalia, 1989;
Bransford et al., 1989, 1990; Palinscar & Brown, 1984; Spiro, et al., 1987).
Knowledge acquisition as enhanced by a problem context is exemplified
by Anchored Instruction, an education approach described by the
Cognition and Technology Group at Vanderbilt (1990). The goal of
Anchored Instruction is that students, motivated by the problem context,
will experience the effects that new knowledge has on their perception
and understanding of these contexts. Awareness of these effects will make
the new knowledge more readily available for use in contexts encountered
later on. Instruction in domain-specific knowledge is anchored in a
macrocontext, or complex problem space.

Knowledge Takes a Part of Its Meaning From Its Application to Problem
Situations (e.g., cognitive apprenticeship). *Cognitive apprenticeship* is the
term given to an educational approach that emphasizes the enculturation
of students into authentic practices in which domain knowledge is used to
address authentic challenges. Collins, Brown and associates (Brown et al.,
1989; Collins, Brown, & Newman, 1989), building on the work of Lave
(Lave, 1977; 1988a; 1988b), observed that knowledge is situated in context, that it can never be completely separated from the context in which
it is developed and used. Knowledge, therefore, takes a part of its meaning from its application to problem situations. They argued that learning,
too, must be situated in contexts of practice in which students can actively come to understand the nuances of meaning imparted by the multiple
purposes and contexts in which it can be used.
    The notions of situated cognition and learning environments con-
ducive to cognitive apprenticeship begin to merge problem solving and
knowledge acquisition into the whole to which we have been alluding.
However, as with the other approaches described, cognitive apprenticeship starts with domain knowledge and situates it in practice. Nesting the
culture of practice within domains such as reading, writing, and mathe-

matics focuses on adapting domain knowledge to context. There remains a need to address the development of the capacity to attune to the inherently multidisciplinary and complex affordances contextualized in problems themselves. The fourth educational approach, Problem-Based Learning, attempts to achieve just that.

PROBLEM-BASED LEARNING AND THE DEVELOPMENT OF THE PROACTIVE LIFELONG LEARNER

Problem-Based Learning[2] as described by Barrows (Barrows, 1992; Barrows & Tamblyn, 1980) is an approach to education that moves away from situating domain knowledge in context; rather, it builds from the knowledge affordances of the problem context itself. It is exemplified here by the Problem-Based Learning Curriculum (PBLC) at Southern Illinois University School of Medicine. The PBLC is an example of radically reshaping the approach to education so that its actual student outcome is congruent with the expected outcome, the proactive lifelong learner prepared to enter the practice of medicine and develop the expertise necessary for practice. Problem-Based Learning does two things. It builds a curriculum from the complex affordances of a set of common and important problems of the profession. Second, it places the responsibility for attuning to and addressing these affordances on the student. Consequently, Problem-Based Learning offers a consistent model as students move along on the continuum from novice to developing expert, and it provides persistent practice in attuning, assessing, addressing and applying with respect to problem affordances. In Problem-Based Learning, students, as novices, are expected to approach problems as a developing expert. However, the more novice the student, the more he or she directs attention to addressing identified deficiencies in knowledge by attending to the learning affordances of the problem. As the student moves through the curriculum, and along the novice–expert continuum, the developing knowledge and skill base allows for freeing up of resources that may then

---

[2]Problem-Based Learning, interestingly enough, was conceptualized in the mid-1970s, before any of the research that is cited here. The PBLC at SIU School of Medicine was developed under the oversight of Howard S. Barrows in line with the principles of Problem-Based Learning in whose development he was intimately involved. The operationalization of the curriculum was the result of the dedicated efforts of a number of basic science, medical education, and clinical faculty who rigorously addressed the many challenges involved in moving from a discipline-based to a problem-based curriculum and in moving from a curriculum in which the responsibility for learning rests on faculty's shoulders to one in which students were required to take responsibility for their own learning.

be reallocated to refining the approach to the problem and adding depth and breadth to the knowledge base. The student gains knowledge and becomes a more proficient problem solver, all the while practicing the patterns that define the proactive lifelong learner.

The Barrows model of Problem-Based Learning (PBL; Barrows, 1992) has been described elsewhere in this volume (see Kelson & Distlehorst, this volume, chapter 7). Here we describe those features as implemented at SIU School of Medicine, which are seen as directly contributing to the development of the proactive lifelong learner. These descriptions are followed by ensuing principles.

• The discipline-oriented basic science years are replaced by a curriculum consisting entirely of patient problem encounters that are selected to achieve two ends: they are representative of the common and important problems physicians encounter in actual practice, and from this "universe" a problem set is selected that will afford the development of a foundation of basic knowledge and skills essential to the practice of medicine.

Principle #1: The acquisition of domain knowledge emerges from learning affordances of common and important problems of future practice.

• Problems are developed from actual patient records and are presented just as patients present in real life. Cases are not scrubbed but present with all of the ambiguity and messiness that characterize actual patient encounters. Although the cases are simulations, they are presented in such a way that students must build the problem by inquiring for patient information, using the inquiry techniques of the profession: taking a history, performing a physical examination, and ordering and interpreting laboratory tests and procedures. In other words, they are ill-structured problems (Barrows, 1990, 1992; Spiro et al., 1987).

Principle #2: The full complement of reasoning skills in which the practicing physician must engage is afforded by the process by which the problem is presented and unfolds.

• Students engage the problems in small groups of five or six, together with a facilitator called a PBL tutor.[3] The tutor coaches the group's collaborative reasoning by means of the Tutorial Process (Barrows, 1992). The tutorial process replicates within the group the hypothetical–deductive reasoning process used by most physicians when encountering a prob-

---

[3]The term *tutor* is used in the sense that the British use it, to mean an educational guide. The terms educational "coach" or "facilitator" are sometimes used for this role.

lem (Barrows & Feltovich, 1987; see also Kelson & Distlehorst, this volume, chapter 7).

Principle #3: Students practice the hypothetico–deductive reasoning process, developing procedural problem-solving knowledge.

• Students are responsible for recognizing and addressing both the learning and problem-solving affordances of the problem, recording as "learning issues" any in which they feel deficient. Following each session in which the group encounters the problem, they research the learning issues and return to readdress the problem armed with new knowledge and skill. This process continues until the group arrives at a well-reasoned resolution and can articulate a systems explanation.

Principle #4: The onus for attuning to problem affordances as well as the responsibility for acquiring the necessary knowledge and skills is entirely on the student. The tutor acts as a coach, taking care to protect this student responsibility.

• The group recognizes that it has a dual responsibility: to arrive at a reasoned resolution of the problem and to fully understand the knowledge and skills it demands. Each problem is finalized in two ways. The group compares its reasoning through the problem with that of the health care professionals who actually cared for the patient, and they are asked to articulate a systems explanation of the present patient problem and its management, incorporating biomechanical, biochemical, and psychosocial mechanisms. They are encouraged to compare and contrast with relevant elements from other cases and to verify their explanation with content experts from the faculty. The systems explanation typically takes the form of a flowchart or a concept map. This knowledge abstraction process serves to unbind knowledge from specific context, fostering its transfer to new problems (Collins et al., 1989). It also contributes to the building of a mental model, which incorporates reasoning from basic mechanisms.

Principle #5: Students see knowledge, problem solving, and knowledge acquisition as an integrated process. Problem solutions are validated by systems explanations.

• At the end of every problem students systematically reflect on their own performance and progress and analyze that of their peers, giving them specific feedback as to strengths and weaknesses and identifying goals for improved future performance. The tutor joins the group in this self- and peer assessment.

Principle #6: Students practice self-reflection and the analysis and articulation of strengths and weaknesses in performances of others, a process that enhances both self-reflection and team building.

Taken together, these features are designed to precisely model the expected outcome of the curriculum. The entire curriculum consists of students practicing the features of proactive lifelong learning.

Curriculum and Assessment in Tandem

Even the most elaborately designed, true-to-outcome curriculum is likely to be undermined by an incongruous assessment system. Many an educational innovation has failed because its students, and consequently the curriculum's own effectiveness, were measured by an assessment system borrowed from the traditional program it was designed to replace. As argued earlier, assessment feeds back on curriculum, shaping it to become more like itself. Because curriculum and assessment by default have such a dynamic relationship, it seems reasonable and necessary to plan for them to work in tandem, "in the spirit of making a virtue of a vice that cannot be shed" (Wiggins, 1989, p. 42).

Frederiksen and Collins (1989; cf. also Madaus, 1988; Wiggins, 1989) pointed out that to introduce tests into a system that adapts itself to the test poses a special kind of validity problem. In such a dynamic system one must ask, "Do the tests continue to measure the student outcome, which they were designed to measure, or have they been co-opted to measure the effects of preparing for the test?" They propose the notion of *systemic validity* to address this issue. A test is systemically valid when in its unavoidable feedback role, it induces changes in curriculum and instructional practice that positively affect the outcomes the test was designed to measure (Frederiksen & Collins, 1989, p. 27). The notion of systemic validity for a test can be extended to the entire assessment system because it is the entire system—anything that counts—that interacts dynamically with curriculum and instructional practice. An assessment system operating in tandem with curriculum would have a high level of systemic validity if, in preparing for any assessment event (educational activity or test that counts), students were engaged in (read "practicing") the behaviors that characterize the student outcome.

Characteristics of a Congruent Assessment System

In order to develop the student outcome we have been describing—the proactive lifelong learner—the assessment system must do three things:

1. It must consistently reinforce and model the approach to problems we expect of the student as an outcome of the program.

2. It must provide explicit feedback on performance within that model.

3. It must provide continuous, seamless tracking of the student's development across the curriculum.

Reinforcing the Model. It is crucial that each component of the assessment system model the approach we expect the student to take toward problems in the real world upon completion of the educational program. We have already noted the characteristics of that approach. The expected student outcome is the individual who

- meets problems proactively;
- attunes to, assesses against, and addresses the problems' affordances;
- has well-developed systems for inquiry and reasoning in order to investigate, frame, and manipulate data associated with the problem;
- has well-developed systems for self-monitoring, self-assessment and creative updating of knowledge and skills;
- has developed an integrated, flexible, dynamic working knowledge base rather than one that is rigid and compartmentalized.

When assessment, either in whole or in part, directs students away from this model, it can be predicted that the curriculum will deviate from its intended purpose, with a subsequent negative effect on student outcome.

Feedback on Performance. All assessment systems provide feedback to students about their performance—feedback that reinforces goals. If the student is given merely an average of grades on assignments or a test score, then feedback reinforces the schoolwork mode, encouraging students' goals and strategies that will lead to higher averages and test scores (Masters & Mislevy, 1993). Feedback provides the data by which students may adjust their internal performance model to some external standard; consequently, it must address the criteria of the model to be internalized. In its best form, feedback not only addresses these criteria, but its delivery is consistent with the model it is reinforcing. In the model we have been describing, delivery should be consistent with the process by which the developing expert reviews performance and reshapes strategies and plans for future problems.

For it to be effective, feedback must be timely, explicit, and consistent. *Timeliness* does not always mean immediate. Feedback that interrupts the problem-solving process is likely to be ineffective and disruptive (Frederiksen & White, 1990). Timeliness does mean that feedback occurs at a time when it can optimally impact on the developing mental model.

Explicitness refers to the citation of specific behaviors in reference to some identified criteria. To say that a certain aspect of a performance is "good," "underdeveloped," or "improving" has no operational meaning, and hence, has little impact on future performance. To cite explicitly the specific behaviors around which these judgments are formed operationalizes the criteria.

Consistency refers to the rigor and regularity with which feedback addresses all components of the model. It is critical to the internalization of that model. Students' behavior can be expected to conform to the desired model to the extent that feedback is timely, explicit, and consistent.

Seamless Tracking. A common strategy students use to address schoolwork can be referred to as "chunking the curriculum." Within this strategy, students treat curricular or instructional segments as compartmentalized entities or goal endpoints. These segments may be marked by ends of chapters, the end of a unit, or the end of a course or they can be temporal in nature, such as "end of the week" or "end of this hour." Usually, though not always, chunks have assessment markers such as examinations, weekly grades, reports due, and so forth. Goal setting by students is often done around the completion of these chunks, especially if they are associated with grades. Chunking tends to be integral to the schoolwork approach described previously. The strategy is effective in most assessment systems because typically there is a grade or set of grades associated with the chunk, and grades are averaged across chunks.

It is easy to recognize the danger of this strategy. Students are at risk not only of adopting goals that make learning incidental to the completion of assignments or passing examinations, they are also at risk of dismissing at the end of every chunk any incidental learning that may have occurred within it.

Chunking the curriculum is also a strategy used by students who are struggling to meet curricular demands. These students seem to treat instructional endpoints as hurdles to clear. Students manage, sometimes with persistent effort, sometimes with minimal effort followed by a last-minute surge, to get over the hurdle, to achieve a minimally passing mark. Once that hurdle is passed, they slump with exhaustion, relax with a sigh of relief, or eye with trepidation the next hurdle. When scores are averaged across grading periods, these students meet the course requirements. However, if performance is reviewed across the entire course, developmental progress is doubtful. If developmental progress is to be maintained, the assessment system must be "seamless," involving tracking students' performance across curricular or instructional segments.

Assessment and the Faculty–Student Dilemma

We have described an approach to educating students that places the responsibility for responding to problem affordances squarely on the students. The role of the tutor is to facilitate all of these processes at the metacognitive level and to urge this responsibility onto the students. The students are responsible for developing expertise, and this can happen only if the full weight of the entire process rests on students' shoulders. This suggests that, in fairness, assessment must also emanate from the student.

Nevertheless there are clear faculty responsibilities involved in an educational program. One of them is assessing students, verifying that they are prepared to meet responsibilities and demands at subsequent levels of education and practice. In short, faculty must evaluate students' progress. Herein lies the dilemma. If we are to have the proactive lifelong learner as an outcome of an educational program, students must be wholly responsible for responding to the affordances of the problems they encounter. Assessment, including examinations, must consistently reinforce this model or it will run the risk of subverting it. If faculty assume their role in certifying competence in the traditional way, then it would appear that assessment must address predetermined, faculty-generated knowledge, skills, and competencies. Students introduced to such a duality quickly express frustration. An assessment system based on predetermined, faculty-generated knowledge and skills sends the unequivocal message that it is the faculty rather than the selected problems that are determining what must be known, and students' goal setting for learning is co-opted by the need to predict what will be on the test and to prepare for it. The challenge, then, is to develop an assessment system in which faculty exercise their responsibility for certifying student competence while preserving student responsibility for learning in response to problem affordances.

ASSESSMENT TOWARD DEVELOPING THE PROACTIVE LIFELONG LEARNER: THE SIU SCHOOL OF MEDICINE PBLC ASSESSMENT SYSTEM

Faculty associated with SIU PBLC have taken on the challenge of developing an assessment system that will work in tandem with the curriculum to provide consistent reinforcement for the proactive lifelong learning model as well as to fulfill their responsibilities as faculty for determining students' progress. The system that they are developing has two major goals: to assess students' progress toward becoming proactive lifelong learners; and to provide consistent reinforcement for the model that preserves students' responsibility for responding to the problem solving and learning affordances of problems encountered. The first goal addresses the faculty's responsibility in assessing students' competence; the second addresses the faculty's responsibility in providing a consistent model for proactive lifelong learning.

Assessment Data

There are two sources of data that together determine a student's progress in the SIU PBLC: the Tutor Group Assessment and the end-of-unit performance-based examination called P.A.S.S. (Performance Assessment of Self-Directed Study).

Tutor Group Assessment. Tutor Group Assessment is systematically organized around five broad curricular goals: knowledge, problem solving, self-directed learning, clinical skills, and collaboration. These broad curricular goals are actually category labels that encompass the characteristics of the proactive lifelong learner. *Knowledge* means the ability to formulate, organize, and articulate the basic biomechanical, biochemical, and psychosocial concepts that can explain the problem and can be employed to resolve an unfamiliar problem. *Problem solving* is defined as demonstrating the ability to employ the clinical reasoning process in the investigation and solution of medical problems. *Self-directed learning* means, when one is unable to articulate the requisite basic knowledge to explain a problem, the ability to design and implement a satisfactory learning strategy to rectify the inability; monitor the adequacy of personal knowledge and skills, and assess the effectiveness and efficiency of self-directed learning strategies employed; and critically assess learning resources for adequacy, quality, and veracity. *Clinical skills* can be seen as a special blend of knowledge and problem solving and involve knowing and applying the specific technical skills needed to interact with a patient as an inquiry source in the problem-solving process. *Collaboration* includes the ability to interact effectively with individuals in an appropriate and responsible manner during group functions (assuming responsibility for shared tasks), and the ability to give and receive constructive criticism in order to fairly assess self, group members, the tutor, and the tutor group process (PBLC Curriculum Committee, 1997).

The Self- and Peer-Assessment Process. Self- and peer assessment occurs at the end of every problem. Each student in the group reports his or her own assessment of his or her current status in knowledge, problem-solving, self-directed learning, clinical skills, and collaboration, the five goals described previously. Every other member of the group then gives the student feedback with respect to each of these categories. This same procedure is repeated until each group member has assessed himself and has been assessed by each of his peers. At the end of every 8 to 10 week unit, this process is formalized and becomes one of the data sets that determine students' progress in the curriculum. In other words, it counts. In the formal report, each student comes prepared with his or her self-evaluation in written form, and every student comes prepared with a peer evaluation of every other student. As a part of this end-of-unit assessment, the group, with the tutor, arrives at a consensus as to each student's performance for each of the five goals. The group is directed to reach a consensus without losing the power of the assessment. This forces them to reconcile rather than dismiss disparate judgments. If a consensus cannot be reached, a "minority report" may be submitted. The results of the group deliberation are compiled within 24 hours, usually by a student other than the one being assessed, and are submitted to the tutor for verification of the completeness and accuracy of the report. This end-of-unit Tutor Group Assessment is then forwarded to the PBLC progress subcommittee and becomes a part of the student's permanent record.

There are several factors that contribute to the effectiveness of the Tutor Group Assessment:

1. Pass–fail system. The effectiveness of self and peer assessment is highly dependent on students' abilities to be honest with one another. One way in which honest feedback is stimulated is by radically decreasing competition. Grading induces competition almost by definition. The SIU PBLC, like many medical school programs across the country, is pass–fail. A pass–fail system frees all aspects of students' evaluation from the need to quantify measures in order to serve a grading system, allowing the entire program to embrace cooperation as the operating principle.

2. Mutual commitment to excellence. Not only is competition actively discouraged, students are actively encouraged to adopt a mutual commitment to the excellence of themselves and of every other member of their group(s). Because students are continually learning and problem solving collaboratively, they are mutually dependent on each other in addressing the patient problems they encounter and in acquiring the knowledge and skills demanded by these problems. This makes it important that each member not just carry his or her share of the load but that each becomes increasingly better at all aspects of the learning and problem-solving process. It is to each student's advantage that all of them strive for excellence.

3. Group accountability. Another feature that makes the Tutor Group Assessment work is a very stringent set of guidelines for group accountability. All students are expected to give thorough and honest appraisals of themselves and of their peers, and they are assessed on their ability to do so. With the exception of producing a confidential report at the end of the unit, assessment discussions are kept within the group. No problems are

dealt with outside of the group. Tutors are discouraged from meeting privately with students to discuss individual or group problems, but rather are encouraged to have the student bring his or her concerns to the group. Any problem that interferes in any way with group functioning or the functioning of individuals within the group is seen as a group problem to be dealt with by the group. All other problems are viewed as irrelevant to the group.

4. Tutor accountability. The tutor participates in the peer and self assessment process not separately, but as a part of the group process. However, the tutor is responsible for the quality of the group's assessment. A significant tutor responsibility is to track performance of individual group members on all five goals and to raise in the group any item of performance that has not been raised by the individual or by his or her peers. The tutor ultimately is responsible for the accuracy and thoroughness of the Tutor Group Assessment for each student. By modeling how to give constructive feedback, the tutor plays a major role in operationalizing the criteria that define outcomes and shape each student's overall development.

5. Nonnegotiable outcomes. A fifth principle that makes the tutor group assessment so powerful is that students are expected to develop fully in all five areas labeled by the goals. Exceptional development in one area is not seen as compensation for underdevelopment in another. A student who is seen to have a tremendous capacity to retain information but who has difficulty applying that knowledge in the problem context might well be considered in academic difficulty, as might the student who manages the knowledge and problem solving but who has difficulty collaborating as a member of a working team. All five goals are seen as absolutely essential.

6. Specificity of data. A sixth principle that contributes to the power of the Tutor Group Assessment is that students and the tutor are asked to cite specific evidence for conclusions drawn with respect to each of the goals or to cite counterevidence when disagreeing with a conclusion. Citing specific evidence or counterevidence serves to operationalize the criteria for performance. An evaluative statement such as "Your knowledge base seems to be developing adequately," although it may have a certain comfort value, has almost no meaning for building the mental model we have been discussing. Consider, however, a statement such as, "Your discussion of the mechanism of action of penicillin was very solid. You took us all the way down to the mechanism by which the drug interferes with bacterial cell wall synthesis . . . much more in depth than you have been going with pharmacologic explanations." This feedback informs the recipient and the entire group of one of the criteria being used to arrive at the "adequate

knowledge" assessment—molecular-level explanations of mechanisms of action for pharmacologic agents. It reinforces development by contrasting present performance with past performance, and it conveys "comfort" in a much more convincing way than the generic statement.

Some Basic Rules

In addition to these principles, there are some basic rules that govern peer and self-assessment. One rule regards the "quiet student." In most collaborative settings the quiet student is problematic. The problem is enhanced when assessment of performance occurs in a group setting. Is the quietness a personality trait or a defense against lack of knowledge or skill? There is a temptation to assume a default position that, in the interest of presumed fairness, says, "If there is no demonstrated evidence of lack of knowledge and skills, we assume that the knowledge is there." In the PBLC system, however, with students' development absolutely dependent on explicit feedback, this default does the student a great disservice, to say nothing of the disservice to the group that suffers the loss of the nonparticipating member's contributions. Articulation of knowledge and reasoning is reinforcing to the learner. It confirms a feeling of knowing or raises gaps, misunderstandings, or errors in logic to the surface. Further, the ability to articulate explanations and reasoning is an absolutely essential skill in the workplace. Failure to give students the support necessary to develop these skills might be viewed as educational malpractice. At the instigation of the students themselves, the SIU PBLC adopted this rule: "Quietness will not be taken as a substitute for the demonstration of knowledge or reasoning." In other words, the student who fails to articulate knowledge, reasoning, or both is presumed to be deficient in them.

A second rule relates to the principle of mutual commitment to excellence. Any time a student difficulty is identified by the group, the group offers its services to help remedy the difficulty. The quiet student can serve as an example. When group members (or the student himself or herself) comments that a student has not participated sufficiently for them to judge the adequacy of knowledge or reasoning, they, or the tutor if necessary, then ask, "How can we help you overcome this problem?" There follows a negotiation in which the group may discover that the student's quietness has been precipitated by some highly aggressive behaviors of others in the group, or that the student is more reflective than his "think-aloud" comrades, or that the student is shy by nature and finds speaking up painful. Together the student and his or her peers agree to strategies that will allow for equitable participation and articulation of knowledge and reasoning.

A third rule is also related to the mutual commitment to excellence. Nothing may appear on a final evaluation that has not already been addressed by the group. It is considered blatantly unfair for students or for the tutor, at the time of the final evaluation, to raise a point the student has not had an opportunity to address. This rule stimulates the tutor and group members to bring to the table early on any behaviors that might potentially lead to poor performance.

Performance Assessment of Self-Directed Study (P.A.S.S.)[4]

The Tutor Group Assessment provides essential data regarding students' performance in a group. Individual performance data is obtained through a performance-based examination that occurs at the end of every unit (8–10 weeks). The discussion here is of the examination as it occurs in the second year of the PBLC. The pivotal criteria for developing this examination is that it should preserve student-centeredness and model the way students should think about patient cases in future practice.

The P.A.S.S. is designed collaboratively by a faculty design team including representatives from each discipline typically encountered in the first two years of medical school (discipline consultants), tutors in the unit, the unit coordinator, and education specialists. The examination centers around three cases specifically selected to engage the student in the biochemical, biomechanical, and psychosocial issues central to the unit. Once the cases are selected, the design team meets to frame the significant issues and an accompanying probe is set for each case, identifying the key issues that the case affords. The probes are distributed to the appropriate discipline representatives who draft an answer key for the benefit of the faculty members who will serve as examiners. The answer key for each probe addresses two levels: a primary level response that spells out the minimal explanation students should be held to when incorporating that concept into explanations, and an extended level response that elaborates on the concept so that the examiner may assess the explanations of students who have richer, more fully integrated knowledge around the concept. After the probes and answer keys are collected and organized into a natural flow, the design team meets again to finalize the exam. The team's challenge is to incorporate only those concepts that are afforded by the case, and equally important, to incorporate all of the concepts that are

---

[4]Walter Myers, Ph.D., D.V.M., worked with the author in conceptualizing this examination. As with the development of the curriculum, P.A.S.S. has been developed, or rather is being developed, by a number of SU School of Medicine faculty committed to building an assessment system that models the performance demands of the physician in practice.

central to a reasoned explanation and to decision making in the patient problem. When the probe set is finalized, the probes, along with their corresponding significant issues, are entered on a master matrix.

The administration of P.A.S.S. is a week-long process. It is considered both a learning and an evaluation process. On each of the first 3 days of the week, students encounter one of the cases presented as a standardized patient.[5] Students interview and examine the patient, after which they complete a formal case write-up on one case and write "Impressions" and "Plans" for the other two. They also draft a list of significant issues suggested by the case, marking those that they identify as learning issues. At least one of these cases is observed by a clinician who assesses clinical skills and reviews the case write-up. On all cases the standardized patient assesses the student's "doctor–patient interaction." After turning in write-ups and learning issues, students are given a written description of the case that provides them with information they should have gathered in the interview and examination of the patient, removing any disadvantage students might have because of the developmental level of their clinical skills. After reviewing the complete case description, students are allowed to revise their list of significant learning issues.

Students then have 2 to 3 days for self-directed learning around the learning issues they have identified. During this time individual matrices are constructed for each student, on which are recorded their learning issues matched with the significant issues and corresponding probes generated by the exam design team. At the end of the week each student meets with an examiner, typically a unit tutor other than his or her own. The examiner is provided with each student's individual matrix along with the probe set and answer key and the description of each case.

Significantly, the examination begins with an open-ended question: "Discuss this case, incorporating rich basic science and psychosocial explanations into your discussion." As the student begins discussing the case, the examiner can track his or her discussion on the matrix, probing when necessary for broader or deeper explanations. Examiners are given license to probe in a tutorial manner from openings that students provide in their case discussion. The correlated student-generated learning issues provide insight into how the student approached researching the concepts he or she found to be key to understanding the case and planning for its management. The matrix, along with the probe key, also allows the examiner to note the quality of the student's explanations, notes that become useful in giving the student specific feedback regarding his or her performance.

---

[5]Standardized patients are actors trained to simulate an actual patient case in every respect (Barrows, 1987).

In addition to giving specific written feedback as to the quality of knowledge and reasoning demonstrated, examiners, taking into account all three cases, rate students as "Satisfactory," "Marginal," or "Unsatisfactory" with the option of commenting on an outstanding performance. Their ratings are based on the accuracy and depth of knowledge the student demonstrates with respect to key issues in the case, and the extent to which that knowledge is spontaneously integrated into the explanation of the case. Examiners are asked to consider four levels of knowledge integration: At the top is the student who spontaneously integrates most or all of the key explanations, with appropriate depth and accuracy, into his or her reasoning through the case. This student would spontaneously discuss the case of sufficient depth and breadth requiring little probing from the examiner. Next is the student who, with probing, is able to generate these explanations, again at appropriate depth and accuracy, and is able to integrate them into his or her reasoning through the case. Third is the student who, with probing, demonstrates the knowledge that is key to the case, but does not integrate this knowledge into his or her reasoning, the knowledge seemingly encapsulated or compartmentalized. Finally, there is the student who fails to demonstrate the knowledge that is key to the case, resulting in inadequate reasoning as well. Students whose performance is characterized by either of the last two levels are of concern. Students are aware of these criteria. What's more, they see them as representing their goal for future practice: the automatic integration of knowledge and reasoning into clinical practice.

The Solution to the Faculty–Student Dilemma

P.A.S.S. provides an acceptable resolution to the faculty–student dilemma by having neither faculty alone nor students alone determine what should be learned. In fact, it is the problem that demands knowledge and reasoning about the concepts and skills to be acquired. Both students and faculty approach the selected patient case in the same way. For students, the oral examination begins with the following query: "Discuss this case, incorporating as much basic science and psychosocial explanation as the case demands," congruent with the faculty approach to drafting the probe set, which is "What basic biomechanical, biochemical, and psychosocial explanations does this case afford?"

The design of this examination is radically different from problem-oriented examinations in which faculty create problem stems to which they attach discipline-generated questions. Such exams represent attempts to test concepts and skills selected from a universe of faculty-determined core knowledge in a more authentic context than that of a straight multiple-choice test. Although such examinations likely increase the perceived relevance of the core knowledge and may test transfer of discipline knowledge to problem contexts, they do nothing to test the student's sensitivity to and ability to address the knowledge and reasoning demands of the problem itself. Rather they divert cognitive goals from sensing and responding to predicting what of faculty-determined core knowledge will be sampled and how. Thus, they fail to reinforce the development of the proactive lifelong learner.

An examination such as P.A.S.S., on the other hand, which demands that both students and faculty take their cues from the problem, precisely tests students' attuning to its affordances and their ability to address these demands. Faculty need not give up their responsibility for seeing that students develop a solid knowledge base nor need they abdicate their role in determining students' progress. Just as faculty shape the knowledge addressed in the curriculum through problem selection, so can they systematically assess the student's developing knowledge base through the selection of examination cases based on the affordances of these cases. However, once cases are selected, they themselves dictate to both faculty and students what is and is not significant knowledge.

The Seamless Assessment System

The final piece in the assessment system of the SIU School of Medicine PBLC is that the system is *seamless*. By this we mean that students are not awarded pass–fail status until they have completed the entire 2 years of the preclinical curriculum. There are typically 10 units in a curricular year. At the end of each unit a progress subcommittee meets to consider the performance of each student across all units, based on data provided by the formal Tutor Group Assessments, which provide information as to individual performance in the group, and by the end-of-unit assessment reports, which provide information as to the independent individual performance. Rather than giving a summative end-of-unit mark or pass–fail notation, each student is given a "Report of Current Status," with one of three statements: "Progressing with these Observations"—indicating that the student is making satisfactory progress and followed by a summary of the students pattern of relative strengths and weaknesses across units to that time; "Progressing with these Concerns"—followed by a summary of performance patterns across units that suggest that special attention is warranted to correct identified deficits; or "Not Progressing Satisfactorily"—followed by a summary of performance patterns, usually persisting despite being previously identified, which are serious enough to warrant special intervention. Failure to respond to such intervention may lead to the student's repeating all or part of the curriculum or even to a recommendation for dismissal.

Work in Progress

The SIU PBLC is committed to developing in students a mental model that we have called here the proactive lifelong learner. This model positions students for the development of expertise. The assessment system, nonetheless, is a work in progress. Its strength is a persistent adherence to modeling the outcome it, along with the curriculum, is attempting to produce. There remain, therefore, things that need to be addressed.

There is a need to assess the developing knowledge base in such a way that students, preparing for such a test, are practicing attuning to and addressing problem affordances. This means avoiding the testing of knowledge and of problem solving as a collection of isolated units. Current efforts are in the direction of constructing a test instrument based on the system's explanation segment of the tutorial process, in which students construct biomechanical, biochemical, psychosocial models of patient cases they had encountered in the curriculum, encounters that presumably build a knowledge base that they carry with them.

There is almost universal agreement among faculty participating in the process that the P.A.S.S. exam gives very powerful information about the student's ability to attune to a problem's affordances, to address deficiencies in knowledge and skills as identified in self-assessment, and to bring newly acquired knowledge and skills back to the problem. There is equally almost uniform concern about the reliability across examiners, about the faculty's intensity of this effort, and about the fact that it is currently the only assessment of individual competence. Present efforts are in the direction of improving training and checks on reliability, and in building in other assessments of individual performance as described previously.

ASSESSMENT: SERVING RATHER THAN DIVERTING LEARNING

I have proposed that the development of expertise may be directly related to the extent to which individuals learn to perceive and respond to the problem solving and learning affordances of problems, and that this general activity ought to form a significant part of educational curricula. Even more significantly, and building on the theme that assessment drives learning, if we are to position the graduates of our programs so that they continue to move along the expertise continuum, then assessment of their progress and performance must focus on their capacity to perceive and respond to these affordances rather than on their capacity to perceive and respond to faculty inclinations as to what constitutes important knowledge and skills.

Incorporating proactive lifelong learning as a seriously pursued outcome of schooling is not a step to be taken lightly. It entails radical rethinking of what learning is, what education is, what assessment is, and what knowledge itself is. Nevertheless, in a world in which complexity and change are the order of the day, and knowledge must continually be renewed or even reinvented in order to address that complexity and keep up with the change, neither can it be dismissed.

An essential step to reform is the radical rethinking of students' assessment. Rather than allowing demands of traditional testing to have unchallenged influence over the goals that direct students' learning and over the educational activities that define the curriculum, assessment must be completely rethought so that it serves the valued outcomes of the curriculum. Whether or not students emerge from their school experience as proactive lifelong learners, positioned for the development of expertise, is largely dependent on the assessment system that has shaped their mental model of what it means to know, what it means to learn, and their capacity and inclination to respond to problems in the real world.

REFERENCES

Anderson, J. R. (1982). Acquisition of cognitive skill. *Psychology Review, 89,* 369–406.

Barrows, H. S. (1987). *Simulated patients and other humans simulations.* Chapel Hill, NC: Health Science Consortium.

Barrows, H. S. (1990). Inquiry: The pedagogical importance of a skill central to clinical practice. *Journal of Medical Education, 24,* 3–5.

Barrows, H. S. (1992). *The tutorial process.* Springfield, IL: Southern Illinois University School of Medicine.

Barrows, H. S., & Feltovich, P. J. (1987). The clinical reasoning process. *Journal of Medical Education, 21,* 86–91.

Barrows, H. S., & Tamblyn, R. M. (1980). *Problem-based learning: An approach to medical education.* New York: Springer.

Bereiter, C. (1990). Aspects of an educational learning theory. *Review of Educational Research, 60*(4), 603–624.

Bereiter, C., & Scardamalia, M. (1989). Intentional learning as a goal for instruction. In L. B. Resnick (Ed.), *Knowing, learning and instruction: Essays in honor of Robert Glaser,* pp. 361–392. Hillsdale, NJ: Lawrence Erlbaum Associates.

Bereiter, C., & Scardamalia, M. (1993). *Surpassing ourselves.* Chicago, IL: Open Court.

Bransford, J. D., Franks, J. J., Vye, N. J., & Sherwood, R. (1989). New approaches to instruction: Because wisdom can't be told. In S. Vosniadou & A. Ortony, *Similarity and analogical reasoning* (pp. 470–497). New York: Cambridge University Press.

Bransford, J. D., Sherwood, R., Vye, N. J., & Rieser, J. (1986). Teaching thinking and problem-solving: Suggestions from research. *American Psychologist, 41,* 1078–1089.

Bransford, J. D., Vye, N., Kinzer, C., & Risko, V. (1990). Teaching thinking and content knowledge: Toward an integrated approach. In B. F. Jones & L. Idol (Eds.), *Dimensions of thinking and cognitive instruction* (pp. 93–110). Hillsdale, NJ: Lawrence Erlbaum Associates.

Brown, A. L., Bransford, J. D., Ferrara, R. A., & Campione, J. C. (1983). Learning, remembering and understanding. In J. H. Flavell & E. M. Markman (Eds.), *Handbook of child psychology* (Vol. 3, pp. 77–166). New York: John Wiley & Sons.

Brown, J. S., Collins, A., & Duguid, P. (1989). Situated cognition and the culture of learning. *Educational Researcher, 18*(1), 32–42.

Chase, W. G., & Simon, H. A. (1973). Perception in chess. *Cognitive Psychology, 4*, 55–81.

Chi, M. T. H., Glaser, R., & Rees, E. (1982). Expertise in problem solving. In R. Sternberg (Ed.), *Advances in the psychology of human intelligence* (pp. 7–75). Hillsdale, NJ: Lawrence Erlbaum Associates.

Collins, A., Brown, J. S., & Newman, S. E. (1989). Cognitive apprenticeship: Teaching the crafts of reading, writing and mathematics. In L. B. Resnick (Ed.), *Knowing, learning and instruction: Essays in honor of Robert Glaser*. Hillsdale, NJ: Lawrence Erlbaum Associates.

Collins, A., & Stevens, A. L. (1982). Goals and strategies of inquiry teachers. In R. Glaser (Ed.), *Advances in instructional psychology* (Vol. 2, pp. 65–119). Hillsdale, NJ: Lawrence Erlbaum Associates.

Darling-Hammond, L., & Wise, A. E. (1985). Beyond standardization: State standards and school improvement. *Elementary School Journal, 85*, 315–336.

diSessa, A. A. (1982). Unlearning Aristotelian physics: A study of knowledge-based learning. *Cognitive Science, 6*, 37–75.

Ericsson, A. (Ed.; 1996). *The road to excellence*. Mahwah, NJ: Lawrence Erlbaum Associates.

Feltovich, P. J., & Barrows, H. S. (1997). *A proposal to establish a center for education for the complex and changing workplace*. Springfield, IL: Southern Illinois University School of Medicine, Internal Document.

Feltovich, P. J., Spiro, R. J., Coulson, R. L., & Myers-Kelson, A. (1995). The reductive bias and the crisis of text (in the law). *The Journal of Contemporary Legal Issues, 6*(11), 187–212.

Frederiksen, J. R., & Collins, A. (1989). Systems approach to educational testing. *Educational Researcher, 18*(9), 27–32.

Frederiksen, J. R., & White, B. Y. (1990). Intelligent tutors as intelligent testers. In N. Frederiksen, R. Glaser, A. Lesgold, & M. Shafto (Eds.), *Diagnostic monitoring of skills and knowledge acquisition*. Hillsdale, NJ: Lawrence Erlbaum Associates.

Gibson, E. J. (1982). The concept of affordances in development: The renaissance of functionalism. In W. A. Collings (Ed.), *The concept of development: The Minnesota symposium on child psychology* (Vol. 15, pp. 55–81). Hillsdale, NJ: Lawrence Erlbaum Associates.

Gibson, E. J. (1991). The concept of affordances in development: The renaissance of functionalism. In E. J. Gibson (Ed.), *An odyssey in learning and perception*. Cambridge, MA: MIT Press.

Gibson, J. J. (1977a). *An ecological approach to visual perception*. Boston: Houghton-Mifflin. Reprint, Hillsdale, NJ: Lawrence Erlbaum Associates.

Gibson, J. J. (1977b). The theory of affordances. In R. F. Shaw & J. D. Bransford (Eds.), *Perceiving, acting and knowing: Toward an ecological psychology* (pp. 67–82). Hillsdale, NJ: Lawrence Erlbaum Associates.

Gibson, J. J. (1979). *The ecological approach in visual perception*. Boston: Houghton-Mifflin. Reprint, Hillsdale, NJ: Lawrence Erlbaum Associates, 1986.

Glaser, R. (1984). The role of knowledge. *American Psychologist, 39*, 105–116.

(GPEP) Panel on the General Professional Education of the Physician (1984). *Physicians for the twenty-first century: The GPEP report*. Washington, DC: The Association of American Medical Colleges.

Lave, J. (1977). Tailor-made experiments and evaluating the intellectual consequences of apprenticeship training. *Cognition and Instruction, 3*, 305–342.

Lave, J. (1988a). *Cognition in practice*. Boston, MA: Cambridge.

Lave, J. (1988b). *The culture of acquisition and the practice of understanding*. IRL report 88-0087. Palo Alto, CA: Institute for Research on Learning.

Lesgold, A. M., Rubinson, H., Feltovich, P. J., Glaser, R., Klopfer, D., & Wang, Y. (1988). Expertise in a complex skills: Diagnosing x-ray pictures. In M. T. H. Chi, R. Glaser, & M. J. Farr (Eds.), *The nature of expertise* (pp. 322–342). Hillsdale, NJ: Lawrence Erlbaum Associates.

Madaus, G. (1988). The influence of testing on the curriculum. In L. Tanner (Ed.), *Critical issues in curriculum: 87th Yearbook of the NSSE, Part I*. Chicago: University of Chicago Press.

Masters, G. N., & Mislevy, R. J. (1993). New views of student learning: Implications for educational measurement. In N. Frederiksen, R. J. Mislevy, & I. I. Bejar (Eds.), *Test theory for a new generation of tests* (pp. 219–242). Hillsdale, NJ: Lawrence Erlbaum Associates.

McDiarmid, G. M. (1996). Challenging prospective teachers' understandings of history: An examination of a historiography seminar. In L. Schauble & R. Glaser (Eds.), *Innovations in learning: New environments for education*. Mahwah, NJ: Lawrence Erlbaum Associates.

National Commission on Excellence in Education. (1983). *A nation at risk: The imperative for educational reform*. Washington, DC: The Commission, Superintendent of Documents, U.S. Government Printing Office.

Palinscar, A. S., & Brown, A. L. (1984). Reciprocal teaching of comprehension-fostering and comprehension-monitoring activities. *Cognition and Instruction, 1*, 117–175.

PBLC Curriculum Committee (1997). *Overview document for the problem-based learning curriculum*. Springfield, IL: Southern Illinois University School of Medicine.

Pellegrino, J. W., & Glaser, R. (1982). Analyzing aptitudes for learning: Inductive reasoning. In R. Glaser (Ed.), *Advances in instructional psychology* (Vol. 2, pp. 269–345). Hillsdale, NJ: Lawrence Erlbaum Associates.

Perkins, D. N., Simmons, R., & Tishman, S. (1990). Teaching cognitive and metacognitive strategies. *Journal of Structured Learning, 10*(4), 285–303.

Salomon, G., & Perkins, D. N. (1989). Rocky roads to transfer: Rethinking mechanisms of a neglected phenomenon. *Educational Psychologist, 24*(2), 112–132.

SCANS (1991). *What work requires of schools: A SCANS report for America 2000*. Washington, DC: U.S. Department of Labor, Secretary's Commission on Achieving Necessary Skills.

Scardamalia, M., Bereiter, C., & Steinbach, R. (1984). Teachability of reflective processes in written composition. *Cognitive Science, 8*, 173–190.

Schoenfeld, A. H. (1988). Problem solving in context(s). In R. Charles & E. A. Silver (Eds.), *The teaching and assessing of mathematical problem solving* (pp. 82–92). Hillsdale, NJ: Lawrence Erlbaum Associates, and National Council of Teachers of Mathematics.

Spiro, R., Coulson, R., Feltovich, P., & Anderson, D. (1989). Multiple analogies for complex concepts: Antidotes for analogy-induced misconception in advanced knowledge acquisition. In S. Vosniadou & A. Ortony (Eds.), *Similarity and analogical reasoning* (pp. 498–531), Cambridge, MA: Cambridge University Press.

Spiro, R. J., Vispoel, W. L., Schmitz, J. G., Samarapungavan, A., & Boerger, A. E. (1987). Knowledge acquisition for application: Cognitive flexibility and transfer in complex content domains. In B. C. Britton & S. Glynn (Eds.), *Executive control processes*. Hillsdale, NJ: Lawrence Erlbaum Associates.

Sternberg, R. J. (1996). *Cognitive Psychology*. Orlando, FL: Harcourt Brace College Publishers.

Sternberg, R. J. (1998). Abilities are forms of developing expertise. *Educational Researcher, 27*(3), 11–20.

The Cognition and Technology Group at Vanderbilt. (1990). Anchored instruction and its relationship to situated cognition. *Educational Researcher, 19*(6), 2–10.

van Rossum, E. J., & Schenk, S. M. (1984). The relationship between learning conception, study strategy and learning outcome. *British Journal of Educational Psychology, 54*, 73–83.

Whitehead, A. N. (1929). *The aims of education*. New York: MacMillan.

Wiggins, G. (1989). Teaching to the (authentic) test. *Educational Leadership, 46*(7), 41–47.

Author Index

A

Abercrombie, M. L. J., 110, 145
Adams, L., 6, 232
Adinolfi, A., 78
Albanese, M. A., 7, 8, 302, 305, 310
Allegheny University of the Health Sciences, School of Public Health, 212
Ames, C., 289
Anderson, D., 320
Anderson, J. R., 190, 251, 324
Anderson, R. M., 38, 39, 78
Aron, J., 54, 57, 67
Association of American Medical Colleges, 75, 79
Astington, J., 63
Atkinson, J. M., 54, 56, 64

B

Bakhtin, M., 149
Bandura, A., 264, 268, 290, 291, 300-301, 310
Barrows, H. S., 1, 2, 3, 6, 20, 25, 26, 35, 53, 54, 55, 56, 60, 63, 67, 82, 111, 112, 129, 167, 168, 169, 171, 172, 173, 175, 177, 178, 179, 181, 182, 185, 191, 228, 230, 246, 252, 263, 264, 319, 320, 325, 327, 328, 329, 339
Barry, W. E., 34
Bassok, M., 234
Beach, W. A., 54
Begg, I. M., 6, 232
Belenky, M. F., 80, 100
Belien, J. J. J, 31, 32
Benn, S. I., 289

Benne, K. D., 78, 87, 92
Bentler, P. M., 28
Berardi-Coletta, B., 231
Bereiter, C., 174, 186, 187, 188, 228, 230, 232, 252, 316, 317, 318, 319, 320, 324, 326
Bielaczyc, K., 230, 231
Bivens, J. A., 232
Black, R., 38
Blake, R. L., 7, 8
Bloom, B. S., 26
Blumberg, P., 8, 54, 202, 203, 205, 206, 207, 208, 209, 212, 214, 215, 216, 218, 219, 220, 224, 233, 254, 259, 263
Blumenfeld, P. C., 110, 186
Boerger, A. E., 172, 175, 320, 321, 325, 326, 328
Bone, R. C., 7
Bonner, S., 299
Boon, L., 36, 38, 39, 40, 41, 202, 205, 308
Boshuizen, H. P. A., 8, 33
Bossert, S., 116
Bossert, S. T., 78
Boud, D., 20, 25
Bouhuijs, P. A. J., 37, 78
Bowles, S., 79
Bransford, J. D., 6, 7, 173, 215, 217, 227, 230, 231, 232, 233, 235, 237, 246, 263, 320, 322, 326
Bretcher, H. S., 167
Brookfield, S. D., 290, 291
Brooks, L. R., 8
Brown, A. L., 110, 194, 227, 233, 246, 247, 320 , 326
Brown, J. S., 110, 230, 232, 233, 246, 325, 326, 329

Subject Index

Contributors

Carl Bereiter is a co-director of the Education Commons and of the CSILE Knowledge Building project at the Ontario Institute for Studies in Education of the University of Toronto. His current work is in the application of epistemology and technology to the solution of educational problems.

Phyllis Blumberg, PhD is the director of the Teaching and Learning Center at the University of the Sciences in Philadelphia. Prior to this position, she worked with others to start several problem-based learning educational programs in the health professions. Her research interests include problem-based learning, self-directed learning, and program evaluation.

Melinda Conlee is a researcher at Southern Illinois University School of Medicine. Her research interests include ethnography, educational research, and conversation analysis. Currently, she is assisting in the design and implementation of PBL in a training program for social work supervisors and researching the impact of medical residency training on the career paths of doctors.

Linda H. Distlehorst, PhD is currently Associate Dean for Education and Curriculum at Southern Illinois University School of Medicine where she is responsible for the implementation and evaluation of the undergraduate medical education program and the longitudinal assessment of its graduates. Her research interests are in developing expertise and learner outcomes, particularly as they are affected by curricula.

Diana H. J. M. Dolmans is an educational psychologist. Since 1989 she has been working at the Department of Educational Development and Research, Maastricht University the Netherlands, first as a PhD student and presently as assistant professor. Her main research interest is in problem-based learning.

JodyLee Estrada Duek earned her PhD from the University of California at Los Angeles. She presently operates an academic consulting firm called FRESCO (Field Research & Educational Services Coalition) that provides in-service and continuing education in medicine, science education, and business.

Dorothy H. Evensen, who earned a PhD in Applied Psychology at New York University, is an associate professor in the program of Higher Education at The Pennsylvania State University. Her research focuses on learning processes and teaching contexts in professional education, particularly within the areas of law and medicine. She is currently conducting a study sponsored by the Law School Admissions Council of group learning in law schools.

Jeff Faidley received his MD degree from Penn State in 1998 and is currently enrolled in a 3-year postgraduate residency training program at Lehigh Valley Hospital in Allentown, PA. During residency, he is conducting research for a new antibiotic undergoing clinical trials for the Merck Corporation.

Jerry Glenn, MD graduated from Penn State and Jefferson Medical College. He served a surgical residency at the University of Florida where he also completed a PhD in microbiology. He trained in surgical oncology at the National Cancer Institute and accepted a faculty position at Penn State University College of Medicine, where in 1992, he implemented a preclinical problem-based curriculum. He is currently a staff surgeon, Associate Professor, and director of the surgery course.

Phillip Glenn, who earned his PhD at the University of Texas, is Associate Professor and Chair of the Department of Speech Communication at Southern Illinois University Carbondale. His primary research interest is in describing patterns of interpersonal interaction in casual and institutional settings, including studies of laughter, sexual harassment, and group processes. Current projects include a book, *Laughter in Interaction*, under contract with Cambridge University Press.

Cindy E. Hmelo is an assistant professor of Educational Psychology at the Graduate School of Education at Rutgers University. Her research examines how people construct knowledge and develop reasoning strategies through problem-solving situations as well as the early acquisition of expertise. In her current work, she is investigating how students construct knowledge in problem-based learning tutorials—focusing on the role of representations and facilitation strategies. She is also interested in the role of technology to support knowledge construction, collaborative learning, and problem-solving.

Ann C. Myers Kelson is currently an assistant professor in the Department of Medical Education at Southern Illinois University School of Medicine. Her responsibilities include faculty development and designing assessment systems. With a background in both education and cognitive science, she is particularly interested in the cognitive science underpinnings of curriculum and assessment systems.

Timothy Koschmann is an associate professor in the Department of Medical Education at Southern Illinois University and a faculty member in the Problem-Based Learning Initiative. The focus of his research is on learning in collaborative settings, with a special interest in how technology might be utilized to foster such learning. He helped to organize the first international conference on computer support for collaboration (CLCS). He recently edited a book on this topic (*CSCL: Theory and Practice of an Emerging Paradigm*, Lawrence Erlbaum Associates, 1996) and, together with Naomi Miyake and Rogers Hall, is working on a sequel.

Robert B. Lebeau is an educational psychologist specializing in cognition and instruction. His research interests include cognitive and social processes linking problem-based learning, learning in informal environments, and uses of technology to support learning and instruction. He currently directs research and professional development efforts conducted in the Advanced Technologies for Learning Lab at LSS (the Mid-Atlantic Regional Educational Laboratory).

Xiaodong Lin is an assistant professor of Education and Technology at Peabody College, Vanderbilt University and a member of the Learning Technology Center. She examines issues related to designing classroom learning activities and evaluating their impact on students' ability to understand, problem-solve, and deal with change in complex subject domains (e.g., science and social studies). She is currently investigating how different cultural and social contexts influence students' theories about themselves as learners in various learning situations.

Jos H. C. Moust, PhD is an assistant professor in the Department of Educational Development and Research, Faculty of Health Science, Maastricht University. His research interests are the performance of tutorial groups and tutors in PBL and the way teachers learn when they are confronted with innovations in education.

Jill Salisbury-Glennon received her PhD in Educational Psychology from Penn State University. She is currently an assistant professor in the Department of Educational Foundations, Leadership and Technology at Auburn University. Her research interests include self-regulated learning, metacognition, collaborative learning, and learner-centered education.

Marlene Scardamalia is a professor in the Department of Curriculum, Teaching, and Learning at the Ontario Institute for Studies in Education of the University of Toronto. She is co-leader of the CSILE Knowledge Building project and is the K through 12 Theme Leader for the Canadian Telelearning Network of Centres of Excellence. Her current work is concerned with applying ideas about the nature of expertise to the design of learning environments and methods.

Henk G. Schmidt is a professor of psychology at Maastricht University in the Netherlands. Before joining the psychology department, he was a professor of health professions education at the same institution. His research interests include problem-based learning, the development of expertise (particularly in medicine) and very long-term memory.

Barry J. Zimmerman is a Distinguished Professor at the Graduate Center of the City University of New York. He has written extensively on social cognitive and self-regulatory processes of children and youth. He was President of the Educational Psychology Division and a recipient of the Division 16 Senior Scientist Award of the American Psychological Association.